The Incas
and their Ancestors

Michael E. Moseley

The Incas
and their Ancestors

The Archaeology of Peru
Revised Edition

With 234 illustrations

Thames & Hudson

Author's Note

Knowledge about indigenous Andeans – ancient, historic, and modern – is blossoming at an ever-increasing rate. I am profoundly indebted to multitudes of colleagues and Cordillera citizens for generously sharing their findings and observations with me. This has shaped my views and I attempt to convey the true marvels of Andean accomplishment in this revised text.

Our knowledge of native achievement is becoming ever more detailed, and here I have tried to stand back and weave together broader evolutionary themes that highlight the fabric and design of indigenous accomplishment. While I address an international audience, I write most pointedly for millions of native Quechua and Aymara speakers because they are the proud inheritors of a past and patrimony that rivals all Old World civilizations.

Younger native Andeans and new scholars will redefine the evolution of indigenous adaptations to the Cordillera, so I dedicate this revised volume to the fresh generation, and to Maya Elena.

Frontispiece: A female Staff God representation on painted cotton cloth found at Karwa.

© 1992 and 2001 Thames & Hudson Ltd, London

First published in the United States of America in 1992 by
Thames & Hudson Inc., 500 Fifth Avenue, New York, New York 10110

thamesandhudsonusa.com

Revised edition 2001
Reprinted 2008

Library of Congress Catalog Card Number 00-108866

ISBN 978-0-500-28277-9

Printed and bound in Slovenia by MKT Print d.d.

Contents

CHAPTER ONE

Introduction 7

The Incas 9 The conquest 11 The historical record 12
The archaeological record 17

CHAPTER TWO

Land of the Four Quarters 25

The Cordillera 25 Geography of the Four Quarters 32
Making a living 43

CHAPTER THREE

The Inca Model of Statecraft 51

The cosmos 51 The ayllu 53 Statecraft 70

CHAPTER FOUR

Colonization of the Cordillera 87

The colonization process 87 Adaptive dispersal 92
Domestication 102

CHAPTER FIVE

The Preceramic Foundations of Civilization 107

Preceramic economies 107 Social formations 114
Arts 115 Monumental architecture 117

CHAPTER SIX

The Initial Period and Early Horizon 131

Irrigation agriculture 133 Monumental architecture 136
Highland developments 143 The Titicaca Basin 154
The Early Horizon 158 The southern sphere 158
Chavín and the northern sphere 163

CHAPTER SEVEN

The Early Intermediate Period   173

North coast 174   The central and south coasts 196
The sierra 203   The altiplano 208

CHAPTER EIGHT

The Middle Horizon   223

Moche upheaval 223   Huari adaptive dispersal 230
Tiwanaku 238

CHAPTER NINE

The Late Intermediate Period   245

The Titicaca region 245   The southern sierra 247
The central and northern sierra 257
The central and south coasts 258
Chimor and the north 261

Epilogue   276

Sources of Illustrations   278

General Bibliography   279

Archaeological Bibliography   280

Index   284

CHAPTER ONE

INTRODUCTION

On the eve of Columbus's Caribbean landfall the largest nation on earth was probably not Ming China or the Ottoman Empire, but Tahuantinsuyu, the 'Land of the Four Quarters' as the Incas called their sprawling realm. Extending more than 5,500 km down the mountainous Andean backbone of South America, the Land of the Four Quarters was the biggest native state to arise in the Western Hemisphere, and the largest empire of antiquity ever to develop south of the equator. By alliance, diplomacy and dint of armed conquest the masters of Tahuantinsuyu governed the longest, most rugged mountain chain in the world, second only to the Himalayas in height and harshness. To the west their sovereignty reached over the dry Atacama desert; to the east it included the flanks of the Amazon rainforest. Inca legions – like their Roman counterparts – marched far beyond the frontiers of civilization to dominate barbarian tribes, and heterogeneous societies. At its height, the imperial capital of Cuzco exercised rule over northern Chile, upland Argentina, Bolivia, Peru, Ecuador, and the south of Colombia. No contemporary Andean nation compares in magnitude or prosperity, and the great wealth of Tahuantinsuyu fostered its downfall.

The conquest of Mexico whetted the Spanish appetite for gold. Yet hopes of securing truly prodigious quantities of precious metal eluded the *conquistadores* until 1532. That year Francisco Pizarro and a small contingent of mercenaries disembarked on the desert coast and ventured into the Andean uplands. At the town of Cajamarca the Inca emperor was enticed to a supposedly peaceful meeting, then kidnapped and ransomed for a room full of gold, and two of silver. After payment of about $50 million by today's bullion standards, the soldiers of fortune garroted the monarch, and marched to Cuzco, the capital and heart of Tahuantinsuyu.

The great metropolis was first sighted by a cavalry vanguard. By all accounts it was unbelievable – it was alien – and it was magnificent. The many distant buildings were clustered so close to the clouds that men and horses of the expeditionary force fought for breath in the oxygen-deficient altitude. Catching and reflecting the sun, towering stone walls shimmered with brilliant hues of gold and silver. Ascending a broad highway into the urban nexus, the party of mounted men was greeted by a brilliantly clad entourage of nobles and attendants, stately but fully foreign in physique and attire. Led across spacious malls with sparkling fountains, and along paved avenues flanked by cut-rock palaces, villas, halls, temples, and shrines, the awe-struck visitors beheld imposing edifices encrusted with precious metals that played dazzling light on all beholders near and far.

Plates 12–14   The city was unbelievable because there was nothing of comparable splendor in the soldiers' Castilian homeland. It was alien because the troops had journeyed from an old, familiar world to a new and unusual one. It was magnificent because Cuzco was the home of the Sun, the god Inti, and gold was his essence. Inti was the sacred patron of the city and its empire. Images of the solar deity and other luminaries of the imperial pantheon resided in an opulent sanctuary, the Coricancha or 'House of the Sun.' A glimpse of this remarkable palace of the gods survives in the thoughtful reflections of Cieza de León, *conquistador* and author of *Chronicle of Peru*. Striding around the temple he found that it measured 'more than four hundred paces in circuit' and was of finely hewn masonry.

> The stone appeared to me to be of a dusky or black color, and most excellent for building purposes. The wall had many openings, and the doorways were very well carved. Round the wall, half way up, there was a band of gold, two *palmos* wide and four *dedos* in thickness. The doorways and doors were covered with plates of the same metal. Within were four houses, not very large, but with walls of the same kind and covered with plates of gold within and without . . .
>
> In one of these houses, which was the richest, there was the figure of the sun, very large and made of gold, very ingeniously worked, and enriched with many precious stones. . . .
>
> They had also a garden, the clods of which were made of pieces of fine gold; and it was artificially sown with golden maize, the stalks, as well as the leaves and cobs, being of that metal. . . . Besides all this, they had more than twenty golden sheep [llamas] with their lambs, and the shepherds with their slings and crooks to watch them, all made of the same metal. There was a great quantity of jars of gold and silver, set with emeralds; vases, pots, and all sorts of utensils, all of fine gold.

Indeed the splendor of the Coricancha and the elegant wealth of Cuzco were so overpowering that the narrator was compelled to conclude, '. . . it seems to me that I have said enough to show what a grand place it was; so I shall not treat further of the silver work of the *chaquira* [beads], of the plumes of gold and other things, which, if I wrote down, I should not be believed.'

If a *conquistador* felt his eye-witness account of Inca accomplishment would be beyond belief, then it is little wonder that centuries later archaeologists confront a uniquely difficult task in attempting to reconstruct this bygone achievement, describe its evolution, and make Andean civilization intelligible to Western society.

Many aspects of Andean accomplishment are only intelligible as adaptations to environmental extremes, particularly life at extremely high elevations. The towering Cordillera is, after all, the only cradle of ancient civilizations where tourists must worry about heart seizures in the rarefied air, and visitors regularly experience altitude sickness due to anoxia. If an eminent empire had once flourished atop the Himalayas, then Tahuantinsuyu could be studied in

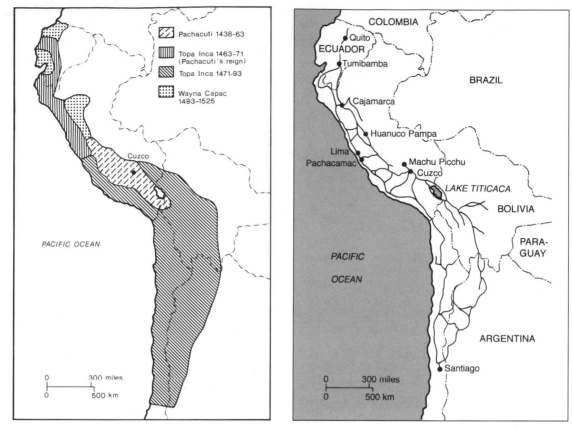

1, 2 (Left) The growth of the Inca empire. Dates for the Inca rulers are the subject of scholarly debate, and are given here as a general guide only. (Right) The Inca road network.

comparative perspective and might seem less alien. Yet, this is not the case, and many aspects of Andean civilization are unprecedented, and thus unique.

Because of these factors we must first understand the geography of Tahuantinsuyu and the nature of Inca rule before turning to the prehistoric record to examine how this way of life and government evolved. An understanding of Inca society and statecraft will serve as a guide for interpreting the archaeological data. However, after reviewing the Inca as an interpretative model, I will turn to the earliest inhabitants of the Andes and trace the evolution of native society and statecraft forward in time to its culmination on the eve of Spanish conquest.

The Incas

It is important to note that the term 'Inca' refers only to a small group of kindred, less than 40,000 individuals, who built a great Andean state by force of arms, and who ruled as the realm's governing nobility. The head of this royal family was the head of state, and at the height of the empire his dominion extended over ten million people or more. These individuals were Inca *subjects*, but they were *not* Incas because this was a closed ethnic body.

The Inca empire incorporated multitudes of polities, chiefdoms, and tribes that the Spanish loosely referred to as *señoríos* and *parcialidades*. Major mountain chains are notorious refuges for divergent types of plants, animals, and people. The many ethnic groups sheltered in these topographic pockets are often not at peace either among themselves or with the greater political order. The rugged Andean Cordillera housed a myriad large and small populations with distinct ethnic identities and strong separatist tendencies. This rich diversity played both for and against empire-building. Ethnic separatism made conquest relatively easy, but consolidation extremely difficult. Small competing polities were played one against another and conquered piecemeal or coerced into allegiance with Tahuantinsuyu. But to integrate these hostile groups into a national whole under a *Pax Incaica* was the single greatest task confronting Cuzco's rulers.

To govern this multitude Inca organizers amalgamated different peoples and polities into larger administrative units. This still left Tahuantinsuyu with more than 80 political provinces, each administratively distinct if not ethnically heterogeneous. Linguistic variance was formidable and incompatible with centralized administration. An official tongue was therefore imposed – *Runa Simi*, or Quechua – as the lingua franca and medium of governmental communication. Communication and contact with the provinces was strengthened by a vast all-weather highway system. Major thoroughfares and trunk lines covered some 30,000 to 40,000 km, and comprised among the best engineered roadways up to the advent of the automobile.

Other integrative policies included relocating entire communities. Called *mitmaqs*, colonists from loyal provinces were resettled in new or hostile territories and subversive villages were moved to consolidated regions. At a higher social level, the offspring of conquered rulers were brought to Cuzco to be educated in Inca ways before returning to their homelands to assume the reins of government.

The formidable task of integrating the New World's largest, most diverse empire was disrupted by European contact. Tahuantinsuyu had not submerged ethnic and political opposition, nor matured into a fully monolithic state by the time Wayna Capac, the last Pre-Hispanic emperor died. Insurrections continued during his rule and revolt became rampant upon his demise. When Wayna Capac became the head of state much of Tahuantinsuyu was controlled by the estates of his predecessors. The greatest potential for his own betterment lay with imperial expansion in the north. The monarch therefore took the best of the Inca officer corps and the empire's elite legions, and spent almost all his reign campaigning in Ecuador, where he consolidated a major power base at Tumibamba. Near the end of his reign there are suggestions that Wayna Capac was planning to create a second imperial capital at Tumibamba, a move not welcomed by the Cuzco nobility. The plan might well have succeeded were it not for the emperor's sudden death in 1526. In many ways the death of Wayna Capac marks the onset of the conquest of Tahuantinsuyu, although almost a decade passed before Pizarro arrived.

The conquest

How could Pizarro's small fighting force of only 260 Spanish mercenaries – 62 horsemen and 198 foot soldiers – topple what in 1532 was potentially the largest nation in the world? This extraordinary event was largely due to the fact that at the time Wayna Capac died so did most of his subjects. Medical historians leave little doubt that Old World infectious diseases, particularly smallpox, worked decisively to Castilian advantage in the conquest of Latin America by swiftly eradicating millions of opponents and occasioning social upheaval in the wake of demographic devastation. The first New World incidence of smallpox was implanted on the Mexican mainland in 1520. It spread further and faster than did the Castilian explorers. Within five years the natives of Panama were largely gone and once across the isthmus there were no barriers to inhibit its southward progress through the Andes and the continent in general, creating the first great New World pandemic. It was the single most severe and far-reaching loss of life that ever occurred in the Americas. Among unvaccinated groups case mortality is about 30 percent. Because the New World peoples lacked immunity, mortality estimates are as high as two-thirds and more of the population.

The impact on Tahuantinsuyu was devastating. Wayna Capac was suddenly struck down, as was his heir apparent, and many of the governing elite in Tumibamba and Cuzco. The tumultuous consequences must have been broadly akin to the upheavals that racked Europe in the aftermath of the Black Death. Demographic collapse ushered in both a power vacuum and a widespread loss of confidence in the established order. Insurrection spread to many quarters of Tahuantinsuyu, and a violent civil war broke out, pitting remnants of the established Cuzco nobility, under one claimant son Huascar, against the survivors of the Tumibamba court led by Atahualpa, one of the dead emperor's many other sons. The war raged on for more than half a decade.

On the eve of the Spanish arrival civil hostilities had only drawn to a partial close. Huascar had been captured, and Atahualpa was marching south through the mountains in slow and stately procession with much of his court and thousands of troops to take possession of Cuzco. Landing on the desert coast, Pizarro learned of Atahualpa's general itinerary and without opposition moved the small Spanish expeditionary force up the Cordillera and into the highland town of Cajamarca. Atahualpa accepted a treacherous offer to go unarmed and without troops to meet the alien interlopers who kidnapped, ransomed and killed the king. This reignited the Tumibamba–Cuzco civil conflict, and aligned Pizarro with the latter faction, who then provided the Spanish with auxiliary troops and welcomed their presumed liberators into the capital. Initiated by disease and concluded with deceit, the conquest of Tahuantinsuyu was largely accomplished without major battles in its early stages. Violent opposition and fierce battles did ensue. However, Atahualpa's ransom and the sack of Inti's golden city produced such immediate wealth that well-armed Castilian *Plate 25* reinforcements arrived in great numbers, and Pizarro's concerns shifted from conquest to consolidation.

The historical record

Demographic devastation by disease, protracted civil war, and Castilian conquest pose problems for understanding what Tahuantinsuyu may have been like in a pristine state. Record-keeping is essential to all empires, and Inca lords kept a vast body of information – ranging from census and tax data to imperial history – recorded upon *quipu*. Deriving its name from the word 'knot' (*Khipu*), a *quipu* consisted of a length of cord held horizontally and from which numerous other yarns of various colors were vertically suspended. Each of these secondary members, in turn, supported a descending hierarchy of dependent colored strings. Different numerical data were entered by different types of knots, and other information was encoded by cord length, color, and hierarchical position. Unfortunately, in the wake of foreign conquest the entire record keeping system disintegrated as rapidly as the royal court that had supported it.

Neither Pizarro nor those under his command were concerned with recording current events, or the achievements of their native adversaries. Indeed, most of the mercenaries were illiterate, and with few members of the initial expeditionary force leaving memoirs there is woefully little information about the Castilian side of the conquest, and even less from the Inca perspective. One insightful account from a native point of view was written by Felipe Guaman Poma de Ayala, who illustrated his observations with hundreds of charming drawings. Yet he wrote long after the fall of the Incas. Almost all records about Tahuantinsuyu were written well after the conquest and extracted from Indian witnesses who were not unbiased by their circumstances. Arriving with troop reinforcements two decades after the death of Atahualpa, Pedro Cieza de León was one of the first chroniclers sympathetic to the natives. Yet even his detailed account of Tahuantinsuyu must be regarded as an historical reconstruction, and all later writings by other authors are of a similar nature. These early accounts about the Inca contain a great deal of fundamental information, but the sources are often contradictory and must be assessed with care. For centuries scholars have taken the early chronicles to be relatively realistic and historically accurate. However, a recent school of analysis sees the accounts as rather idealized expressions of Inca values and norms shaped by how the surviving lords of Cuzco and other native informants wished to have the nature and history of Tahuantinsuyu portrayed to their alien conquerors. No doubt there is a mixture of fact and fiction.

I believe that what colonial sources reported about matters such as native organization and statecraft is substantially more reliable than what is reported about Inca history. Historical information about Tahuantinsuyu suffers from the problem that Andean people conceived of time as cyclical. This was little understood by the Spanish, who framed what the Incas said about history in lineal time. There has been little awareness of this problem and Inca historical lore has traditionally been accepted at face value. This viewpoint has had a pervasive and lasting impact on Western perceptions of Andean civilization, and on the development of Andean archaeology. For example conquerors often ration-

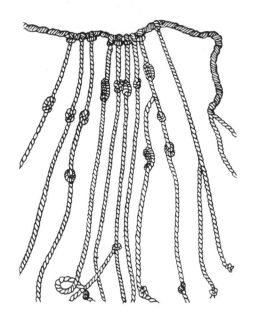

3 Part of a quipu recording device of cord and string.

4 Guamán Poma's sketch of an imperial clerk with a quipu record made of cord and string.

alize their acts both to themselves and to their new subjects. For the lords of Cuzco the rationalization process came to include a special creation myth. Inti, the essence of the Sun, was declared the progenitor and spiritual father of the Inca. By this doctrine, the Incas were Inti's chosen 'children of the sun,' and the emperor, a demigod, was his executor on earth. From Inti came divine edicts for his children to transform Cuzco into the imperial navel of the universe and to conquer the world as its empire. Dogma held that before Tahuantinsuyu there was only savagery and barbarism, while in the wake of Cuzco's holy wars came civilization and enlightenment. Two remarkably able emperors, Pachacuti and his son Topa Inca, reputedly spread this enlightenment and conquered more than three quarters of Tahuantinsuyu. The historical message was simple: civilization originated at Cuzco and then spread over the Cordillera as a vast horizon of enlightenment within a span of two generations. This is the basis for what may be termed the *origin center → civilization horizon* concept by which Western society has long interpreted the Andean past.

The oral traditions behind this concept reach back several centuries before the coming of the *conquistadores*, to times when the Cuzco or Huatanay Valley housed a number of small peasant populations who were hostile to one another. These rude conditions purportedly typified the universe in general following its relatively recent creation. Called Viracocha, the Creator had caused the sun to emerge from the waters of Lake Titicaca. He then went to the ancient lakeside metropolis of Tiwanaku, which in a former time had been inhabited by a race of giants. Here he gathered primordial clay and modeled animals and people. On the human models Viracocha painted the different clothes and distinct costumes that would distinguish the many different ethnicities of the Andes, and each group was instructed in its different language and customs. The creator ordered the people to descend deep into the earth and mountains and then to emerge separately from caves, springs, lakes and hills in different homelands.

In some stories the founder of the Inca royal family, Manco Capac, along with three brothers and four sisters, emerged from Lake Titicaca, while in other versions they emerged from a cave southeast of the Río Huatanay. Gathering a small following, the siblings set off in search of a place with rich soils to settle. A long and adventurous journey sees several of the brothers turned to stone, entombed in mountains, and the like. Eventually, Manco Capac and his sister, Mama Oqlyo (his bride and wife) arrived near the spot where the Río Tullumayu joins the Huatanay. Here the founder plunged a golden staff into the soil to test it. Finding it auspicious, they drove away the local inhabitants and established a settlement at the locality that would become the Coricancha. After founding Cuzco and establishing a family, Manco Capac turned to stone. This ancestral stone was one of the Incas' most sacred objects or *huacas*.

By official accounts Cuzco remained a simple village through the reign of its eighth headman, Viracocha Inca. Late in life, after rule had been passed to his chosen heir, Inca Urcon, a powerful chiefdom from the northwest, the Chanca, amassed to attack Cuzco. The threat was so great that Viracocha and his heir fled the town and took refuge in a distant fort. However, a once-troublesome royal son, Yupanqui, some capable generals and various settlers refused to desert their homes. Defenses were hurriedly organized under Yupanqui's command and reinforcements from neighborhood groups secured. When the more numerous Chanca pressed their attack and tried to take Cuzco by storm, they were heroically resisted. In the heat of the great battle, just when it appeared defences might give way, Yupanqui cried out that the very stones in the fields were turning to armed men to repel the attackers. Cuzco's forces rallied and the Chanca were bloodily repulsed. The thankful commander immediately had the field stones collected and distributed among the city's shrines which they had helped to save.

The victorious Yupanqui, Cuzco's savior, then turned his attention to practical matters and usurped the throne. Although his father was allowed to live out the rest of his life in disgrace, his brother Inca Urcon's name was stricken from the dynastic king lists. I suspect that the usurper – who assumed the imperial title of Pachacuti or 'Earthshaker' – recast far more Inca history than simply striking his brother's name and memory from the royal record. This is because his reign marks a sudden, major change in Inca official history. After having rallied Cuzco's forces behind the banners of defence, Pachacuti Inca Yupanqui unfurled the banners of offense for a long series of aggressive foreign wars. He united the inhabitants of the Huatanay Valley and made local Quechua-speakers honorary Inca citizens, and then turned to the great Titicaca Basin, the largest demographic center in the Andean uplands. Credited with subjugating the Lupaka, Colla, and other kingdoms around Lake Titicaca, the great defender of Cuzco had amassed a tremendous power base and became concerned with developing institutions of statecraft that would consolidate Inca gains. He therefore returned to Cuzco, relinquishing the imperial legions to his son, Topa Inca. While Topa pursued a victorious career, Pachacuti invented statecraft and institutions such as the national taxation system, the highway and communication system, and the state's extensive warehousing system.

Inti, the Sun God, had appeared to Pachacuti in a vision when he was a young man and provided inspiration for the great deeds that had to be accomplished for humanity's betterment. In appreciation the emperor elevated the cult of the sun to that of Cuzco's patron god and commissioned construction of the marvelous Coricancha. Cuzco had been little more than a humble village until the defeat of the Chanca. Pachacuti tore down the old settlement and designed *Plate 15* a new one befitting Cuzco's status as the navel of the civilized universe. By some accounts streets and buildings were laid out so that the new celestial city looked, in outline, like a vast puma. At his death in 1471 the deeds and accomplishments of Pachacuti were so numerous and far-reaching that he had literally transformed the Inca realm from the Creator, Viracocha's, humble and somewhat unfinished handiwork, to that of Inti's divinely commissioned center of the civilized universe.

Although not the reputed inventor of statecraft that his father was, Topa Inca was by official accounts the Alexander the Great of the continent. From the time of first assuming command of the army to the end of his reign one year after Columbus' discovery of the Caribbean, this gifted tactician expanded the imperial frontiers along more than 4,000 km of the Cordillera, from central Ecuador to central Chile. Subsequently, Wayna Capac's reign was one of consolidation, with relatively modest imperial expansion into the tropical frontiers of Tahuantinsuyu before the chaos of the first smallpox pandemic and the ensuing civil war.

This brief synopsis of Inca historical lore does injustice to its rich but often contradictory detail. It does, however, capture two basic tenets of imperial propaganda: first, that civilization did not exist before the Incas; second, that it was invented at Cuzco and spread from there with remarkable rapidity to the rest of the Cordillera. The first tenet denied any time-depth to Andean development, and it took almost four centuries for Europeans to discover this to be in error. The second tenet limited development of civilization to a single ancient city serving as the fountainhead for invention and diffusion, and it has taken even longer to assess the legitimacy of this notion.

It did not befit the Incas' self image to admit that powerful states had contested Cuzco's rule, or that great civilizations had thrived long before the rise of Tahuantinsuyu. Yet, there were a few great cities in their vast realm that the masters of the Inca realm did not claim. Ultimately each would rise like an archaeological phoenix to challenge the claims of Cuzco. One was the venerable monument of Tiwanaku (Tiahuanaco) on the shores of Lake Titicaca. *Plates 79–83* Renowned for towering stelae in human form, the site figured as a primordial center, built and inhabited long ago by giants whom Viracocha had turned to stone before he created people. Cieza de León visited the site and wrote that the Incas had found it in ruins and regarded it with great reverence.

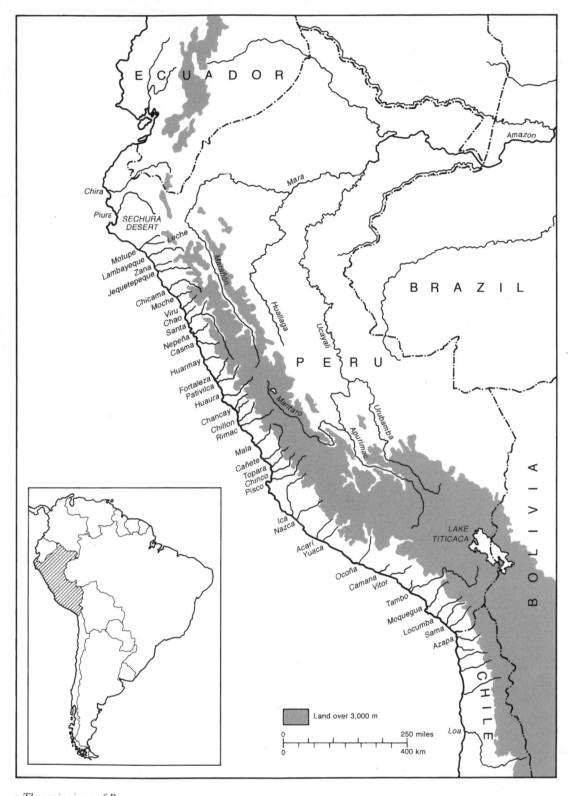

5 *The main rivers of Peru.*

Pachacamac was another great city that the Incas could not claim. Located *Plate 6* near the sea at the mouth of the Río Lurin, south of Lima, it was the home of a widely sought oracle with a powerful cult following. Drawing pilgrims and devotees from all quarters of the Cordillera, Pachacamac was the most revered city in the Andes. Probably something of a thorn in the imperial side, the Incas told Pizarro that the city contained immense riches, whereupon the *conquistador* dispatched his brother and a contingent of troops to sack the sacred center. Although great wealth was not found one officer did provide a short eyewitness account of finding and destroying the idol which was the oracle.

Finally, the Inca admitted to conquering the sprawling metropolis of Chan *Plate 99* Chan at the mouth of the Río Moche on the northern coastal desert. This was the capital of Chimor, the second largest New World empire, whose frontiers were recorded by Spanish ethnohistorical sources. Spanning 1,000 km and encompassing two-thirds of the irrigated Andean coastlands, Chimor reached from southern Ecuador to just north of Pachacamac. It was the largest nation to contest Tahuantinsuyu and a protracted struggle was won by the Incas several generations before Pizarro's arrival. The official history of Cuzco made but passing mention of their greatest adversary, but survivors of the old empire made the Spanish aware that it had not been of Inca origin.

The archaeological record

Just as the historical accounts of Tahuantinsuyu are not without prejudice, the archaeological record did not remain unbiased by the Spanish arrival. The conquering forces quickly learned that great stores of precious metal existed in the ground. Much was purely geological in context, but the tombs of past lords and nobles also contained enormous stores of gold and silver. Within a generation of the conquest, looting operations grew so large and financially rewarding that they became legally synonymous with mining. Ancient monuments were divided into claim areas with titles registered in notarial archives. Title holders established chartered corporations to mobilize massive work forces and systematically quarry ruins. As with geological mines, the Castilian king was entitled to a 20 percent tax on all wealth extracted from the ground. Within a short span the Crown established a royal smelter in the Moche Valley, not because of any local geological wealth but because the royal mausoleums of Chan Chan had been discovered and looting of the nearby Pyramid of the Sun was underway. By rendering the plundered treasures into bullion, overseers of the Crown foundry ensured collection of the royal tax.

From these lucrative beginnings commercial exploitation of antiquities has remained a large-scale business, and the Andean Cordillera is probably the most intensively looted ancient center of civilization in the world. Early in the 1960s several men plowing a field in a northern desert valley discovered the entrance shaft to a deep tomb with rich accompaniments of gold and silver work and fine pottery. The find revealed a cemetery, known as Loma Negra, and within several days 800 looters, called *huaqueros*, reportedly amassed to pillage the newly discovered graveyard. Grave robbing is not limited to *huaqueros* but is now a national pastime tied to the religious calendar and reverently pursued by multitudes at Easter. *Semana Santa*, as the annual occasion is known, is considered a particularly auspicious time for discovering ancient tombs and families regularly go to the countryside to picnic atop ancient cemeteries where child and adult alike dig about searching for treasures and trinkets.

One by-product from the four centuries of monument-mining and ruin-quarrying has been the exposure of vast quantities of artifacts. Enormous quantities of fine ceramics, exquisite textiles, wood and lapidary work survived as curios and gradually stocked the shelves of museums and private collections around the world. But apart from the fact that these collections came mostly from graves, there was little information as to where they were found and with what monuments or other materials they were once associated. Therefore as Andean archaeology began to develop as a discipline, analysis and interpretation was largely art-historical. Objects were grouped on the basis of physical similarities and organized into styles, and subsequent excavations concentrated on establishing the spatial distributions of pottery and art styles and on fixing their stratigraphic positions in time.

Although pillaging was the norm, a few individuals pursued a more enlightened attitude, and sought to preserve ancient works by describing, illustrating, collecting, and safeguarding them. In the 16th century Cieza de León was a pioneer of this attitude. Near the end of the eighteenth century another was Martínez de Compañón, Bishop of Trujillo in the Moche Valley. He commissioned the mapping of ancient monuments, including Chan Chan and the Huaca del Sol (Pyramid of the Sun), probably the largest mud brick mound ever erected in the continent. Extensive looting had already taken place at the Huaca del Sol, including the diversion of the Río Moche to undercut it, causing two-thirds of the monument to be washed away by the time the Bishop mapped the pyramid.

The Prussian-born naturalist, Alexander von Humboldt, was the first to draw international attention to Andean antiquities and those of Latin America in general. Traveling widely in Spain's colonies, he took notes on ancient monuments, buildings, and works such as the vast highway system of the Cordillera, and in 1814 published *Vues de Cordillères et Monuments des Peuples Indigènes de l'Amérique*. This bold study set a very important precedent by making the investigation of Latin American monuments a legitimate field of scholarship. Consequently, accounts of Andean antiquities became more numerous and more rigorous.

The German scholar, Max Uhle, was the first to elicit time-depth and stratigraphic change from the archaeological record. As a young museum worker in Dresden, he analyzed artifact collections from Cuzco and familiarized himself with the style of the Incas. Uhle also worked on the study and publication of a large corpus of material from the ancient metropolis of Tiwanaku (or Tiahuanaco) near Lake Titicaca. The art and architecture of this city were stylistically distinct, and Uhle knew Tiwanaku was old because the Incas reported that it lay in ruins when they took control of the lake region.

Fired with the desire to study the Andes in person, Uhle first excavated at the great oracle center of Pachacamac in 1896–7. His research was supported by supplying museums with quality artifacts commonly encountered in graves. Attentive to stratigraphy, he recognized that burials with Inca-style artifacts were underlain by graves with a local style of pottery; beneath these were interments with materials related to the Tiwanaku style, and deeper still were burials with a second local style of pottery. Thus, Uhle identified a stratigraphic succession of two local styles, interspersed with two widespread styles, Inca and Tiwanaku. He found similar successions, but with different local styles, during subsequent excavations in the Ica and Nazca valleys of southern Peru, and in the northern Moche Valley. Earliest of all were coastal middens, which Uhle correctly attributed to 'Fisherfolk,' and in northern Chile he discovered that some of these maritime folk artificially mummified their deceased.

Rightfully impressed by the widespread occurrence of tombs containing artwork broadly similar to the Tiwanaku style, Uhle looked to far-flung Tahuantinsuyu for interpretative analogy. In Uhle's view, Inca lore held that an era of intranquility and unsophistication had prevailed before an epoch of civilization was invented at Cuzco and then flashed across the Andean landscape. Thus, he inferred that the former condition was represented by times of local stylistic diversity in the archaeological record, whereas Tiwanaku and Cuzco were the origin centers of civilization that episodically united the Cordillera.

This interpretative framework was initially codified in the 1920s and 1930s by A. L. Kroeber, at the Berkeley campus of University of California, where the majority of Uhle's collections were deposited. However, the framework of 'horizons' and 'intermediate periods' had to be adjusted because Andean societies rarely changed in concert at the same time throughout the Cordillera. In the 1950s, John Rowe of Berkeley used Uhle's collections from the Ica Valley and radiocarbon dates to establish a 'master sequence' of chronologically defined periods and horizons. For example, the Late Horizon is a unit of time defined by the Inca occupation of the Ica Valley. The Ica sequence of time units has its greatest use among foreign scholars.

The founder of a more indigenous view of Peruvian prehistory was born in 1890. At this time Peru's native Indian population was viewed with contempt, but one superbly energetic and talented native youth, Julio C. Tello, won a fellowship to Harvard and from there worked his way to the first fully international career in Peruvian archaeology. Well known for directing the national archaeological museum in Lima, this charismatic scientist was also elected to the country's senate. Tello's popularity and international success as a scholar attracted talented young students to archaeology and established it as a respected national discipline.

Tello concentrated on elucidating the early aspects of civilization that had eluded Uhle. He located and excavated the rich seaside necropolis of Paracas, and the enormous coastal mound of Sechín Alto and its associated architectural complexes in the Casma Valley. Yet, Tello's ethnic ancestry drew him to the

Plates 43, 47–49

little-known eastern flanks of the Cordillera. Here his most far-reaching discoveries were at the primordial platform complex of Chavín de Huantar, a great masonry monument rich in stelae and artistically carved stonework displaying a vivid iconography dominated by felines, raptorial birds, and serpents. The naturalist E. W. Middendorf had previously visited the ruins and thought them to be early, but it was Tello who demonstrated that Chavín de Huantar was the most elaborate and ornate center of a previously unknown stylistic complex which had been widely disseminated across the central Andes at an early date. He viewed Chavín de Huantar as the upland origin center of a 'mother culture' which drew upon Amazonian roots to nurture the rise and perpetuation of civilization in Peru. Tello read ancient art and iconography through indigenous eyes that elicited rich symbolism and meaning, which he believed was reiterated over the course of time. Emphasizing continuity, Tello viewed Andean evolution as an organic flow of life that repeatedly diverged and converged again, whereas Uhle emphasized discontinuities and temporal successions of distinct cultures.

Assuming the directorship of the national museum from Tello in 1930, Luis E. Valcarcel furthered the vision of continuity and unity. Valcarcel began his career in Cuzco, which remained an indigenous center, and he saw the Spanish conquest as threads of change that Indian populations had adaptively interwoven into the fabric of ongoing life. At the national museum, Valcarcel worked for decades to promote ethnology, ethnohistory, and archaeology to make the wholeness of the Andean past and present intelligible not simply to scholars but to today's six million or so native Quechua and Aymara speakers.

The foundations laid by Uhle, Tello, and Valcarcel have been built upon by increasing numbers of scholars. Concerns with chronology and successions of ancient styles and societies are now justly tempered with concerns for understanding the past in terms of indigenous people and their institutions. Due to a tremendous escalation in Andean studies, more archaeological, historical, and anthropological research has been carried out during the current generation than during all prior centuries. The great surge of new information defies succinct synthesis because it has occasioned a profound and exciting revolution in archaeological interpretation that remains ongoing. The *origin center → civilization horizon* concept certainly does not work the way Uhle thought it did, and intermediate periods are by no means times of lesser development but times of coastal prosperity.

Nor is change in the archaeological record without evident input from nature. There is a wealth of new information on environmental dynamics. The theory of plate tectonics has shown the Andes to be the New World's most actively growing cordillera, associated with high rates of tectonic, seismic, and volcanic activity that produce natural disasters of regional scope. The theory of ocean–atmosphere interaction has identified recurrent catastrophes of pan-Andean scope in the forms of profound droughts, and severe El Niño perturbations of normal marine and meteorological cycles. Thus, a dynamic landscape must be woven into our appreciation of Andean civilization.

The chapters that follow are brief. Therefore, they selectively touch upon major evolutionary processes and high points of the archaeological record represented by some better-known Andean civilizations. The chronological framework I employ is presented on the following two pages. It begins with a long Lithic Period and a shorter Preceramic Period. Following an Initial Period of pottery use there are Early, Middle, and Late Horizons, separated by Early and Late Intermediate Periods. The Periods and Horizons are units of time defined by the Ica Valley 'master sequence.' This sequence is most applicable to central Peru where Uhle worked. It is less satisfactory to the north and south, where cross-correlations must be projected to distant regions that are geographically and culturally distinct.

Time Scale	North Coast	Central Coast	South Coast	Periods/Horizons
1500 —	INCA	INCA	INCA	Late Horizon
1250 —	CHIMU	CHANCAY	ICA	Late Intermediate Period
1000 —	SICAN			
750 —				Middle Horizon
		HUARI		
500 —		Pachacamac		Early Intermediate Period
250 —	MOCHE	LIMA	NAZCA	
A.D.				
B.C.	GALLINAZO	Miramar		Early Horizon
	SALINAR	Baños de Boza		
500 —	CUPISNIQUE	Ancon	PARACAS	
1000 —	Caballo Muerto Cerro Sechin	Garagay		Initial Period
2000 —	Huaca Prieta	La Florida El Paraiso		Preceramic Period
4000 —		La Paloma		
6000 —				Lithic Period
	PAIJAN			
8000 —		Luz		
10000 —				

6 *Chronology for coastal Peru.*

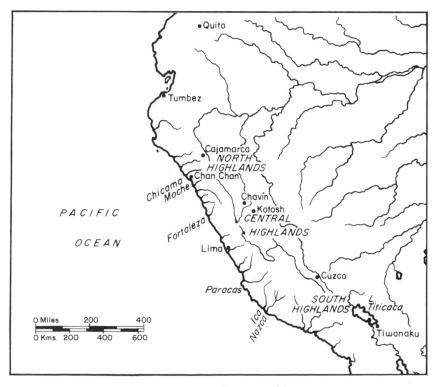

7 *Some of the main archaeological sites and modern towns of Peru.*

Time Scale	North	Central	South	Periods/Horizons
1500	INCA	INCA	INCA	Late Horizon
1250		Wanka	KILLKE	Late Intermediate Period
1000				
750		HUARI	Pikillaqta	Middle Horizon
500	Marcahuamachuca			
250	RECUAY	HUARPA		Early Intermediate Period
A.D. B.C.				
500	Kotosh CHAVIN		Chanapata	Early Horizon
1000	Huacaloma		Marcavalle	Initial Period
2000	Galgada			Preceramic Period
4000		Pachamachay		
6000	Lauricocha			Lithic Period
8000	Guitarrero			
10000				

8 *Chronology for highland Peru.*

Time Scale	Moquegua	Arica	Titicaca-Altiplano	Periods/Horizons
1500	INCA		INCA	Late Horizon
1250	CHIRIBAYA	GENTILAR	AYMARA KINGDOMS	Late Intermediate Period
1000	Tumilaca			
750	Chen Chen			Middle Horizon
500	OMO		TIWANAKU	Early Intermediate Period
250				
A.D. B.C.	HUARICANI	Faldas el Moro	PUKARA	
500			CHIRIPA	Early Horizon
1000				Initial Period
2000		CHINCHORRO		Preceramic Period
4000			Asana	
6000				Lithic Period
8000	Ring Site		Toquepala	
10000				

9 *Chronology for the Titicaca region.*

COLOMBIA

ECUADOR

BRAZIL

PERU

ANTISUYU

CHINCHAYSUYU

Cuzco

LAKE TITICACA

CUNTISUYU

BOLIVIA

PACIFIC OCEAN

PARA-
GUAY

CHILE

COLLASUYU

ARGENTINA

0   300 miles

0   500 km

10 The four quarters of the Inca realm emanating from Cuzco, the imperial capital.

CHAPTER TWO

LAND OF THE FOUR QUARTERS

Thanks to the rugged Cordillera, which is characterized by global extremes in environmental conditions, Andean civilization differs from other great civilizations of antiquity. If thriving civilizations had matured atop the Himalayas while simultaneously accommodating a Sahara desert, a coastal fishery richer than the Bering Sea, and a jungle larger than the Congo, then Tahuantinsuyu might seem less alien. Fundamental contrasts in the Andean Cordillera's habitats confronted humans with radically disparate conditions and dissimilar resources. Simultaneous adaptation to all niches by a single population or society remained an untrodden evolutionary avenue. Instead people pursued more selective proficiency in making a living in one or another environment. The mountain, marine, desert and jungle habitats required distinctive adaptive strategies and promoted different evolutionary pathways, called Arid Montane, Maritime-Oasis, and Tropical Forest lifeways. The Incas were a montane society, but the land of the four quarters incorporated people adapted to other conditions.

The Cordillera

Two sources of energy, tectonic and solar, have molded the South American Cordillera into a land of ecological extremes. Tectonic energy compels the westward-moving continental plate to override the eastward-moving sea floor of the Nazca plate at high rates up to 15 cm per year. The ocean floor bends down into

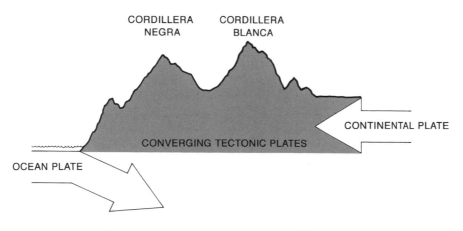

11 Converging tectonic plates created two parallel Andean ranges.

an abyssal ocean trench as it is subducted under the mainland. The over-riding continental margin is compressed, thrust up, and buckled into long parallel mountain ridges that stretch from the Caribbean coast of Colombia to Tierra del Fuego. Weather is a product of solar energy conveyed by the atmosphere and ocean, and millions of years ago the central Cordillera grew high enough to split the continental climate between wet eastern and dry western regimes. Normally all Andean precipitation comes from the distant Atlantic Ocean. The high eastern escarpment captures most of the moisture creating rain shadows to the west where the arid Pacific regime prevails.

Where the Andes are highest and widest the mountain plan forms a gigantic H, the cross-bar formed by the Nudo de Vilcanota peaks. The western range, the Cordillera Negra, fronts the Atacama desert. The taller eastern range, the Cordillera Blanca, fronts the Amazon and buffers clouds from the Atlantic carrying almost all of the Andes' rainfall. South of the Vilcanota peaks the two ranges diverge to frame the altiplano, an immense landlocked trough of high plains some 800 km in length. Drainage flows south through a string of lake basins. In southern Chile these form salt pans and the sparse grasslands there are called salt puna. As the Andes become higher they become drier, but the puna pasturage is not salty in the northern altiplano, which forms the largest expanse of uninterrupted agricultural flatlands in the Andes, around Lake Titicaca, which drains south to Bolivia's Lake Poopó.

North of the Vilcanota mountains the uplands splinter into long, narrow ranges paralleling the Cordilleras Negra and Blanca, cross-cut by numerous short ranges which frame high, but fractured, puna grasslands and a string of lower sierra basins, eventually reaching a slim tropical low point in Ecuador. As altitude decreases rainfall increases and the grasslands and sierra basins of northern Peru are relatively lush. About 90 percent of Andean runoff descends to the Atlantic watershed, while only 10 percent descends to the Pacific.

The Andes also channel marine currents. Strong daily winds off the ocean are deflected northward by the Cordillera Negra causing the sea to flow northward along the continental margin. Upwelling currents rise from the depths of the tectonic trench propelling extremely cold but nutrient-rich waters to the surface, and supporting a prodigious maritime food chain. The cold currents generate a temperature inversion, inhibiting coastal rainfall and producing the Atacama desert. From central Chile to the mouth of the Río Santa in northern Peru there is little or no continental shelf. The Río Santa breaks through the Cordillera Negra and disgorges abundant runoff into the ocean. North of it the Andes pull back from the shore as a wide continental shelf and coastal plain emerge and expand northward, comprising agricultural lands irrigated by abundant runoff from the lower, wetter Cordillera and large oasis valleys in northern Peru.

Chronic stress

The Cordillera exerts many severe forms of chronic and episodic stress upon humans. Feeding people is not easy because low primary productivity and limited biotic diversity typify desert and high mountain ecosystems. In the central Andes the majority of people traditionally resided above 2,500 m, where adverse corollaries of altitude include rugged terrain, fragile topography, steep slopes, poor soils, limited farm land, short growing seasons, high winds, aridity, elevated solar radiation, erratic rainfall, precarious nutrition, cold, and hypoxia. Hypoxia is the technical term for low oxygen tension due to elevational decrease in barometric pressure. It is a pervasive source of chronic stress on all life. At sea level arterial blood is 97 percent saturated with oxygen, but around 5,000 m this is reduced by 30 percent because there is less oxygen in the air. Affecting all physiological functions, anoxia, or low oxygen availability at the beginning of the biological supply systems, causes modified cellular metabolism, higher red blood cell counts, as well as increased circulation and ventilation associated with large chests and lung capacity. Rest and work are more strenuous and energy-demanding above 2,500 m due to increased respiratory and circulatory needs. Furthermore, to maintain body temperature in the frigid upland requires additional energy to sustain elevated basal metabolic rates. Thus, cold and anoxia oblige people to eat more, and highlanders are estimated to need around 11.5 percent more calories than lowlanders. Consequently, it costs measurably more to support life and civilization in mountains than in lowlands. Life is also more precarious because comparable food shortages, caused by drought and other disasters, exert greater nutritional duress at higher elevations than at lower ones.

Hypoxia exerts a strong negative stress on the reproduction of plants, animals, and people that is compounded by other adverse corollaries of altitude. Human colonization of progressively higher elevations was certainly a step-by-step process, with people moving up to one altitude and adjusting to it reproductively and economically before descendants moved to a still higher rung. Highlanders and lowlanders can acclimatize to different altitudes most easily when young and tolerably when mature. Yet childbearing women indigenous to high Andean altitudes have placentas of a different configuration, size and weight from their lowland counterparts. Anecdotal evidence suggests that the experience of seventeenth-century Spanish colonists at anoxic altitudes was one of low sperm counts, infertility, inability to carry a fetus to full term, and, in the event of live birth, neonatal death. Reproductive concerns have traditionally contributed to European preferences for residing at low altitudes. How native lowlanders faired with hypoxia is not clear. However, comparisons of ancient skeletal remains from the coast and from the highlands reveal that desert populations are generally much more closely related to one another than to mountain populations and vice versa. Therefore, anoxia probably reinforced economic and cultural separations of Arid Montane, Maritime-Oasis and Tropical Forest adaptations.

Episodic stress
High rates of tectonic activity are stressful for Andean populations. Subduction of the sea floor slowly pushes the Cordillera upward a few millimeters per

decade and tectonic creep exacerbates erosion and strains slope-sensitive canals. Episodic earth movement generates at least one Magnitude 7 or greater earthquake per decade that causes fatalities, property damage, and thousands of mountain landslides. Along the desert watershed the millions of tons of earthquake debris will lie in loose repose for years until El Niño rainfall flushes it into the sea where it is ground up and deposited as beach sand. It is then picked up by strong winds off the sea and moved inland as sprawling sand dunes that can bury farmland and settlements alike. Volcanoes are active in Colombia and Ecuador, as well as south of the Nudo de Vilcanota. In February AD 1600, Mount Huaynaputina in southern Peru exploded with such power that the entire volcano was reduced to a gaping crater. Thousands perished in the violent upheaval which natives construed as a battle between their indigenous gods and victorious Christian ones.

Andean rainfall is both the blood of life and life's tormentor. Precipitation is irregularly distributed due to rugged topography and mountain rain shadows. It is markedly seasonal, peaking between December and March and generally vanishing between June and September. It is also exceptionally fickle, swinging well above or below statistical norms that see 'average' precipitation but once every four or more years. This irregularity is stressful because plant growth and farming fluctuate in response. High-altitude rainfall farming fluctuates less severely than low-elevation runoff farming and irrigation. Arid mountain soils, like sponges, absorb fixed amounts of moisture and must reach saturation before rainfall will produce runoff. For example, soil saturation requires 260 mm of moisture in the Río Moquegua basin of southwestern Peru. Precipitation only exceeds this value in headwater altitudes and between 3,900 and 4,900 m annual rainfall averages about 360 mm, which produces around 100 mm of runoff. At higher elevation, moisture is largely locked into permanent glaciers and ice fields. Therefore, if rainfall fluctuates by 10 percent, dropping to 334 mm or rising to 396 mm in the 3,900–4,900 m zone, then runoff will fluctuate on the order of 36 percent. This is because the soil always absorbs 260 mm, which leaves runoff residues of either 74 mm or 136 mm respectively. The Moquegua calculations are approximations, but they demonstrate the asymmetrical relationship between rainfall and runoff and show why the flow of Andean rivers fluctuates dramatically from year to year.

The rainfall regime is turned topsy-turvy by El Niño disruptions of meteorological and marine currents. Generally lasting 18 months, strong disruptions can slow the earth's rotational momentum, alter the length of day, and cause temporary reordering of terrestrial and marine food chains. Severe El Niño events generate torrential storms and cataclysmic flooding along the normally rainless coast, while devastating drought often envelops the southern mountains and Titicaca Basin.

Longer-term climatic fluctuations beset the Andes and civilizations have waxed during wet periods then waned during long droughts documented in glacial ice cores and Lake Titicaca sediment. Pronounced desiccation between about 2200 and 1900 BC contributed to increased atmospheric dust revealed in

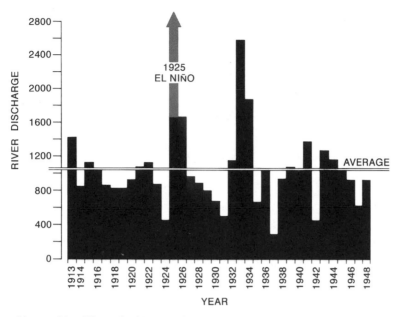

12 Measured in millions of cubic meters between 1913 and 1948, annual coastal discharge of the Rio Chicama fluctuates markedly due to soil absorption, accentuating variation in mountain rainfall.

glacier ice. The Titicaca region remained drier than today until increased rainfall led to lake filling after 1600 BC. However, water levels later dropped during attenuated droughts between about 900–800, and 400–200 BC as well as between AD 1–300, and AD 1100–1450. During the last episode, called the 'long drought,' rainfall declined on the order of 10–15 percent. Between AD 562 and 594 shorter 'extreme drought,' with a 20–25 percent precipitation decline, is also documented in ice cores. In some cases it was both drier and cooler. The long drought saw a 0.6° C drop in temperature, resulting in a 70-m downward shift in ecological zones in some high mountain regions. In all cases drought stress upon runoff farming was disproportionally greater than upon rainfall farming due to dry mountain soils spongeing up scarce moisture. Alternatively, wet periods conferred disproportional benefits on runoff farming and coastal irrigation. Andean rainfall exceeded long term norms by 25 percent or more at the beginning of the Little Ice Age between AD 1500 and 1700, and wet periods are documented around AD 900–1000 and AD 400–500.

Distribution of resources

Human adaptations to the Cordillera have been shaped by the distribution of natural resources. Resources are broadly similar over vast tracts of the tropical lowlands where societies, even thousands of kilometers apart, relied upon similar resources including manioc, maize, and the same kinds of wild plants and animals. Likewise, the Andean coastal desert is very long, but the basic

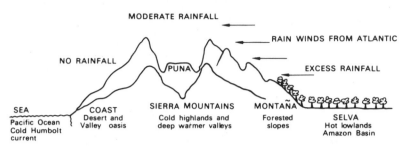

13 Cross-section of the Andes, showing general environmental conditions.
Irrigation was vital to agriculture in the dry coastal zone.

resources in different oasis valleys are generally comparable. Environmental similarities in the coastal and tropical lowlands are reinforced by limited fluctuations in annual temperatures that allow crops to grow year-round when adequate quantities of water are available.

Seasonal variation increases with elevation, and plant-growth cycles are successively shorter at progressively higher altitudes. In the towering mountains, ecological zones are compressed and stacked atop one another. Andean people can trek 100 km as the crow flies and go from hilly jungle to alpine tundra, crossing counterparts of the major continental life zones. Mountain populations around the world pursue farming, herding, and the exploitation of multiple ecological zones because stacked habitats with different growing seasons are close together and the productivity of different zones fluctuates from year to year. In the Andes, this exploitation pattern moves people and produce up and down the mountains, and it is called 'verticality,' in contrast to 'horizontality' which typifies lowland movement.

Verticality and horizontality are associated with different means of procuring resources. Mountain families typically exploit three or more ecological zones, such as high pasturelands, lower potato lands, and still lower farmlands. Consequently, they *directly* procure commodities from a series of habitats by moving produce along a vertical or elevational axis with the aid of llama pack animals. Alternatively, in desert and tropical lowlands people generally make their living in a single continental life zone. Because major zones are far apart, resources from distant habitats are procured *indirectly* by trade, barter, or exchange with other people, which benefits from watercraft transporting commodities along the Humboldt Current or the Amazon and its tributaries.

Farming the Andes

In addition to favorable sunshine, temperature, and soil nutrients, Andean farming depends upon domesticated plants, arable land, and appropriate moisture. The Cordillera is plagued by the problem that where there is land there is often little or no water and vice versa. Furthermore, moisture supplies are fickle, vacillating between wet and dry years, decades and centuries. To cope with these problems, people moved prodigious quantities of earth and water to

	Annual Mean Temperature °C	Annual Rainfall (dm)	Altitude (m)
Aracacia xanthorrhiza (arracacha)	15-23	7-15	850-956
Arachis hypogaea (peanut)	11-27	3-40	46-1000
Capsicum annuum (chili pepper)	9-27	3-40	2-1000
Capsicum frutescens (chili pepper)	8-27	30-40	385-1000
Chenopodium quinoa (quinoa)	5-27	6-26	28-3878
Cucurbita ficifolia (squash)	11-23	3-17	850-956
Cucurbita maxima (squash)	7-27	3-27	385-1000
Cucurbita moschata (squash)	7-27	3-28	28-1000
Erythroxylon coca (coca)	17-27	7-40	450-1200
Gossypium barbadense (cotton)	9-26	5-40	320-1006
Ipomoea batatas (sweet potato)	9-27	3-42	28-1000
Lagenaria siceraria (gourd)	15-27	7-28	850-956
Manihot esculenta (manioc)	15-29	5-40	46-1006
Nicotiana tabacum (tobacco)	7-27	3-40	57-1000
Oxalis tuberosa (oca)	12-25	5-25	850-1700
Persea americana (avocado)	13-27	3-40	320-1750
Phaseolus lunatus (lima bean)	9-27	3-42	28-1000
Phaseolus vulgaris (common bean)	5-27	3-42	2-3700
Psidium guajava (guava)	15-29	2-42	28-1000
Solanum tuberosum (potato)	4-27	3-26	2-3830
Tropaelum tuberosum (mashwa)	8-25	7-14	850-3700
Ullucus tuberosus (olluco)	11-12	14	3700-3830
Zea mays (maize)	5-29	3-40	2-3350

14 Approximate elevational growing ranges of Andean domesticated plants.

create artificial agrarian landscapes based upon a marvelous array of techniques. Rainfall farming on relatively flat land at elevations of 2,500–3,500 m is the simplest means of agrarian production, if not the oldest in the Cordillera.

During drought, customary quantities of mountain precipitation and soil moisture still occur, but only at higher altitudes some 100–400 m above their normal distribution. Topographic slopes and roughness, as well as inclement weather, increase with altitude. Therefore, reclaiming rugged drought-tolerant terrain requires great labor to build and maintain agricultural terraces vital for curtailing the erosion of thin mountain soils. Dry centuries during the long AD 1100–1450 drought witnessed the construction of millions of terraces, called *andenes,* and by some debatable accounts the Spanish named the Cordillera after these ubiquitous works. Multitudes of these terraces lie abandoned, because they are costly to maintain in earthquake country and crops fair better at lower, warmer elevations. Andenes are an apt reminder that there is much more arable land at high elevations than at low ones, but fewer than 20 percent of major Andean cultigens grow well above 3,000 m, whereas 90 percent of all indigenous crops thrive below 1,000 m. This elevational inversion of land availability and crop diversity created far-reaching supply and demand problems that underlie verticality and Arid Montane adaptations.

Normally, runoff farming generates much higher yields than rainfall farming. During eras of abundant runoff expansive tracts of low terrain around

Plate 2

the saturated margins of Lake Titicaca were reclaimed by mounding up soil to create 'ridged fields' – long, wide planting ridges that are elevated and separated by deep parallel troughs filled with slow-moving water that warms during the day and releases frost-protecting heat at night. When lake levels fell by 12 m or more during the long drought no less than 50,000 hectares of ridged fields were left dry stranded and abandoned.

Along the arid Pacific watershed at least 85 percent of sierra farming and virtually all desert farming is sustained by runoff irrigation. However, channeling stream flow across rugged terrain requires long, often large canal systems that must be built and maintained cooperatively. More than 60 short, steep rivers descend the western watershed to cross a stretch of desert longer than that traversed by the Nile or Tigris rivers. Whereas Near Eastern rivers tend to unite people living along their banks, the multitude of Andean rivers promotes separation and segregation. Furthermore, every river supplying an oasis valley or sierra basin feeds a series of separate canal systems each capable of operating independently and supporting an autonomous population. During drought, rainfall farming is depressed less severely than runoff farming and coastal irrigation suffers the most because it is furthest away from mountain precipitation. Desert people had few means of mitigating the long drought, other than digging 'sunken gardens' down to the water table where subsurface runoff could sustain plant growth. This required great labor and it was only practical where ground water was near the surface. Called *cochas* in the altiplano, sunken gardens were also dug in the Titicaca Basin during dry times.

Geography of the Four Quarters

The Incas viewed Cuzco as a sacred city and they structured it according to Andean cosmological principles, which included dual organization. Hence, the capital was divided into upper, *hanan,* and lower, *hurin,* sectors with five royal lineages occupying each. Boundary lines that quartered Tahuantinsuyu originated in the main plaza of the metropolis. One divider ran roughly northwest–southeast along the axis of the Milky Way, while the other boundary pursued a perpendicular course. Consequently, Cuzco sat at the nexus of the four quarters, midway between lowland desert and jungle, and close to the Nudo de Vilcanota, which divided the northern sierra from the southern altiplano.

Collasuyu was the largest and southernmost quarter of Tahuantinsuyu, stretching from the Pacific shores of the Atacama desert, over the mountains to the eastern tropical forest. It was dominated by the high plains of the altiplano, where in the region of Lake Titicaca seasonal rainfall was 50 cm or more, with cool but tolerable temperatures. Here the Aymara-speaking kingdoms were densely settled and became the first target of Inca conquest. The lands along Lake Titicaca formed the bread basket and power base of highland Tahuantinsuyu.

1 Modern highland Indians still pursue many of the traditional adaptations to mountain life that evolved centuries ago, providing insights into the beliefs, languages and customs of their ancient Andean ancestors.

Arid Montane adaptations

2 (left) Terracing is vital to farming the rugged Andes mountains, and steep flights of stone-faced terraces such as these in the Urubamba Valley (center) were an Inca tradition not duplicated by modern farmers.

3 (right) The Inca city of Machu Picchu overlooks the rugged mountains of Antisuyu.

4 (below) Llamas and alpacas, which pasture on the puna, above the elevational limits of agriculture, are essential to survival in the high mountains.

5 *(above) The Río Paramonga (bottom) supplies water to large canals that transformed the barren desert into agricultural oases. Built late in prehistory, the imposing hill-top bastion sanctuary of Fortaleza de Paramonga overlooks the verdant valley.*

6 *(below) View of the coastal city of Pachacamac from the air.*

7 *(opposite) A space shuttle view of the desert coast showing (from top to bottom) the Moche, Viru, Chao, Santa and Nepeña Valleys.*

Maritime-Oasis adaptations

Coast and Tropical Forest adaptations

8 (left) A fisherboy on a balsa raft. Watercraft were fashioned from reeds because the desert yields no wood.

9 (above) Supplying fish and other foodstuffs, jungle rivers were vital to life in the tropical forest. Seasonal flooding enriched adjacent soils for farming, and the waterways provided routes for long-distance trade and commerce.

10 (right) Feathered cloth, such as this coastal tunic, was highly prized and manufactured by skilled specialists.

11 (overleaf) Mountain adaptations united herding and farming, with llamas supplying both fertilizer for crops and a means of transporting produce between far-flung mountain habitats.

The huge lake holds a wealth of resources and its deep waters trap and release warmth which mitigates frost damage to adjacent fields. Abundant, relatively flat farm land lies mostly within a narrow zone between about 3,500 m and the upper alpine limits of plant growth. Altitude, frost, hail, erratic rainfall, a short growing season, and poor soils that must be fallowed frequently allow only the most hardy and specialized of crops. Staples included a variety of tubers, such as oca (*Oxalis tuberosa*), ulluco (*Ullucus tuberosus*), and potatoes (*Solanum*), of which there are more than 60 varieties tended by altiplano folk. Robust chenopods called quiñoa and cañihuas (*Chenopodium quinoa* and *Chenopodium pallidicaula*) were domesticated for grains. Above about 3,900 m vast expanses of dry puna grasslands provided grazing for herds of llama and *Plate 4* alpaca, which in turn provided fertilizer critical to crops when pastured on the stubble of harvested or fallowed fields. This reciprocal arrangement between farming and herding, called 'agropastoralism', transformed the Titicaca altiplano into the most populated region of the Andes, and its rich archaeological heritage includes the ancient cities of Pukara and Tiwanaku at the northern and southern ends of the lake.

South of Titicaca the Atacama Desert sweeps over the Cordillera Negra and transforms the uplands into salt puna and salt lakes. There are occasional highland oases but runoff from rainfall is scarce and even the coastal valleys are small. Maritime exploitation, however, dates back 11,000 years along the narrow band of upwelling currents that hug the desert shores and provide the richest fishery and marine biomass of the Western Hemisphere. Mollusks, large fish, sea mammals, and marine birds were taken; and small fish such as anchovies were harvested throughout the year with simple nets from small water craft, then dried whole or after being ground into meal, and stored. This maritime adaptation remained basically independent of valley oasis agriculture.

Antisuyu, the eastern quarter of Tahuantinsuyu, stretched into the rugged montaña forests overlooking the Amazon. The boundaries of this province are less clear, but included the rugged sierra and puna uplands forming the eastern rim of the Cuzco Basin. The steep eastern Cordillera dominates the landscape, the sheer mountainsides drained by fast-flowing streams and rivers in deep canyons and valleys providing negligible flat land. Here the highest degree of natural diversity found in the continent is compressed into narrow stratified ecological zones that follow the horizontal, but irregular contours of the mountainsides, creating a vertical series of stacked agricultural zones. From potatoes and quiñoa near mountaintops to manioc and tropical fruits on the jungle floor, each habitat is characterized by particular patterns of rainfall, sunshine, and temperature, and calls for different techniques and times of cultivation. The rugged topography provides relatively little land suitable for farming, but is highly prized because of the many different types of crops that can be grown. Altiplano and sierra villagers regularly descend to the montaña to tend fields of maize, coca, cotton, and other staples.

The extremely broken topography could not accommodate large populations. The Inca empire incorporated much of the montaña but their penetration of the jungle below about 1,500 m was negligible. The lords of Cuzco actively developed their Antisuyu holdings, particularly in the Urubamba Valley where the hillsides were carved into great flights of terraces. A string of monumental *Plate 3* settlements were built, including the mountaintop retreats of Machu Picchu and Wiñay Wayna as well as the larger complexes of Pisac and Ollantaytambo. Antisuyu provided a refuge for the Inca court following Pizarro's capture of Cuzco, and a base for guerrilla warfare.

Cuntisuyu, the small, southwestern quarter of Tahuantinsuyu, stretched from Cuzco to the Pacific coast near the Ica Valley in the north and the Moquegua Valley in the south, including sierra habitats. However, the dominant geographical features of the province were the dry western slopes of the Cordillera and the bleak coastal desert. Normally there is no annual rainfall below elevations of about 1,800 m, leaving the western Andean escarpment and Pacific coastlands barren. Stratified ecological zones occur along the mountain slopes, but extreme aridity leaves these habitats impoverished in comparison with those of Antisuyu. The Cuntisuyu desert is crossed by 15 short rivers, which support terrace farming along the sierra headwaters where irrigation supplements seasonal rainfall. At mid-course they flow in deep canyon-like courses offering few farming potentials. Near the ocean they widen out to form V-shaped valleys with greater agricultural potential, but decreasing runoff from southern mountain rainfall leaves populations small.

Here desert dwellers made intensive use of marine assets and another resource complex called *lomas*. During the cool southern winter the coastlands are enveloped by dense sea fogs, which condense on certain slopes and plains to support a remarkable flora for a few short months. These lomas provide feed for cattle, sheep and goats, and during very moist years and El Niño years can support crops. In the past, herds of guanaco – wild camelids related to the llama and alpaca – pastured on the fog plants and were intensively hunted.

Chinchaysuyu, the second largest quarter of Tahuantinsuyu, encompassed Ecuador and more than two-thirds of Peru. Reaching from the Pacific coast to the montaña, it stretched north from Cuzco, past Quito where the Cordillera is low and tropical, and ended on the fringes of present-day Colombia. Chinchaysuyu embraced the fractured sierra and included large expanses of dry grasslands gradually giving way to wet puna splintered into long meandering ridges and mesas separated by deep streams and rivers. At high elevation near their headwaters, sierra drainages tend to be wide and basin-shaped, with steeply sloping sides sometimes called the *quichua* zone. But with decreasing altitude, the rivers cut into deep gorges with little farmland.

By flowing north and then east to feed the Amazon, the sierra drainage pattern tended to draw highlanders into closer contact with the montaña and jungle. In Ecuador Chinchaysuyu loses its purely Andean characteristics as tropical vegetation envelops both the Atlantic and Pacific watershed, and mangrove swamps dot the humid coast.

Plate 7   The desert in the northern quarter is crossed by 40 streams and rivers, including 10 of the 12 largest that descend the desert watershed. Along the wide flat coastal plain above the Río Santa it was possible to construct canal networks fed by two or more rivers. The largest such system united the Ríos Motupe, La Leche, Lambayeque, Zaña, and Jequetepeque and formed the so-called Lambayeque canal complex. To the south the Ríos Chicama and Moche were also once linked. The ten valleys from the Río Motupe south to Río Viru comprised almost one-third of all land reclaimed along the desert coast and held about one-third of the coastal population. As the heartland of Chimor, the Incas' greatest rival, this region imparted a duality to Andean geopolitics: northern coastlands and southern uplands.

The largest desert river, Río Santa, disgorges where there is no coastal plain for agriculture. Although streams and rivers to the south are largely isolated from one another by mountains, canal link-ups between adjacent valleys were built across the difficult terrain between the Ríos Supe, Pativilca and Fortaleza and at the mouths of the Ríos Chillon and Rimac. These irrigated oasis valleys of the western desert gave the highest yields per unit in the Inca realm, and it was in this setting that Pizarro founded Lima as 'the City of Kings', after his sack of Tahuantinsuyu.

The area of coastal desert used for agriculture was less than 10 percent of the total and therefore small in comparison with the Titicaca altiplano or the sierra basins. Many more people lived in the mountains than along the littoral. However, the mountain populations were scattered while those on the coast were densely concentrated in oases. Andean civilizations were products of large numbers of people living close together, and the distribution of large architectural monuments broadly mirrors the past distribution of dense populations. The highland cities of Cuzco, Huari, Pukara, and Tiwanaku reflect the southern, upland demographic pole, while the large architectural complexes of the coastal valleys of Chinchaysuyu reflect the northern counterpart, including the biggest pyramidal mounds of South America in the valleys of the Ríos Lambayeque, Moche, and Casma.

Making a living

Evolutionary pathways diverged in the central Andes because the arid Cordillera offers very different types and spatial arrangements of basic resources. There is greater biological diversity at low elevations where many different types of crops can be grown. Diversity and crop types diminish with altitude, but mountain habitats are narrow and stacked, allowing several to be worked concurrently. Farming and herding provide carbohydrates and protein and each vocation can be pursued individually when mountain farmland and pastureland are widely separated. Yet, upland farming and herding are more productive and reliable when practiced together. Consequently, Arid Montane adaptations are characterized by people doing both. Maritime-Oasis adaptations, on the other hand, are characterized by economic specialization, because marine fishing and desert-valley farming produce higher, more secure yields when they are perused individually on a full-time basis. However, Tropical

Forest adaptations combined the activities of river fishing, hunting, and farming.

Contrasts between horizontally spaced and vertically stratified life zones required different solutions to supply and demand problems. Highland agropastoralists secured essential plants and animals directly because each mountain community produced its own. By contrast, coastal fishing and farming specialists acquired each others' produce indirectly by barter, or *trueque*. Although direct and indirect procurement strategies characterize the highlands and lowlands respectively, they were not mutually exclusive and people often engaged in both.

Arid Montane adaptations

Life in the towering Cordillera depends upon herding and farming, which people pursue concurrently when possible. This is because animal fertilizer enriches nutrient-poor mountain soils and harvested or fallow fields offer grazing areas for herd animals, which provide food, wool, and pack transport. Large populations are sustained where puna pasture lies near high-altitude potato and tuber farmland. Agropastoral communities in the potato zone typically grow other crops in still lower ecological tiers in order to reduce the many risks of mountain farming. Annual fluctuations in rainfall, temperature, frost, and hail often produce poor yields at one altitudinal zone without affecting harvests in another ecological tier. To allay the unpredictable, people exploit a series of vertically stacked environmental zones in order to spread risks and rewards, favoring economic generalization over specialization.

By exploiting a vertical series of life zones, each with a different crop growth cycle, herding and farming can go on throughout the year. Yet, poorly developed, nutrient-deficient mountain soils that sustain potato and tuber farming require many years of regenerative fallowing after a few years of cultivation. Village land management was and is traditionally a corporate affair, with consensus decisions as to whether to farm or leave fallow large sectors of communal holdings. Sectoral farming and fallowing makes llama and alpaca herd management easier by blocking out large tracts of land for either pasture or cultivation. With old fields going out of use and fallow ones coming into production, there is always much to do, and because labor is a scarce commodity, both men and women work in the fields while children tend herds. Although multiple zones are worked and everyone toils, drought, hail, frost, and pestilence concede only one good harvest every three to five years. Therefore, storage for lean times is exceptionally important. To this end, certain varieties of potatoes are freeze-dried to produce *chuño*, while llama and alpaca meat is sun-dried to make *charqui* (jerky), an equally durable commodity.

Plates 4, 11

In the world's highest mountains many forces of natural selection are similar, including anoxia, cold temperatures, frost, hail, poor soils, short growing seasons, very limited crop diversity, rugged topography, and marked rainfall variation over short distances. Consequently, human populations in the Alps, Himalayas, and Andes exhibit many parallel adaptations, including symbiotic

15 Grown at low altitudes, coca leaves are chewed with lime kept in small gourd vessels. The lime is removed with a thin spatula and transferred to the mouth as depicted in this Moche ceramic painting.

integration of agricultural and pastoral production, exploitation of multiple ecological zones, reliance on different crops from different altitudes, sequential timing of work in different ecological tiers, dependence upon dung fertilizer, frequent fallowing of fields, emphasis on long-term storage of food products, relatively little sexual division of labor in subsistence tasks, and a mixture of household and communal control of land use.

The Cordillera's Arid Montane adaptations are set apart by a proclivity for people traversing great distances to directly secure distant resources. Walking two, three or more days to farm a faraway field, in a distant ecological niche that produces fruit, grain, or other matter not found in one's mountain homestead, is called 'ecological complementarity' by ethnohistorian John V. Murra, who first defined this adaptive pattern. More generally, the pattern is called 'verticality' because people and produce move elevationally or vertically up and down the mountain topography. Although highland agropastoralists produce self-sufficient quantities of carbohydrates and protein, people want lower-altitude products such as maize, fruit, coca, and salt from iodine-rich marine products that mitigate goiter. The model of vertical complementarity posits that mountain communities maintained satellite colonies of villagers in far-flung ecological zones in order to secure distant commodities. Occupied on a seasonal or year-round basis, colonists work their community's economic satellites to grow low-altitude produce or to obtain resources such as salt and seaweed. Products from distant enclaves are returned to the home settlement for redistribution in the community. Villagers reciprocate by looking after the colonists' fields, herds, and kindred, and expatriates retain full rights and privileges in their highland homeland. Indeed, unwavering commitments to reciprocity bind economic satellites to their home community by insuring just recompense for those who work distant holdings.

Many mountain settlements are located more than a day's walk from puna pastures. Consequently, many communities maintain economic satellites in the

16 Guamán Poma's illustrations of Inca agriculture: left to right, maize planting, guarding the young shoots from birds and animals, and harvesting.

grasslands where herding takes place on either a rotational or a full-time basis. John Murra labeled the puna a 'multi-ethnic' ecological zone because it is exploited by enclaves from many different social groups. There is mixed evidence for more restricted multi-ethnic colonization of lower altitudinal zones. At elevations of 1,000 and 2,000 m, maize, coca, and numerous other crops grow in irrigated drainages descending the arid Pacific sierra. Important to both mountain and coastal societies, control of this zone often vacillated between autonomous local populations, lowlanders, and highlanders. Yet, when highlanders pushed into a low sierra drainage they generally came from only one or two adjacent ethnic groups.

Directly procuring resources via economic satellites and ecological complementarity varies in form with elevation, topography, and the relative proximity of different habitats. It can be 'compact,' with few foreign enclaves where resource tiers are closely spaced and within easy walking distance, or it can be 'dispersed,' with many separate enclaves where ecological zones are widely separated. The forested eastern flanks of the Cordillera foster compact expressions, while the arid Pacific watershed favors dispersed expressions. Relative to longitude, complementarity is least developed in the equatorial north where the mountains are low and tropical. Elaboration and intensity increase to the south as the Cordillera becomes higher, wider, and drier.

In the Titicaca region Lupaka and other Aymara kingdoms maintained numerous, often large colonies on both flanks of the range. Discontinuous land holdings distributed among scattered colonies made these kingdoms *extensive* in terms of being far-flung, but not *intensive* in terms political hegemony because their colonies were separated by vast tracts of land belonging to others. Further south the altiplano is drier still, with brine lakes, dry pans, and stubby grasslands called salt puna. Here Chilean archaeologists maintain that herders made seasonal rounds between sparse widely scattered farming communities moving goods from one to another by llama caravans. Although *trueque* barter played a role, herders and farmers maintained real and fictive bonds of kinship, reinforcing their symbiosis.

The origins of verticality and ecological complementarity reach far back in time and vary in different regions of the Cordillera. They were certainly intertwined with the domestication of plants and animals. Domestication exacerbated natural disparities in the elevational distribution of resources. As we have seen, few crop types grow at high altitudes where farmland is most abundant, whereas many domesticates thrive in low life zones. Furthermore, mountain farming requires fertilizers, as well as llama pack animals for movement of bulk cargo. As highland populations grew in size and low altitude domesticates grew in diversity, demand for foreign products certainly increased.

Direct procurement of distant resources via colonization is a central Andean folk adaptation that likely intensified in tandem with the rise of agropastoralism. Its initial development was undoubtedly constrained by the difficulties early autonomous communities confronted in establishing folk enclaves within lower territories permanently occupied by other people. Along the arid western watershed would-be colonists had to either irrigate new lands or obtain land already in production by coercion or reciprocally beneficial arrangements. Conflict and contention over holdings in the lower sierra were common when the Spanish arrived. By this time satellite land holdings and colonists were not generally identified with individual highland communities, but with large ethnic groups and strong political bodies. Thus, the development of ecological complementarity was furthered by the rise of social and political formations capable of forcefully engaging in colonization. Ultimately, the longstanding integration of direct resource procurement with both folk communities and the political economies of highland states suppressed the development of monetary systems, merchant classes, and vibrant marketplaces – all hallmarks of great empires elsewhere in the ancient world.

Most Andean people live at high altitude where crop diversity is the least. Consequently, for mountain people agriculture imparts a downward economic thrust to obtain products from low elevations where crop diversity is the greatest. The archaeological record is characterized by the recurrent presence of upland commodities and cultural influences in lower ecological settings. The

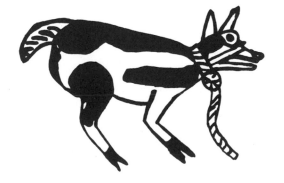

17 Important on the coast as well as in the mountains, llamas were depicted on Moche ceramics.

direct or indirect means by which such goods and ideas moved down is often unclear. However, evidence of lively commodity flow points to longlasting interaction between the Titicaca Basin and the Moquegua and Azapa Pacific drainages; the Ayacucho sierra and the coastal Ica and Nazca valleys; the Callejon de Huaylas and valleys from Santa to Casma; and the Cajamarca sierra and Jequetepeque Valley. Mountain political centers, such as Cuzco, Huari, and Tiwanaku, expanded both through the uplands as well as down into the lowlands where resource diversity was greatest. In contrast, coastal centers, such as Chimor and Moche, expanded along the Pacific littoral, with little penetration into the highlands above 2,000 m because their aim was to monopolize the most productive of Andean ecological settings: the lower Pacific watershed and its near-shore fishery.

Maritime-Oasis adaptations

Maritime-Oasis lifeways rely on vocational specialization and *trueque* exchange, beginning with the basic production of protein and carbohydrates. This is because coastal fishing and farming produce higher, more secure yields when each is pursued individually on a full-time basis. The two vocations entail different risks and technological demands, tied to different production cycles – one lunar, governed by tides and fish movement, and the other solar, governed by precipitation and plant growth. The two are also spatially distinct because farmers reside inland along rivers that cross the desert perpendicular to the sea, while fisherfolk reside by the shore.

The Andean fishery is by far the richest in the Western Hemisphere, and its near-shore upwelling currents support a prodigious biomass. Small craft, with small crews, can net-harvest schooling fish 280 days a year, and the diversity of *Plate 8* marine life allows fisherfolk to extract products ranging from seaweed and mollusks, through small and large fish, to sea birds and mammals. Exploitation of marine resources began at least 11,000 years ago, and persisted as an uninterrupted economic adaptation.

Peru's distinguished ethnohistorian, Maria Rostworowski de Diez Canseco, has shown that fishing and farming were non-overlapping ethnic specializations when the Spanish arrived. Fisherfolk in northern Peru spoke their own language or dialects, married among themselves, resided in separate communities under their own hierarchy of leaders, and venerated their own deities. Using sunken gardens dug along beaches they grew *totora* bulrush reeds for watercraft, cotton for fish nets and lines, and gourds for net floats, thus focusing upon industrial cultigens essential to maritime technology. In northern Chile similar ethnic specialization characterized Chongos fisherfolk who used log rafts to ply their trade. There are some archaeological cases of people residing at small coastal springs engaging in both fishing and farming. Yet the separation of the two enterprises is the long-term norm that still prevails.

Whereas all coastal waters can be fished, less than 10 percent of the desert *Plate 5* can be farmed due to sparse water. Irrigating the driest of deserts with runoff from the most rugged of mountains in the hemisphere is taxing and typically requires long canals that are corporately constructed and managed. Cultivation can go on year-round with water, but river flow is markedly seasonal and smaller drainages are dry part of the year. The most secure rights to annual river flow are enjoyed by upstream irrigation systems, whereas the lowest and last of downstream canals often have little flow to draw upon. Maintenance of irrigation systems takes place during the dry season, and is ever demanding due to stress from tectonic creep and frequent natural disasters.

Yields per hectare are the highest in Tahuantinsuyu, but they are irregular owing to irrigation's dependency on runoff from rainfall high in the Cordillera Negra where the soil soaks up substantial moisture. Consequently, large as well as small desert rivers have marked differences in yearly flow, and annual yields from irrigation vacillate between very good and very bad. Because drought depresses rainfall proportionally less than runoff, crop losses for coastal irrigation farmers are two to three times greater than those for mountain rainfall farmers. Nonetheless, irrigated oasis valleys supported large, densely packed agrarian populations.

The fundamental division between marine (fishing) and terrestrial (farming) adaptations underlay a coastal tradition of more complex economic specialization. Some social groups were named for particular tasks they engaged in, such as cooks and deer hunters. Specialization extended to art, craft, and construction: metallurgy in Chimor was in the hands of skilled technicians organized in a guild-like manner and subsidized by the state; the design and engineering of irrigation systems was similarly in the hands of experienced technicians. Specialty tasks permeated the royal courts, where nobles held titles such as steward of the shell trumpet, drink master, and master of feathered clothmakers.

Technological specialization was fostered by both coastal and highland nobility, because the lords of Chan Chan as well as Cuzco sought to monopolize the production of valued goods, such as fine textiles and precious metals. Similarly, *Plate 10* the nobility furthered *trueque* barter and indirect procurement with their demands for exotic goods from far away. Long-distance seafaring to secure foreign commodities was an ancient littoral tradition. Ecuador was the focus for maritime exchange because its warm tropical waters, and low, forested Cordillera offered unusual products not found in the higher, drier Andes. It was home to exchange specialists called *mindala*, who supplied local chiefs and rulers with foreign goods including precious metals and gems. To engage northern commerce lords in the Lambayeque region had coppersmiths produce *naipes* or 'axe money' as a medium of exchange for a short period around AD 1000. Later Chimor monopolized the Ecuadorian sea routes, only to have them stripped away by the Incas and refocused upon the Chincha Valley which the Spanish found home to 6,000 maritime tradesmen who regularly sailed to tropical Ecuador to procure alien goods, including colorful *Spondylus* shells, held sacred by Andeans and the Inca nobility.

Whereas fisherfolk and farmers exchanged produce, coastal señoríos and parcialidades sought economic autonomy by expanding their territories to include

18 The Moche were seafaring people, as suggested by this vase painting depicting sailors with a boatload of pottery vessels.

both maritime and agrarian communities. As opposed to extensive mountain states with far-flung colonies, coastal states were more intensive and incorporated adjacent valleys to form continuous political dominions. Nonetheless, seafaring capabilities facilitated the establishment of distant economic enclaves and coastal colonies.

In overview, Maritime-Oasis and Arid Montane adaptations were not separated by great distances because, on a clear day, fisherfolk could easily see aloof mountaintop fields. The two sets of adaptations were kept apart by extreme topographic relief, elevation, climate, and anoxia, which created ecological differences that demanded distinct strategies for making a living. Yet both populations arose from a common ancestral stock and were interlinked by direct and indirect exchange, with close physical proximity contributing to basic shared beliefs about social and cosmological organization. Andean traditions were also enriched by those of the Amazon, and where the Cordillera lowered and narrowed in the north tropical forest, rainforest adaptations submerged and replaced those geared to the high mountains and coastal desert.

CHAPTER THREE

THE INCA MODEL OF STATECRAFT

Many aspects of Inca statecraft differ from those of other ancient civilizations because Andean institutions of rule were adapted to unusual, multifaceted environmental conditions. The Incas and their political predecessors elaborated basic principles of organization that first evolved among local communities. Therefore, it is useful to review folk organization before describing the imperial order of Tahuantinsuyu.

The cosmos

Andeans revere a wide variety of sacred phenomena known as *huacas*. Some are ancient human works, but most are works of nature. Nature is believed to be highly animate, charging the landscape with interactive forces. This befits a dynamic Cordillera of smoldering volcanoes, frequent earthquakes, and recurrent El Niño crises. There are male and female forces within the indigenous cosmology of gender duality, balance, and equality. Deep reverence of *Pacha Mama* (mother earth) is pervasive, and she receives offerings and prayers on all agricultural occasions by all who till the soil. Sharing procreative powers, women feel particularly close to Pacha Mama. They also share a close relationship with the moon – the female counterpart of the male sun. Prominent mountain peaks, called apu, are influential spiritual forces and primary sources of water, the life blood of mother earth.

The Andean cosmos is one of layers with outer celestial and inner terrestrial spheres overlaying and underlying the earth's surface. In the remote mythical past giants and superhumans emerged from within to frolic and fight over this world. A great deluge swept away multitudes, but many were transfigured into the landscape forming alpine *apu*, and other topographic features. Primordial humans then ascended from the inner sphere and heroically colonized the earth, leaving behind puzzling ruins and huacas of the distant past. Eventually, a more steadfast existence arose when the forebears of living people settled the landscape and gave rise to contemporary communities. This all-encompassing cosmology provides deep identification with the environment. Andean people literally read their physical surroundings as a resonant text of sacred places and spaces that commemorate a trip across time and changing landscapes from super beings to human beings to present beings.

Past beings interact with present ones because life and death are a continuum and expiration entails no loss of vital essence. Explained in vegetational metaphors, this notion finds analogies between chili peppers and common people. Buds and babies bloom forth moist, fleshy, and fat. Both mature to solid adult fruit. Then growth gives way to parching, wrinkling, and shrinking. Eventually the shriveled old expire, falling to the ground where they dry further, mummifying. Yet desiccated peppers remain potent hot givers and bearers of life, and people are no different. For Pre-Hispanic people the 'afterlife' was not a metaphysical sphere, but a corporeal realm where the deceased remained puissant, requiring food, clothing, and care. To enter the ancestral realm a corpse had to be intact, because physical dismemberment by enemies, carnivores or carrion eaters condemned a soul to eternal damnation. Colonial accounts of looting at Chan Chan, the capitol of Chimor, indicate that indigenous people formerly distinguished at least two classes of sacrosanct buildings. One, called *huacas sepulturas*, were burial places and mausoleums of important deceased. The other, called *huacas adoratorios*, were sanctuaries and temples for the adoration of divinities. Thus, the cosmos was animated by forces of afterlife and forces of nature, each with their own devotional huacas.

The galaxy

Water, vital to life in the arid Cordillera, is believed to originate in a cosmic sea that the earth floats upon. Moisture is picked up from the sea and transported heavenward by the Milky Way – *Mayu*, the 'celestial river.' The star stream then releases rainfall on high apu peaks where essential moisture descends in runnels and rivers to feed crops, canals, and Pacha Mama who nourishes humanity. Farmers watch Mayu closely, because solstices of the Milky Way coincide with onsets of the wet and dry seasons. To scrutinize the Milky Way is to follow the course of galactic rotation, which is noticeably inclined by 26 to 30 degrees from the plane of the earth's rotation. Seen from South America, the difference in orbiting planes means that Mayu slants left to right half the year. Then a spectacular reversal transpires when the Milky Way crosses zenith. During 24 hours, the celestial river flips to a right-to-left slant for the next six months. The annual galactic turnabout creates two intersecting, intercardinal (NE–SW and SE–NW) luminary axes dividing the heavens into four quarters, known as *suyu* in Runa Simi (Quechua).

Using apu peaks as skyline sighting points, the annual movement of astronomical phenomena can be tracked by the quarters of Mayu that they arise in and the suyus they travel across. Long ago people observed that celestial cycles often correlated with biological cycles. With Mayu girding their heavens, Andeans used many astronomical phenomena to time impending conditions and to schedule work in different ecological zones. Celestial luminaries such as the sun, moon, planets, pleiades and other constellations forecast plant cycles and scheduled sowing. Galactic quartering also facilitates tracking of the great stellar voids. These 'dark-cloud' constellations include an adult and a baby llama, a fox, a partridge, a toad, and a serpent. Their movements are used to predict animal behavior and schedule herding.

Keeping track of cycles in the heavens and cycles on earth is aided by spatial association. Therefore, villagers have used the four intercardinal quarters of Mayu to divide their terrestrial homelands in to suyus aligned with the galactic

NE–SW and SE–NW axes. Naming their imperium 'the land of the four quarters' indicates that the Incas applied these principles on an imperial scale.

The ayllu

Integrating farming and herding, Arid Montane adaptations often demand that several tasks are executed at the same time, but in widely separated places. A married couple is the minimal economic unit that can do this. Yet, newlyweds working alone cannot erect adequate housing or transform wilderness into fertile fields. Nor can they efficiently cope with the agricultural cycle during labor-intensive times of plowing, planting, and harvesting. Thus, a couple – a nuclear family – is a basic economic entity, but not a self-sufficient one. Because additional helping hands are needed, the most desirable marriage partners are those with the most kin. Relatives bring commitments to share work, resources, and returns. Therefore, in the Andes the autonomous unit of production and reproduction is an alliance of households and kindred that exchange labor and jointly own land and other resources. These collectives are called *ayllu* in Quechua. This institution is not simply a group of people, property, and things. The ayllu is an organizational charter that allows problems of different scope and scale to be addressed by folk collectives of variable size and inclusiveness.

Ayllu charters are kinship charters based on real or fictive descent. They emphasize unity, duality, hierarchy, and replicative organization. Unity is established by a founding ancestor who provides the collective with its identity. Duality is a cosmic and gender principle applied to the founder's heirs which

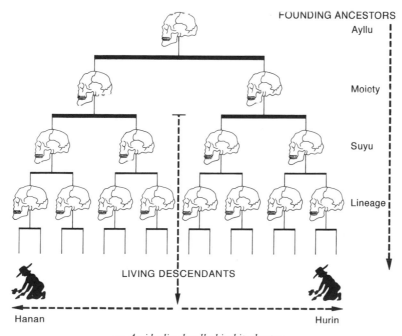

19 An idealized ayllu kinship charter.

include a pair of prominent forebears, such as older and younger siblings who gave rise to separate descent lines or lineages that divide all living households into two groups of intermarriageable families, called moieties. Replication occurs when moiety founders, in turn, have two heirs who further subdivide living descendants into quarters, or suyus that can be split yet again. Hierarchy is ingrained because ancestors who were older sons and daughters produce descendants who are senior to kin lines arising from younger siblings. Therefore, individuals are ranked by genealogical proximity to their ayllu, moiety, suyu and lineage founders. At birth, different members of the same ayllu inherit different relationships – responsibilities to others and claims upon them – that determine access to labor, land, water, and other collective assets. Although ayllu are communal organizations, not everyone is equal. Some individuals belong to prosperous families and kin lines, others do not.

At the time of contact, the most prevalent ayllu were small kin collectives that traced descent from a human mummy or *mallqui*. In addition to exchanging labor, members of mallquis ayllu collectively held and managed pastureland, farmland, canals, water, and other assets. Preserving corporate assets within the kin collective was vital to corporate survival, and this was promoted by moiety organization. In harsh environments with limited resources and scattered populations, dual organization of marriageable descent groups was highly adaptive for small groups because it allowed members to wed within their own community. The economic benefit of intra-ayllu matrimony lay in retaining property and durable resources within the collective, thereby fostering corporate autonomy and survival.

20 *A woman weaving with a back-strap loom. Textile production occupied more people for more time than any other Andean craft and fine fabrics served as a form of currency.*

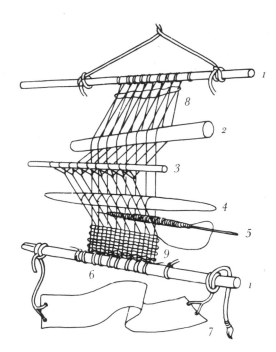

21 *The components of a back-strap loom – an instrument still employed by traditional native weavers. (1) Warp beam, (2) shed stick, (3) heddle rod, (4) sword, (5) bobbin with yarn, (6) warp attachment, (7) belt or back-strap, (8) warp threads, (9) weft threads.*

Related families live near one another in suyu quarters and moiety partitions. Moiety organization split Inca Cuzco into upper, *hanan*, and lower, *hurin*, residential areas. When women marry, they generally move to their husband's moiety or suyu, but retain full membership in their lineage and moiety of origin. In Pre-Hispanic times, women often traced descent and inheritance through their mothers, whereas men traced ancestry and birthrights through their fathers. Gender parallelism in kinship charters divided people into dual, interdependent sexually linked spheres, and at the folk level marriage rituals emphasized an ideology of gender equality between wife and husband.

Rights and responsibilities

Although ranked descent charters condone inequities, people sometimes marry into or are adopted into other ayllu if they are willing to meet the responsibilities of membership. Obligations entail the most fundamental of Andean essentials, labor and work, and responsibilities are based on the creed of reciprocity – the belief that when something is rendered, something of equal kind or value will be returned. The Aymara word *ayni* designates a service rendered with obligatory repayment of equal kind. The Quechua word *mit'a* designates a 'turn' of labor and the equal exchange of work. Ayni and mit'a allow a household to temporarily mobilize more labor than that for which it has workers, and this is essential for mountain agropastoralism. An individual's brothers, sisters, their offspring, nieces, and nephews, comprise the nucleus of kin with which mit'a and ayni are exchanged for agricultural tasks, for house building, and for other jobs that a couple cannot do alone.

Ideally, the type of labor rendered is the same type of labor that will be returned. Strict accounting is involved. When male and female kin assemble to execute a job, such as plowing a relative's field, they do not work as a gang. Instead each couple works a different field row and then another. By clearly segmenting work the tasks that kindred render are clearly defined. Subdividing jobs into repetitive, modular tasks also characterizes large undertakings. When a number of ayllu are concerned with common endeavors, such as building churchyard or cemetery walls, each constructs and maintains a specified section.

Although work is carefully accounted for, among kindred it is often repaid with another type of service, or with goods resulting from other labor. Goods traditionally include textiles, and the time devoted to producing fabrics of a particular quality and size is well understood, but food is the commodity most frequently exchanged. When people render mit'a, they expect to be fed, and it is the obligation of those who are receiving labor to feed those who are rendering service. Beyond this, certain types of service are regularly repaid with staples. The exchange of food and other commodities fosters the redistribution of staples and dietary elements, thereby contributing to the health and well being of the collective.

Reciprocity obligations are passed from one generation to another. For example, when labor or food are loaned to help newlyweds build a home, the couple is obligated to repay the debt when their creditors' offspring wish to set up housekeeping, even though the original lenders of labor may be deceased. Consequently, reciprocity is a means of 'banking' labor and perishable commodities that can be loaned to others and then recalled in kind, decades later. This allows members of prosperous households and lineages to inherit investment credits for work, food, and goods from their progenitors.

Ancestors

Ethnographically, people who depend on circumscribed resources transmitted down kin lines often believe that their well being is fostered by forebears who remain vigilant and forceful. Ayllu autonomy and identity were traditionally based on collectively held resources. Communal assets were secured by primordial founders, while more immediate forebears established rights to use certain resources. Thus, the deceased had active economic roles among the living, and ancestor veneration was ubiquitous in the Andes at the time of contact. Veneration generally involved preserving, mummifying, and curating corpses of forebears. Mummies provided tangible documentation of relationships and responsibilities, and they reinforced commitments to social organization based upon descent and collective economic holdings. Artificial mummification began some 7,000 years ago, and then developed sporadically with a variety of expressions. When the Spanish arrived, evisceration, organ removal, embalming, skin tanning, and posing the deceased in lifelike postures were generally reserved for rulers and important people. Commoners were conserved by controlled desiccation.

The Inca fort of Sacsahuaman

12 (above) Crowning the heights of Cuzco, the great fortress of Sacsahuaman was completed in the fifteenth century only after decades of labor by a workforce of 30,000.

13 (below left) The imperial-style Inca architecture at Cuzco impressed the conquistadores.

14 (below right) Imposing polygonal masonry faced the great terraces of Sacsahuaman.

Inca architecture

*15 (left, above) Fine masonry embellished the terraces and ornamental
niches of Tampu Machay, site of a sacred spring where the emperor
Pachacuti is said to have lodged when he went hunting.*

*16 (left, below) Built of superb masonry, most buildings at Machu Picchu were rectangular.
Built atop a carved rock of special significance, the oval 'Torreon' (center right) was a sacred
building, its trapezoidal window perhaps providing a viewpoint for astronomical observations.*

17 (above) General view of Machu Picchu.

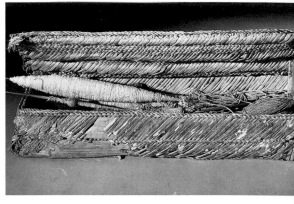

Andean textiles

18 (above left) A coastal native picks and cleans cotton. First cultivated for the manufacture of fishing-nets and clothing, cotton has dominated coastal textile traditions for 5,000 years.

19 (above right) Women were often buried with their weaving baskets, such as this one which contains spindles, thread, and loom implements.

20 (below) Paracas weavers 2,000 years ago produced ornate embroidered fabrics rich in iconography. The wool used for embroidering was dyed in a wide range of colors and was probably supplied by highland herders.

21 (right) This embroidered feline motif from a Paracas fabric depicts a costumed figure with a cat-like nose ornament and carrying a trophy head.

Inca ceramics

Opposite:

22 (top left) A classic Inca aryballoid vessel, displaying the distinctive shape and decoration of the imperial style.

23 (bottom left) After the fall of the city of Chan Chan to the Incas, Chimor's artisans toiled for their new overlords producing aryballoid vessels such as this, which is typically Inca in shape, but with ornamentation in the coastal Chimú tradition.

24 (center right) Holding birds, Inca women with shawls and long dresses are depicted in this late imperial style vessel. At Cuzco the style persisted into the initial decades of Spanish rule with increasing Hispanic influence as native artisans toiled under new rulers.

Inca metallurgy

25 (above) After sacking Cuzco, the conquistadores began looting ancient cemeteries for treasures such as this sheet gold funerary mask from Chimor.

26 (right) Inca silver figurine from Moquegua.

Farming origins: Guitarrero Cave

27 (above) Excavations at the mouth of
Guitarrero Cave in the central Andes.
Thomas Lynch found evidence here for the
oldest cultivated plants in the New World,
dating back 10,000 years.

28 (left) A stone scraper discovered at the
site was wrapped in deer hide and secured
with a cord binding.

During a year of mourning, cadavers were placed in a cave or sheltered placed and allowed to dry naturally. Then the mallquis were ritually received by the living, and ceremonially reunited with other deceased kindred in communal repositories of the dead.

Although most ayllus occupied their homelands for many centuries, common folk ignored unimportant forebears and compressed or 'telescoped' their genealogies around a few nodal mallquis. Yet notions of kinship and descent extended to prominent elements of the physical environment, therefore back in time to the primordial human and the superhuman past. Today similar sentiments of relatedness are evoked by huacas, such as Camelot, or majestic apu, such as Mount Fuji. Kinship, along with the environment, allowed Andean folk to identify tangible ancestral founders for higher, more inclusive levels of ayllu organization. Claiming an ancient monolith or other object to be a mutual founder sanctioned the integration of adjacent communities and kin groups for pursuits of common interests. Due to small size, mallquis ayllus with human founders were commonly allied with other such groups in larger 'huaca' ayllus that claimed objects as their founders. Thus, Cuzco's ten royal lineages claimed descent from the sacred rock representing Manco Capac, the first emperor. Maximal levels of folk integration were attained by claiming descent from a superhuman mountain. 'Apu' or mountain ayllus embraced entire ethnic groups numbering in the thousands. These large social formations were nested hierarchies of mirror-image smaller formations, because a single organizational charter, the ayllu, structured all levels of folk integration.

Ayllus were often named after their founders. Similar to King Arthur, founders were heroic figures. They battled formidable opponents to secure the homelands for their people. Models of morality, they established codes of proper behavior. They were venerated and honored in annual ceremonies. Their mortal or immortal remains ranked among an ayllu's most sacred holdings. If outsiders captured these vital relics, an ayllu could be held hostage and forced into submission.

Mallquipavillac

When the Spanish arrived, each small sierra ayllu had or shared a *llacta* mortuary complex constituting a huaca sepultura. Here mallqui reposed in aboveground mausoleums, or in subterranean caverns, tombs, and cemeteries. The tombs of important forebears were generally well marked so that they could be venerated, and many mortuary repositories allowed physical access to the deceased so that they could be curated, and propitiated. The deceased were regularly consulted on important matters ranging from planting and harvest to marriage and health. Reciprocity obligations extended to ancestors – they had given all to their heirs and therefore were owed much in return. Respected mallquis were endowed with lands and herds. Ancestral debt, obligation, and endowment were managed by sanctified attendants called *mallquipavillac* in Quechua and *ministros* by the Spanish. In addition to overseeing mourning rites for the recently departed, the mallquipavillac gave consultations and replies on

 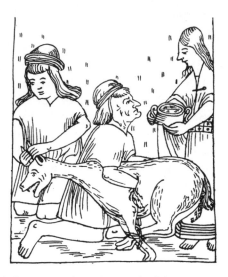

22 Mummies of important ancestors were paraded about on ritual occasions: a sketch by Guamán Poma.

23 Llamas were sacrificed on ritual occasions. Here Guamán Poma depicts removal of the heart.

behalf of the dead. They also supervised annual rituals to feast, praise, and placate the ancestors. All observances required the living to make very substantial outlays of food, drink, coca, and property for the dead that mallquipavillac lucratively garnered. Thus, the cult of the dead empowered a small but potent folk ministry that directed much of an ayllu's political economy by speaking for the deceased on everything from propitious mortuary endowments to auspicious marriage and kin alliances.

Tinku

Although mountain peaks are physically remote, each supreme apu ancestor was venerated at a regional shrine, a huaca adoratorio, visited annually by multitudes of pilgrim progeny. Ritual was essential for maintaining collective solidarity, which was fragile at all levels of ayllu organization. Hierarchical descent lines fostered 'asymmetrical' relationships, with senior kin groups drawing resources from junior counterparts, but not vice versa. Social fission was continually mediated by rituals of unity best labeled by the Quechua term *tinku*, which refers to the joining of two to form one. A pair of streams unites in tinku to create one river. Yet people are more fluid, because they can converge to form a social whole, only to diverge again into discrete moieties and descent groups. Therefore, uniting the dual divisions of society has long been the focus of elaborate rituals. Ancient iconographic depictions of tinku pageants include dual processions of figures converging jointly upon a temple gateway from opposite directions. Historically, tinku rituals can also unite people by releasing tensions through fierce competition or bloody ritual battles. Combative tinku often involves an equal number of participants from each social division, and in some cases there are but two combatants who duel hand to hand, each armed with a large stone.

Ayllu members do not drink alcohol on a daily basis, but copious libations of chicha beer and ritual intoxication are essential elements of tinku and almost all folk ceremonies. Etiquette demands toasting and drinking and people are seated, served alcohol, imbibe and speak in formal order governed by status. Because liquor is an essential accompaniment of commemorative oration and ritual participation, it is dispensed and consumed in stupefying quantities over the course of ceremonies that can endure for several days. Ritual intoxication is an ancient Andean tradition to judge from the common occurrence of libation vessels in prehistoric graves.

Cargo systems

When the Spanish arrived, millqui ayllus were internally governed by office hierarchies with civil and religious posts, called *cargo* systems. Today, as in the past, there are civil cargos akin to mayor, vice mayor, treasurer, clerk, constable, bailiff, and other municipal offices. Religious cargos organize annual observances of church holidays and patron saints that have replaced earlier huacas and gods. Each moiety has its own administrative hierarchy and cargo posts are filled on a rotational basis for a year or so. Holding office is truly a public service that entails substantial outlays of personal time and resources, as well as serving prodigious quantities of food and drink on required occasions. Indeed, one year in office can consume two or more years of family savings. Ideally, individuals begin young by holding lesser cargos and with maturity assume higher positions. The final goal is to retire from the apex of the office hierarchy as a prestigious elder with a distinguished title acknowledging years of service. Celebrated retirees are generally limited to the well-to-do who can shoulder the expenses of community service. Due to the public esteem accorded office holders, cargo regimes are also called 'prestige hierarchies.'

Governance based upon office hierarchies through which people rotate probably goes back to the dawn of Andean civilization. Each important cargo post is symbolized by a distinct ceremonial staff, or *vara*. Embued with huaca-like essence, these beautifully carved and ornamented scepters are grasped vertically and paraded about by their office holders on all formal occasions. Vara are important emblems of authority in ancient iconography, but they are often wielded by deities or by nobles who inherited their privileged rank.

Creeds

Commoners and nobles venerated multitudes of local huacas that defined common identity and group solidarity. However, ayllus, señoríos and native states were also cross-cut by potent religious creeds that people could embrace regardless of social affiliation or whether other ayllu members shared similar beliefs. Of regional to Pan–Andean scope, these ecclesiastical formations were broadly similar to contemporary religions, but much more ecumenical because individuals could adhere to more than one Andean faith. Most creeds coalesced around a particular deity from creation's dawn of primordial super beings. Some were otiose, others active, but all communicated with devotees through omens, auguries, or oracles manipulated by priests.

In the altiplano and south sierra Viracocha, a creator, Inti, a sun, Mama Kilya, a moon, and Illapa, a lord of lightning and tempest were focal divinities of older creeds that the Incas incorporated into their imperial pantheon. As in life, everyone was ranked and Inti headed the Incas' hierarchical pantheon. The Rock of the Sun, a stone outcrop on the Island of the Sun in Lake Titicaca, was the original home shrine of the sun, which first arose from adjacent lake waters. It was a potent huaca in Tiwanaku times, and highly venerated by the Incas who also created an imperial residence for Inti in the Coricancha. Elsewhere other spiritual hierarchies and other deities prevailed. Important gods associated with human betterment, lightning, thunder, and deluge included Paricaca in the central mountains and Catequil in the northern sierra. The sea was venerated by millions. She was called Cocha Mama by the Incas, and Si by the people of Chimor. In Chimor, the moon was considered more powerful than the sun because it controls tides and can be seen in day as well as night. Little is known about the north-coast gods of Aiapec and Con, a creator, other than that the cult of the latter was displaced in antiquity by devotion to Pachacamac.

Located at the mouth of the Lurin Valley, the temple city of Pachacamac vied with the Island of the Sun as the most sacred place in the Andes. The creator of humans and agricultural plants, Pachacamac was also the lord of earthquakes. Seismic shocks were reminders of his power and wrath, and cult members considered him superior to the sun and moon. Crafted from hard wood, his idol occupied a darkened chamber within an opulent, mound-top temple sacked by Pizarro's brother. The idol was a commanding oracle, drawing devotees from as far away as Ecuador in the north through Bolivia in the south. Similar to Mecca, thousands of pilgrims trekked to the sacred city to undergo days or months of preparatory penance and rituals appropriate for a Pachacamac prophesy.

Pilgrimage was both arduous and costly, because the deity required substantial propitiation in the form of food, coca, fabrics and other gifts ultimately garnered by the oracle's clergymen. The powerful religious order held sway over señoríos in the Lurin and Rimac valleys. The priesthood was hierarchical and chroniclers mention ranks similar to bishops and archbishops that were apparently held on the basis of ability, not inheritance. The clergy advanced the cult by establishing satellite shrines for one or another of Pachacamac's offspring and kindred among devout populations willing to make beneficent tithes. Indeed, one Spaniard reported that many coastal populations paid tribute to Pachacamac, not Cuzco. The exceptional prosperity of the sprawling city was manifest in its monumental architecture, dominated by numerous magnificent huacas and platform temples. Some housed representatives from other pantheons, such as the Sun Temple erected by the Incas for Inti's veneration. Although the full-time resident population of clergy and religious personnel was not very large, the mortuary population was enormous because Pachacamac was a prime burial place for commoners and kurakas alike.

24 A staff – the symbol of high office and authority – is carried by a winged figure in this Huari textile motif.

25 Staff emblems of authority probably evolved from clubs as wielded by this early Cerro Sechín figure incised on a monolith.

Kurakas

When Pizarro encountered Atahualpa, cargo governance of ayllus was subsidiary to rule by hereditary nobles called *kurakas*. There were at least two nobles, one for each moiety. The sovereign of the senior division was called the kuraka *principale* by the Spanish, and his junior counterpart the *segunda persona*. Each suyu subdivision generally had a kuraka and most ayllus were governed by a hierarchy of four or more lords, while señoríos generally had many nobles. There were female kurakas, but most were males and they had the important prerogative of taking more than one spouse or mate. This was a significant economic advantage, because women were a major source of labor. Polygamous households outproduced monogamous ones of commoners where gender balance was the norm. Kurakas and their offspring formed a separate, hereditary class of people who married among themselves. Although distinct, this class was organized by ayllu-like principles of ancestry, duality, and hierarchy. The kurakas of large polities, such as Chimor or Tahuantinsuyu, portrayed themselves as grand royal families, with a king or principale and a segunda persona as patriarchs.

Interceding with the cosmos on behalf of their subjects' well-being, kurakas ruled as intermediaries between heaven and earth. They claimed this special position on the basis of special descent. Lords of small ayllus professed closer kinship with founding millaquis, huaca, or apu, than their subjects. Yet mundane forebears, even towering mountains, were unsuitable for the aristocracy of great señoríos and states. Pushing ancestry to the heavens, the nobility of Chimor claimed descent from two bright stars, while commoners purportedly arose from lesser luminaries. In a similar vein, the Inca sovereign saw himself as a child of the sun, with extraordinary origins, superior to the rest of humanity. Claims of special origins rationalized a cast-like separation of the social classes. Kurakas defined their privileged status with sumptuary vestments, opulent dwellings and lavish huacas sepulturas. These markers of the nobility can be traced back in time to a few centuries before the beginning of the Christian era, when the kuraka class first became widespread.

Claims of celestial descent and rule as cosmic mediators were associated with regal elaboration of calendrical rituals designed to maintain the social and natural order of life. The lords of Cuzco ritually initiated and supervised the annual agropastoral cycle, making sure that important tasks were executed in a timely manner. The more humble kurakas of small ayllus directed similar scheduling, while also mediating disputes and allocating the use of land, water, and other collective assets. In return, ayllu members worked for their leaders by weaving cloth, tending their fields and herds, and rendering other services. Although kurakas extracted more than they returned, communal and cosmological reciprocity was expected. Leaders were supposed to be hospitable and generous, plying their subjects with food, and drink on ritual occasions, and rewarding special service with cloth or other gifts. Nobles were expected to keep nature on an even keel and when disaster struck, kurakas were responsible. According to coastal lore Fempellec, a powerful potentate in Lambayeque, was put to death by his subjects when a severe El Niño flooding devastated their desert homeland.

Statecraft

Tahuantinsuyu arose during the difficult dry times of the long drought, and Inca statecraft benefited from adaptive principles drawn from earlier polities and from ayllu organization. Extracting taxes and tithes, in civil or religious form, is a cornerstone of government. Yet payment is subject to considerable negotiation and manipulation, particularly in an ethnically heterogeneous realm such as Tahuantinsuyu. Therefore, Inca imperial revenues are best reviewed in an idealized form, as the lords of Cuzco might have wished to see their income.

Labor was the coin of the realm and the imperial economy extracted tribute in the form of work. The local community or ayllu was the basic unit of taxation, and tribute obligations were distributed among households by the local kurakas. Labor taxation required accurate inventorying of people, resources, and conditions. When Tahuantinsuyu incorporated a new province its people were counted, along with their livestock, fields, and pastures. Topographic models were made, and the data sent to Cuzco to be acted upon. Males and heads of households were graded by age and decimally organized. The smallest unit comprised 10 taxpayers overseen by a foreman. In turn, 10 such units were overseen by a 'Chief of 100' and the system scaled up through to *Hunu Kuraka*, a 'Lord of 10,000,' who reported directly to the Inca provincial governor. The decimally organized masses rendered three types of labor for the state that can be called agricultural taxation, mit'a service, and textile taxation.

Agricultural taxation

Agricultural taxation extracted work from both men and women. Commoners did not own land – it belonged to the ayllu. It was Inca practice to divide conquered agricultural land into three categories, ideally of equal size, all of which the peasantry was obliged to farm. The first category was dedicated to the support of the gods, including the imperial pantheon and huacas of local importance. These lands were cultivated first, before other categories of fields. Yields went to support religious functionaries, priests, and shrine attendants. Stores were also held to provide food and drink on holidays when particular gods, huacas, or ancestors received public veneration.

The second category of fields belonged to the emperor, as head of state, the governing nobility viewed proprietary ownership as theirs by divine right. Imperial fields were tended after religious ones, and yields went to support the imperial court and the needs of government. Because the emperor was head of state as well as a god king heading the state religion, agrarian tribute from both religious and imperial lands was largely under Cuzco's direct control. Food storage is crucial during uncertain times of drought, and the Incas invested in widespread construction and display of warehousing facilities. These generally comprised numerous one-room masonry structures known as *qollqa*: circular ones for maize storage, and square ones for potatoes and tubers. Both forms had

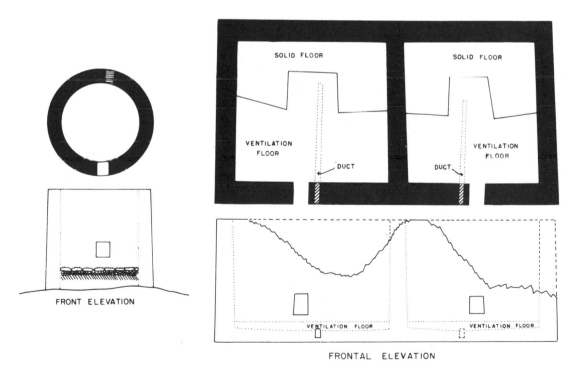

26 Circular qollqa storehouses were often used for maize.

27 Rectangular qollqa buildings at Huánuco Pampa stored potatoes and tubers.

ingenious ventilation systems that allowed air to enter through an underground channel in the floor and then escape through an opening at roof level. Designed for display, long rows of finely built qollqa were erected on hills and high places where they could be seen from great distances.

The third category of land was assigned to the local community for its support, redistributed annually to village members by the local kuraka. This allotment was not in equal parts, but proportional to the size of a family and the number of dependents under each head-of-household. As households grew or shrank, their share of land changed. When an individual was absent working on a government project or attending official business, other members of the ayllu tilled his lands and fulfilled his agricultural tax obligations. Puna pasture lands, and llama and alpaca resources were organized in a similar three-fold manner. Systematic administration of pasture was critical because it encompassed more terrain than was under cultivation, and highland polities controlled immense herds for the production of wool and food. Thus, just as the highlanders were agropastoralists, so too was the tax system.

Mit'a service

While agricultural taxation extracted work from both sexes, mit'a service was an annual draft that extracted labor from able-bodied males. It was an ancient form of tribute that embraced activities ranging from work on construction projects to participation in military campaigns. So long as reasonable numbers of men remained at home to attend fields and ayllu needs, flexible numbers of draftees could be mobilized for variable length of service. With millions of male subjects to draw upon, mit'a gave Tahuantinsuyu a labor-intensive economy seen in the monumental splendor of Cuzco, which amazed the *conquistadores*. Indeed, a rotating force of 20,000 corvee laborers reputedly worked for decades *Plates 12–14* to erect Sacsahuaman, the grand acropolis of cyclopean masonry crowning the imperial capital.

It profits government to expend returns from one tariff in ways that expand the returns from another tax. To this end, the Inca and earlier polities invested mit'a labor in the acquisition of agricultural land that could then be taxed and yields stored to augment imperial coffers. This strategy was pursued both by conquest and by agrarian reclamation of unproductive terrain. Over the millennia, opening new land required ever greater effort undertaken by progressively larger señoríos and polities capable of mobilizing mit'a from multiple communities. Beginning with Pukara, all major Andean political centers expended great labor on turning their adjacent hinterlands into agrarian parklands. The Incas pursued these policies on a grand scale, adjusting them to drought and later to wetter conditions.

Highland populations responded to the long AD 1100–1450 drought by gradually shifting the farming focus from lower, warmer elevations to higher, cooler altitudes where rainfall was still relatively abundant and to the better-watered eastern Andean escarpment. In both cases, the adaptive shifts were to steep, *Plate 2* rugged terrain that required construction of agricultural terraces to curtail

*28 Inca forces storm a fortified
hilltop pukara in this illustration
by Guamán Poma.*

erosion of thin mountain soils. The lords of Cuzco employed such construction
on a grandiose scale to majestically resculpt their rugged sierra homeland. They
unleashed legions of mit'a laborers to reclaim the sacred Urubamba Valley that
transects the Cordillera's verdant eastern slopes. Descending the canyon from
Pisac to Ollantaytambo and Machu Picchu, multitudes of dramatic masonry
terraces confront visitors with an epochal story of eastward agricultural
expansion.

Centuries of scarce rainfall not only changed where mountain populations
farmed, but where and how they lived. Because drought heightened competition for scarce resources, many people resettled in communities on high prom-
ontories and steep ridges frequently fortified with dry moats, high walls with
parapets that also made up the defenses of their pukara safe havens. Such bulwarks were deadly to take by storm, thereby deterring assault from raiders. Yet
they were completely vulnerable to drawn-out siege that deprived hilltop
defenders of food and water. The Incas exploited this weakness and transformed indigenous warfare by fielding mit'a conscript forces for long periods of
time under the command of professional officers from Cuzco's royal families.
Most of Tahuantinsuyu's foreign conquests transpired as the long drought
broke and rainfall gradually returned to normal and then to above-normal
levels. This opened the way for mountain farming to shift from higher drought-
tolerant altitudes back to lower, warmer elevations where more types of crops
flourished. As conditions ameliorated, the Incas used mit'a labor to reactivate
land abandoned during drought and to open new terrain with improved water
supplies. To change agricultural patterns the lords of Cuzco often changed settlement patterns. In some cases large populations, known as *mitamaq* colonies,
were moved great distances for agrarian as well as political purposes. More
commonly, communities that grew up during drought on high-fortified prom-
ontories were locally resettled in undefended villages adjacent to lower-

elevation farmland. Andean drought requires people, produce, and information to move over greater-than-normal distances, and the Incas prudently invested mit'a labor in the construction and maintenance of tens of thousands of kilometers of well-built road networks. Young men doing mit'a served as relay runners, or *chaskis*, carrying quipu and messages to and from Cuzco, while also reputedly supplying the emperor with fresh seafood from the coast.

Textile taxation

Weaving is a highly valued labor-intensive Andean craft and females have long rendered tribute by cloth production. They wove for ayllu kuraka overlords. To home-bound taxpayers, the Cuzco government annually doled out specified quantities of raw fiber, cotton, or wool. Men made cordage and rope, while women spun and wove. Spinning involved a drop spindle and weaving was done on several types of looms. Vertical loom frames were preferred by residents of Chinchaysuyu's north coast, while Aymara people of Collasuyu regularly wove on a horizontal loom. The finished goods were collected by the state and fine *Plates 18–21* cloth was used as a monetary-like medium of wealth and exchange. Pride in clothing one's family is a hallmark of Andean femininity, and clothmaking occupied more people for more time than any other craft. All women wove, from the humblest of peasants to the wives of kings. Queens and empresses wove as an Andean symbol of their femininity. Many grades of cloth were produced, and very fine fabrics were very highly esteemed, culminating in the most elegant of Inca fabrics, known as *qomba*.

29 A painting from a Moche ceramic vase of women weaving beneath a ramada.

What people wove and wore – decoration, iconography, and quality – established their ethnic identity and indicated their rank and status. Heads of state wore the finest of materials, rich in color and design, and often fashioned from exotic fibers such as vicuña wool, embellished with threads of gold and silver, *Plate 10* or with bright feathers of tropical birds. As a commodity highly valued by all, cloth fulfilled certain functions analogous to currency. Cloth was the Inca reward for government service, and the army received regular allocations of textiles.

State expenditures

With millions paying taxes, Tahuantinsuyu had enormous revenues. In addition to labor, the agricultural and textile taxes were used to support two types of expenditure. The agricultural tax was used to provide people with food and drink, termed 'staple' finance. The textile tax was used to reward people with valued goods, termed 'wealth' finance. The two systems operated rather differently: the kuraka and kingly elite sought to monopolize items of wealth, whereas commoners and masters expected sustenance when rendering state service.

The greatest bulk of Tahuantinsuyu's agrarian staples were budgeted for feeding the millions who worked for the state. Many more people worked for the government on a temporary basis than on a permanent one, and the largest expenditures presumably supported vast numbers of males rendering mit'a service. A small portion of the population, perhaps 10 percent, was permanently subsidized because it occupied the highest ranks of local and national government. There were two tiers: the upper, decision-making one was occupied with rule and administration, while a lower technical tier was occupied with the implementation of rule and the support of governmental institutions. At the apex stood the royal families of hanan and hurin Cuzco, then the people of the Cuzco Basin, who were Incas by appointment and honor but not by ancestry. From the royal families came the heads of state and the heads of Inti's imperial church. From the body of Incas by birth or honor came the military and gubernatorial heads of the empire, and, it is assumed, the heads of all branches of the imperial bureaucracy. Allied with this apex by forced and voluntary allegiance, and by the exchange of sons and daughters in marriage, were the noble families and hereditary rulers of subject states. These ranks ranged from the conquered potentates of Chimor down to the kurakas of formerly independent ayllus.

Beneath those enjoying great power and prestige was a significantly larger tier of people who were subsidized because of their occupations, hereditary

30 Building monuments, roads, and suspension bridges required technicians skilled in surveying, engineering, and architecture.

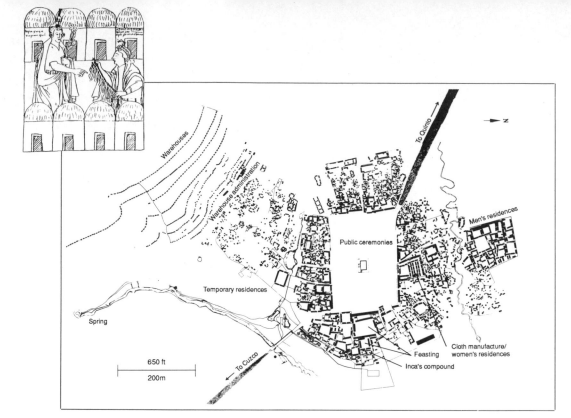

31 Standing in a complex of qollqa storehouses (above left), a noble reviews the quipu record of an accountant. The plan of Huánuco Pampa shows the hundreds of qollqa prominently displayed in ten hillside rows overlooking the site.

knowledge or training relating to technical matters. The profusion of professional accountants, the *quipukamayoqs*, drew considerable attention from early chroniclers. Other technicians must have included agronomists, architects, surveyors, engineers, hydrologists, and the like. Another large body of support personnel comprised skilled artisans and craft specialists. Entire colonies of specialists – from ceramicists, through lapidarists, to metallurgists and jewelers – were removed from subject provinces and resettled in the Cuzco environs to serve the lords of the sacred city. These professionals were both numerous and important because 'wealth' finance, as opposed to 'staple' finance, depended not only upon textiles, but upon multitudes of other valued commodities culminating in finely wrought artworks of gold and silver.

At Cuzco's great rival capital of Chan Chan the vast majority of residents were artisans. Women were weavers of fine cloth, while men were predominantly metalsmiths and jewelers. By supporting tens of thousands of skilled craft personnel the government used staple finance to generate commodities for wealth finance, which made artisans essential to the national economy. Thus at Chan Chan artisans enjoyed the privilege of wearing earspools, albeit very simple wooden ones, a privilege otherwise reserved for the governing elite, who wore elaborate earspools as the hallmark of their status and rank. (Indeed, the *Plate 51* Spanish referred to the Inca elite as *orejones*, or 'big ears,' because of the large, round earspools that set them apart from the masses.)

Staple reserves

In the Cordillera, storing surplus food is a critical household adaptation essential to risk management because frost, hail, rainfall, and runoff vary dramatically seasonally and annually. Without reserves of charqui, chuño, tubers, cereals, and legumes there are few means of mitigating stress from frequently poor harvests in different ecological tiers. Food storage is particularly essential during protracted drought. The Incas responded to dry times with prodigious elaboration of warehousing facilities unprecedented in the annals of world prehistory. Mit'a labor was lavished on the construction of multitudinous qollqa. Both round and square storehouses had ingenious ventilation systems allowing air to enter through an underground floor channel and flow out from roof-level vents.

To assure people that the state could adequately manage the risks of drought and natural disasters, rows of qollqa were audaciously placed on lofty hills and high, cool places where they were readily seen from great distances. Thousands surrounded Cuzco; and Cotapachi in Bolivia had 2,400. The provincial center of Hatun Xauxa had an enormous warehousing complex, and 497 qollqa, arranged in hillside rows, overlooked the center of Huánuco Pampa. Excavations at the last two centers revealed locally produced agricultural commodities, indicating the government was not stocking exotic produce from distant provinces for local redistribution. Qollqa stores were national reserves for state purposes, but when disaster struck they could be dispensed to the common populace.

Staple reciprocity

The taxation system did not entail a unidirectional flow of labor from commoners, and of its fruits to the government. There were fundamental beliefs that both kurakas and kings had reciprocal obligations of hospitality and generosity, particularly with food and drink. Staple finance was critical to the symbiosis between the ruled and the rulers and allowed the latter to schedule activities within a framework of public celebrations. In civil or religious guise, fiestas provide a major release from the somber drudgery of peasant life. Past rulers sponsored such festivities to coincide with plowing, planting, harvest, canal cleaning, and other labor cycles, so that work proceeded on a voluntary rather than a coercive basis.

Toasting and libations with chicha beer were integral and ancient aspects of Andean ceremonialism and festivities. Seating, serving, swilling, and speaking order were no doubt hierarchical, as today. Status was indicated by an individual's drinking vessel: the lowly used gourd bowls, the well-to-do drank from finer containers, while gold and silver were reserved for the highest echelons. During the first millennium BC, different forms of ceramic libation vessels *Plates 46, 59* became firmly established in different regions. For example the lords of Chimor toasted from 'stirrup-spout' goblets that were traditional to the north coast, while the nobility of Cuzco drank from beaker-shaped *keros*, vessels indigenous to the Titicaca Basin, and used by rulers of Tiwanaku a millennium earlier. As markers of status and rank libation vessels regularly accompanied people to the grave.

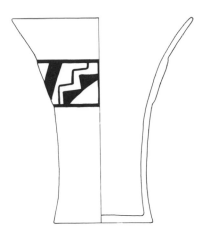

32 (left) A Moche Phase V stirrup-spout libation vessel.

33 (above) A Tiwanaku kero beaker from Moquegua.

Wealth reciprocity

Reciprocity to the masses largely entailed food and beverage, but the elite required more. Anticipating rewards appropriate to their rank, administrators confronted government with a hierarchy of reciprocal obligations. Military troops received cloth, but officers expected better cuts.

Carefully graded by quality, textiles were the most common reward for service. But for yet higher ranks the rewards included superb ceramics, lavish libation vessels, woodwork, lapidary arts, and splendid metalwork. Thus fine arts critical to wealth finance were the end returns of an elite investment strategy that used mit'a labor to gain agricultural lands. In turn the land was taxed and the staple revenues were used to subsidize skilled artisans who produced commodities to satisfy reciprocity among the elite. This system of transforming the fruits of unskilled labor into fine durable goods was an ancient one at least as old as the emergence of the kuraka class.

Arts and crafts

Reciprocity based on valued goods placed fine arts and skilled crafts in direct service of the state. Artisans and tradesmen were subsidized, and their products were geared to serve corporate ends. As a result, aesthetic canons, design motifs, and iconography were dictated by the political and religious organizations supporting the artisans, commissioning their work, and controlling its distribution, creating 'corporate styles' that were characteristic of particular polities, religions, and organizations. In modern society, national coinage and currency convey such styles, depicting political founders, past rulers, heroic figures, totemic animals, and emblems appropriate to a nation. Postage stamps and church art convey similar corporate symbolism.

In the Andes there were two levels of economic organization: the self-sufficient community or ayllu, and the imposed señorío or state economy. Likewise, there were two levels to the production of arts and crafts, and to architecture. The base level comprised the ayllu and their folk traditions. These tended to be simple, conservative, and long-lasting. Above these were the corporate styles, the canons and composition which conformed to particular political or religious dictates. Their duration depended upon the rise and fall of the corporate bodies they served, and they changed more frequently than did the basal stratum of folk traditions.

The great art styles of the Cordillera were all corporate styles, but the nature of the organizations that underwrote them varied in terms of political, religious, and social composition. Inca corporate arts and architecture illustrate a number of basic characteristics of such styles. First, the styles emerged well after the corporations that they identify came into existence. The Incas established their ethnic identity and their homeland generations before Pachacuti decided a corporate style was in order and rebuilt Cuzco as its architectural hallmark. Second, once a corporate body was established, a corporate style could be put together rapidly, either newly created or borrowed. Third, critical to the creation of a corporate style was the amassing of artisans and specialized technicians. Transforming peasant farmers into skilled craftsmen was not easily done. In later prehistoric times complicated technical expertise generally passed from parent to child and was therefore kin-based, with artisans forming guild-like kin corporations. The lords of Chimor not only subsidized cadres of kindred artisans, but sought to monopolize the production and circulation of precious metal. Upon conquering Lambayeque, metallurgists from the region were resettled at Chan Chan. In turn, when Tahuantinsuyu subjugated Chimor, tens *Plate 23* of thousands of craftsmen at Chan Chan were moved to the environs of Cuzco to serve new rulers. To the degree that fine arts constituted the coin of the realm, Chan Chan was thus stripped of the mint it needed to finance revolt.

Fourth, corporate styles generally spread as far as their supporting reciprocity systems reached. But reciprocity was not uniform. For example, the Incas exploited Ecuador more intensively than central Chile, and elements of Tahuantinsuyu's corporate style are more numerous and sharply defined in its northern holdings than in its southern. Fifth, stylistic unity at the corporate level had little relation to ethnic homogeneity or cultural cohesion at the folk level. The lords of Cuzco imposed widespread artistic cohesion over much of their empire, but this did not reflect a fundamental rise in ethnic unity among the diverse populations of the realm. Sixth and finally, change in corporate style and replacement of one by another did not necessarily reflect population change or the replacement of one ethnic group or cultural group by another. Conservative folk styles were more sensitive indicators of population dynamics, but these traditions also changed without entailing ethnic change.

The most dramatic expressions of Inca corporate style are new cities, towns, and installations erected where none had previously existed. Tumibamba, Wayna Capac's incipient Ecuadorian capital, closely cloned the imperial masonry and architectural styles of Cuzco, as did other new settlements founded along the great highway system radiating out of Cuzco. Inca imperial buildings were power emblems intended to impress, if not intimidate, and were generally executed in close accordance with Cuzco's canons. The urban administrative centers of Huánuco Pampa, and Hatun Xauxa are well-studied new Inca cities, whose fine masonry and buildings, elite pottery and status goods conform to Cuzco patterns. Yet, close scrutiny of these materials indicates that most were produced by local personnel working under state overseers rather than imported from the capital.

Imperial heartland

The capital of Tahuantinsuyu was not large because the Inca royal families were the only people who resided in the metropolis. The chronicler Cristobal de Molina says that when the Spanish first entered the area Cuzco may have contained up to 40,000 souls, whereas some 200,000 resided within 10 to 12 leagues. Large numbers of technical personnel, artisans, and other people who worked for the government, but were not Inca by birth, lived in suburban communities near the capital. Great labor was expended upon agrarian reclamation and transformation of the imperial heartland into a park-like landscape. Magnificent terraces sculpted the hillsides, which irrigation kept verdant and luxurious. Here the nobility had sumptuous estates, and hundreds of huacas and shrines graced the scenery.

Cuzco and its environs were the quintessence of Inca corporate construction and architecture. Only the finest stonework was used, employing precisely carved blocks that fitted together without the need of cement. There were two *Plates 13, 14* styles: one consisted of fine ashlars laid in even horizontal courses; the other was of bold polygonal blocks. Each multi-sided stone was a unique work laboriously cut to a special size and faceted shape that would fit the angles of adjoining blocks. The two styles of masonry were used for two different classes of structures: polygonal blocks for solid structures, such as terraces and platforms; and ashlar blocks for buildings with freestanding walls and open interior space, *Plate 16* often surmounting solid structures. The doors, windows, and niches of Inca buildings were distinctly trapezoidal, being wider at the bottom than at the top. Roofs were gabled and of thatch. Typical of the Andes, roofed buildings were usually one-room structures. If two or more rooms shared a roof, they were treated as separate structures, each room having an outside entrance but no interior doorways between compartments. Covered buildings ranged from vast assembly halls, or *kallanka*, to small rectangular quarters called *masma* and *wasi*. The masma form was U-shaped with one side of the building left open. They were rare, but perpetuated an ancient tradition of erecting U-shaped ceremonial buildings.

The one-door, one-room *wasi* was the most common form of dwelling for people and for their idols and gods. Wasi were erected alone and in patio groups, framing a secluded outdoor activity area for work and relaxation. Extended families and near kin often occupied adjacent houses and patio groups. The Incas and other Andean people had a penchant for building dwellings and patio clusters within spacious, high-walled enclosures called *kanchas*. Generally having a single entrance, the fine masonry enclosures of Cuzco framed entire city blocks and housed ruling families in elegant wasi. The kancha-wasi architectural pattern was ancient and perhaps derived from herders whose humble dwellings are still erected within the corral, safekeeping their animals. Although Inca construction drew on earlier foundations, the lords of Cuzco added their own distinct corporate stamp, transforming their imperial heartland into a majestic parkland.

Navel of the universe

Opulent construction and extravagant embellishment were lavished upon Cuzco, making it one of ancient America's greatest wonders. This befitted Inca beliefs that their sacred city was literally the navel of the universe from which Tahuantinsuyu unfurled. Four grand highways and four cosmic lines radiated out of the central plaza, called the *Huacaypata* quartering the empire along intercardinal axes much as Mayu, the Milky Way, quartered the heavens. A nexus of tinku, the spacious plaza accommodated stately rituals uniting the royal lineages, or *panaka*, of hanan and hurin Cuzco. It held the umbilicus of the Inca world, the *usnu*, a multifaceted dais of finely hewn rock with a vertical

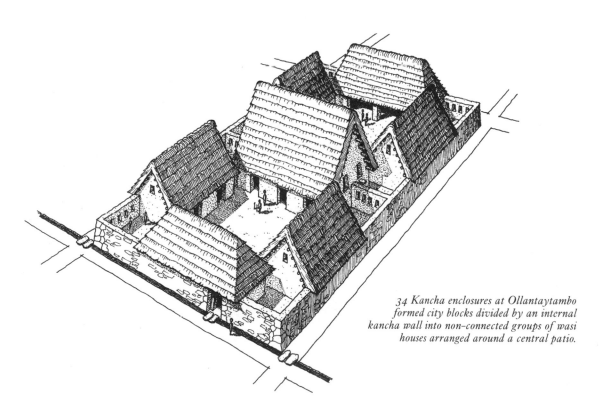

34 Kancha enclosures at Ollantaytambo formed city blocks divided by an internal kancha wall into non-connected groups of wasi houses arranged around a central patio.

pillar and a carved seat. The jutting pillar was a celestial sighting rod for track-ing heavenly luminaries and dark constellations. The sculpted seat was an ada-mantine throne where the emperor, the 'son of the sun,' maintained terrestrial order. The lord of the realm ascended the stunning dais to review ritual proces-sions, to toast the gods and to placate the ancestors. Copious libations of chicha beer were poured into the 'gullet of the sun,' a majestic stone basin sheathed in gold at the foot of the usnu. Nearby towered the tallest of all edifices, the *Sunturwasi*, a grand spire of exquisite masonry that cast no noontime shadow at zenith.

The highways and suyu dividing lines emanating from the Huacpata reflect radial organization of space, which the Incas used in addition to orthogonal organization. Within the plaza, the usnu pillar and windows in the towering Sunturwasi were used to sight outward to distant horizons where mountains and huaca shrines provided visual points for tracking heavenly movements. The Incas also erected distant masonry pillars and stone pylons against the skyline to sight upon the sun and predict planting times in different ecological zones. Cuzco's most extraordinary temple, the Coricancha, was the sighting center for a remarkable system of radial organization. A sun dial is perhaps the nearest analogy, but the grand temple was more akin to the hub of a cosmic dial for tracking and timing movement of heavenly phenomena and correlating them with terrestrial phenomena. Radiating out of the Coricancha, 41 sighting lines, called *ceques*, stretched to the horizon or beyond. On these rays, or adjacent to them, some 328 huacas, pillars, and survey points were arranged in a hierarchi-cal manner. Archaeoastronomers note that the 328 stations represent the days in 12 sidereal lunar months. Given drought and the importance of irrigation, it is not coincidental that one-third of the *ceque* points comprised the major springs and water sources of the region.

It appears that *ceque* lines were grouped into upper and lower sets and further divided into four quarters. The upper set was associated with hanan Cuzco, Chinchaysuyu and Antisuyu, the lower set with hurin Cuzco, Collasuyu and Cuntisuyu. Each quarter was in turn subdivided into three parts by *ceque* rays, and each third was again divided by three more lines. Owing to terrestrial and celestial realities, the angle of arc between lines was variable and some may not have been straight lines. Individual rays and their huacas were associated with and administered by specific panaka kin groups. In part, the lines and huacas distinguish panaka holdings, established ritual responsibilities and defined annual activity schedules. Thus, the spatial and temporal reference points along the rays were instrumental in organizing land, water, work, and ritual activities of Inti's noble children.

The navel of the imperial universe was intimately connected with a marve-lously complex cosmos, and one must suppose earlier Andean capitals were also cosmologically structured. Curiously, although the Incas commanded the largest nation of the Americas, the ruling nobility never abandoned tenets of organization founded in the ayllu and traditional folk beliefs. Cuzco's organiz-ing principles were poorly understood by *conquistadores* who left but five short,

35 With Sacsahuaman as the head, the outlines of a great puma are traced on
E.G. Squier's early map of Cuzco.

eyewitness accounts of the capital before native rebellion incinerated the
metropolis in 1535. Colonial records are often contradictory and modern scholars interpret them in different ways. The Spanish thought indigenous rule was
similar to the Castilian monarchy where the crown passed from father to first
son. The chronicler Betanzos lists ten Inca emperors he took to be a dynastic
succession of rulers. Some historians propose that the great hero Pachacuti was
crowned the eighth emperor in AD 1438 and later retired to remodel Cuzco in
1471, when his son Topa Inca took the reins of state. Yet, with its hanan and
hurin divisions, the capital was clearly structured by indigenous principles of
dual organization, and diarchy or dual rule most likely prevailed: hanan Cuzco
being led by a principal potentate while a segunda persona counterpart headed
the hurin moiety. Therefore, king lists recorded by the Spanish are open to
several very different interpretations. One holds that figures such as Pachacuti

and Topa Inca were not father and son, but senior and junior coregents, in which case Betanzos' list spans but five generations. Another interpretation holds that the lists are not of individuals, but of imperial offices that operated concurrently and were held by the heads of the ten royal panaka kin groups. Consequently, what *conquistadores* construed as dynastic history was a fictionalized kinship charter joining ten ayllu in a ruling alliance. Differing interpretations of royal history are to be expected, because the archaeological record indicates that Inca political development began as a gradual process shortly after AD 1000. Thus, what survives as Inca 'history' is centuries short on content and, at best, reflects truncated remembrances and myths.

Inca lore associates the transformation of Cuzco from a simple community into a monumental capital with the name of Pachacuti, who might be either a ruler or an office of rule. Nonetheless, the lore outlines a three-fold succession of happenings that is logical and historically plausible. First, the Incas consolidated their homeland. Second, they expanded to the south. And third, they then remade their city in an imperial corporate style befitting the navel of the cosmos. Archaeological data indicate that early political consolidation in the imperial heartland spanned three or more centuries. This transpired while unelaborate Killke and Lucre styles of ceramics were used respectively in the western and eastern sectors of the greater Cuzco Basin. Radiocarbon dates indicate that imperial-style corporate arts and architecture were formulated around AD 1350–75. Impressive temples and large buildings were constructed in the Lucre area prior to this. However, the Cuzco region did not have a tradition of fine stonework and legend holds that the imposing masonry of Tiwanaku inspired Pachacuti to rebuild the capital in similar megalithic elegance. Thus, historical lore and archaeological information jointly demonstrate that imperial-style corporate architecture emerged only after a solid political base was in place to sustain the new emblems of power. Although core area consolidation was a lengthy process, it later supported rapid expansion that carried imperial-style arts and architecture to the distant quarters of Tahuantinsuyu.

Built as centuries of drought broke, the metropolis was replete with numerous fountains and underground drains. The Ríos Huatanay and Tullumayu were canalized to border Pachacuti's new-built city and, where the rivers converge in tinku, they frame a narrow triangle of land known as the *Pumachupan*, or puma's tail. The Inca's heroic founder, Manco Capac, resided at the start of the tail before his transmutation into a revered stone huaca. The founder's sacred home site was later transformed into the Coricancha. This opulent kancha of exquisite masonry enclosed six wasi-like religious chambers arranged around a courtyard. One chamber, richly bedecked with gold, was dedicated to the sun and held Inti's golden image; a second chamber clad in silver belonged to the moon, considered female and held her sterling image. Other religious wasi contained images or symbols of Viracocha, *Illapa* the lord of thunder, *Cuychu* the rainbow, and various celestial bodies. In an attempt to harmonize their heterogeneous empire through symbolic integration, a hallowed idol or object from each subject population resided in the temple's confines. These hostage huacas were rotated when the kings and kuraka of their subject populations observed compulsory residence around Cuzco for several months each year, learning the ways of their overlords.

Some scholars argue that the Pumachupan was the tail of an imperial metropolis shaped like a vast puma seen from the side. Others deny this, and what the builders had in mind is debatable. Still, the outline of a great cat can be drawn over remnants of the ancient city. The Huacaypata plaza with its royal usnu creates an open space between the uphill front quarters of the puma and its rear legs and down hill tail. Forming entire city blocks, vast kancha-wasi compounds of the royal panaka occupy the upper hanan and lower hurin sectors of the beast.

The head of the putative feline is the loftiest and largest of imperial edifices, Sacsahuaman, reportedly built by 20,000 laboring over several generations. *Plates 12, 14* Perched atop a high hill, one side of the complex runs along a cliff with a commanding view of the city. The opposite side of the promontory is relatively low and encased by three imposing zigzag terraces with few entrances. Each retaining wall employs the finest and most impressive of Inca polygonal masonry, including crafted blocks weighing 90 to more than 120 metric tons. The flattened hilltop behind the terraces held a marvelous complex of fine ashlar buildings with tall towers, as well as round and rectangular structures. There are remnants of an ornate system of conduits, drainages, and finely cut stone channels suggesting ritual manipulation of water.

When Inca forces were besieged in 1535, Sacsahuaman served as a native bulwark against the Spanish, where Pizarro lost a brother and other men. Yet it was probably not designed as a fort when foreign wars were originally far afield. Cieza de Leon says that Pachacuti intended Sacsahuaman to be a temple that would surpass all other buildings in splendor. The chronicler Garcilaso de la Vega relates that only royalty could enter the sacrosanct complex, because it was a house of the sun, of arms and war, and a temple of prayer and sacrifice.

The *conquistadores* were justly impressed with the navel of the Inca universe. Today thousands of visitors marvel at Sacsahuaman, at the Coricancha, remnants of old Cuzco and its monumental parklands, which spread to Ollantaytambo, Machu Picchu, and beyond. The chapters to come will probe the ancient foundations of Andean statecraft and the folk adaptations that underlay the Incas' extraordinary achievement.

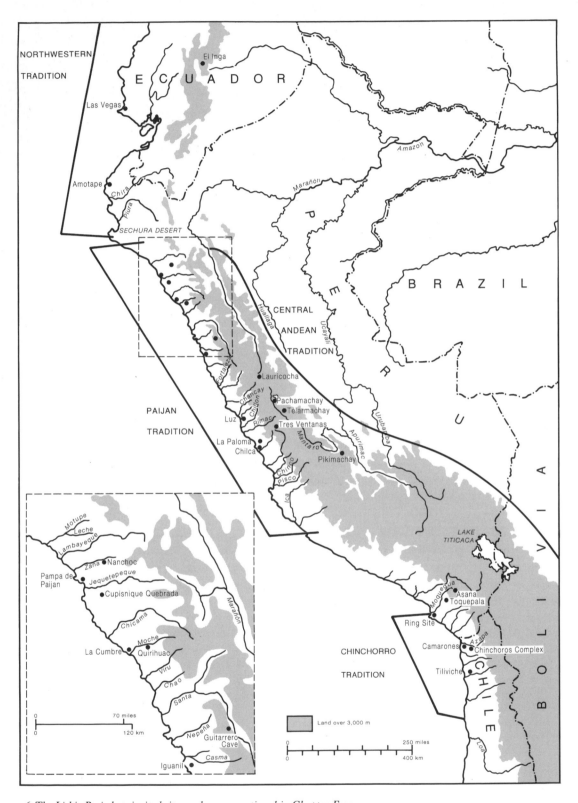

NORTHWESTERN
TRADITION

ECUADOR

El Inga

Las Vegas

Amotape

Chira

Piura

SECHURA DESERT

CENTRAL

ANDEAN

TRADITION

Huallaga

Ucayali

Marañón

Amazon

BRAZIL

PAIJAN

TRADITION

Fortaleza

Lauricocha

Chancay
Chillon

Pachamachay
Telarmachay

Luz
Rimac

Tres Ventanas

La Paloma
Chilca

Mantaro

Pikimachay

Ica

Chinco
Pisco

Apurimac

Urubamba

P
E
R
U

LAKE
TITICACA

BOLIVIA

Motupe
Leche
Lambayeque

Zaña
Nanchoc

Pampa de
Paijan

Jequetepeque

Cupisnique Quebrada

Marañón

Chicama

Moche
La Cumbre
Quirihuac

Viru

Chao

Santa

Nepeña
Guitarrero
Cave

Iguanil
Casma

0   70 miles
0   120 km

Moquegua
Asana
Toquepala

Ring Site

CHINCHORRO

TRADITION

Camarones
Azapa
Chinchoros Complex

Tiliviche
CHILE

Loa

Land over 3,000 m

0   250 miles
0   400 km

36 The Lithic Period: principal sites and areas mentioned in Chapter Four.

COLONIZATION OF THE CORDILLERA

Humans entered the Western Hemisphere during the last Ice Age by crossing the Bering land bridge between Siberia and Alaska. Pushing south, vanguards penetrated the Andes when the Cordillera was markedly different from today. Mountain peaks were heavily glaciated and ice drew moisture from the sea, lowering ocean levels more than 100 m. Ecological zones were stratified at lower elevations and tropical conditions extended into northern Peru, but the central Cordillera remained very dry. A great metamorphosis then transpired between 15,000 and 5,000 years ago as glaciers melted, ocean levels rose, biotic habitats migrated upward, and marine and meteorological currents shifted into their modern configuration. Pleistocene large game died out, but plants and animals were domesticated as people adjusted to making a living in diverse environments of the desert coast, sierra basins, high puna, and tropical jungle. This chapter examines human colonization of the Cordillera during the Lithic Period, which ended around 5,000 years ago when post-Pleistocene sea levels stabilized and climatic as well as environmental conditions assumed their current configuration.

The colonization process

Human reclamation of the Western Hemisphere was a remarkable adventure, but one about whose beginnings we can only speculate. Spreading down the Americas, people reached the southern Chilean site of Monte Verde around 12,500 radiocarbon years ago, or about 14,850 calendar years ago given ancient fluctuations in atmospheric carbon. The long trek south spanned many generations, but earlier sites in the Americas are uncommon and their authenticity and antiquity are vigorously disputed. Consequently, I can only offer a speculative scenario about the initial colonization of the continent and the Cordillera. This begins with the molecular biology and DNA of contemporary Native Americans, which points to their descent from three or four biologically distinct populations that separately entered the New World. Only one stock, called Paleo-Indians, pushed south into Middle America. Advance guards then traversed the narrow Isthmus of Panama and gave rise to millions of South American progeny.

Because southern colonists were neither numerous nor biologically diverse their descendants exhibit less genetic variation than Native North Americans. For example, blood type B is absent and A is rare while the frequency of type O exceeds 90 percent. Geneticists explain this by the so-called 'Founder Principle.' This holds that when reproductive forebears are few in number their descendants will inherit circumscribed variability dominated by the limited gene pool of the original founders. Therefore, the prevalence of certain genetic traits, such as blood type O, and the absence or rareness of others among Andean and Amazonian people is attributable to the finite genetic make up of the continent's scanty pioneers. Linguists employ analogous principles when they work back in time from historical dialects and tongues to reconstruct extinct parental languages. In a similar vein, it is reasonable to infer that South America's original founders passed on patterns of belief and behavior that descendants perpetuated when the traits proved advantageous or adaptively neutral.

Beliefs widely shared by ethnographic populations suggest that the founders' cosmology envisaged a multi-layered universe with the earth suspended between celestial outer and cavernous inner spheres, and that nature was charged with vital, anthropomorphic qualities which influenced peoples' well being. Incest taboos underlay reproductive well being and the colonists were organized by principles of kinship based upon lines of descent or lineages that determined who could and could not marry. Moiety or dual organization was advantageous for small founding populations because people could wed certain cousins within their kin group, whereas exogamy – the marriage of outsiders – would require wandering the vacant continent vainly searching for foreign spouses. Decision-making was a communal affair, and leadership positions were held on the basis of ability and group consent. Shamans accompanied the immigrants, and mediated between the living and the multi-layered cosmos by joining healing and religion in an extricable whole.

Securing more to eat from plants and small animals than from large game, food was roasted or pit-baked with fire ignited by a wooden shaft drilled against a softer stick. Plant reproduction was well understood, and natural vegetation was burned to benefit the regrowth of useful foliage. Plant fiber provided bedding, and was hand spun and plied for yarn and cord that was looped and knotted to produce mesh bags and netting. Mats and fabrics were made by twining, also known as 'finger weaving.' Wood was used to fashion digging sticks, throwing sticks, mortars, tool handles, spears, and atlatl spearthrowers. Hide supplied covers, containers, and lashings. Reeds, fiber, cordage, wood, and hide were used to fashion snares, traps, netting devices, and watercraft. Bone was made into awls, perforators, gorges, and hooks. Naturally rounded rocks were used for bolas and sling stones. Irregular chips, flakes, and bifacially worked stones were produced opportunistically for cutting, scraping, perforating and manufacturing other objects of fiber, wood, hide, and bone. Spears had simple fire-hardened tips, as well as points fashioned from dense, solid wood, or chipped stone. While simple, this postulated technology was sufficiently flexible to facilitate early exploitation of the continent's diverse habitats.

Upon crossing the Panamanian Isthmus, it is very unlikely that people migrated directly down the high Andes. In addition to anoxia, the upper Cordillera was glaciated, cold, and sparsely vegetated until the waning of the Ice Age. It is more likely that pioneering groups moved along the continental

37 The atlatl or spear thrower probably armed the continent's first human colonists.

margins, exploiting the terrestrial and aquatic assets of rivers, deltas, and fresh-
or salt-water lagoons. Colonization of the Pacific Rim proceeded on a step-by-
step basis, with vanguards moving into a pristine habitat, settling there, and
reproducing in growing numbers. Daughter colonies then budded off from
parental hearths to claim fresh homelands and repeat the process. Over the
course of multiple generations humans advanced sequentially down the littoral
desert, establishing home territories around one and then another river mouth
or water source. Coastal homesteaders ventured into the lofty sierra to retrieve
resources, such as obsidian and game. Yet glaciers, cold, and anoxia made the
high Cordillera a relatively late frontier of permanent settlement, which awaited
the close of the Ice Age. Colonization of the high mountains presumably transpired in a stair-step manner, with people acclimatizing to moderate elevations
before their altitude-adapted progeny ascended a step further to more lofty habitats.

This conjectural colonization scenario has people moving down the continental margin in Pleistocene times along routes now submerged by post-glacial
sea-level rise. Still, radiocarbon assays from coastal sites in Peru and Chile
confirm that the littoral desert was inhabited by at least 11,500 calendar years
ago, and this is a widely accepted base-line date for evidence of humans elsewhere in the hemisphere. There are disputed claims for significantly greater
human antiquity in the Americas. While these should not be dismissed, most
are rather nebulous about the nature of early human activities. Therefore, let us
begin with the best current case for ancient people in the Andes, Monte Verde,
an encampment in south-central Chile.

Monte Verde

In the subarctic pine forests of the low southern Cordillera people lived briefly
along the sandy banks of a little creek until it backed up and capped their former
settlement with a thin layer of peat. In addition to one human footprint, the peat
preserved dwelling remnants, wooden artifacts, other tools, remains of plant
foods such as wild potatoes, and animal bones including those of five or six mastodons – extinct cousins of elephants, which were scavenged or hunted. The
product of a small group of people, the occupation spanned an annual cycle

some 12,500 radiocarbon years ago (14,800 calendar years ago), to judge from more than a dozen dates. Excavations by Tom Dillehay and Chilean colleagues yielded round rocks the size of an egg. Some might have been sling stones, but others were grooved for suspension as bolas stones. A long, spike-like stone cylinder may have served as a drill. Rare flaked artifacts include one core and one chopper, and partial remains of two long leaf-shaped projectile points similar to so-called El Jobo Points found in early Venezuelan contexts. Wooden artifacts included a sharp-pointed lance, digging sticks, three handles with stone scrapers mounted on them, and three rough-hewn wooden mortars.

Wood was employed in the construction of two different types of structures found in two different site areas. To form foundations for rectangular dwellings, small logs and rough-cut hardwood planks were laid on the ground and held in place by stakes. Next to these, vertical saplings were then driven into the ground every meter or so to form frames for the huts. On some fallen poles were traces of animal skin, suggesting that hides formed the walls of the dwellings. Measuring 3–4.5 m on a side, the 12 excavated rooms were joined at their sides and arranged in two parallel rows. Inside the huts there were tools, plant remains, and shallow clay-lined pits that once held embers and served as braziers. Cooking was apparently a communal affair and took place around two large hearths.

Separated from the dwellings, a very different type of building was erected in an isolated setting at the western end of the site. This was a wishbone-shaped structure with foundations of compacted sand and gravel. Fragments of upright wooden poles were present every half-meter along both arms and served as a pole frame for a hide covering. A small raised platform protruded from the rear of the hut, resulting in the 'Y' or wishbone configuration. The platform was about 3 m wide and almost 4 m long. The open front of the structure faced a small clearing or courtyard that contained small clay-lined braziers. The area yielded pieces of animal hide, burned reeds and seeds, and several species of medicinal plants, including leaves that had been chewed or masticated. Around the building and court there was a concentration of hearths, woodpiles, tools, medicinal plants, and bones, including most of the mastodon remains found at the site. It is evident that this open-fronted structure was the focus of special activities that included the processing of game, if not ritual feasting, preparation of herbal medicines and perhaps practice of shamanistic healing. The wishbone structure stands at the beginning of a long evolutionary tradition of special-purpose architecture that served special corporate activities, which we know little about.

Monte Verde people either scavenged or killed elephants and hunted camelids and small game in the countryside. Plant gathering was of equal, if not greater, importance. In addition to wild potatoes, botanical remains included edible seeds, fruits, nuts, berries, leafy vegetables, tubers, and rhizomes. Flora was secured from nearby marshes, from inland forests, and from the Pacific coast, with algae and lagoon vegetation rich in iodine and salt. By exploiting widely dispersed ecological zones with different growing regimes, the inhabitants obtained plants that matured during all months of the year and brought them back to Monte Verde, which was inhabited during all seasons. This evidence of residential permanence runs contrary to the notion that very early foragers were always migratory. Although Monte Verde lies in cool moist forests far beyond the frontiers of Tahuantinsuyu, the occupation adumbrates many adaptations that would be pursued in the Andes.

Unfortunately, there is scant evidence of contemporary occupation elsewhere in the Andes. The central Chilean sites of Taguatagua, dated 11,400 years ago, and Quero, dated 11,100 years ago, produced remains of mastodon and horse, as well as some stone flakes, and lithics thought to represent unifacial tools, scrapers, and choppers. However, it is not until about 11,000–10,000 radiocarbon years ago that there is more widespread evidence of human activity in the Cordillera, by which time mastodons were gone, but Pleistocene horse and ground sloth still lingered on.

Fluted projectile points

Horse was the most ubiquitous animal to have been hunted and remains have been found at a number of sites with different lithic technologies, including Pikimachay, Jaywamachay, Huarago, and Ushumachay in Peru and Los Toldos in Chile. In Tierra del Fuego, Junius Bird excavated horse, sloth, and guanaco – wild relatives of the llama – remains associated with fluted points in Fell's Cave and Palli Aike Cave near the tip of Chile. Beneath deposits of later hunters, the lowest cave strata yielded dates of 9050 ± 170 BC and 8770 ± 300 BC, and produced simple stone tools and finely crafted spearheads called 'fluted fishtail points.' Similar in shape to a fishtail, the points expand slightly at the base and have a channel or flute on each side. Fluted projectiles are rare in South America and their distribution is limited to the Andes and southern plains, or 'pampas.' Occasional surface finds are reported from southern Brazil, Uruguay, and Los Toldos in Argentina. Near Quito, Ecuador, the highland site of El Inga yielded 21 specimens of fishtail projectiles in a shallow deposit mixed with later remains. These are not the remains of generalized hunters who mastered different environments, but they reflect an adaptation focused on the

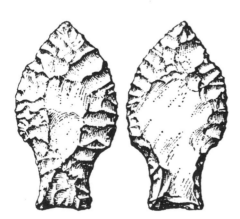

38 Fluted Fishtail points from Tierra del Fuego.

resources of the open grasslands and of people who avoided the tropical forests and the western desert, where there are but two surface finds of fishtail points in northern Peru. The occurrence of similar projectiles in Panama suggests that fluted points may represent a second penetration of South America by a small Paleo-Indian population.

Adaptive dispersal

Because the Andean landscape confronted human colonists with global extremes in desert, mountain, and tropical conditions, adaptive dispersal entailed early economic specialization. Distinct ways of life unfolded in the forested lowlands, the high Cordillera, and the arid coast by 10,000 years ago or shortly thereafter. To varying degrees the divergent adaptations are associated with different types of stone tool assemblages known as the Northwestern Tradition, the coastal Paijan Tradition, the Central Andean Lithic Tradition, and the Atacama Maritime Tradition.

Northwestern Tradition

Because rock is often scarce in the jungle, people living in tropical forests rely more on bone and various botanical resources. Stone is reserved for choppers, scrapers, and sharp flakes that can be used to produce other tools such as spears and arrows tipped with hardwood projectiles. The Northwestern Lithic Tradition is characterized by simple but variable stone artifacts, but no stone projectiles. Tropical adaptations of this tradition are found in coastal Ecuador on the Santa Elena Peninsula north of the Guayaquil Gulf. Here the Las Vegas culture is defined by more than 30 camps and settlements dating between 10,000 and 6,600 years ago. The type site is a dark midden about 1 m deep that accumulated during an early occupation and later served as a burial ground. People lived in circular houses c. 2 m in diameter with mud-plastered walls of cane or poles secured in a narrow trench cut below floor level. Small size suggests these were quarters for a couple and their offspring. With the exception of several axes, stone tools were simple and hunting must have relied upon weapons of wood, reed, and fiber. Land animals, particularly deer, accounted for about 54 percent of the dietary protein, the remainder coming from fish and mangrove mollusks from the sea some 3 km away. Gathering of wild flora is reflected by midden pollen, which also indicates that people had begun to cultivate the bottle gourd (*Lagenaria siceraria*) c. 7,000 to 8,000 years ago. Some 192 individuals were interred at the site in the form of secondary burials of disarticulated bones jumbled together some time after the flesh had decomposed or been removed. Secondary burial among tropical forest peoples contrasts markedly with central Andean peoples' concepts about the hereafter and it is evident that belief systems as well as economic systems diverged at a very early date.

During the Pleistocene warmer, moister conditions pushed down the Cordillera several hundred kilometers into northern Peru into areas that are now desert. Along the coast the Northwestern Lithic Tradition extended south to the Ríos Piura and Chira. Here it is represented by a succession of shallow or surface sites with occupations beginning some time between 11,000 and 8,000 years ago during the Amotape phase and then continuing through Siches, Estero, and Honda phases. During the early phases people hunted and camped along the shore, gathering shellfish from mangrove swamps, but about 6,000 years ago the mangroves disappeared as the northernmost coast reverted to desert.

At higher elevations a belt of montane forests extended southward during Pleistocene times, and survives today as relic stands of tropical trees and thorn steppes in the headwaters of the Zana and Lambayeque river drainages. People using the Northwestern Lithic Tradition settled the upper Zana by 8,000 years ago and their ongoing occupation left behind more than 47 prepottery sites situated along small streams or atop adjacent hill spurs. One site, Nanchoc, is of particular interest because it has a pair of small mounds. In plan the flat-top platforms are oblong, lozenge-shaped, and wider in the southwest than in the northeast. Roughly aligned, they are about 15 m apart, and measure 32–35 m in length and 1.2–1.5 m in height, rising in three tiers faced with stones. The mounds were not all built at once, and radiocarbon dates from basal samples fall between 6000 and 5500 BC. Each consists of a series of superimposed floors separated by layers of artificial fill that gradually added height to the structures. This pattern of incremental building, in which periods of use and epochs of construction alternately succeed one another, is typical of later Andean platform mounds. From an organizational perspective episodic construction was an important means of reaffirming corporate identity by bringing people together periodically to work on an established symbol of unity. The excavators of Nanchoc, Tom Dillehay and Patricia Netherly, suggest that the twin mounds reflect dual social organization and the ceremonial architecture of moieties.

Most of the early Zana sites represent small residential areas about 35 m in diameter, defined by thin middens with hearths, carbonized plants, animal bones, and occasional secondary burials. Near some settlements there are traces of buried furrows and short feeder ditches that may date to the latter half of the Lithic Period. These are the earliest garden plots known to survive, although it is not certain what types of plants were cultivated. Lithics are limited to unifacial tools and grinding stones, but the discovery of part of a Paijan projectile and some marine shells indicates contact with the coast, less than 75 km away, where different adaptations were pursued.

Paijan Tradition

Sites in the Paijan Tradition have given numerous dates between 12,000 and 7,000 years ago. The tradition's hallmark is the long, slender Paijan point, averaging 10 cm in length. The piercing tips are exceptionally long and narrow, and they may be described as 'needle-nosed' projectiles. The noses rarely survive intact, and long broken tips have been mistaken for stone awls. The bases are characterized by long, narrow tangs indicating that the points were mounted in

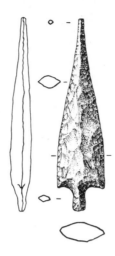

39 *A Paijan projectile – the tip of the point is missing.*

hollow shafts of cane or reed. The breakage tendencies of needle-nosed projectiles made them ineffective against large game with thick hides and they appear to have been designed for spearing fish, whose bones are found in inland middens. Yet the shoreline sites where Paijan people presumably obtained much of their food were inundated long ago by rising sea levels. Thus, all that survives of this tradition are sites associated with secondary activities that drew people inland for brief periods.

Three types of interior sites are known: stone quarries, lithic workshops, and short-term camps. Projectiles are commonly found at the first two, but rarely at the last, suggesting that the weapons were not used for hunting. Covering one square kilometer, the site of La Cumbre on the north side of the Moche Valley combined quarry and workshop activities and yielded more than 4,500 artifacts. Long, foliate, bifacially chipped pieces were the most numerous, and were probably preforms from which finished tools would be made, including projectiles, knife-like *limaces*, side scrapers, notches, beaks, denticulates, pebble scrapers, pebble tools, cores, and flakes or blocks modified by use alone. The base of a fluted point, fashioned from foreign stone, was found on the surface.

Further inland on the north side of the valley, a huge tilted boulder provided an overhang, known as the Quirihuac Shelter. Here a few Paijan people camped to collect land snails and left behind tool fragments, chipping debris, and burials of a child and an adult. These and other Paijan interments were primary burials of intact corpses. Bones of the adult were dated to 9,000 years ago; whereas the burial of the child was a millennium earlier. With the exception of one young date, assays of small bits of charcoal in the rockshelter ranged between 8,645 and 12,795 years ago.

Land snails appear in shallow camp deposits left by Paijan peoples in the Quebrada Cuculicote on the north side of the Chicama Valley. In addition to grinding stones for processing plant foods excavations show that people ate lizards, birds, and vizcacha (*Lagidium peruanum*), a rabbit-sized mammal, as well as fish and crabs brought in from the sea. To the north, in the adjacent

Cupisnique drainage, Paijan quarry sites, manufacturing sites, and camp sites have also been found. Although not rich in artifacts, two camps had midden deposits 20 cm deep. Charcoal associated with a human burial was 10,200 years old, and other midden remains produced dates of 9,800 and 7,700 years ago. Grinding stones were present, and, in decreasing order of importance, animal remains included land snails, fish, lizard, fox, and one deer bone.

The Paijan Tradition reflects a highly specialized adaptation with a sharply circumscribed geographic focus. The tradition is absent north of the Río Omo where more tropical conditions existed. It is also absent in the forested headwaters of the Río Zana where the Northwestern Tradition prevailed, but Paijan people were present at lower elevations on the coastal plain crossed by the Zana River. The primary focus of the Paijan adaptation was the wide coastal plain and broad continental shelf between the Ríos Omo and Santa where hundreds of needle-nosed projectiles have been found. As the coastline narrows to the south, the frequency of Paijan remains begins to diminish. Three surface sites near the Casma shore yielded a dozen or so needle-nosed projectiles, and several were discovered at high elevations in the Río Casma headwaters. The tradition is present during the Laz phase in the Ancon-Chillon area near Lima, and the most southerly occurrences of Paijan points comprise two surface finds in the Ica desert.

In overview needle-nosed Paijan points vie with fluted fishtail points as the most distinctive early projectiles on the continent. Paijan stands apart from other traditions in its circumscribed geographic focus, principally along the wide coastal plain of the north, with some southward penetration to Ica. It is curious that this wider distribution coincides with the later distribution of large architectural monuments along the coastal desert. The earliest of these monuments were erected by preceramic fisherfolk who relied on nets and hooks, but not harpoons. Paijan was certainly ancestral to these later developments but rising sea levels have submerged shoreline sites which would reflect their early evolution.

Central Andean Tradition

Fluted fishtail and Paijan assemblages are distinct yet repetitive, each probably representing people who pursued similar customs and spoke the same language. This is not the case with the Central Andean Tradition, which is a widespread, but generalized lithic technology shared by populations pursuing several environmental adaptations. It is characterized by projectiles that resemble willow leaves, with tapering points and rounded or blunt bases. The leaf shape is a simple configuration that constitutes a 'generic' weapon form, with minimal elaboration on the functional necessities of a projectile point. Leaf-shaped points are widely distributed from the Río Santa headwaters into Chile and Argentina and range in size from short, stubby blades to long, thin ones. There is such variation in leaf shape and associated tool assemblages, and they occur over such a vast area, that authorities do not agree on where the tradition begins and ends. It has been most often applied to northern and central Peru, but in a generic sense it encompasses much of the south central Andes as well. Leaf-shaped projectiles are associated with puna, sierra basin, and coastal adaptations. In the north each represented a separate way of life, but in the arid south impoverished resources led to combined adaptations.

Puna hunters. Except for the rich marine food chain, Andean animal life was most abundant in the high elevation puna grasslands of the north. The selective pressures of altitude kept the variety of puna wildlife small, but plentiful. The vicuña (*Vicugna vicugna*), a deer-sized wild relative of the llama, is frequently found along streams and creeks draining the grasslands. Vicuña live in two types of groups: bands and troops. Bands are reproductive groups consisting of one dominant male and an average of seven females that occupy a small, fixed territory. Troops are herds of up to 40 males that wander near the reproductive groups and are constantly being expelled from band territories by dominant males. The northern herds are not characterized by seasonal migration. These facts and the abundance of game have led John Rick to argue that if hunting bands numbered about 25 individuals sufficient vicuña could be hunted within a radius of 9 to 10 km to support puna occupation year round. Rick's interpretation has been based on excavations at Pachamachay Cave, surrounded by grasslands at an elevation of 4,300 m, and located *c.* 10 km from Lake Junin. The first two phases of occupation are dated at 10,500–9,000 years ago, and 9,000–7,000 years ago, and are associated with leaf-shaped points as well as with triangular and shouldered forms. Carbonized seeds indicate the collecting of wild grasses and other plants. Bone was common and no less than 97 per cent came from camelids. Phase 1 is thought to reflect the presence of relatively mobile hunting groups, who were in the process of formulating puna adaptations; but from Phase 2 onwards occupation was probably permanent by a small population that used the site continually for many millennia. To maintain a stable adaptation people had to limit their own numbers and avoid over-exploitation of the vicuña herds.

A number of other high altitude caves with stratified deposits reflect similar economic adjustments to the wet puna. They include the first two phases of occupation at Lauricocha Cave, 100 km northwest of Pachamachay. Located at an elevation of about 3,900 m, the site is in rugged terrain near camelid pasture as well as lower zones inhabited by deer. The earliest occupation dates to *c.* 9,500 years ago and is characterized by the presence of leaf-shaped projectiles that become longer in the Phase 2 occupation. The Lauricocha people were probably permanent residents and seem to have complemented their game diet with a remarkable variety of local edible roots and tubers.

Sierra basin foragers. At the time Paijan people occupied the Casma coast, highland people of the Central Andean Tradition pursued a very different living in the mountains only 80 km away. The sierra lifeway has been documented at Guitarrero Cave and at higher open-air sites in the Callejon de Huaylas by Thomas Lynch and his associates. The Callejon is one of the great Andean

Plates 27, 28

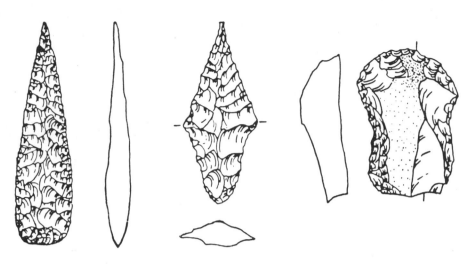

40 Projectile point and stone tools from Guitarrero Cave, shown actual size.

basins that drains from south to north, but it forms the headwaters of the Río Santa and is the only sierra basin to empty into the Pacific. At an elevation of 2,580 m, Guitarrero Cave overlooks the river and narrow floodplain a short walk away. The principal occupation of the cave – called Complex II – was short-lived and took place about 10,000 years ago. Lithic remains resemble those from higher local sites and those from Lauricocha and Pachamachay. However, the animal remains from Guitarrero are rather different. Here small rodents such as rabbits and rabbit-like vizcacha are common, as are birds, including pigeon and tinamou. Larger game consisted principally of deer, which outnumbered camelid remains by seven to one. The bones reflect a sierra valley fauna which is more diversified than that of the higher puna, but less plentiful in numbers. Sierra game did not provide the hunting resources that favored year-round residency. The Callejon sites probably represent seasonal transhumance that brought people to the grasslands above 4,000 m when the sierra began to dry after the December to March rains. The recovery of only one marine shell at Guitarrero suggests limited contact with the coast. Thus, although only 80 km apart, marked differences in lithic assemblages and economic adaptations show that highland and lowland populations were already diverging culturally if not biologically.

Altiplano hunter-gatherers. The resources to support separate hunter-gatherer adaptations in the puna and sierra decrease as the Cordillera becomes higher and drier. The turning point seems to be in the Ayacucho uplands of central Peru. Research in this region suggests that from about 10,000 years ago successive phases of occupation reflect a relatively mobile way of life. The pattern of annual movement saw families congregating at mid altitudes in sierra drainages when the rainy season brought forth a rich bloom of plants attractive to animals

41 Deer were never abundant in the arid Andes and by Moche times stag hunting had become a sport of the nobility. Wounded by an atlatl spear, a buck is dispatched by club in this ceramic painting.

and humans. Drier times necessitated a dispersal of people to other elevations, particularly to the higher puna hunting grounds.

The Lithic Period occupation of the Lake Titicaca basin is largely unexplored, but due west, in the Río Moquegua area, early sites from the dry puna down to the coast have been investigated. At an altitude of 2,000 m, the painted caves of Toquepala yielded radiocarbon dates as early as 9,500 years old. The long occupation of the cave was characterized by seasonal residence during the moister months between October and April. Painted and unpainted caves and rockshelters with Lithic Period occupations are common in the higher altitudes, but the open-air settlement of Asana in the high sierra is unique because of its architecture. Not far below the puna, it is situated on the banks of a Moquegua tributary at an elevation of 4,500 m. Its occupation spans the Lithic Period, with radiocarbon dates between 9,580 and 3,640 years ago. Beginning about 7,000 years ago the stratified deposits contain floor outlines of small circular dwellings that were apparently walled with brush, hide, or some other perishable material. From about 5,000 years ago they clustered around a larger, central ceremonial structure. Defined by a well-made clay floor 10 m in diameter, the structure may have been 'C' shaped in plan with an open front that was largely destroyed by a rock slide. The interior was kept clean and its most noteworthy feature was a cairn-like pile of rocks perhaps representing an altar. The excavator, Mark Aldenderfer suggests Asana was a wet season residential area for people who focused their efforts on exploiting the nearby puna much of the year and spent time camping in puna caves. The dry season affects both sierra valleys and higher grasslands, but the dry puna is dotted with seeps and springs that support moors, or *bofedales*. Contemporary pastoralists often channel the springs to irrigate and expand the lush bofedal vegetation. As a source of pasturelands where wild herds would congregate during the dry season, the moors were no doubt vital to past hunter-gatherers. Analysis of tools and the types of stone from which they were fashioned at Asana demonstrates substantial similarities in sierra and puna lithic assemblages, but marked differences with coastal assemblages.

From Lake Poopó south the altiplano is enveloped by the Atacama Desert. The salt puna and small sierra valleys of northern Chile become progressively more impoverished and this required greater seasonal mobility on the part of hunter–gatherers and a merging of what were separate adaptations to the north. A merger of highland and coastal exploitation patterns seems to have characterized the arid Cordillera from the Río Loa–San Pedro de Atacama region south. Here Chilean investigator Lautaro Nuñez postulates a pattern of transhumance with Lithic Period people utilizing coastal resources between May and September and then migrating high into the mountains for the remainder of the year.

Atacama Maritime Tradition

Fishing is the oldest enduring way of making a living in the arid Andes and Paijan people were not the only folk to harvest the ocean. Seafood was consumed by their southern neighbors, who made opportunistic informal stone tools, stubby barbed harpoon points, as well as leaf-shaped projectiles. Some of the earliest surviving evidence of maritime adaptations in the Americas comes from southernmost Peru and northern Chile. Here the Atacama Desert is at its bleakest, but alluring seeps and springs occur in some dry coastal drainages, called *quebradas*. In Quebrada Jaguay, near the Río Camana, early encampments are radiocarbon-dated between 10,000 and 11,100 years ago. From an initial emphasis on collecting clams and netting corvina, consumption of seafoods broadened over time. Accumulations of garbage or midden and traces of a brush dwelling suggest people resided locally much of the year, yet ventures into the high sierra are indicated by obsidian from a mountain source more than 100 km away. Further south near the Río Moquegua shellfish from the bottom midden of the deeply stratified Ring Site produced a date of 10,575 years ago. Within a millennium or so this large settlement was permanently occupied on a year-round basis by people who obtained all their protein by angling if not by netting. The center of this ring-shaped settlement was apparently a plaza, with families living in a circle around it where 2 m of shellfish garbage mounded up. Some 35 km to the south, there are 10,500- to 10,750-year-old charcoal dates from a temporary camp at Quebrada Tacahuay. Here modest quantities of mollusks and anchovies were consumed while people cleaned and processed large numbers of cormorants and seafowl. Bird butchering focused on removing the breast meat and these prime cuts were apparently packed off for consumption at more permanent settlements.

Across the Chilean border near the Río Azapa, early fisherfolk at the Asia settlement resided in small circular, dome-shaped structures of poles and thatch. An adult buried in one hut produced a 9,000-year-old carbon date and chemical analysis of the human bones implied a diet of more than 90 percent seafood. Further south, occupations in the Tiliviche and Conchas Quebradas are dated to 9,760 and 9,680 years ago. In the inland Tiliviche drainage seafoods were consumed as well as land animals, hunted with leaf-shaped projectiles including some fashioned from mountain obsidian. A greater focus upon marine foods is evident in the occupation of Quebrada Las Conchas where refuse deposits produced preserved fragments of fish net dated at 9,730 years ago.

Over time, seaboard folk of the southern Atacama Desert diversified their fishing tackle to secure broader returns. Float nets were complemented by fishhooks fabricated from sturdy cactus thorns, shell, and bone, and bone points were attached to cigar-shaped stone shafts to create composite fishhooks. Wooden harpoons with stone points were used to take large fish and perhaps sea lions. The latter were of dietary important for their fat and organ meat, and sea-lion ribs were used as pry bars to extract marine snails and other gastropods from their rocky perches. Maturing abilities to harvest the sea allowed people to increase their numbers and reside in sedentary communities of modest size, which were organized by kinship and descent lines to judge from mortuary practices.

Chinchorro mummies

Among ancient civilizations, artificial mummification of corpses was a social distinction conferred upon important people who were generally born to privileged status, such as Egyptian pharaohs and nobles of yore. Remarkably, the very earliest mummies in the world were the daughters, sons, and parents of Chilean fisherfolk whose bone chemistry points to a 90 percent seafood diet. Known as Chinchorro, those societies who engaged in this unprecedented cult of the dead focused upon physically conserving the deceased in a quasi-lifelike state between about 8,000 and 3,600 years ago. Most corpses were buried without special treatment and fewer than 250 Chinchorro mummies have been recovered. The majority are neonates, children, and adolescents, while adults of both sexes are less common. Chinchorro morticians perfected unusual skills: in defleshing and disassembling bodies; in removing cerebral and visceral matter; in treating the skin to arrest deterioration; in reassembling the skeleton; in implanting cane or wooden shafts to support the skull, trunk, arms, and legs; in adding fiber, feather, clay, or other fill to body cavities; in applying an exterior coat of clay to permit the sculpting and painting of facial details; and in replacing pelage with wigs of human hair. Although there was great variation in corpse treatment, the end products tended to be ridged and statue-like. Significantly, some mummies exhibit surface damage and others damage that was later repaired. Thus, preserved cadavers were kept accessible to the living for considerable time prior to final disposal by interment. Some were interred as family groups of children and adults, and one group spanned three generations with infants, adults of reproductive age, as well as very old adults. One must wonder if Chinchorro mummies were not prepared by specialists who also oversaw subsequent ritual curation of conserved corpses as later mallquipavillacs did. It cannot be said that ancestor veneration was central to this early cult of the dead, because the majority of Chinchorro mummies were adolescents and

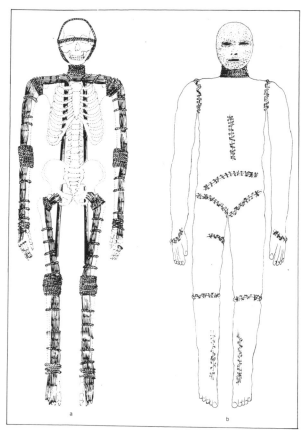

42 After bracing the skeleton with reed supports (a), Chinchorro mummies were reassembled (b) and facial details were modeled in clay covering the head.

children, and not ancestors or progenitors. Consequently, the distinct privilege of being mummified must have been a social entitlement that a few children inherited from their parents and lineages. Presumably, a mummy's display and curation endured as long as its lineage remained entitled to distinct social position, but when the latter waned corpse interment ensued.

Chinchorro folk were not alone in their concern with preserving the deceased. Around 6,000 years ago corpses were salted to arrest deterioration at the settlement of La Paloma on the central Peruvian coast. In sharp contrast to secondary burial practices of disarticulated corpses among tropical forest people, these early coastal mortuary complexes reflect very ancient and very profound Andean beliefs that the deceased had to be physically intact to enter the afterlife and join the realm of the ancestors. Ranging from the common ayllu to the imperial Inca, Andean social formations were held together by kin bonds based upon veneration of the deceased. Mummies were the preferred symbols of corporate identity and founding fathers. Thus, the Chinchorro and Paloma mortuary complexes reveal an ancient inception of kin concepts and mortuary beliefs critical to the rise of civilization in the Cordillera.

Domestication

The evolution of Andean civilization was intimately interwoven with the domestication of robust plants, hardy animals, and with the arduous transformation of inhospitable terrain into farmland. Yet plant and animal husbandry has never been an idyllic way of life, nor one free from famine in a rugged landscape of environmental extremes with frequent natural hazards. Under lengthy human care, domesticated species experienced genetic changes that biologically distinguish them from their wild progenitors. These changes in behavior, morphology, and genetic structure transpire over many generations of tending and cultivation, but tending species does not always result in domestication. To construct watercraft Andean fisherfolk have long cultivated bull rushes that do not exhibit genetic modifications qualifying them as domesticated plants. With very ancient remains, it is often difficult or impossible to tell if an organism was gathered wild or matured under human care, because there are no genetic or morphological signatures distinguishing between the two. Consequently, the vital first step in the domestication process, human tending of wild plants and animals, is very elusive.

Theories

Although there is ancient evidence of cultivation and plant domestication at some early Andean sites, there are fewer facts than theories about domestication. Pioneering insights about agropastoral origins were put forth by the great naturalist Alexander von Humboldt several centuries ago. As the first European scholar to systematically explore the Cordillera and to report upon the archaeological monuments of Latin America, he wrote voluminously about the flora and fauna of the hemisphere. Aware that tens of thousands of plants and animals thrived, but fewer than 1 percent were domesticated, a notion of risk lay at the heart of his ideas. Von Humboldt believed that early experiments with tending organisms and altering their characteristics were more likely to fail than succeed. Therefore, well-off people living in productive habitats had little reason to engage in such hazardous activity. The motivation for tending wild resources would instead be found among the inhabitants of marginal settings and harsh environments where trial and error in the care of plants or animals offered more acceptable risks as potential means of stabilizing or increasing food supplies. The Prussian scholar reasoned that people were gradually pushed into harsh settings conducive to experimentation as population growth filled in more favorable habitats. To this push we may add the environmental changes at the end of the Pleistocene as well as the swings in Holocene climate.

Although von Humboldt saw necessity as the mother of invention, people never consciously sought to domesticate plants and animals. In the Andes, a major route to domestication lay with experiments that promoted plants and animals inhabiting one place or zone to live in another. Herders altered the distribution of wild resources when they used bofedal springs to irrigate pasturage and people often transplanted organisms closer to where they lived. Moving potential domesticates entailed seeding in the case of beans and cereals, and certainly transplanting of root parts or cuttings in the case of tubers. Distances between natural occurrence and human transplant were often short. Yet in the rugged Cordillera living conditions change over very short distances and habitats can vary within a few hundred meters of elevation. Therefore, moving organisms and altering their placement injected both human selection and natural selection into the Andean domestication process. That is why the Cordillera is home to over 3,000 genetic varieties of potatoes.

Traveling the Cordillera, von Humboldt recognized that domestication was an unending process in which the harsh highlands are still undergoing agricultural and pastoral transformations. Plants and animals are continually moved from tolerant to less tolerant settings. Cultigens are shifted laterally at their established elevation to new fields with different soils, moisture, pests, and other growing conditions. However, the thrust of agropastoralism has long been into ever-higher mountain regions where vast tracts of open land lie invitingly beyond the altitudinal limits of farming. This dynamic economic frontier fluctuates up and down continually in response to short- and long-term changes in temperature and precipitation. The upward assault is spearheaded with a few varieties of exceptionally robust root crops. Nature defends her elevational boundaries with the greatest stress and risks in the continent, resulting in frequent crop failures, and minimal yields. The uphill battle is waged in small, scattered plots where a few farmers believe that microenvironmental conditions might be less hostile than average. These peasants suffer the risks of fighting the frontiers of agriculture because they are the land-poor and economically marginal members of local ayllu communities with nowhere else to go.

Many Andean domesticates and the majority of highland crops likely originated at different points along the Cordillera's tropical eastern slopes, where rich biotic diversity is compressed in narrow, stratified habitats. Some types of potatoes may have derived from wild forms from the eastern flanks of the Titicaca Basin, and similar origins may hold for tubers such as oca and ulluco, as well as for the grains of quinoa and cañihua. Camelids were almost certainly domesticated in the highland grasslands.

Botanists believe that the wild ancestors of upland or lowland cultigens came from many places, with domestication transpiring in many different settings. Peanuts have their nearest wild relatives in Argentina and may have originated there, while cotton has wild relatives on the north coast of Peru. Fruits such as avocado, and chirimoya along with coca originated to the north where the range is tropical. Finally, the Amazon or Orinoco Basins supplied the important lowland root crop of manioc. Ultimately, it was much easier to tend plants in the low, warm, well-watered tropics than in those bleak deserts or anoxic mountains where farming was not merely a matter of acquiring domesticates, but also demanded the acquisition of land with adequate water supplies. Thus, domestication and farming advanced accordingly.

43 Grown for containers and fishing floats, gourds were domesticated very early.

Early evidence

Dating to 10,000 years ago, the well-preserved botanical assemblage of Complex II at Guitarrero Cave, in the Callejon de Huaylas of northern Peru, includes the oldest cultivated plants yet found in the New World. In order to assess the Guitarrero finds, it is important to recognize that native flora provided many more things than food. Medicinal plants were vital to health care, while so-called 'industrial' plants provided clothing, containers, weapons, bedding, and shelter. Therefore, plant tending need not have arisen exclusively from concerns with food. The dry deposits of Guitarrero reveal a plant assemblage dominated by wild vegetation that served not diet, but technology, and products ranging from beds to apparel. Furthermore, it was a technology emphasizing fiber over wood. The latter was used for weapon shafts, dowels, and fire-drills. However, the bulk of the assemblage consists of fiber debris from hemp-like plants including *Tillandsia*, *Puya*, and *Furcraea*. People slept on, wore, and made mats as well as mesh containers out of fiber. Cordage was the basic element of production, and it was used for many things including the production of textiles and netting. One fragment of an open mesh bag or net was recovered from the lower cave deposits, while other fabrics were made by simple twining, with weft elements manually twisted around the warp elements. The Guitarrero assemblage stands at the beginning of a major Andean tradition focused upon fiber technology that later incorporated domesticated plants (cotton), and animals (alpaca), and made textiles uniquely important to statecraft.

In Guitarrero Cave the amount of fiber-plant debris was very large in comparison with food-plant remains. Tubers and rhizomes were a major source of carbohydrates, and oca as well as ulluco have tentatively been identified among the remains. A number of Andean fruits were represented, including lucuma

Plate 27

Plate 28

(*Pouteria lucuma*), pacay (*Inga* sp.), *Solanum hispidum,* and *Trichocerus peruvianas.* Because these fruits and tubers are native to the general region, they may have been gathered wild, or they may have been tended. Excavations yielded a few specimens of domesticated common beans (*Phaseolus vulgaris*) and lima beans (*P. lunatus*) and one specimen of chili pepper (*Capsicum* sp.). The beans and pepper represent cultivated plants because they do not grow naturally in the region; rather, their wild range was probably the eastern slope of the Cordillera. To occur at the cave the plants must have been tended perhaps in small plots near the river. If people were cultivating foreign plants then they may well have propagated the local fruits, tubers, or industrial plants. The Guitarrero cultigens were sturdy ones that could be sown and left unattended while seasonal hunting and gathering were pursued elsewhere.

Guitarrero Cave was certainly not the only place in the Andes where early plant tending transpired. In the headwaters of the Chilca drainage, at an altitude of 3,925 m, Tres Ventanas Cave produced tubers thought to be ulluco and potato also dated to about 10,000 radiocarbon years ago. Fragments of gourd (*Lagenaria siceraria*) of comparable or somewhat greater antiquity have been reported from cave deposits in the Ayacucho region. We need not pursue further evidence to say that domestication began at a remarkably early date in the Andes, but it did not usher in an agricultural revolution. Plant and animal tending in the Cordillera served secondary roles complementing other ways of making a living thousands of years longer than they played primary roles as economic mainstays.

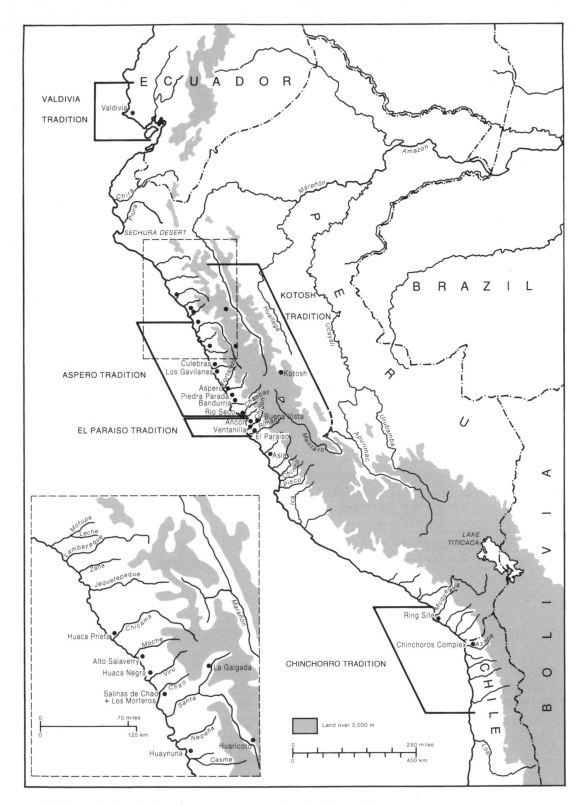

VALDIVIA
TRADITION

ECUADOR

Valdivia

Chira

Piura

SECHURA DESERT

PERU

Marañón

Amazon

BRAZIL

KOTOSH
TRADITION

Huallaga

Ucayali

Kotosh

ASPERO TRADITION

Culebras
Los Gavilanes

Aspero
Piedra Parada
Bandurria
Rio Seco

EL PARAISO TRADITION

Ancon
Ventanilla

Buena Vista
Rimac
El Paraiso

Asia

Chancay
Chillon
Fortaleza

Mantaro

Apurimac

Urubamba

LAKE
TITICACA

BOLIVIA

Ica
Chincha
Pisco

Ica

Moquegua

Ring Site

Chinchoros Complex

Azapa

CHINCHORRO TRADITION

CHILE

Motupe
Leche
Lambayeque

Zaña

Jequetepeque

Marañón

Huaca Prieta

Chicama

Moche

Alto Salaverry
Huaca Negra

Viru

Chao

La Galgada

Salinas de Chao
+ Los Morteros

Santa

Nepeña

Huaynuna

Huaricoto

Casma

0   70 miles
0   120 km

Land over 3,000 m

0   250 miles
0   400 km

44 The Preceramic Period: principal sites and areas mentioned in Chapter Five.

CHAPTER FIVE

THE PRECERAMIC FOUNDATIONS OF CIVILIZATION

A great environmental turning point provides a convenient subdivision of the long prepottery era into two periods: Lithic and Preceramic. The first coincides largely with dynamic changes accompanying the retreat of the Ice Age. The second, sometimes called the Late Archaic, begins with the abatement of glacial meltback and relative stabilization of sea levels which transpired as marine and meteorological currents entered their contemporary regimes about 3000 BC. Because the ecology of the Cordillera shifted into its current configuration, the survival of ancient sites improved dramatically and much can be said about the preceramic foundations of civilization.

All ancient civilizations were based upon institutions promoting integration and social fusion. Yet extreme environmental diversity in the Andes fostered counterforces of fission and division. Consequently, customs and lifeways certainly diverged during the Lithic Period. Thus Preceramic populations were challenged to forge integrative unities out of individualistic groups. At the community level segmentary lineages, moieties, and cargo-like governance presumably structured organization. Nonetheless, by 2000 BC some Preceramic populations integrated their efforts to erect the continent's largest architectural monuments of the time. This organizational fusion must have transpired under religious guise, because there is scant evidence of kurakas, or hereditary political leaders.

Preceramic economies

Although plants were often cultivated, Preceramic people derived most of their food from the wild. Therefore, archaeologists posit that civilization did not emerge until pottery came into use, because ceramics are associated with societies that obtain most of their calories from domesticates. The spread of intensive farming and pottery followed the path of least resistance, moving from low to high and moist to dry environments. In the well-watered tropical north of Colombia and Ecuador, agriculture was adopted well before 3000 BC. However, extension down the arid Cordillera lagged, and only after an episode of dusty, and apparently dry, climatic times did farming take hold in northern and central Peru around 1800 BC. Further south there was again a lag until 1600 BC when rainfall increased in the Titicaca region and supported the rise of agro-pastoralism. From here it still took many hundreds of years for farm plants and pottery to diffuse into the hyper-arid environments of San Pedro de Atacama and the very dry Chilean coast.

45 The sea influenced the art and iconography of Preceramic fisherfolk who depicted crabs and serpent-like fish or eels in this Huaca Prieta textile motif.

In the Peruvian Andes, where plant tending began in the Lithic Period and continued through Preceramic times, cultivation came first to self-watering lands where mountain rainfall or river runoff favored plant growth. Coastal fisherfolk grew cotton (*Gossypium barbadense*), gourd (*Lagenaria siceraria*), squash (*Cucurbita* spp.), beans (*Phaseolus vulgaris, P. lunatus and canavalia* sp.) and fruit (*Lucuma bifera*, and *Psidium guajava*) in seasonally inundated stream bottoms without the aid of large irrigation works. Their sierra neighbors tended these and other plants where there was sufficient mountain rainfall and in small canal systems along river channels. Although hunting and foraging in high mountain grasslands remained important, increasing reliance upon cultivated plants pulled sierra populations into lower settlements where conditions were less hostile to plant tending. Due to environmental variation, all plants did not prosper equally well in all settings. Therefore, cultivation exacerbated the demand for distant commodities, procured either directly via verticality or indirectly by trueque and exchange.

Sierra uplands

As mountain populations decreased their dependence on wild resources and increased their reliance on cultivation, they were slowly drawn away from the higher elevations to lower settings where warmer temperatures and milder conditions favored plant tending in the bottomlands of sierra drainages. A gradual downward shift in the locations of camps and residential sites is well documented during prepottery times in the quasi-tropical headwaters of the Río Zana, where the use of irrigation began at an early date. A parallel shift, perhaps a little later, is also evident in more arid drainages to the south, including the western Callejon de Huaylas and its eastern sierra counterparts formed by the headwaters of the Ríos Marañón and Huallaga.

In these mountain drainages the shared beliefs about ritual and special purpose architecture is called the Kotosh Religious Tradition. The type site of Kotosh, near modern Huanaco, is located on the bank of the Río Higueras, a tributary of the Río Huallaga, at an elevation of *c.* 2,000 m. The climate is temperate and seasonal rainfall is limited, but supports subtropical vegetation and scattered thorn trees. The site comprises two large platform mounds flanked by lesser constructions and a number of small structures on a nearby river terrace. Perhaps the twin mounds reflect moiety organization. With a basal diameter of almost 100 m, the largest mound was a mass of superimposed structures that reached a height of 8 m and reflected long building activity and ceremonial use. Deep trench excavations exposed ten superimposed constructions. The two lowest and earliest, called the Kotosh Mito Phase, are preceramic but lack radiocarbon dates. Subsistence remains included unidentified charred seeds, domesticated guinea pig, deer antler, and bones of camelids that may have been hunted or herded. Hunting is indicated by a chipped-stone industry with leaf-shaped points similar to those found in the Lauricocha Cave. Crops could have been tended along the nearby river, or by irrigation, but there is no surviving evidence of cultivated plants. There are indirect suggestions that higher and lower ecological zones were exploited, perhaps adumbrating verticality adaptations. The camelid remains suggest hunting or herding in the puna. The mid-range elevation of Kotosh afforded access to lower habitats along the Amazon tributaries. The site produced ground stone axes that are typically Amazonian, and when pottery appeared at Kotosh it had many lowland characteristics.

Ornamental products from high and low altitudes have been found at the site of La Galgada, a complex of two ceremonial mounds and surrounding dwellings in the Callejon de Huaylas on the east bank of the Río Tablachaca, a major tributary of the Santa River. The drainage forms an east-west corridor for crossing the Cordillera and La Galgada is located at midpoint *c.* 80 km from the Pacific coast and an equal distance from the tropical reaches of the Río Marañón. The arid Tablachaca Canyon cuts through a highland plateau and the site lies at 1,100 m, below the elevation of seasonal rainfall. The architectural complex includes two platforms and numerous other small structures. Consisting of a mass of superimposed buildings, the largest mound has produced dates between 2200 and 1200 BC and is associated with Preceramic and early ceramic occupations. Cultivated plants included beans, squash, fruits, chili peppers, gourd, a great deal of cotton and one corn cob. Irrigation was needed to grow the plants and nearby remains of ancient canals are thought to be of Preceramic origin.

The excavators of La Galgada believe the economy was based on more than farming, and see the site as a hub for the movement of goods between distant habitats. Funerary objects included marine shell beads and disks of coastal origins, as well as finely fashioned pins and ornaments of bone. There were also colorful feathers that may have come from Amazonian birds. It is unclear from evidence thus far uncovered at the site whether these foreign products were obtained by exchange, or by direct collection from the coast and Marañón. However, the foreign items are small and light because pack animals had yet to enter the economy.

Kotosh and La Galgada provide but fleeting glimpses of Preceramic economies in the sierra uplands. At the same time vital developments were taking place within and without the Titicaca Basin. Cave sites in the grasslands above the altitudinal limits of farming continued to be occupied as herding gradually replaced hunting, but evidence of the processes that later linked puna herding and sierra farming to produce agropastoralism remains elusive for this early period.

Desert coast

In the 1960s, a number of Andean, American, and Soviet scholars independently concluded that the stage of development known as the 'Neolithic revolution' could be sustained by more than one type of economy, and they proposed a maritime hypothesis for the arid coast. The theory holds that exceptionally rich, easily accessible marine resources provided calories to sustain sedentary residence, population growth, large communities, and the rise of complex organization capable of erecting large architectural monuments. Cold up-welling currents make the Andean fishery the richest in the Western Hemisphere, but the frigid waters create a temperature inversion that inhibits rainfall in the world's driest desert. Whereas all the littoral waters can be fished, less than 10 percent of the desert can be farmed even with very large irrigation works; and self-watering river floodplains are narrow, entrenched and offer little arable land. The construction, maintenance, and use of coastal irrigation systems entail multitudes of corporately organized people. Conversely, the anchovy fishery is most efficiently exploited by net-harvesting small schooling fish from small craft manned by small crews. By 1970, Peru and Chile earned far greater foreign revenues from fishmeal than from mechanized coastal plantations growing crops for international export. This is because commercial anchovy yields averaged 100 metric tons per year per square kilometer over the 2,000 km length of the near-shore fishery. Even if Preceramic fisherfolk cropped the stock more modestly and ate only anchovies, a population of six million could be sustained. Near the northern end of the anchovy belt, around 8°,11°, and 15° South Latitude there are fishery hot spots with annual yields of 1,000 tons. Significantly, adjacent to this 600-km stretch of water where the fishery is richest is where the greatest social complexity arose and largest Preceramic monuments were erected. Although anchoveta have long been the 'staple' of the Andean fishery, other marine life is abundant and fisherfolk enjoyed diversified maritime victuals sometimes complemented by wild or cultivated plants from nearby river valleys.

Dietary evidence. Chemical analysis of human bone from Chinchorro interments indicates a diet of more than 90 percent marine foods for Chilean fisherfolk who settled along the coast early in the Lithic Period. Because human colonization of the Andes was a gradual matter of sedentary parental communities giving rise to more mobile daughter colonies seeking new terrain, infilling of the Cordillera and its coast was an attenuated process. This is evident at the settlement of La Paloma located in a lomas vegetation area some 4 km inland of San Bartalo Bay, 15 km north of the Chilca drainage in central Peru. About 4500 BC a small group of relatively mobile people moved in to the site, opening the first phase of occupation. Their descendants became more fully sedentary during two subsequent phases of residence which ended shortly after 3000 BC. Although the Paloma community may never have numbered more than 30 to 40 individuals, more than 900 individuals lived, died, and were interred during the 1,500-year occupation and a sample of more than 200 burials has been analyzed by bioanthropologists from the University of Missouri. Making their living principally from the sea, Palomans lived in circular dome-shaped structures, with about 11 sq. m of floor space, that were built in shallow, flat-bottomed pits about 40 cm deep. Cane was used as wall supports and reeds and grass as thatch. The structures were used for storage, sleeping, and often as repositories of the dead, including children and adult members of both sexes representing family members. The deceased were often conserved with salt, warped in reed mats with few accompaniments, and then interred. A ceremonial fire was sometimes ignited over the shallow grave and may have contributed to corpse desiccation and conservation. This treatment was not extended to all deceased, and a low frequency of female neonates and infants suggests infanticide was practiced and the corpses disposed of elsewhere. Nonetheless, the Paloma practice of keeping corpses in their homes presages much later customs of keeping the mummified emperors of Chimor and Tahuantinsuyu in their palaces.

A shallow midden at the 15-ha site contained considerable charcoal from stems and twigs of lomas plants that became smaller over time, pointing to over-exploitation of scarce fuel resources. The trash also included bone fishhooks, net fragments, and abundant mollusks, sea birds, sea mammals, and fish, dominated by small species such as anchovies and sardines. The latter are the primary constituent in human feces and in corpse stomach content, which also contained small seeds from wild grasses. The chemistry of human bones was characterized by exceptionally low levels of strontium due to an exceptionally high intake of protein. The latter certainly came from the sea, and diving in cold water is evident in a very high incidence of osseous damage to the ear structures of males. Popularly known as 'surfers' ear,' such auditory damage typified Chinchorro populations, as well as later fisherfolk. During the initial phase of occupation, Paloman males consumed more protein than females. Dietary parity improved during the subsequent occupation phases as the incidence of childhood anemia decreased and adult stature increased. Although the population grew, people sought to control their numbers by delaying age of marriage and reproduction, and by female infanticide. Thus, while the Palomans were a so-called egalitarian society, everyone was not equal.

There is evidence of far-ranging outside contacts in the form of obsidian from the mountains, a pet rainforest forest monkey, and colorful *Spondylus* shell from the tropical waters of Ecuador where intensive agriculture was taking hold. These distant contacts, either direct or indirect, suggest that fisherfolk were well aware of farming, and traces of gourds, squash, and beans appear in the Paloma midden and the latter two in the intestines of corpses. Cultigens were most likely grown in the self-watering floodplains of the nearby Chilca drainage. Contemporary with the later phases of Paloma, a community of similar nature, called Chilca I, arose on the local stream bank about 3 km inland. It was occupied between 3500 and 2500 BC by fisherfolk who grew and consumed gourd, beans, and perhaps squash. They also tended or collected junco reeds (*Cyperus* sp.) for making house thatch and twined mats.

Industrial and comestible cultigens. If the bounty of the Andean fishery has sustained millions for millennia, why then should fisherfolk farm? At the time of contact fishing and farming formed separate, but symbiotic, ways of making a living, in part because angling activities are scheduled by lunar and tide cycles that are often at odds with solar and rainfall cycles which schedule agronomic activities. Nonetheless, plants are essential to fisherfolk because the sea does not supply fuel, shelter, clothing, fishing line, netting, net floats, or watercraft. Consequently, terra firma provides the fundamental infrastructure of maritime adaptations, and interdependence of the aquatic and terrestrial components results in change in one affecting the other. For example, population growth and intensification of net fishing were tied both to expanding fiber supplies which, in turn, fostered the cultivation of cotton, and to watercraft production which led to bulrush cultivation for reed boats. Thus before there were coastal farmers, early seaboard populations had to collect or cultivate plants in order to fish.

Preceramic fisherfolk procured wild and cultivated plants both directly and sometimes indirectly. Flora requiring little care, such as perennial cotton, gourds, squash, beans, and certain fruit trees, were most commonly tended. When crops are represented by high frequencies of unusable and inedible plant parts in early middens, harvests were presumably acquired directly from river floodplains and returned to the community for processing and waste discard. While valley-mouth settlements were well positioned to exploit floodplains and to control them, plant discards are reported from some littoral sites far from rivers. Rights to self-watering river land gained in importance as maritime populations grew, yet very few Preceramic sites have been found in valley interiors other than the Supe drainage. The apparent dearth of interior settlements reinforces the proposition that floodplain farming was an intermittent, seasonal activity pursued by maritime people residing along the shore.

Although direct acquisition of riparian resources was the apparent norm, a precocious exception – a fishing-farming symbiosis – is now evident in the Supe Valley. This drainage and the adjacent Pativilca and Forteleza valleys contain a substantial number of early sites, and a recent survey of the Supe by scholars from Lima's National Museum of Archaeology and Anthropology has identified 17 Preceramic civic-ceremonial centers ranging from 10 to more than

70 ha in size. This is the largest concatenation of prepottery architectural monuments in the continent, and the inland location of many is attributable to the Río Supe being shallowly incised and to numerous valley-floor springs capable of supporting simple, extensive irrigation systems. Situated 22 km inland at an elevation of 350 m, the 50-ha mound and residential complex of Caral is the focus of ongoing excavations by Ruth Shady and National Museum archaeologists. The ancient residents farmed and consumed two root crops, achira and sweet potatoes (*Ipomoea batatas*), in addition to squash, beans, and pacae and guayaba fruit, while also growing the industrial cultigens of cotton and gourd. Their protein came abundantly from the sea – as attested by anchovies and small fish remains in storage facilities, and by numerous shellfish discards – yet no fishing tackle has been found at the settlement. Shady argues that this reflects a carbohydrate-protein exchange system involving barter of industrial and comestible cultigens for seafoods. If a similar economic symbiosis linked other inland and coastal Supe settlements as is likely, then the valley foreshadows patterns of subsistence specialization that became widespread during the Initial Period.

The Caral domesticates constitute a relatively common core of Preceramic crops. Other fruits and cultigens are more sporadically represented at desert settlements. For example, jicama tubers (*Pachyrhizus tuberosus*) are reported from five sites, and yuca (*Manihot esculenta*) from one. Absent at Caral, the Supe coastal center of Aspero produced a small cache of maize (*Zea mays*) and several isolated midden cobs. To the north, maize was a more common midden constituent at the Río Huarmey littoral community of Los Gavilanes, and a small Preceramic sample was reputedly found near the mouth of the Río Culebras. In the Río Casma region the situation is mixed, with small amounts of maize present at the sites of Cerro El Calvario and Cerro Julia, but the crop was not found at Huaynuna where potatoes were found. The sierra distribution is similarly spotty, with one cob found at La Galgada, and human bone chemistry suggesting moderate maize consumption at Huaricoto in the Río Santa headwaters. The sporadic distribution of some domesticates is a product of long-distance procurement. Preceramic settlements at Ventanilla and Ancon Bays north of Lima produced three specimens of oca (*Oxalis tuberosa*), two of ulluco (*Ullucus tuberosus*) and one of white potato (*Solanum* sp.), which are highland cultigens, difficult or impossible to grow on the coast. Shellfish occasionally occur at some sierra sites and other iodine-rich marine products were probably of dietary importance for mitigating goiter. On the edge of the now dry Ventanilla Bay, the small Preceramic encampment of Camino was a collecting and processing station for kelp seaweed. After removing root holdfasts, stems and air bladders, the edible kelp leaves were consumed elsewhere, either on the coast or in the mountains. Evidence of economic interaction with the highlands is important, because we must look to the lower sierra for early development of irrigation technology that eventually opened desert valleys to intensive farming.

Social formations

Andean people experienced a many-fold increase in their numbers during the Preceramic Period. In the sierra, residential sites became more numerous and scattered, on the coast fisherfolk filled in the littoral around sources of potable water, and large civic-ceremonial complexes arose in the mountains and deserts of northern and central Peru. It is likely that some people maintained dual residences, living in a rural setting for much of the year but moving to larger monumental centers during cycles of ceremony and civic activities. Erecting monumental works, maintaining them, and coordinating their use required corporate organization and chains of hierarchical command that allowed a minority to mobilize and direct activities of the majority. Debate surrounds the nature of early corporate organization, with scholars who investigate small sites emphasizing simplicity and counterparts studying large sites proposing complexity.

The proposition that early Andean populations were kin-based segmentary lineages grouped into moieties is applicable to smaller and mid-sized Preceramic settlements, including Río Seco situated behind a long sandy beach, 10 km north of the Río Chancay. Dating to the closing centuries of the Preceramic Period, 1–1.5 m of dense refuse covers 11.8 ha, which systematic testing suggests contains a mortuary population of 2,500 to 3,000 individuals. Compact floors with traces of cane or mat walls constitute the remains of undifferentiated residential quarters. Built in several stages interspersed with episodes of use, Río Seco has twin platform mounds of modest size 2–3 m high, potentially reflecting dual organization. These communal facilities were likely erected by the local populace alone, coordinated by hierarchical organization akin to later 'cargo systems,' with offices held by capable individuals on a rotational basis. From this perspective, early community organization need not have differed markedly from that of later ayllu collectives to account for much of the Preceramic archaeological record.

Larger huaca complexes reflect a more complicated organization. For example, coastal Aspero and interior Caral each have half-a-dozen sizeable platform mounds. If each huaca represented a different constituency, then multifaceted organization characterized the apex of order at these centers. Shady's excavations at Caral have identified two distinct classes of residential buildings. One, attributed to the majority of inhabitants, entails compacted floors with wooden supports for walls and roofs of reed, mats, or thatch. The other, used by a minority, entails plastered floors and walls with the latter built of masonry and interspersed vertical wooden beans capable of supporting large roofs of perishable material. These unusually well-built quarters are found immediately adjacent to platform mounds, indicating that they were privileged housing for special personnel managing activities associated with the contiguous huacas. Shady postulates that Caral organization was not simply hierarchical but class-structured, with a minority of hereditary elites coordinating activities of the majority. More provocatively, she hypothesizes that the 17 Preceramic civic-ceremonial complexes within the lower Supe drainage could not have been built and maintained without drawing upon human resources from outside the valley. This proposition is based on the notion that the Río Supe assumed early sacrosanct status as home to multiple supernaturals that attracted the devotion of disparate populations. If correct, Shady's hypothesis provides ancient precedents for the pluralistic pantheons and plentiful pilgrimage centers that characterized the Cordillera at the time of contact.

The extent of Preceramic class distinctions in living quarters is not known, because residential architecture remains poorly explored at other large centers. Differential treatment of the dead has mixed social implications. Random disposal of newborns, without accompaniments, in shallow midden pits suggests that social recognition hinged upon attaining a certain age in some societies. At the Asia site near the Omos drainage, eight severed heads, including juveniles, were wrapped in a mat and interred, foreshadowing later concerns with 'trophy *Plate 21* head' rituals, a practice which survived in modified form among tropical Jivaro people renowned for shrinking their enemies' heads. Three times as many males as females were buried in the occupation areas of Asia and the Culebras site at the mouth of the Río Culebras, indicating that deceased men were kept closer to the living than women. Preceramic people generally went to the grave with at least a cloth garment and a mat wrapping. At Asia, 133 cloth accompaniments were distributed among 28 normal interments, with most individuals having 2–4 textiles, although a few had twice the norm. The most fabrics, 12 – as well as gourd containers, bone tools, wooden tubes, a sling, a slate tablet, a comb, and other goods – accompanied a young male, yet this rich grave could reflect high status that was either inherited or achieved through personal deeds. As we will see, the best potential case for inherited high status comes from La Galgada, where a limited number of males and females with fancy accompaniments were entombed in ceremonial chambers. Yet, other than the Galgada burials and the Caral residential architecture, there is scant evidence of separate Preceramic classes.

Arts

Developed arts are another criteria of civilization, and Preceramic people laid enduring aesthetic foundations. Prepottery media included stone, shell, bone, baked clay, gourd, wood, basketry, bark cloth, and fabrics. Textiles were by far the most important. From garments to wraps and bags, textiles served many purposes and are a prevalent artifact at Preceramic sites. People lived in, sat and slept on, and went to the grave in twined mats of reed. At Huaca Prieta, the coastal Preceramic-type site near the mouth of the Río Chicama, as well as at La Galgada, and elsewhere, twined baskets and looped satchels of reeds and sedges fulfilled the need for containers, as did gourd vessels; but the greatest time and care was lavished upon twined textiles of cotton. Twining with spaced wefts and exposed warps was the most common construction technique, but looping, knotting, and simple weaving were also employed.

46 Condors descend to the coast to feed upon fish and inspired this Huaca Prieta textile motif.

47 A double-headed fish or eel is indicated by the fins on this preceramic textile motif from the site of Asia.

Plates 20, 21   The lattice-like structure of the fabrics imparted geometric undertones to the arts, which have an angular quality, emphasizing symmetry and interlocking elements. The roster of design elements falls into two classes – abstract and representational. Stripes, diamonds, squares, and chevrons make up the former, and occur individually, as repetitions, and in combinations making up more complex patterns. Representational designs depict people, birds, serpents, crabs, fish, and other animals. When used individually such motifs are often repetitive and interlocking. They also appear in compositions showing several creatures. Frequently attributes of two animals are combined to form compos-

48 An enduring tradition of embellishing gourd containers with incised designs made its first appearance at Huaca Prieta.

49 Double-headed 'serpent' motifs persisted in Paracas textiles and later coastal arts.

ite beings. In one case, perhaps showing the heraldic overtones of an insignia, a large bird, perhaps a condor, with spread wings is depicted from the front, while on the chest or in the stomach a spotted serpent or elongated fish is shown. In other cases, artisans crafted preternatural beings. One Huaca Prieta fabric depicts a double-headed serpent with a pair of rock-crabs appended to its elongated body. A double-headed bird with a serpentine body was engraved on the cap of a gourd bowl.

Double-headed serpents and birds, and composite beings with animal, avian, reptilian or invertebrate features persist into later Andean arts. As with griffins and unicorns, these composite creatures were surrounded by lore and beliefs that made the iconography intelligible to the general populace, and Preceramic motifs were the building blocks of symbolic communication that came to dominate the later corporate styles.

Monumental architecture

During the third millennium BC distinct forms of civic-ceremonial architecture crystallized in tropical, sierra, and desert settings. In the forested north, Ecuador's Valdivia farmers often arranged their houses around an oval, circular, or central plaza with two types of oval, dome-shaped structures sometimes erected atop low earthen mounds. One type, called 'Charnel' houses, were used in mortuary rituals and the preparation of corpses for secondary burial. 'Fiesta' houses, the other type, were for feasting and drinking and have analogies with 'Men's' houses in tropical ethnographic communities. At the same time, the very largest architectural monuments in the hemisphere were being erected in Peru by people who relied secondarily upon agriculture in a fractured physical environment conducive to social fission and division. Here corporate construction bespeaks of fusion and amalgamation as well as of formality and convention. Every Preceramic plaza was a place for prescribed behavior, every platform mound a place for precise protocol and people consented to expected conduct whenever they built or used a particular facility.

These corporate works are called civic-ceremonial facilities because they presumably served public and municipal ends as well as sacrosanct and religious ones. The mix of secular and sacred activities varied and are difficult to sort out because the edifices were swept out and kept clean. Space was divided horizontally by walls as well as vertically between below-ground, ground-level, and above-ground planes. Special building materials, including fresh stone and clean mortar, differentiated corporate works from surrounding midden and mundane structures. Dry conditions limited roofing to small structures and favored activities and assemblages in open courts and plazas, some of which served as processional ways while others held audiences. Demarcation of entryways and stairways was elaborated because portals demarcated changes in space and prescribed behavior.

Platforms. Due to size and solid construction, platform mounds are the most conspicuous and commonly preserved corporate works. Elevated architecture conferred status segregating extraordinary from ordinary space and some mounds were probably meant to emulate mountain apu. Platforms sometimes began as ground-level buildings that were subsequently filled in to create an artificial eminence. As with the two Lithic Period mounds at Nanchoc, the final size was a product of 'temple interment,' entailing multiple construction stages interspersed with periods of use. Platform construction required substantial fill, and freshly quarried rock, not midden, was the preferred material. As noted in Chapter Three, Andean people keep close account of their labor when working on group undertakings and quarried rock was hauled in large open-mesh satchels, called *shicra*, made of sturdy reeds capable of holding up to 26 kg of stone. The satchels were not emptied at the construction site, rather the shicras and their fill were deposited intact. This practice reflects the segmentation of corporate work into repetitive tasks and was probably a means of accounting for labor expenditures. Mound exteriors were generally inclined and sometimes stepped. They were faced with rounded boulders or angular quarry stone set in mud mortar and often plastered. Summit access was by a central flight of stairs that could be recessed into the mound or projected slightly outward.

Coastal Preceramic platforms were generally rectangular, while their sierra counterparts often had rounded corners and sometimes oval shapes. Mounds were both freestanding and banked against hill slopes. They could rise as a single flat-topped eminence, or they could rise in steps or as terraced structures with tiered front courts. Platform summits were occupied by courts and smaller compartments that facilitated secluded activities, but accommodated relatively few people. Therefore, on ceremonial occasions central stairways were likely stages for ritual display to multitudes assembled in front of the facilities. Far more people helped build platforms than could ever fit into the summit quarters, and on terraced platforms accommodations were hierarchical, progressing from small facilities at the top to larger ones on lower tiers, culminating in spatial forecourts at ground level. Gradation in the elevation and size of platform facilities presumably mirrors gradation in the status of their users, with commoners occupying the base of a social pyramid capped by a privileged few. Privilege presumably accrued with communal service in cargo-like hierarchies. With isolated exceptions, there are always two or more platforms at mound centers, expressing pluralism in organization and belief. Propositions of dual organization are reasonable where there are twin mounds, as at Río Seco, La Galgada and Kotosh. Where more were erected, organization was certainly more multifaceted. In this vein, each Preceramic platform was individual and unique. At Caral, for example, each of the six major mounds differs in layout, form, orientation, and size. These were certainly intentional differences intended to distinguish one facility and its clients from another. Although mound building was an enduring Andean practice, platforms served many ends and it cannot be said that Preceramic examples express a particular set of beliefs. However, several other forms of early corporate construction do reflect shared ideological notions about sacrosanct space that archaeologists employ in defining long-lived 'traditions' in civic-ceremonial facilities.

The Plaza Hundida Tradition

Vertical segregation of space included not only positive or elevated planes of platform mounds, but also negative or inner-earth plains of *plazas hundidas* or sunken courts. Large flat-bottomed pits were excavated into the ground, lined with masonry, and provided with opposing stairways allowing people to pass into and out of terra firma. Plazas hundidas arose in circular form during the third millennium BC in northern Peru. A transition to rectangular form occurred at Chavín de Huantar during the Early Horizon, and this form then persisted in the altiplano south until the collapse of Tiwanaku around AD 1100. The highly enduring emphasis on sunken sacrosanct space brings to mind Andean origin myths in which humanity ascends from an inner cavernous sphere to the outer terrestrial one it now occupies. Perhaps plazas hundidas were places for re-enacting the dawn of creation when people emerged from caves, springs, and holes in the ground. Perhaps the courts were places to venerate Pacha Mama, mother earth, by reverently descending into and out of her womb. Alternatively, the cult of the sunken court may well have merged both notions, ensuring long-lasting appeal.

Sunken courts and their underlying ideological conventions were stand-alone constructs and a plaza hundida is the only corporate work at Alto Salavery, an early maritime community on the south side of the Moche Valley. Most Preceramic examples occur in front of platform mounds, as at La Galgada, Salinas de Chao, Piedra Parada, and Caral. The pairing of an elevated mound and a subterranean plaza with aligned stairways evokes images of ritual processions descending into mother earth and then ascending to father apu. Initial Period and later examples were also erected beside or behind mounds and on the wings and summits of platforms. Because sunken plazas occurred in

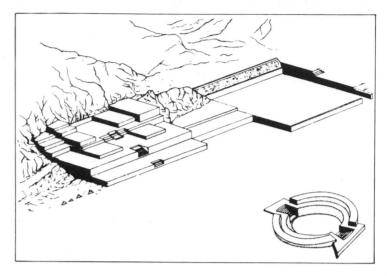

50 The circular sunken court and terraced platform at Salinas de Chao are aligned in this idealized reconstruction.

variable contexts associated with different architectural traditions, we can infer that they reflect a distinct cult or set of beliefs and rituals that could be ecumenically combined with other civic and religious orders. Preceramic sunken courts are generally smaller than the mounds they front, perhaps because they were meant to be paraded through prior to ascending the aligned platform. However, the size relationships were reversed at Caral's large 'amphitheater' complex, where a wide, centrally aligned causeway led to stairs descending a large deep court, 29 m in diameter, with stepped masonry sidewalls formerly plastered and painted white or yellow. Behind the ascending stairs two aligned rectangular plazas opened to a modest platform mound half the width of the plaza hundida.

The Kotosh Tradition

Named after its sierra-type locality of Kotosh, this tradition is defined by detached, one-room, enclosed sanctuaries accommodating small, private congregations – probably kindred – focused upon burnt offerings made in a central hearth. Development and variation in these special chambers is well explored at Huaricoto, situated in the Callejon de Huaylas at an elevation of 2,750 m. Few large works were built at this ritual center, but many Kotosh sanctuaries were erected beginning about 2260 BC and lasting into the Chavín Horizon almost two millennia later. With walls of waddle and daub, the early examples were both relatively flimsy and variable. The intent was to create an enclosed cubicle with a single entry that could be sealed. Floors were carefully plastered and kept clean and in good repair. The essential feature was a central hearth and excavated fire basins exhibited intense burning and frequent replastering and repair. What was fed to the fires is not clear, but fragmentary marine shell and animal bone were recovered from one of the latest Huaricoto hearths, and refuse outside Preceramic chambers included sea shells and fish bone as well as bones of deer and large camelids, probably guanaco. Coastal contact is not surprising, and while uncommon in littoral Preceramic contexts, several Kotosh-like chambers have been found in the Río Casma region.

A relatively standardized sanctuary form emerged at other Preceramic sierra sites and at Huaricoto in ceramic times. Rectangular or square, the chambers were of masonry with an entry that could be tightly closed. Plastered floors were split-level: a higher surface against the interior walls created a wide bench for an audience, surrounding a central recessed rectangular floor area housing the focal hearth. Outside oxygen was fed to the fire by a slab-lined ventilator, which passed horizontally beneath the bench to the chamber exterior, thereby allowing tight sanctuary closure during ceremonies. As with plazas hundidas, Kotosh chambers and their underlying ideological convictions were constructs that could stand alone or conjoin with other orders of organization and belief.

The Preceramic Mito Phase at Kotosh saw the initial construction of twin platform mounds, which grew by temple interment to heights of 6.5 and 8 m during the Initial Period. The platforms had wide terraces and flat summits surmounted by numerous chambers that define the Kotosh ceremonial tradition. The most elaborate Preceramic chamber of standardized form was uncovered on the middle terrace of the largest platform. Measuring about 9 m on a side and built of cobbles set in mud mortar, this sanctuary had thick, plastered walls with interior rows of ornamental niches. The wall opposite the entry had a central, over-sized niche flanked on either side by a smaller niche. Below each of the two smaller recesses there was a clay frieze depicting a set of human arms crossed at the wrists, leading the excavators to dub this the 'Temple of the Crossed Hands.' Mito people later filled in the structure while elevating the platform, and then erected a similar chamber, the 'Temple of the Niches,' which had ornamental wall recesses, but no friezes. Embellishing high-status architecture of niches and friezes is a practice that began at Kotosh and other Preceramic centers and then endured into Inca times.

Situated in the Río Santa drainage, La Galgada is an elaborate and well-preserved sierra mound center with Kotosh chambers atop two elevated platforms of unequal size. Oval in shape, the larger platform was faced with fine masonry and fronted by a circular sunken court. Mound construction began about 2400 BC, and periods of Preceramic use were interspersed with episodes of Preceramic enlargement. Summit chambers had rounded corners creating an oval shape. The well-built sanctuaries were of stone set in mud mortar, then clay plastered, painted pearly white, and always ornamented with rows of symmetrically arranged interior niches. Each chamber was generally entered from the east and equipped with a horizontal ventilator shaft that passed under the door to feed a central hearth on the lower surface of a split-level floor or floor-bench arrangement. White, orange, and green downy feathers of tropical birds were encountered on some floors as was deer antler. Plant remains and chili peppers were found in firepits. Burnt offerings of chili would certainly have brought tears to the eyes of the ritual participants!

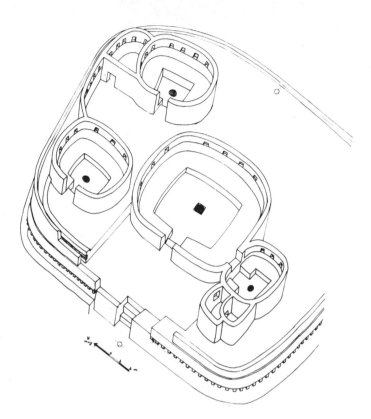

51 The isometric view of mound-top chambers at La Galgada reconstructs the hearths, benches, and niched walls of the ritual sanctuaries but not their roofs.

When the Galgada platforms underwent temple interment, old summit chambers were not filled in. Instead they were re-roofed with large rock slabs, left hollow, then connected by vertical shafts to the newly elevated mound top and transformed into mausoleums, each housing two or more adult bodies. Females were well represented as were unusually fancy accompaniments including ornate textiles, baskets, seashell jewelry, and bone ornaments inlaid with stone. The crypts and their venerated dead were kept accessible for generations and in one case seated mummy bundles were added directly atop earlier extended corpses. As with Chinchorro mummies, we may speculate that curating and communing with the deceased was orchestrated by ritual specialists akin to later mallquipavillacs. During the Initial Period chamber mausoleums were replaced by long hall-like galleries within the mound tops. These catacombs contained numerous seated mummy bundles of adults and children, both with high-value grave goods. The children no doubt inherited their rights to special enshrinement, and the same is presumably true of the privileged adult interments. Thus, La Galgada exemplifies three hallmarks of the later kuraka class: hereditary elites, veneration of the deceased, and huacas sepulturas. Yet, these seem to be unprecedented local innovations that did not take hold elsewhere for a millennium or more.

Ceramics and heddle-loom weaving make their appearance during the two final episodes of platform construction at La Galgada, which produced radiocarbon ages falling between 1700 and 1200 BC. This era of economic and ideo-logical change saw the replacement of Kotosh chambers by a single, very large mound-top sanctuary of unroofed, rectangular form with an over-sized fire basin. Capable of accommodating 50 or more people, the new facilities mark a shift to larger burnt offering ceremonies integrating more participants. An even bolder transformation occurred with the final epoch of construction when the summit assumed a U-shaped configuration, with three elevated platforms sur-rounding a spacious lower central court opening to the front of the mound. Although there was court space for numerous ritual participants, burnt offer-ings were now of secondary importance and confined to a small chamber on one corner of the U-shaped platform.

The Supe Tradition

The largest prepottery monuments in the hemisphere were erected along the arid coast between the Ríos Chicama and Chillon. Sites with noteworthy corpo-rate construction include Huaca Prieta, Salinas de Chao and Los Morteros near the Río Chao; Huaynuna near Casma, Culebras, Bandurria near the Huara Valley, Río Seco; and El Paraiso. Other than El Paraiso, the coastal monuments can be assigned to the Supe Tradition, named after the valley with 17 Preceramic mound centers. These range from coastal Aspero and Piedra Parada to the inland complexes of Caral and its larger, unexplored neighbor of Chupacigarro. The architectural emphasis is upon flat-topped mounds as stages of ritual display for very large audiences assembled in front of the platforms. This is a more public-oriented doctrine of civic-ceremonial activity than the Plaza Hundida and Kotosh Traditions, but it lacks their standardization due to the variable form of coastal platforms. Although burnt offering rituals were important, their context and location were variable. For example, the mound at Caral's large 'amphitheater' complex sits within a spacious walled plaza that holds, in one corner, a 'fire altar.' About 4 m in diameter, this feature is a low-walled circular dais with a heavily burned central hearth aired by two vents. With traces of cream, yellow, and gray paint, the altar stands in a rectangular court, measuring about 10 m on a side, that was tangential to the main axis of the larger complex.

The Supe Tradition includes works that reflect different orders of organiza-tion. The corporate constructions at Río Seco, Bandurria, Culebras Huaynuna, and Huaca Prieta are of modest size and associated with midden deposits and domestic remains of sufficient size to suggest that the public works were built by their local communities. A different order is reflected in grander works at Salinas de Chao, Los Morteros, Piedra Parada, and El Paraiso, where sizeable resident populations are either lacking or less evident. Many of these monu-ments were likely built and sustained, in part, by people who did not reside in the immediate neighborhood. Presumably, people in small settlements were linked by real or fictive kinship to residents of larger centers where civic-cere-monial facilities served both the local and rural populace. Finally, there is the proposition that the multitude and magnitude of Río Supe monuments reflect a regional support base extending well beyond the immediate valley and coast. If this was the case, then regional organization and mobilization of popular folk were potentially based upon institutions presaging those of later great pilgrimage centers such as Pachacamac and Lake Titicaca's Island of the Sun. To reach the paramount Rock of the Sun, devotees pursued a long ritual route with numerous stops, observances, and offerings at multiple mainland and island shrines and huacas, and perhaps Supe's many mound centers were similarly integrated in a revered landscape. Such organization is not without hierarchy, but ecclesiastic status and office tend not to be hereditary.

With 11 smaller mounds 1–2 m high and 6 major platforms surrounded by 15 ha of dark midden, the coastal center of Aspero probably served a broader populace than lived at the site. The complex occupies a shallow basin surrounded by hills that jut into the sea at the north end of a long sandy beach formed by the mouth of the Río Supe. In 1905, the discoverer, Max Uhle, noted that 'from a distance, the settlement appears black, like an old foundry site.' Dark midden rich in carbon due to baking in earthen pits is typical of many Preceramic maritime settlements. The Aspero midden was dug over in the past and ground-level residences, courts, and terraces are not well preserved. The larger freestanding mounds range up to 4 m or more in height, and to over 10 m where the platforms were banked against or set atop hills. Alignments varied within 20°, with some platforms facing out to the valley and others back into the basin. Investigations by Harvard University personnel in the 1970s focused upon two of the larger mounds, Huacas de los Idolos and Sacrificios. Sacrificios was a freestanding platform and summit. Excavations were limited to the last phases of construction and use, which produced radiocarbon assays that averaged to 2857 BC. Basal dates would certainly be far older, and construction of this huaca probably began and ended earlier than at other Aspero mounds. Many of the walls were built of basaltic blocks and some exhibited 'H'-type masonry in which long blocks were set vertically upright and apart from one another to form the uprights of the letter H, with smaller stones laid horizontally between the uprights. This type of masonry occurs in Preceramic and early ceramic contexts on the coast and in later times in the Titicaca region. Ascent to the huaca summit was via an eastern stairway that led to a large entry court, which was flanked by an irregular grouping of smaller compartments. The court center held a hemispherical fire pit about 50 cm across and 25 cm deep, burnt bright orange and replastered several times with ash dated to 2533 BC.

Huaca de los Sacrificios derives its name from two burials, an infant and an adult, found 3.5 m apart on the same floor level of a summit compartment. The poorly preserved adult was very tightly flexed and some joints may have been cut to force the corpse into a cramped position in a tight pit. The individual was bound or wrapped with cloth and accompanied only by a broken gourd. This apparent sacrifice contrasts with the two-month-old infant which was slightly flexed, placed on its right side with the skull to the north, facing west. The head was covered with a cap or hat adorned by 500 shell, plant, and clay beads, and the body was completely wrapped in a cotton textile. Along with a gourd bowl, the bundle was placed in a basket, which was wrapped in textiles. A cane mat was rolled around the bundle and tied with strips of white cloth. This was placed on the ground with two large pieces of cotton cloth waded together. The assemblage was then covered with an inverted basin carved from stone. The stone basin is one of the finest Preceramic objects ever found. Carefully crafted from a single boulder, it has four legs, stood 9 cm high and measured 38 by 44 cm. The upper surface had been used for grinding and traces of red pigment adhered to the inner lip. The infant burial was obviously one of exceptional importance.

Perched against a small hill, Huaca de los Idolos is one of the higher platforms. Summit structures cover an area of 20 by 30 m and excavations penetrated the last three stages of often complex construction dating from 2558 to 3055 BC. From ground level, a wide slightly projecting ramp led to the summit and to the gateway of a high-walled, spacious entry court with smaller courts and rooms behind it. The most important was a centrally located compartment, measuring c. 4 by 5 m, on the main axis of the platform. Each interior wall had a row of three small rectangular niches at chest level and the niched compartment was subdivided by a thin wall, faced with a geometric adobe frieze consisting of horizontal bands of raised plaster. The ornamented wall had a distinctive 'T'-shaped central doorway that was wider at the top than bottom. Immediately north there was another important summit room reached by a separate hallway system. On the rear wall, aligned with the single entry, there was an isolated recessed niche. The bottom of the niche was level with the top of a centrally positioned altar-like bench built against the center of the rear wall.

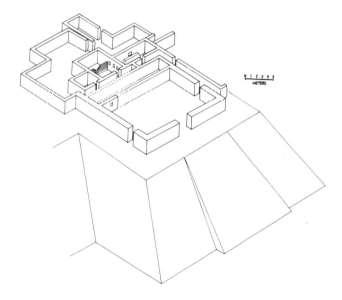

52 A summit entry court on Huaca de los Idolos leads to the interior compartments without roofs. In one room an altar-like bench sat in front of a wall niche. Another room with niches was partitioned by a low wall with a frieze of horizontal adobe bands.

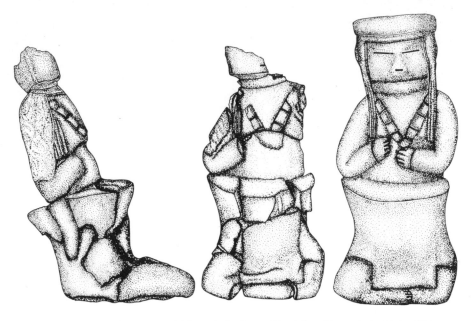

53 Figurines of unbaked clay were deliberately broken and buried at Huaca de los Idolos. This fragmentary figure, 16 cm tall, is shown in side, front, and reconstructed view.

The overall configuration of the niche and altar impart a shrine-like impression, but how the sanctuary was originally used is uncertain.

The altar sanctuary had a small alcove with a cache of objects spread over its floor before the compartment was filled in to support a new, higher floor. The cache included twined baskets, matting, plant material, animal fur, and at least 13 figurines all broken, but seemingly the work of a single artist. The images ranged from 5 to 14 cm in height and give Huaca de los Idolos its name. Eleven represent females, with four possibly pregnant. Portrayed in a seated position with crossed legs, the figures held their arms against the torso, bent at the elbows so that the hands meet at the chest. Eyes were represented by narrow slits; the mouth by a shorter, wider slit; and the nose by a slightly raised triangular ridge. Some wore turban-like hats with flat tops. Necklaces of square red beads were occasionally indicated, and two such beads were found at Aspero. Thigh-length skirts covered the lower body, but no footwear was shown. This is the largest cache of early clay figurines known from Peru, although other specimens come from Río Seco, Bandurria, El Paraiso, and Kotosh. While their production continued in Peru, it was never as prevalent as in the tropical north, where in historic times shamans transferred patients' ills to figurines, which were then disposed of. Although Aspero people acquired tropical *Spondylus* shell, it is not known if the figurines were used in healing.

Over time, bilateral symmetry came to characterize the arrangement of courts and compartments atop many coastal platforms. For example, the small terraced mound at Huaynuna had equal-sized rooms and courts on either side of a central access structure that ran from the base to the top of the platform, which was banked against a low hill. Midden from the associated maritime community produced late dates between 2250 and 1775 BC. Huaynuna also produced an example of a Kotosh ceremonial chamber, which certainly points to ideological interchange with the sierra, as do sunken courts. One of the latter appears at Piedra Parada, which is located 2.5 km inland in a small basin on the southern margin of the Supe Valley. This unexcavated complex includes three large platforms banked against hills, several smaller masonry monuments, and a thin midden deposit of small size.

The main monument at Piedra Parada was built against a low hill and consists of a terrace platform symmetrically fronting a large forecourt housing a smaller circular sunken court. Square in plan, the low-walled forecourt measures 40 m on a side. The centrally positioned sunken court is 20 m in diameter. Faced with boulders and then plastered, the circular pit had two opposed passageways symmetrically aligned with the central axis of the forecourt and the terraced platform. About 10 m behind the forecourt, the first boulder-faced terrace rose to a height of more than 5 m and was 80 m long by 65 m wide. A central stairway provided ascent to an entry court that was 26 m wide. On either side of this, there was one additional court 20 m wide. The three summit courts were in turn subdivided into front and back halves by a single wall running the length of the terrace. An entrance connected each half. However, the rear compartments were higher than the front ones. The second terrace of the platform rose about 5 m above the first and was of equal length but only 20 m in width. Its courts were similarly divided into three parts and two levels. The rear of the platform stood about 75 cm above the hill it was built against.

The main mound at Caral was of equally imposing height, but entirely man made. Fronted by a circular sunken court, the structure was c. 140 m wide, with each end rising in three large steps to create a broad basal platform which, in turn, supported a higher central platform. On the midline a sunken stairway led to a recessed summit atrium which contained a natural, lance-like obelisk measuring 1.70 by 0.45 m. This center-line rock was certainly a sacred huaca, as no doubt were two other partially worked stone columns on one wing of the platform, and yet another slab in the Caral 'amphitheater' complex. It is not known if the obelisks embodied distant gods or were akin to the huaca rock of Manco Capac, which united the Incas with a mythical founder, but they were undoubtedly of great significance. Many of Caral's platforms were associated with flanking surface-level compounds. These facilities contained courts and patios, some with ceremonial hearths, as well as ancillary quarters, and they are apt reminders that a great deal of formal activity transpired beyond the mounds.

The Paraiso Tradition

El Paraiso is the largest prepottery masonry monument in the hemisphere. More than 100,000 tons of stone were quarried to erect nine architectural complexes that occupy 58 ha of the Chillon Valley, 2 km from the sea. The buildings survive as jumbled rock piles up to three stories in height. The two largest

Plates 29, 30

ruins are elongated, parallel mounds that form the wings of a giant 'U'. Each wing is more than 50 m wide and more than 250 m long and they frame a spacious 7-ha plaza. The base of the U is only partially demarcated by several smaller ruins, but cardinal orientation of the wings and plaza is exactly the same as later U-shaped ceremonial centers in the region. Other masonry complexes are scattered around the periphery of the monumental core, suggesting El Paraiso grew in a piecemeal fashion.

The stone piles are remnants of platform mounds erected in multiple stages by piling mesh bags with fill into interconnected courts, corridors, and compartments with thick walls that once stood 2 m or more in height. Adjacent hills were quarried for rock that was set in mud mortar for walls, which were then plastered with adobe. A French investigator excavated and restored one complex at the base of the U. This structure was roughly square, measuring 50 m on a side, stood about 8 m high, and had two separate flights of stairs leading to summit compartments. The main entry was the larger, more elaborate western flight of stairs with aligned compartments behind it. The second compartment was a ceremonial court, painted red, with a sunken central floor area measuring 4.5 by 4.25 m. The finely made recessed floor was burned to a bright orange with a dark oval stain in its center. The bench-like floor surrounding the central depression had four large circular pits, each 1 m in diameter and each containing abundant charcoal, symmetrically positioned behind each corner of the sunken court. Here again we see evidence of ancient concerns with fire and incendiary rituals. Yet behind this special chamber the summit structures were highly compartmentalized, left clean except for some stones used to grind red pigment, clay figurine fragments, and a small sling.

Investigations in other complexes indicate that they also consist of interconnected courts and compartments that lack domestic hearths or evidence of residential activities. Unlike the extensive midden deposits at Río Seco or Aspero, accumulations of trash were not common at El Paraiso, because the majority of people who built and used the facilities apparently resided elsewhere. In front of the restored complex an 80-cm-deep midden area revealed that all dietary protein came from the sea and from small fish in particular. Industrial cultigens were common and plant foods included fruits, achira, squash, and jicama tubers. El Paraiso is located next to 150 ha of wide river floodplain that was probably irrigated with small canals and used to grow cotton and other crops. Land suitable for flood-water farming or simple ditch irrigation was seemingly in short supply by the close of the Preceramic Period, and the quest for arable land led to the establishment of several Preceramic sites over 40 km up the Río Chillon.

Radiocarbon assays indicate that construction was underway by 2000 BC at El Paraiso. Yet one third of the assays fall after 1800 BC, when pottery and intensive agriculture appeared in the area. This raises the possibility that Preceramic maritime adaptations persisted for a century or so after ceramic-using people began large-scale reclamation of the desert. Transforming coastal valleys into agrarian oases may have been undertaken by either of two populations. Sierra people, such as those at La Galgada, may have expanded farming downstream,

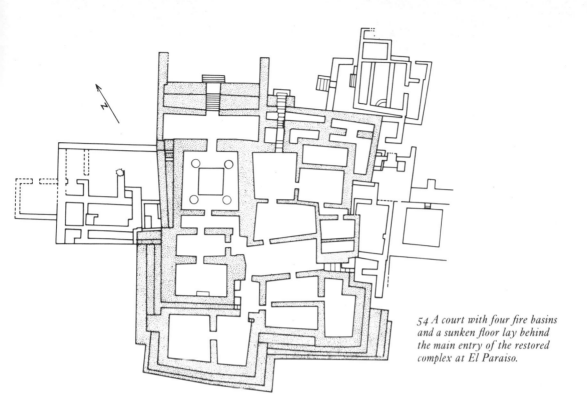

54 A court with four fire basins and a sunken floor lay behind the main entry of the restored complex at El Paraiso.

gradually radiating into the littoral valleys. Alternatively, segments of the maritime population may have turned to agriculture. This was the case in Chile's Azapa Valley, where biological analysis of skeletal remains indicates that some descendants of early Chinchorro people became inland tillers of the soil while others continued to pursue a seaboard existence. Transforming fishermen into farmers was certainly a complex process because tide and lunar cycles govern the latter and solar and rainfall cycles the former. The risks of each adaptation are also dissimilar: fishermen worry about sharks and turbulent seas, farmers about insects and droughts. Today these distinctions are expressed in divergent beliefs, with fishermen and farmers praying to different saints and observing different religious holidays.

Where then does El Paraiso stand in the transformation process? The ceremonial center could be the product of imitation, and thus built by Preceramic maritime people copying the U-shaped centers of contemporary farming societies. On the other hand, if El Paraiso assumed its U-shaped configuration by about 1900 BC, then it would be in the vanguard of things to come. Architect Carlos Williams proposes that the masonry complex represents the first phase of a long tradition of U-shaped civic-ceremonial centers that subsequently dominated the inland valley bottoms, where they were associated with irrigation agriculture. The association was both physical and ideological, because U-shaped centers literally turn their back to the sea to face the mountains, with their great arms reaching out to the rising sun and the sacred apu sources of desert water. Thus, El Paraiso is certainly the architectural expression of the ideological and organizational transformations of an impending new era.

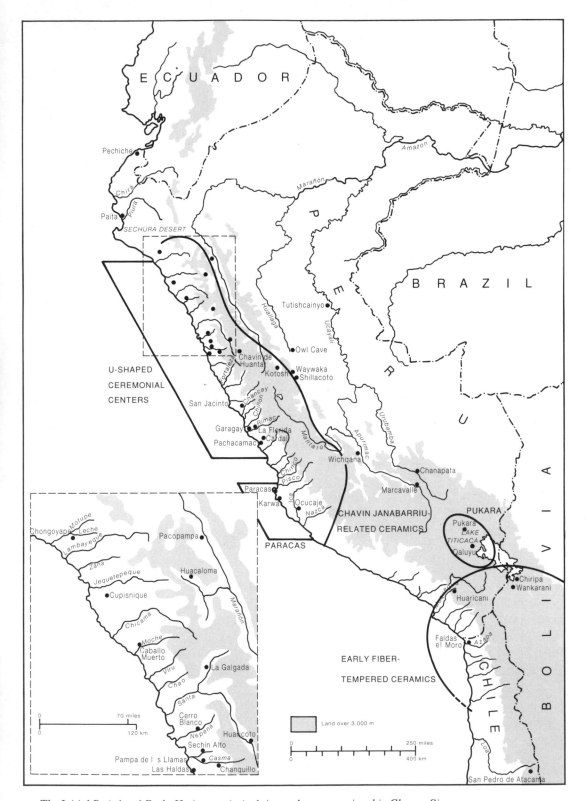

55 *The Initial Period and Early Horizon: principal sites and areas mentioned in Chapter Six*

CHAPTER SIX

THE INITIAL PERIOD AND EARLY HORIZON

The southward expansion of intensive agriculture into the drier and higher Cordillera correlates with climatic amelioration and improved rainfall, which were underway in northern Peru by 1800 BC and after 1600 BC in the Titicaca Basin. In the sierra, farming integrated with herding laid the foundations of agropastoralism. Along the arid coast, irrigation added the new dimension of agrarian oases to older maritime pursuits. By opening new habitats to new ways of making a living, farming created 'boom times' in economic prosperity and demographic growth. Highland basins and desert valleys with favorable land, water, and climatic conditions became evolutionary nodes and the mountain and coastal poles of Andean civilization began to crystallize. Arid Montane adaptations supported the largest of high-altitude populations in the south where upland basins are the biggest. Alternatively, Maritime-Oasis adaptations sustained the densest coastal populations in the north where desert rivers are the biggest. In the north, the advent of intensive farming and ceramics marks the beginning of the Initial Period, while in the Titicaca region this era is often referred to as the Formative Period.

New concerns with the cosmos and religion accompanied the economic and social transformations which swept the Andes. I suspect that growing dependency upon agriculture set the stage for pervasive veneration of Pacha Mama,

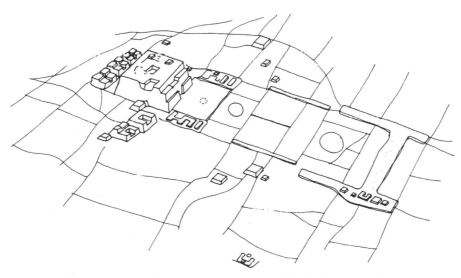

56 By 1200 BC the U-shaped ceremonial center of Sechín Alto was the largest architectural monument in the New World.

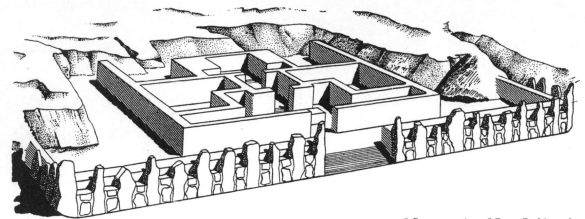

57, 58 Reconstruction of Cerro Sechín and (opposite) part of its megalithic mosaic wall.

while worries about rain and runoff fostered reverence of towering apu. Similar roots are likely for the tracking of Mayu, the Milky Way, and for observances of other heavenly bodies crucial for scheduling agricultural and pastoral activities. Farming harsh environments brought many new risks and new anxieties, which heightened concerns with religiosity expressed by an exceptional spate of plat-form-mound and huaca construction. Highland civic-ceremonial centers became widespread. In the coastal pole of civilization the Initial Period saw more mounds erected in many valleys than at any other time in Andean prehis-tory. While most facilities were small or modest, some were enormous.

By 1400 BC, work was under way on the largest of all early ceramic monu-ments in the Americas – Sechín Alto, a colossal, stone-faced platform that still stands some 40 m high. Measuring 300 m in length by 250 m in width, the enor-mous mound formed the basal cross-bar of a vast U-shaped center. The elong-ated wing mounds bracketed a succession of aligned plazas 1,100 m long by 400 m wide that held two circular sunken courts. Erected on the Sechín branch of the Casma Valley, the gigantic U anchored a 10.5 sq. km sprawl of large *Plates 31–34* buildings and platforms that comprise the Sechín Alto Complex. The adjacent Casma branch of the drainage housed the somewhat smaller Pampa de los Llamas-Moxeke Complex of imposing civic-ceremonial facilities.

Beyond the Casma, a plethora of large and small civic-ceremonial facilities were erected in other valleys reflecting the new prosperity of agrarian adapta-tions. Then something went profoundly amiss. Beginning about 900 BC, virtu-ally all the coastal centers were abandoned within a century or two. The sierra was not unscathed, but some civic-ceremonial sites continued to function. This momentous turning point in early coastal development coincides with several hundred years of severe drought identified in sediment cores from Lake Titicaca. Although rainfall eventually returned to normal, littoral populations seem to have lost much of their confidence in temple-mound construction. Conservatism was justified, because protracted drought struck again between about 400 and 200 BC. Coincidentally the cult of Chavín de Huantar spread over

much of the northern Andes, giving rise to the Early Horizon. In this chapter, we will probe the rise and fall of Initial Period accomplishments and then examine the new social and religious synthesis of the Early Horizon.

Irrigation agriculture

Although intensive agricultural economies emerged at different times in the north and south they generally appeared in conjunction with pottery and heddle weaving; ceramics were vital for storing, cooking, and brewing agrarian comestibles; farming and herding increased cotton and wool supplies; while heddle weaving allowed for the mass production of cloth. South American root crops were the primary staples, complemented by beans, legumes, squash, and fruits. Maize tending and llama herding took place in the sierra, but remained rare or absent in most early coast settings. Irrigation was an integral aspect of the new economic order in both the mountains and coast, with canal systems influencing how people worked and where they lived.

Canals. Herders irrigate bofedal pastureland and the basic concepts of channeling water to plants are not complicated. The sierra uplands receive sufficient rainfall to support high-elevation tuber and quiñoa farming. In somewhat lower zones, irrigation works (fed by mountain springs and streams) allow other plants, including squash, beans, and maize, to be sown earlier and harvested later than nature would otherwise allow. With artificial watering it is possible to plant and reap several times a year and irrigated land is valued for its high yields. Steep mountain slopes must be terraced if they are to be irrigated. Below *Plate 2* this the sierra basins provided limited bottomlands that are relatively flat and enjoy favorable growing conditions. These lands were reclaimed first, and in the upper reaches of the Ríos Zana and Santa channeling runoff to crops was underway in Preceramic times if not earlier. These activities drew mountain people into lower elevations both permanently and seasonally. By opening the sierra bottom habitat, below and separate from higher-rainfall farming, mountain irrigation contributed to verticality.

On the coast irrigation supported human dispersal into an otherwise inhospitable ecological niche – the desert. Pacific drainages exhibit three relationships between river water and arable land. First, rivers descend narrow canyons;

here steep gradients allow short canals to reach arable land, which is scarce and occurs in isolated pockets. Second, they pass through the necks of coastal valleys that fan out to the sea. Necks are prime canal locations because short leadoff channels supply canals that open outward as the V-shaped valleys do and thereby irrigate a great deal of land. Third, rivers slow down as they near the sea, and relatively long canals must be built to irrigate modest amounts of land, which can suffer salinization or drainage problems due to high water-table conditions near the sea. In many valleys it seems that irrigation developed along the path of least resistance, and most canal systems were situated well inland. Development began in canyons and valley necks where river gradients are relatively steep, and these areas generally have substantial numbers of Initial Period monuments. Reclamation then advanced downstream where shallow gradients required greater investments in canal construction. In many valleys land immediately behind the coast was either never irrigated or only reclaimed very late. Because canal irrigation pulls farmers inland, the Initial Period is marked by split patterns of residence, with fisherfolk living along the littoral and farmers settling inland.

Fishing can go on almost any day of the year, but farming is structured by the seasonal runoff and weather. Coastal rivers discharge more than 75 percent of their runoff between February and May, after which smaller drainages are dry. Annual variation in discharge is dramatic: the flow of large rivers can vary between 500 and 2,500 million cubic meters within a 10-year period. Such a great source of uncertainty to farmers must have fostered the prominent development of rites and rituals intended to placate the life-blood of irrigation.

Construction. On the coast intensive agriculture gives the surprising impression of rapid implementation. Irrigating the New World's driest desert with runoff from its most rugged mountain ranges is a taxing undertaking and more than 90 percent of the land in production today is corporately worked in one way or another. Initially, canals may have been built by independent farmers as well as by corporate groups. But less than 5 percent of the desert that is farmed today could be easily reclaimed by individual effort, and this condition certainly worked against the rise of independent farmers during the Initial Period.

Preceramic economies supported the evolution of corporate organizations capable of executing large building projects. The ability to build sizeable canals by collective labor favored corporate reclamation of land. And, as easily irrigated land became scarce, the collective had greater resources for reclaiming additional land than did the individual entrepreneur.

Numbers. Given water, most canals can operate independently and therefore *Plate 5* support an independent group of people. Most rivers sustain a series of canal systems that maintain a number of separate agrarian collectives and in most cases a single canal is associated with a single group of people. Hence, irrigation agriculture is a segmentary phenomenon, with separate canals supporting autonomous groups of people. Similarly, rainfall farming maintains self-sufficient collectives that are agriculturally independent of one another. Consequently, early Andean reclamation fostered the rise of multitudinous self-supporting communities. Since these were largely self-governing collectives, most erected their own local civic-ceremonial facilities, just as any respectable town today has its own town hall and church. Early communal facilities could oftentimes grow to monumental scale, because many settlements endured and prospered for centuries and local labor was not diverted elsewhere under the political pull of kurakas and señoríos, which had yet to evolve. Thus, a great plentitude of early civic-ceremonial works commemorated the rise of innumerable autonomous collectives sustained by independent farming systems.

In the Moche Valley, early reclamation supported three independent ceremonial centers in irrigated pockets of narrow canyon land. There was a large cluster of big platforms – the Caballo Muerto Complex – on the main valley neck canal. In addition, there was a separate ceremonial mound in mid-valley. In succeeding millennia ceremonial centers moved downstream, became fewer in number, and eventually the entire valley was dominated by a single vast center, Huaca del Sol, and later Chan Chan. This suggests that irrigation underwrote the rise of independent corporate groups with separate ceremonial facilities long before the populations fused into larger political formations. *Plate 39*

Plates 56, 99

Initial Period monuments reflect significantly larger populations than in Preceramic times, and intensive agriculture certainly brought about a major demographic revolution. Reclamation of relatively accessible land supported growth of larger workforces capable of opening progressively more difficult terrain. Once underway, the expansion of reclamation and population was potentially self-propelling until limitations on water and land outstripped the labor, organizational, and engineering capabilities required for further reclamation. Yet the limitations confronting early farmers were not static but dynamic, and with the onset of protracted drought around 900 BC the agrarian bubble burst as prosperity gave way to centuries of austerity.

Organization. Having hypothesized that people first entered the Andes as moiety-based lineage groups, it is reasonable to suppose that early agrarian communities were organized by similar descent principles and by cargo-like office hierarchies. It is likely that the advent of farming heightened concerns with kinship and descent as sources of entitlement to collective resources. Canal builders generally monopolize the land and water they bring into production, and the same is true of rainfall farmers. In both cases, working arable lands of the Cordillera requires pooling labor during work-intensive times of plowing, planting, and harvesting. If early reclamation was undertaken by collectives that also pooled farm labor, then the means and modes of agrarian production were always corporately controlled and owned. Individual farmers were similar to sharecroppers, and access to the means of making a living was based on kinship and paid for by contributing to corporate undertakings. Thus farmers prospered and increased their numbers, but under a rather totalitarian yoke of their larger kin conclaves. If individuals did not own the land they tilled at the onset of agriculture, then it is not surprising that peasant farmers worked collective holdings in Inca times.

Because the mortuary practices and domestic settlements of early agriculturalists are little explored, much about their organization remains debatable. At La Galgada there are deceased elite, but elsewhere interments are unelaborated and relatively egalitarian. In the Casma some households enjoyed better quarters than their contemporaries, but elsewhere such distinctions are less evident. Other than imposing friezes adorning temple mounds, elaboration of the fine arts was infrequent and there is little suggestive of wealth finance. Yet, staple finance certainly underlay the construction and operation of larger, regional civic-ceremonial centers and most authorities agree that regional corporate organization was based upon religion and the supernatural.

Monumental architecture

The Initial Period was the great age of civic-ceremonial architecture, propelled by local communities building their own huacas and contributing support to provincial sanctuaries. Along the coast, large works and numerous small ones were erected from the northern La Leche Valley down through the Río Pisco. Even in later times, sizeable desert monuments were seldom erected south of the small Nazca drainage due to the latitudinal decline in coastal agrarian potential as the Cordillera becomes higher and drier. Highland building activities reached from the Cajamarca Basin to the environs of Lake Titicaca. Early agrarian monuments are so numerous, variable, poorly dated and little explored that they defy easy summation. Certain Preceramic practices persisted, including temple interment and the use of mesh bag construction fill, as well as H-type masonry. Irrigation built up soils suitable for producing mud bricks, and adobe construction became more common, employing hand-made bricks of

Plates 101, 102   conical, cylindrical, or bullet shape. Enormous adobe friezes, often painted in rich polychromes, were applied to the exterior facades of great mounds to
Plates 35, 36   impress huge audiences. With many centers flamboyantly vying with one another, ostentatious display was certainly a conscious concern of religious policy and sacrosanct power.

Coastal traditions

With little to suggest that early mounds incorporate elite tombs, we may presume that platforms and their attendant buildings were similar to later huacas adoratorios, while also serving civil and political ends. A variable and pluralistic pantheon would help explain the marked variation in early ceremonial architecture. In Inca times, different ethnic groups maintained shrines and huacas dedicated to local deities and doctrines and similar practices may be inferred for early kin corporations. Local beliefs were cross-cut by broader cults and creeds associated with ceremonial structures of repetitious form, such as sunken courts, Kotosh chambers, and U-shaped centers. Local interpretation of these cults and creeds was flexible and ecumenical, to judge from architectural variation. Sunken courts could differ in numbers and placement relative to other structures. Ceremonial structures that occur together in a group are rarely of equal size, and creeds and congregations were likely of different size and status.

At least three Initial Period traditions in ceremonial architecture, with overlapping distributions, can be recognized on the coast. In the north between the Ríos Jequetepeque and La Leche, a variable tradition emphasized low, wide, rectangular platforms, often aligned with rectangular forecourts. Rogger Ravines located 30 such monuments in the middle Jequetepeque drainage, with a majority of them occupying the canyon flanks at an elevation of 400 and 450 m. In addition to U-shaped complexes and sunken courts, there were isolated platforms, ones with forecourts, as well as terraced mounds with and without summit structures. The associated ceramics exhibit many elements of styles found at adjacent highland centers, such as Huacaloma in the Cajamarca basin. Thereafter strong linkages between coast and sierra persist up to the time of Spanish arrival.

Between the Ríos Santa and Huara, architect Carlos Williams recognizes more of a defined tradition emphasizing circular sunken courts in front of rectangular platforms, possibly derived from the style at preceramic sites such as La Galgada. There are some 30 pit-platform combinations in the Supe Valley that probably date to the Initial Period, and even larger numbers in the adjacent Pativilca and Fortaleza valleys. With a hundred or more examples altogether, the three drainages were the nexus of pit-platform construction.

Williams postulates an evolutionary sequence for the Supe Valley structures, in which the pits were at first physically detached from the platforms, as at Piedra Parada. Next, sunken courts were connected to mounds, and wide, flat collars built around the pit. Collared structures had upper court walls above ground level that were widened as causeway-like connections with platforms. After this fusion of the two structures, pits became much larger relative to pyramids and this trend culminated in complexes where the sunken court was the dominant structure. Finally, the structural proportions reverted to earlier norms, but platforms were low and square rather than tall and rectangular. This sequence suggests that for a time rites in sunken courts became more important than those on associated platforms.

The Paraiso Tradition

Sanctuaries built in the shape of a U are the most enduring form of ceremonial architecture in the Andes. Their evolution spans four millennia. During the Initial Period U-shaped complexes on the coast were the largest and most elaborate of all early monuments in the Americas. Over time their size was reduced, but not their importance. The lords of Chimor ruled from open-fronted throne rooms called *audiencias*, and U-shaped masmas served Inca potentates. *Plate 100*

Contemporary Aymara people near Lake Titicaca worship in a mountain-top shrine that is U-shaped. The one-room stone structure is open to the sky. An interior altar of slabs projects from the middle of the rear wall and there are

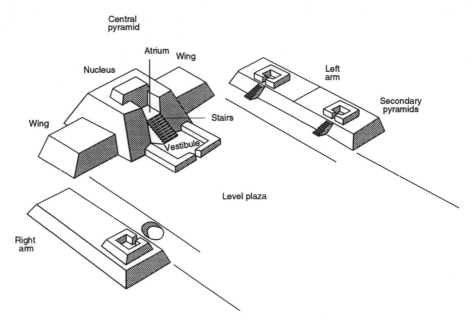

59 The basic elements of a large central mound flanked by two lower lateral platforms are shown in this idealized view of a U-shaped civic ceremonial center.

three exterior altars, one against the center of each outside wall. All are blackened and ash-covered from burnt offerings. The sanctuary serves a powerful mountain spirit that influences meteorological phenomena and the shrine is employed for rain-bringing rites to benefit crops. In a similar vein an intimate association with agricultural concerns characterizes the ancient U-shaped centers on the coast. These monuments almost always face inland mountains, opening their ceremonial wings to the mountain headwaters of desert rivers.

Carlos Williams considers the Preceramic ruins of El Paraiso to be the starting point of the U-shape tradition, and the inland orientation and general shape of the ruins make this a reasonable typological argument. But the Paraiso economy was more maritime than agrarian. Origins are also uncertain because a U-shaped configuration was found to be superimposed atop La Galgada when pottery and elaborate arts appeared at this Santa center about 1900 BC.

Monuments of the Paraiso tradition have an Initial Period coastal distribution between the Ríos Jequetepeque and Mala. In terms of numbers, they were most common between the Huaura and Lurin valleys where more than 25 centers were erected. However, the north includes both the biggest complex, Sechín Alto, and one of the most elaborate, Huaca Los Reyes, a member of the Caballo Muerto Complex.

Plate 39   Located more than 25 km inland, Los Reyes yielded dates that begin early in the Initial Period and span more than six centuries. Over the course of generations, the complex grew to a final size of 200 by 200 m. Architect William Conklin envisages eight phases of building that started in a two-fold manner. A small platform, with a U-shaped summit was erected at the rear of two aligned courts facing up-valley to the east. This little mound was never modified again. At the same time, to the south, work began on the rear buildings of what later became a higher, dominant platform. In phase two the platform was elevated and became a two-tiered huaca, with an added lower frontal mound with a central entry court. The facade of the lower mound was ornamented with six large niches, each framing an enormous cat-like head of adobe executed in high relief. Proceeding outward from the mound, later episodes of construction added detached lower wings framing a spacious court in front of the central platform. In the fourth phase the builders began to erect colonnades of square pillars in front of wing platforms and later on the main mound. The colonnades became more grandiose over time and pillars were transformed into frieze panels, each depicting a large human-like figure facing forward toward audiences assembled in the center of the U-shaped complex. Colonnades and monumental friezes made Los Reyes more ostentatious and ornate than most other centers.

Plates 35, 36

No two centers of the Paraiso tradition were exactly alike and their friezes are not standardized. Nonetheless, the direction of orientation, ground plan, and spatial organization of U-shaped complexes were broadly repetitive. As huacas adoratorios, they invite analogy with cathedrals and mosques in terms of recurrent structural canons and sacrosanct character. Commemorating the initial flowering of civilization, the magnitude of early U-shaped complexes is often

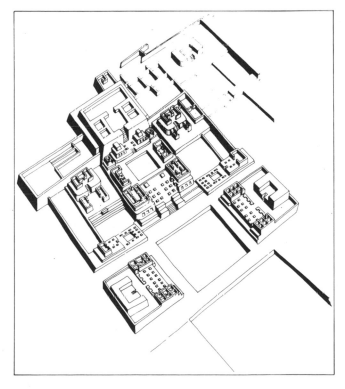

60 *A reconstruction of Huaca los Reyes. The smaller, presumably older temple sits in a separate court at the top.*

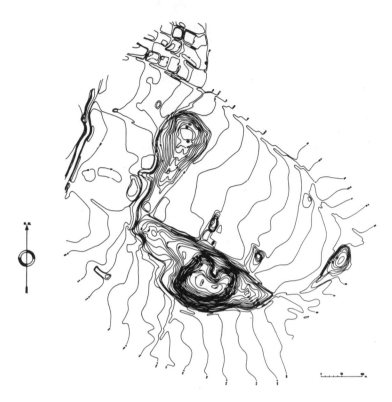

61 A topographic plan of Garagay, a U-shaped center in the Chillon Valley.

astounding. Including Sechín Alto, there are at least ten cases where size equals or greatly exceeds the Early Horizon complex of Chavín de Huantar. The Ríos Chillon, Rimac, and Lurin each contain two centers larger than Chavín, as well as one or more smaller complexes of nearly equal dimensions. One estimate calculates that the monuments in these three valleys represent in excess of 12 million man days of work.

Based upon architectural considerations, Williams has proposed a six-phase sequence of development. Following El Paraiso, there was increasing standardization and size. Size increased especially from Phase 3, with complexes such as La Florida. Florida is located near Lima, dates from between *c.* 1750 and 1650 BC, and is estimated to have required 6.7 million man days of labor to construct. Garagay, the largest of the Chillon complexes has a projected labor expenditure of 3.2 million man days. Yet in all such cases work was interspersed with long episodes of use spanning centuries. Emphasis on size persisted into Phase 5, when the largest of six U-shaped Chancay centers was completed at San Jacinto, which was three times the size of Chavín. Size then decreased at the end of the sequence, at centers such as Cardal.

Large populations are implied not only by the labor needed, but also by the design, which seems oversized in relation to human scales. For example Cardal, one of the smaller centers of four in the Lurin Valley, has a 3-ha court. By

today's architectural formula for standing room, it was designed to accommodate an audience of some 65,000 people – more than six times the population
that has traditionally resided in the lower Lurin! Excavations at Cardal by
Richard and Lucy Burger indicate that occupation and construction began relatively late, at about 1100 BC, and ended about 850 BC. It is intriguing to note
that two circular sunken courts were cut into one of the wing platforms of this
U-shaped center, while a third was placed between the main mound and the
other wing. Each of the unroofed courts could accommodate a small standing
audience of 150 or so. Walls exhibited traces of red, white, and black paint.
Except for a central hearth with ash, floors were clean, but beneath one a votive
offering was found consisting of a child's cranium.

Clearing the central facade of the main mound revealed a polychrome clay
frieze depicting a giant mouth of interlocking triangular teeth and large canines
each a meter long. Painted cream, yellow, rose, and black, the band of great teeth
had seen long exposure and was renovated at least four times. The imposing
frieze was centrally positioned on both sides of the entry to the summit atrium,
so that one stepped into the fanged aperture to reach the top of the mound.
Seen from the court of the U, the great size of the artwork was certainly
intended to impress. Cardal's builders may have drawn on work forces that did
not live at the site, but the monument was not a vacant ceremonial center,
because adjacent excavations revealed small domestic dwellings and refuse consisting of cultivated plants and sea foods. It is significant that construction and
use of Cardal overlapped with similar activities at the nearby U-shaped centers
of Manchay Bajo, 1 km away, and Mina Perdida, 5 km away. As in the Moche
Valley, the concurrent operation of multiple ceremonial centers suggests that
they served different audiences and, by inference, different kin corporations.

Religious formations

In the center of Cardal's summit, atrium burials of both sexes were encountered. Grave position indicates that these were important individuals, but
accompaniments of common pottery and little else suggests that they were not
wealthy people. One old man was noteworthy for his necklace of sea-lion teeth
and earspools fashioned from porpoise vertebrae, but entitlement to this distinctive attire was presumably achieved by the elder through service at Cardal
rather than through social inheritance. If concerns with natural and supernatural forces underlay the great spate of huaca construction among early farmers
then we must acknowledge that beliefs were associated with ritual specialists
and primordial cults and creeds which gave rise to later ones pervading the
Andean landscape at the time of conquest. Although most early belief systems
elude us, Kotosh chambers and sunken courts were certainly associated with
distinct doctrines and clerical personnel, probably ranging from lay leaders or
deacons to professional practitioners. Yet the architectural facilities do not
suggest that these creeds were necessarily centralized or hierarchical. This is
not the case for U-shaped facilities. By analogy with Christendom, Cardal and
Garagay resemble local churches while huacas La Florida and San Jacinto are

similar to provincial cathedrals, and I believe an organized priesthood was associated with these facilities and their faith. Beyond individual doctrines, Andeans also created ecumenical nexuses akin to Jerusalem, where multiple cults and creeds shared holy sites and sanctuaries. For example, Pachacamac had a grand platform temple dedicated to the prophetic deity Pachacamac, as well as numerous other huaca sanctuaries devoted to diverse gods, including supernaturals from afar. The Incas added to this holy landscape by erecting an opulent Sun temple for their own patron Inti. I believe that the pluralistic qualities of Andean religiosity are expressed at early sites such as Aspero, and that a penchant for sacred multi-faith landscapes can be seen in the Casma Valley during the Initial Period.

The colossal monument of Sechín Alto stands at the very apex of the U-shaped religious tradition. The five largest attendant mounds – three at the back and two on one side – are also U-shaped, leaving little doubt that this was the nexus of a specific creed where its largest, most elaborate rituals were enacted. Perhaps it was Vatican-like, but the broader landscape is studded with multitudes of other large and small monuments of variable form suggesting something more eclectic, possibly akin to Jerusalem.

Along the Río Sechín other monuments of exceptional size include Sechín Bajo, which is U-shaped, and Taukachi-Konan, which is not, as well as the elaborate but much smaller shrine of Cerro Sechín, which is different again. Cerro Sechín began very early as a modest multi-room sanctuary with adobe walls that were ornamented by large polychrome paintings of felines as well as a fish. Before 1200 BC it was filled in to create an expanded one-story-high rectangular platform mound ornamented on all sides by a unique megalithic facade of incised monoliths. The monoliths form a giant mosaic that depicts a dual procession of armed men carrying axe-like clubs that diverge from the back of the structure, with one line marching down and around one side of the structure and the other parading along the other side. In the front of the building, each line converges on the platform's central entrance, both sides of which are demarcated by monoliths depicting fluttering banners. This expression of twin processions uniting at a temple ingress is our first grand iconographic statement of tinku rituals and duality convergence – a long-lasting ritual theme. Yet the most common motifs in the imposing mosaic are dismembered humans. The weapon bearers are interspersed among numerous depictions of severed corpses, heads, limbs, and other body parts, but what they symbolize is not known.

Less than 10 km away, in the Casma branch of the valley, there is still another assemblage of imposing monuments, the Pampa de los Llamas-Moxeke Complex that is architecturally and ideologically very different. It is dominated by two large, rectangular platforms about 1 km apart, that are aligned and centrally situated on either side of a spacious square court measuring more than 350 m on a side. Multitudes of small low mounds and domestic dwellings flank the court. Huaca Moxeke, which stands at least 25 m high and measures some 165 m on a side, had an imposing facade ornamented with giant niches framing high-relief friezes painted in red, blue, white, and black. Two friezes depicted human faces, two illustrated richly garbed individuals facing forward, and one showed the back of a person with arms bound at the rear in a manner similar to later Moche renditions of prisoners. The lower Llamas platform, some 12 m high and about 130 m on a side, had two entrances; one facing Moxeke led to a long central corridor connected to the other entrance, or exit, which faced a circular sunken court. Three rows of symmetrically arranged courts and rooms occurred on both sides of the corridor, and excavations indicate that they were elaborate food-storage facilities and presumably related to an early form of staple finance.

The Casma and its Sechín branch form a modest drainage that has traditionally supported a modest population of 14,000 people, but larger numbers were certainly needed to erect and sustain its many early monuments, which have been investigated by Thomas and Shelia Pozorski of Texas Pan-American University. They see the Sechín Alto Complex and Moxeke-Pampa de los Llamas Complex as complementary moiety-like formations exerting a six-valley sphere of religious influence between the Ríos Chao and Huarmey. To the south they postulate two other spheres, one in Supe extending between the Ríos Huaura and Fortaleza where pit court and platform centers were common, and *Plates 37, 38* then another between the Ríos Chancay and Lurin where U-shaped facilities were prevalent. To the north, Caballo Muerto may have held sway between the Ríos Viru and Jequetepeque. Such spheres are tenable yet speculative because the frontiers of creeds and faiths are generally permeable and dynamic. While peaceful coexistence was the apparent norm among early creeds, violence was not absent in the macabre megaliths of Cerro Sechín, where men in arms with *Plates 31–34* pike-like clubs parade among dismembered corpses. One must wonder if the pikes were not emblems of authority that later evolved into staffs of office.

Highland developments

In the highlands Initial Period settlements and monuments were widely dispersed between northern Peru and the Titicaca Basin. Built of stone and adobe, ceremonial centers were elegant but generally smaller and more widely scattered than on the desert. The more widely scattered distribution of highland centers reflects larger but more dispersed populations engaged in agropastoral pursuits. Domesticates vital to these pursuits came into use during the Initial Period, but, as we have seen, their evolutionary origins are poorly understood. Herding did not replace hunting at Pachamachay Cave until about 1600 BC, yet, less then 100 km away at Telarmachay Cave, the transition is dated shortly after 3800 BC.

Llama and alpaca domestication opened the highest of economic zones, the *Plates 4, 11* puna, to controlled exploitation, while irrigation opened sierra bottomlands to farming. As highlanders increased their dependency upon plant and animal husbandry they increased their reliance upon domesticates that prospered at different altitudes. If nature operated in the past as it does at present, then yields of different crops in different habitats varied and counterbalanced each other year by year, and encouraged reliance on a range of domesticates adapted to different altitudes, or verticality.

Northern frontiers

In the north and east where the Cordillera is low and forested, people pursuing tropical adaptations engaged in rainfall farming long before agropastoralism emerged in the mountains and irrigation transformed the desert. Altitude set boundaries on tropical agriculture because its major crops, such as manioc, fare poorly above 1,500 m. Similarly, its southward spread along the coast was inhibited by the prerequisites of large-scale irrigation. With the later rise of powerful states, such as Moche and Chimor, the frontiers between Andean and Amazonian spheres of influence were pushed northward from an ancient divide at the Sechura Desert that had persisted into the Initial Period. In coastal Ecuador Valdivia farmers were producing pottery by 3000 BC. Yet more than a millennium passed before ceramics and agriculture spread the 400 km down the desert coast where intensive farming required irrigation and land reclamation. Dating between 1800 and 400 BC, early ceramic phases in northernmost Peru include Santa Rosa and Pechiche in the Tumbes Valley, Paita in the lower Chira and Piura drainages, and Encantada in the upper Piura. These assemblages are Ecuadorian in affiliation and they are associated with settlements of moderate size, but not with large monuments.

Mountain adaptations prevailed in the highlands east of the Sechura Desert. Situated at an elevation of 2,410 m in the Chamaya Basin, Pacopampa is among the most northerly of early Peruvian ceremonial centers. Initial Period and Early Horizon corporate architecture covers some 10 ha, and the habitation area is probably more extensive. The crest of a natural hill was modified to create a series of terraced platforms that were faced with massive masonry walls and fronted spacious courts, lined with stone colonnades and a modest number of stone carvings.

Early sierra adaptations are also evident in the Cajamarca-Crisnejas Basin at the ceremonial centers of Huacaloma and Layzon. Each center consists of one or more rectangular platform mounds that were generally terraced, stone-faced and sculpted from a natural hill or eminence. Huacaloma is the type site for the Early Huacaloma Phase, which dates between c. 1500 and 1000 BC and is characterized by ceremonial chambers of the Kotosh Religious Tradition. These were covered during the Late Huacaloma Phase, c. 1000 to 500 BC, to create masonry platforms embellished with polychrome paintings. Camelid and llama remains increase sharply during the Layzon Phase of 500 to 200 BC, when sizeable platform construction was undertaken at the nearby center of Layzon. Huacaloma was also remodeled with the significant addition of two stone-lined, stone-roofed canals to one of the mounds. One channel was straight, but the adjacent one was serpent-like and rather impractical. Elaborate stone conduits are a recurrent feature of early ceremonial architecture in the highlands.

El Paraiso: a Preceramic monument

29 (right) With nine complexes of collapsed stone buildings, El Paraiso was the largest New World monument ever erected by people who neither made pottery nor relied principally on agriculture. The two largest masonry complexes parallel one another, similar to the arms of later U-shaped ceremonial centers.

30 (below) A small, restored masonry complex at El Paraiso is more than two stories high.

Cerro Sechín: an Initial Period site

31 (left) A severed body and severed head incised on a monolith at this important site, dating to 1290 BC, near the Sechín Alto complex on the north coast.

32 (above left) A club-wielding figure on an incised Cerro Sechín monolith.

33, 34 (above right and below) The iconography of these Cerro Sechín severed heads reflects a concern with conflict and dissonance.

35, 36 *Feline heads of adobe ornamented the façade of Huaca Los Reyes in the Caballo Muerto Complex, Moche Valley.*

37, 38 *The north coast Cupisnique style, contemporary with Huaca Los Reyes, had early prominence in the Viru, Moche, and Chicama valleys. These Cupisnique ceramic vessels portray (above) an aged individual and (right) a woman and child.*

39 (below) *An aerial view of Huaca Los Reyes, its U-shape clearly visible. Above the main huaca sits a smaller platform in a separate court. A later prehistoric canal course lies uphill. In the desert beyond (center left), two parallel lines are traces of an ancient road leading to an outlying mound.*

Huaca Los Reyes

Pukara: an Early Horizon center

40 (left) A Pukara stone figure holding a trophy head.

41 (above) A Pukara-style incised polychrome vessel fragment with a feline head.

42 (below) Occupying a broad terrace, the sunken court at the site of Pukara, northwest of Lake Titicaca, was surrounded on three sides by detached one-room buildings built of stone blocks.

Opposite:

43 (above) General view of the Castillo façade at Chavín de Huantar, the magnificent site in the northern highlands whose rise in the first millennium BC defines the onset of the Early Horizon.

44 (left) An incised vessel of the coastal Paracas culture, with a feline motif, attributed to Chavín influence.

45 (below left) An incised polychrome Paracas vessel.

46 (right) A coastal stirrup-spout vessel with incised decoration probably influenced by Chavín.

The Chavín style

Chavín de Huantar

47 (above) Stone heads with human and animal attributes were once tenoned into the façade of the Chavín Castillo, and are now stored for their protection in an interior gallery.

48 (below) A New Temple anthropomorphic tenon head from Chavín, with exaggerated canine teeth.

49 (right) Head of the so-called Lanzón stela in an inner chamber at Chavín.

Some conduits were certainly drains. Others were inefficiently designed and over-built for useful ends, and probably served as conduits for the ritual manipulation of water. People apparently thought natural rainfall and runoff could be influenced by the ceremonial maneuvering of water flow.

Although Cajamarca was Andean, the basin was flanked by relict stands of tropical forest in the upper Lambayeque and Zana drainages. Sandwiched between the Pacific desert and the high sierra, the Zana held a southern enclave of people who pursued more tropical adaptations well into the Initial Period. To the east, lowland forest envelops much of Peru and here human development remains elusive until the introduction of pottery resulted in durable artifacts. Near the jungle city of Pucallpa on the Río Ucayali, the site of Tutishcainyo has early ceramics with an estimated date of 2000 BC. The pottery is associated with a sedentary farming community that presumably emphasized manioc cultivation and perhaps maize tending, while lake and river fish supplied protein. Similar ceramics occur at the Río Huallaga site of Owl Cave near the mountains. Along the mountain fringes tropical adaptations probably gave way to Andean ones at elevations around 1,500 m.

At Kotosh, in the upper Huallaga drainage, the Initial Period opens with the Waira-jirca phase. Waira-jirca pottery is well made and shares attributes with the Owl Cave assemblage less than 100 km away. Similarities are expectable if Waira-jirca people descended into the lower montaña to grow crops or procure tropical produce. Movement into the high mountains is attested by a significant increase in domesticated camelid remains at the site. Ceremonial construction focused on the elaboration of earlier platform mounds, but ritual chambers of the Kotosh Religious Tradition were no longer built. Beliefs may have changed as the local economy changed. However, a very large chamber was built nearby at Shillacoto, and the Kotosh Tradition persisted at other sites including Huaricoto.

Across the mountains to the west, at La Galgada, irrigated farming of scant canyon lands persisted. The Initial Period saw the addition of a few new crops, but herding is not in evidence. In Preceramic times Kotosh-type chambers had served first as seats of ritual and then as burial crypts, but they ceased to be built. When pottery was introduced the summit of the main platform was remodeled into a U-shaped configuration. This new design was accompanied by internal construction of long, narrow galleries within mounds and platforms. The slab-lined sanctuaries were then used as repositories for corpses. Some mummies were accompanied by textiles and jewelry that rank among the finest of Initial Period grave goods yet recovered. The latter includes shell disks with engraved birds and a stone disk mosaic with a cat-like face that are rather similar to later Chavín artwork. The grave goods are highly suggestive of personal wealth and status, while the gallery crypts are equally suggestive of sepulchral huacas of later-period nobility. This is by far the best early evidence for elite individuals and kindred who inherited wealth and status, thereby adumbrating the later kuraka class. Yet parallel developments are not evident elsewhere in the Cordillera for more than a thousand years! If kuraka rule is considered a social adaptation, then La Galgada suggests that local adaptations often flowered but failed because conditions were not conducive to their spread or evolutionary perpetuation.

Central highlands

In the Ayacucho region Initial Period settlements have yielded pottery assemblages, called Andamarca and Wichqana, with limited decoration and few suggestions of tropical influence. The Wichqana site has a ceremonial structure, reputedly in the shape of a U, associated with the buried skulls of decapitated women. In the nearby Andahuaylas Valley, excavations in the Muyu Moqo sector of the Waywaka site produced a 3,440-year-old stone bowl containing metalworking tools and gold beaten into thin foil. This is the earliest evidence of precious metalworking in the Andes.

Some 250 km to the east, in the Cuzco Basin the valley-bottom settlement of Marcavalle was occupied as early as 1300 BC. Continued use over almost half a millennium produced dense midden around dwellings with thin walls built of adobe. In addition to plain utilitarian containers, Marcavalle pottery includes painted vessels, some of which were decorated with metallic pigment. Thousands of years later Inca residents of the region looked to Lake Titicaca for their mythical origins. Thus, it is of interest that Marcavalle is not the only Initial Period pottery to appear in the Cuzco region. John Rowe identified examples of a second ceramic complex, known as Qaluyu after its type site on the northern shore of Lake Titicaca. The most common forms were open vessels such as bowls and plates, often decorated with incised geometric designs or painted with black and red motifs on cream-colored surfaces. Dating to *c*. 1300 BC, the site of Qaluyu is a low mound of habitation debris covering about 1 ha. Superficial explorations suggest that it was a long-lived community supported by farming, herding, and a collection of lacustrine resources. After abandonment the site was taken over later by Pukara people who resculpted the mound into the shape of a catfish. Although not the earliest ceramic complex in the region, Qaluyu attests to ancient links between the lake area and Cuzco. The persistence of links in tangible and mythical form through to Inca times simply reflects the fact that agropastoralism transformed the vast Titicaca Basin into the demographic and cultural nexus of high-altitude civilization.

The Titicaca Basin

After 1600 BC, rainfall gradually increased in the Titicaca Basin, facilitating the spread and elaboration of Arid Montane adaptations, which marks the beginning of the local Formative Period. Until protracted drought set in around 900 BC, agropastoral communities grew in number and prospered. Many erected their own civic-ceremonial facilities, which often combined three components: a rectangular sunken court, a platform mound, and a low-walled rectangular enclosure.

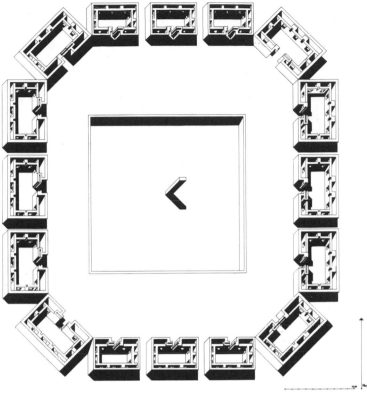

62 A reconstruction of the Chiripa mould-top buildings and sunken court. Emphasis on detached one-room buildings persisted through Inca times.

Chiripa

Located on the southern shore of Lake Titicaca, the site of Chiripa dates between 1400 and 850 BC and has been explored by a number of U.S. and Bolivian investigators. Large quantities of fish, waterfowl, snails, and aquatic plant remains were recovered from early deposits, as were totora rushes likely used for reed watercraft, as is the practice today. Small seeds and tubers may represent cultivated quiñoa and potatoes, while bones of llama, alpaca, and wild camelids were also found. Thus, food remains point to the early integration of lacustrine resources with agropastoral pursuits. Cooking took place in undecorated utilitarian ollas that sometimes include vegetable matter as ceramic temper. Open bowls with flat bottoms and vertical sides saw frequent decoration, with designs first outlined by thin incision and then painted in polychrome, emphasizing red, cream, and black. Further embellishment included appliqué felines, animal heads, and human faces. Potters also produced ceramic trumpets that rank among the earliest musical instruments found in the Andes. Chiripa-style ceramics occur at a number of settlements on the Bolivian side of Lake Titicaca, but it is not clear whether this reflects ethnic, religious, or political affiliations.

Plate 8

People resided at Chiripa for a number of centuries before erecting a plat-form mound in about 1000 BC. During its long use the structure underwent several construction stages before brief abandonment was followed by extensive remodeling and use by Tiwanaku peoples, who brought it to a final height of 6 m and dimensions of *c*. 55 m square. The platform was initially stone faced, and the summit seems to have had a square sunken court surrounded by small rectangular buildings. This basic configuration was enlarged upon during a second major phase of remodeling and use between 600 and 100 BC. At this time the stone-faced sunken court measured 23 m square and 1.5 m in depth. Carved stone plaques were set in the masonry walls of the court and ornamented with serpent, animal, and human motifs, beginning a stelae and stone-carving tradi-tion in the Titicaca Basin that persisted for millennia.

Atop the Chiripa mound 16 small, rectangular buildings ringed the court and opened to it. The facilities were symmetrically arranged and apparently com-prised a row of three aligned structures on each side of the court, and one build-ing diagonally placed at each corner. Each building was similar and built of earth and adobe. They were double-walled, the exterior walls forming an outer shell, while parallel but detached interior walls created a smaller rectangular chamber. Long narrow cells separated the two sets of walls. Niche-like interior windows provided access to the cells, which might have stored ceremonial par-aphernalia. Walls were stuccoed and painted with terracotta and green pigment, forming a chevron design in one case. Opening to the court, each building had a single rectangular entrance that was 'stepped': the exterior wall entry was wider than the interior wall entry. The appearance was of a smaller doorway set within a larger one. The entries were fitted for a sliding door that could be pulled back into the wall. Finally, plastered door jambs were stepped in a two-tiered manner, reinforcing the door-within-a-door appearance.

Architect William Conklin cogently argues that Chiripa features mark the onset of Titicaca architectural traditions, which lasted into Inca times. The door-within-a-door entries provide antecedents for the monolithic gateways at Tiwanaku which are similarly tiered. The single-entry, detached, one-room structure eventually evolved into the Inca wasi. Interior wall niches, sunken courts, and structures arranged around a central court also persist as architec-tural themes.

Chiripa and Qaluyu pottery belong to a family of early ceramic complexes that differ in decoration, yet share forms and, to varying degrees, employ veg-etable matter as temper. Other complexes include Huaricani in the middle Moquegua Valley, Faldas el Moro in the lower Azapa drainage, and Wankarani in the Lake Poopó highlands. Similarities among these assemblages are prob-ably due to the diffusion of ceramic technology out of the Titicaca Basin. West of the basin the long Preceramic occupation at Asana in the Río Moquegua headwaters indicates that scarce resources in the arid high sierra encouraged seasonal movement to the dry puna. Opening the sierra to year-round occupa-tion required creation of an artificial niche based on domesticated plants and animals as well as on irrigation. This was a gradual transformation that pulled people into lower settings favorable for crops. Beginning in the first millennium BC, the Huaricani complex is represented by valley-side settlements in warmer elevations around 2,000 m. Here stone outlines of rectangular one-room dwellings are scattered above traces of ancient canals. Adjacent to some sites there are cemeteries where seated, flexed burials were interred in cylindrical pits lined with stone. This pattern of interment is typical of the Titicaca region, and it supports propositions that the lower sierra was reclaimed by highlanders.

The coast had a long occupation by maritime folk such as those of the Chinchorro tradition of northern Chile. Here archaeologists see ceramics, woven textiles, and irrigation agriculture as introductions from the outside that were adopted by local people by 1200 BC. The introductions are thought to be from the Titicaca Basin, because the pottery, called Faldas el Moro, has highland similarities. However, some crops came into use that were not of highland origin, and squash, cotton, or gourd may equally have diffused down the coast from one valley to another.

The far south

Lake Titicaca drains south to the more arid region of Lake Poopó, where early ceramics, with general similarities to those of Chiripa, are represented by the Wankarani complex. Defined by Bolivian archaeologist Carlos Ponce, this complex may have arisen as early as Chiripa, and then persisted into Tiwanaku times as a conservative agropastoral adaptation to a harsh environment. The Poopó region and drier reaches of the southern Cordillera lack elaborate ceremonial architecture, and there are few expressions of corporate constructions other than defensive walls enclosing settlements. Walled and open Wankarani villages consisted of circular adobe houses that were probably thatched. The number of households ranged from 15 to one extreme case of over 700. Metallurgy is in evidence in the form of copper-smelting slags that radiocarbon assays date between 1200 and 800 BC. This marks the beginning of a southern Andean metallurgical tradition, emphasizing copper, tin, and bronze, that developed independently of a more northern tradition, associated with copper-arsenic ores and gold-working. Some eastern Wankarani villages occur at lower altitudes near the Cochabamba Valley. These settlements may have been established to exploit temperate maize-growing lands, and if so, they represent an early expression of verticality on the eastern slopes of the Cordillera.

In arid Chile, Nuñez and Dillehay propose that altitudinal movement of people and produce was somewhat different from in northern verticality adaptations. The southern salt puna and hyperarid reaches of Chile are where hunter-gatherers probably pursued seasonal transhumance between the coast and puna. Agriculture came late to this harsh environment, appearing after the last century BC in the highland oasis of San Pedro de Atacama and in the Río Loa desert valley. Here farming and herding seem to have been independent pursuits managed by different groups of people. Widely separated communities of sedentary farmers arose in highland oases and small coastal valleys. Apparently farmers did not travel up and down the mountains to obtain distant resources, but relied for the transport and exchange of goods on herders, who moved their herds between high and low pastures on a seasonal basis. Herders did not cultivate the produce they transported, nor were they colonies of the communities they connected, but their symbiotic relationship with farmers served the same ends as verticality did in the north.

THE EARLY HORIZON

At the same time as coastal civic-ceremonial centers along the desert coast were forsaken, Chiripa and other Formative settlements waned as rainfall declined and the level of Lake Titicaca dropped for several centuries after AD 900. The impression is that Andean farmers simply could not cope with protracted drought – a disaster they had never experienced before. When rainfall increased again, societies were more somber, although natural and supernatural forces were still of fundamental concern. The Early Horizon is associated with Chavín de Huantar, a civic-ceremonial center founded by 800 BC in the northern highlands. Technically, the horizon is a unit of time that begins when Chavín artistic influence first appears in the ceramic arts of the Ica Valley about 400 BC. This is broadly coincident with another protracted plunge in rainfall. Yet this disaster was met with greater adaptive response. Let us briefly examine developments in the southern pole of Andean civilization before turning to Chavín, which was a northern phenomenon.

The southern sphere

Many Formative populations arose in the Titicaca region that produced locally distinct ceramics, but by about 500 BC they came to share crosscutting iconographic and ideological beliefs called the 'Yaya–Mama Religious Tradition,' named by Karen and Sergio Chavez after its hallmark monoliths depicting a male or 'yaya' on one side and a female or 'mama' on the other. The spread of this creed no doubt facilitated communication among diverse populations, and this was very important during prolonged drought when information, produce, and people had to move greater-than-normal distances.

Pukara

Plate 42

Located some 75 km northwest of Lake Titicaca, the modern town of Pukara lends its name to a nearby sprawl of ruins demarcating an ancient civic-ceremonial center that arose around 400 BC and assumed regional prominence three or four centuries later. Monumental construction was banked against a range of hills. Elegant corporate works and finely built quarters were erected on massive hillside terraces. Faced with large boulders and rock slabs, the biggest terrace had centrally positioned masonry stairs. The spacious summit was occupied by a rectangular sunken court with well-made stone walls. On three sides it was surrounded and enclosed by a series of detached, one-room structures, creating an arrangement very reminiscent of the court-and-room complex at Chiripa.

63 Rollout tracing of a Yaya-Mama stela depicting a female on one side and a male on the other.

There were also flanking plazas and other structures with dressed-stone foundations that supported adobe walls. An extensive residential zone spread across the plain below the elevated civic center, and may have held a population of urban dimensions.

Pukara artisans produced corporate-style ceramics that were complex and beautiful. Motifs were outlined and subdivided by incision to demarcate intricate zones, which were then slip-painted in red, yellow, and black that firing transformed into harmonious tones. The style passed through several phases of development, combining stylized and realistic motifs. The latter included birds, *Plate 41* llamas, felines, and humans. Human and cat heads were often modeled in relief on flat-bottomed opened bowls. Richly ornamented kero beakers were used as libation vessels and music was played on delightfully decorated ceramic trumpets. Drawing on aspects of the Yaya-Mama tradition, Pukara stone carvers created both fully round and flat-relief sculptures. Incision and champleve (cutting the pattern out of the surface) techniques were used to fashion low-relief carvings on stone slabs and stelae depicting felines, serpents, lizards, and *Plate 40* fish, and human-like figures. Sculptures carved in the round tended to emphasize relatively realistic humans or supernaturals often accompanied by trophy heads, which also figure prominently in the few surviving examples of Pukara textiles.

Pukara art was seemingly geared to elites, but archaeologists have not found the mortuary remains of kurakas. Perhaps corporate organization was akin to that of a maximal or apu ayllu. Pukara populations were well-enough organized to mitigate the effects of protracted dry times by excavating enormous sunken gardens with sloping sides called *cochas* that tapped water-table moisture. Interconnected by canals and ditches, water ponded in cocha bottoms during the rainy season, then as the pits gradually dried crops were planted along their sloping banks and eventually in their bottoms. This increased agricultural yields by allowing farming to go on over a much longer time than scant rainfall alone would support.

Although Pukara flourished in the northern limits of the Titicaca Basin, its arts made sporadic appearances much further afield. Several specimens of Pukara textiles from the Azapa coast, and occasional Pukara ceramics in the Moquegua Valley, point to distant western contacts. In the mountains examples of Pukara stone sculpture are known from the department of Cuzco. These widely scattered remains are suggestive of economic interactions rather than imperial hegemony. There is little evidence that Tiwanaku, at the southern end of the lake, was politically incorporated by Pukara. The first two phases of the Tiwanaku occupation produced radiocarbon dates ranging between 400 BC and AD 100. It was thus contemporary with Pukara, but seems to represent an independent course of development. The two corporate styles share certain similarities, but this is thought to reflect common ancestry in earlier stone carving and artistic concerns of the Yaya-Mama Tradition.

Paracas

The distinguished Peruvian investigator Luis Lumbreras cogently argues that Pukara polychrome wares and those at Tiwanaku exhibit affinities with contemporary Paracas pottery and textiles found at the famous coastal necropolis of Paracas and nearby valleys from Chincha through Nazca. The artistic and iconographic affinities between this coastal corporate style and the Titicaca Basin are of a rather generic nature, but nonetheless align Paracas with the more southerly sphere of civilization. The ceramic tradition includes both monochrome and polychrome wares. Framed by incised lines, polychrome motifs were rendered in resin paints applied after vessel firing. Richly ornamented libation vessels have squat bodies mounted by two short spouts connected by a bridge, and such double-spout-and-bridge bottles long remained a preferred drinking vessel in the region. The Paracas style has been subdivided into a ten-phase sequence, and by the third and fourth phase local potters occasionally produced stirrup-spout libation vessels ornamented with relatively realistic depictions of feline heads. These vessels lack local antecedents and are attributed to Chavín influence which marks the opening of the Early Horizon. Later

Plates 44–46

64 *A Paracas vessel depicting a feline face attributed to Chavín influence.*

ornamentation becomes simpler and more naturalistic, and during the last two phases Lumbreras sees particularly close ties with the south highlands and Pukara. From the early beginnings, flamboyant polychrome endured through later Nazca and Ica cultures in their namesake southern valleys, which always maintained close interactions with the sierra and south.

First explored by Julio Tello, the seaside Paracas necropolis contained numerous well-to-do individuals interred as seated mummy bundles with remarkable finery. Many bodies showed evidence of cranial surgery, known as trepanation, in which small pieces of the skull were removed after being cut out by incision, scraping, or drilling. For burial, the unattired corpse was first placed in a flexed seated position and bound with cords to maintain the pose,

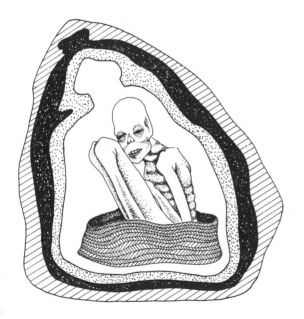

65 *Schematic reconstruction of a Paracas mummy bundle.*

66 *Paracas underground burial vaults included 'Cavernas'-type pits (top) and 'Necropolis'-type masonry crypts.*

which is typical of interments in the Titicaca region. Next, the body was wrapped in textiles and seated upright in a large shallow basket containing elaborate garments and other offerings. Then the basket and body were wrapped together in many layers of plain cotton cloth to form the final bundle. The deceased were enshrined in large subterranean crypts that took the form of bell-shaped pits or rectangular masonry mausoleums. Used over generations, the vaults held up to 40 other mummy bundles, which were presumably kindred who inherited their kuraka-like status.

67 Wool in this Paracas embroidered motif probably came from herd animals in the highlands.

Plate 20

Plate 21

Due to its extreme dryness, the Paracas necropolis has yielded more fine attire and elaborate fabrics than any other early site, and the textiles are more advanced than those found in coastal areas to the north. Among these advances is the use of alpaca wool, no doubt imported from the highlands. Wool takes and holds a far greater range of dye colors than cotton, and exquisite polychrome embroidery is the hallmark of Paracas fabrics. Embroidered mantles, cloaks, tunics, and headgear depict mythical creatures as well as ornately garbed humans wearing gold nose ornaments that look like cat whiskers, and carrying trophy heads as well as staves that were probably emblems of status and office. Indeed, may assume that rituals based in myth were regularly acted out by Paracas elites bedecked in rich garb and ostentatious costumes that accompanied the actors to their graves.

The stages for such rituals were not the necropolis, but at civic-ceremonial centers of a highly distinctive form that Lumbreras and colleagues have identified in the Chincha Valley. Built of hand-made adobes, their most basic form consists of two aligned rectangular platform mounds on the front and back of a high-walled central court recessed to near ground level. Because the court side walls are exceptionally thick and almost as high as the platforms the ruins often look like a single elongated mound with a sunken summit court. One complex, Huaca Soto, stands 15 m high and measures 70 by 200 m and has two interior courts as well as a thick-walled frontal entry court. Similar facilities have not been reported from other valleys within the Paracas domain, which may have been more ideological than political in nature.

Chavín and the northern sphere

After the fall of Sechín Alto and other coastal centers, beliefs associated with sunken courts and U-shaped ceremonial facilities persisted in the highlands and at the sanctuary of Chavín, home of an oracular deity. The later ensuing spread of the Chavín cult during protracted dry times cross-cut old social boundaries and fostered the flow of ideas, information, products, and people within vast reaches of what would become the northern sphere of Andean civilization.

Chavín de Huantar

At an elevation of 3,177 m, Chavín de Huantar is situated at the confluence of two small streams, the Mosna and Wacheksa, the Mosna eventually feeding into the Río Marañón. The site includes a substantial residential area of stratified refuse and remains of unimposing dwellings investigated by Richard Burger, who divides the occupation into three phases. Initial radiocarbon dates for the Urabarriu Phase fall around 800 BC, although settlement might have begun a century or two earlier. Initially the community was modest in size, with some 500 individuals spread over 6 ha. During the short middle phase between 500 and 400 BC the population doubled and spread across 15 ha. During the final Janabarriu Phase of 400–200 BC numbers again doubled and 2,000–3,000 people occupied an urban core of 42 ha before the site went into decline.

The rise and demise of the local populace were tied to the fortunes of the adjacent complex of masonry buildings, known as the Castillo. Less than one-tenth the magnitude of the great platform at Sechín Alto, what the Castillo lacks in size is compensated for by remarkable engineering, fine masonry, and marvelous stone art. The engineering is fascinating because a quarter of the Castillo interior is hollow and occupied by a labyrinth of narrow galleries roofed by great slabs of stone. Built at different levels, some galleries are connected by stairways and by an elaborate maze of small drains and vents that pass beneath the exterior plazas. We have discussed early concerns with the ritual manipulation of water and at Chavín analysis of the hydrological and acoustical characteristics of its conduits and chambers by Lumbreras and colleagues in engineering suggests that by flushing water through the drains and venting the sound into the chambers and then out again the temple could, quite literally, be made to roar! Galleries served more than acoustical purposes, however. Several contain slabs with traces of incised and painted figures, including a fish with feline attributes and four examples of what might be shrimp. Another gallery, excavated by Lumbreras, was filled with votive offerings of fine ceramics. Systematic mapping of the galleries and internal features by Stanford University archaeologists reveals a very long and highly complex history of construction.

Plate 43

Traditionally, the masonry-faced Castillo has been divided into two adjoining temple complexes, the old and the new. Flourishing during the Urabarriu Phase, the Old Temple measured approximately 109 by 73 m, and *c.* 15 m in height, with block-like wings framing a U-shaped plaza that opened to the east.

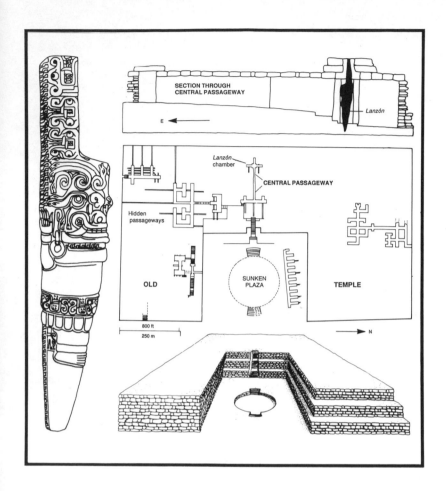

Within the plaza there was a circular sunken court with descending and ascending stairs leading to the central temple staircase. Each side wall of the court was ornamented with a banded masonry frieze depicting a procession of anthropomorphic figures above a procession of jaguars. Marching from the descending stairs, the dual cavalcades converged upon the ascending stairs in tinku fashion. Human processions presumably passed through the court and ascended the mound in a similar two-fold manner. Access to the various internal chambers of the Old Temple may have been through summit passages.

In the midline of the mound there are two galleries, one above the other, with the lower, more finely constructed, sanctuary having the unusual form of an elongated cross. Built into the center of the cross is a truly imposing stela, the Lanzón. Slender and some 4.5 m tall, the great stone is knife-shaped, with the blade point embedded in the floor, and a narrow tang projecting into the ceiling and floor of the higher overhead gallery. Carved in low relief, the stela depicts a being with a human body whose fingers and toes terminate in claws. Garbed in simple but fine attire with large, bangled earspools, the figure has a markedly feline face. Thick lips curl up and back, exposing two tusk-like canines, while

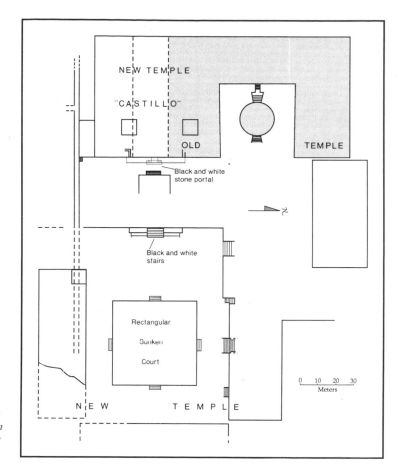

68, 69 The 'Castillo' of Chavín de Huantar began as a U-shaped ceremonial center - the Old Temple (left) – with a circular sunken court. The Lanzón stela, or principal cult image (shown enlarged), stood in the central passageway. Then (right) the Old Temple, shaded, was expanded southward in two construction stages, and eastern platform mounds were erected to create the New Temple. The new complex held a rectangular sunken court that was aligned with a stairway and portal of black-and-white stone.

eyebrows and hair are depicted as snakes. Variously called the 'Smiling' or 'Snarling God,' the deity gazes eastward down the long axis of the dark, windowless gallery, forcefully confronting any arriving viewer. By lifting a floor stone in the gallery immediately above the Lanzón, an unseen attendant could speak for the deity below. This has led to the proposition that the Lanzón was an oracle which spoke to privileged supplicants who gained access to the inner sanctum.

The cult of the Lanzón grew after 500 BC, as did the monumental facilities. A detached platform was built immediately in front of the north wing of the Old Temple. More importantly, the southern wing of the temple was expanded laterally to the south more than 30 m in several construction phases to create a large block-like platform constituting the base of the New Temple. To the east, two detached mounds were erected to create the lateral wings of a U that framed a spacious rectangular plaza, which held a square sunken court measuring 50 m on a side. From the plaza, the temple was reached via a massive megalithic stairway, one side of which was hewn from black rock and the other from white limestone. Flanked by large stone columns with intricate carvings, the

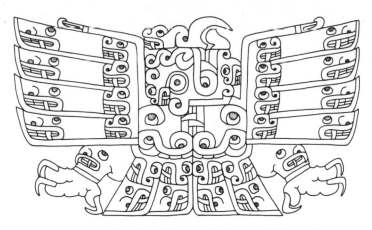

70 A Chavín New Temple bas-relief of a raptorial bird with serpent motifs indicating feathers.

stairway led to an elevated landing or patio with a small stone-faced rectangular sunken court in its midline. To the rear stood an elaborate gateway called the black-and-white portal because half was fashioned of light stone and the other of dark rock. Behind the portal, a long narrow corridor ran along the face of the temple mound, which had no frontal entrance. However, 6 m up the masonry facade there were two rectangular openings with stairs from the interior that apparently allowed priests to miraculously appear above and on either side of the black-and-white portal.

The Castillo was ornamented with splendid artwork of stone, only traces of which remain in place. High on the exterior walls of the New Temple there were one or more rows of round heads mounted on tenons so that carved heads projected out from the wall. These are the only three-dimensional sculptures at Chavín, and included stylized birds and canines, as well anthropomorphic

Plate 47

71 With exaggerated canine teeth denoting preternatural status, an anthropomorphic figure carries a hallucinogenic San Pedro cactus instead of a club.

72 Gender dualism is commemorated in rollouts of the columns of the Black and White Portal of Chavín's New Temple with light female (left) and dark male (right) holding saber-like arms.

beings rendered with curved tusks, and hair in the form of serpents. Near the top of the temple facade there was an encircling row of bas-relief cornices depicting spotted jaguars and raptorial birds with feline attributes. They apparently formed a dual procession that divided and departed from the back of the platform. Each cavalcade then advanced around one side of the temple before converging with the other cavalcade above the black-and-white portal. A line of stylized hawks converging beak-to-beak with a counterpart line of eagles is carved in low relief on the usable bottom face of the portal lintel. The lintel was supported by two circular stone columns, one black and one white, with contrasting engraved images. One was an anthropomorphized male with a hawk head; the other, eagle headed, was female replete with 'vagina dentata.' Both were winged, richly attired and significantly each was armed with two staffs or sabers, one wields in each hand. In gender and portal color, the supernaturals bespeak of duality, convergence, and tinku.

Among many artworks not found in original context, the latest and most elaborate expression of Chavín art is the Raimondi Stela, a 2-m-high monolithic plaque discovered in the 19th century by the naturalist of the same name. It depicts the Lanzón god, after 500 years of evolution, as a forward-facing supernatural, still with clawed digits and snake-like hair. Yet now there is very rich adornment culminating in a towering rayed headdress larger than the deity itself. Telling of synergistic powers, the supernatural holds two elaborate vara, one grand staff in each hand, thereby uniting the dual spheres of Andean society and cosmos. Crystallizing first at Chavín, this 'Staff God' motif of supernatural synthesis will resonate through the Andes again in much later time frames. I concur with Lumbreras' suggestion that the Raimondi Stela was originally situated above or behind the black-and-white portal where winged

73 *Two skyward-facing jungle caymans (crocodiles) are revealed in this rollout of the Tello Obelisk, each with plant and animal symbols.*

supernaturals converged upon the paramount deity, as is shown in later iconography. Having proposed that earlier multi-mound centers in the Casma and Supe valleys accommodated multifaceted pantheons, I think there is much greater focus upon one paramount deity at Chavín around which the temple architecture is integrated. Yet some monoliths may represent beliefs from further afield. The Tello Obelisk, discovered by Julio Tello outside the Castillo, is a 2.5-m-long shaft of stone with complex, shallow carving with dual representations of a great cayman, the South American crocodile. The cayman is depicted with manioc, gourd, pepper, and other cultigens in a manner suggesting that the beast might have been the mythical donor of these crops.

Spreading God's word

The stonework at Chavín de Huantar was unquestionably the product of master craftsmen, and the Castillo reflects professional engineering as well as substantial corporate labor. How this marvelous center came to command such resources is linked to the way in which tribute and support were obtained from distant populations. This was not done by exporting locally produced objects of stone or ceramic. The monumental stone artwork defining Chavín corporate iconography stayed at the center itself. When carved stone is occasionally found at contemporary centers in other regions it represents local productions that may or may not include stylistic attributes found at Chavín, which is also true of ceramics.

What was being exported was the word and cult of a god who smiled or snarled at first and then later carried the dual staffs of social and cosmic unity. Dissemination perhaps involved proselytizing missionaries; more likely it entailed devoted pilgrims who were ritually anointed at the Castillo to spread the faith, because there is great regional variation in expressions of Chavín ideology. The later cult of the Pachacamac oracle was promulgated by nodes of secondary oracles, portrayed as wives, sons, and daughters of the prophesying patriarch. Promising appropriate tithes and tribute, people could petition the oracle's priesthood to establish kindred shrines in their homeland, thereby adding a Pachacamac-related presence to local pantheons and huacas. Richard Burger suggests the Lanzón cult spread by similar means. In the absence of paper, textiles traditionally served as the means of graphically disseminating ideas and ideology in the Andes, due to their flexibility and portability. The largest single body of undisputed Chavín-style art found beyond the type site is a cache of several hundred cotton fabric remains from a looted tomb at Karwa on the Paracas Peninsula. These were not garments, but large panels of cotton cloth with Chavín motifs and at least 25 Staff God representations painted in red–orange, tan, brown, green, and blue. The majority of these iconographically

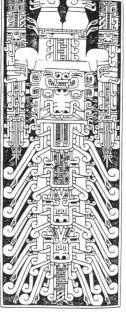

74 (left) The Staff God depicted on the Raimondi Stela could also be 'read' when inverted, as shown in the right-hand image.

75 (above) The Staff God painted on cotton cloth found at the coastal site of Karwa.

charged works were of substantial size, well suited for public display as banners, tent flaps, or wall hangings. Karwa depictions of the Staff God are noteworthy because gender is frequently indicated and it is always female. Thus, the reputed satellite oracle could have been the wife or daughter of the Chavín patriarch.

Changing times

The spread of Chavín ideological influence during the Janabarriu Phase of 400–200 BC was in part related to a concurrent drought in the Cordillera. If rainfall declines and food production is depressed then people, products, and information must move over greater distances to satisfy basic wants. By allowing 'pilgrims' to travel peacefully across countryside, the cult of the Lanzón facilitated mobility and interaction beneficial to commerce and the spread of innovative technologies in many media, including textiles. Twining had persisted for the production of ornate, high-status cloth, but was now completely replaced by heddle weaving. Coastal cotton cloth saw the supplemental use of dyed camelid wool. Tapestry came into use along with supplemental, discontinuous warps. Painted, tie-dyed, and batik cloth appeared. These innovations revolutionized Andean textile production. On the coast this new order of cloth included a widespread, but dispersed, corpus of specimens with Chavín-related motifs analyzed by William Conklin. He concludes that these fabrics do not exhibit regional distinctions in technology or style, as do ceramics, and thus
Plate 46   constitute the purest expression of a horizon marker for Chavín times.

The broader distribution of Janabarriu elements reflects extensive communication networks for exchanging goods and ideas. For example, obsidian use at Chavín de Huantar increased five-hundred-fold during Janabarriu times, with more than 90 percent of the stone coming from the Huancavelica region 470 km to the south.

The Ayacucho region yielded Initial Period specimens of hammered sheet goldwork – the earliest in the Andes. Yet, precious metal only came into widespread use during the Early Horizon when metallurgy experienced a technological revolution comparable to the one in textile production. Innovations included soldering, sweat welding, repoussé decoration, and the creation of precious mixtures of gold alloyed with silver or copper. These inventions allowed three dimensional gold and alloyed objects to be fashioned from preshaped metal sheets that were joined together by complex means to create magnificent artifacts. These bold works are a hallmark of the metallurgical tradition that came to characterize northern Peru and to distinguish it from traditions in the Titicaca Basin and in the northern highlands of Ecuador and Colombia.

There is scant evidence that artisans at Chavín de Huantar produced fine pottery for export. Thus, assemblages of pure Janabarriu pottery only occur in the vicinity of the type site. Less than 80 km away, the contemporary ceramic assemblage at Huaricoto is local. In such situations Chavín influence may be defined by the appearance of certain new vessel shapes such as stirrup spout bottles, and of certain modes of plastic ornamentation, including surface

76 A Chavín-style tapestry motif from the coastal Supe Valley.

texturing by combing or rocker-stamping, repetitive rows of incised or stamped circles, circles with central dots, concentric circles, and occasional motifs such as eyes and feline mouths that also appear in stonework.

The distribution of such elements indicates that the northern frontier of Chavín influence coincided with the Sechura Desert, while in the northern highlands recognizable Chavín traits occur at Pacopampa. On the eastern flanks of the Cordillera a strong veneer of Janabarriu-related elements appears at Kotosh and during the Kotosh Chavín Phase. On the coast evidence of Chavín attributes diminishes south of the Río Mala. However, limited influence does appear early in the Ocucaje sequence. In the sierra the southern limits of Janabarriu-like traits are manifested in ceramic assemblages from Atalla near Huancavelica and from Chupas near Ayacucho. In overview, the regional distribution of Chavín-related traits represents a counter-pole to the southern Pukara-Paracas culture sphere.

Changes during Janabarriu times were not simply economic, but social and political. Richard Burger's excavations in residential areas surrounding the Castillo indicate that during the 400–200 BC epoch of drought people who resided close to the monument enjoyed a better diet and more camelid protein than those living on the margins of the settlement. The pulling apart of social classes is evident at Kuntur Wasi in the north highlands, where University of Tokyo scientists recovered four shaft tombs, averaging 2.3 m deep, cut into the top of an earlier platform mound. Each contained a single individual with rich offerings that characterized later kuraka elites. Gold crowns accompanied two males, as did a plaque, a pair of earspools, and pectorals of gold. In addition to pottery, the tomb of an elderly female held a carved stone cup, a pendant of gold and silver and some 7,000 shell and stone beads that once ornamented a fine garment. The tombs of Kuntur Wasi and those of the Paracas necropolis gentry point to a spreading process of class formation. In part, this process is explained by 'circumscription theory,' which holds that there are finite limits on arable land and water in coastal valleys and sierra basins. When population growth reaches these limits then competition arises over the scarce resources and conflict promotes the rise of secular, authoritarian leadership. Because resource circumscription is much more constraining during dry times than wet ones, drought probably contributed to the rise of secular leadership and social differentiation during the Early Horizon.

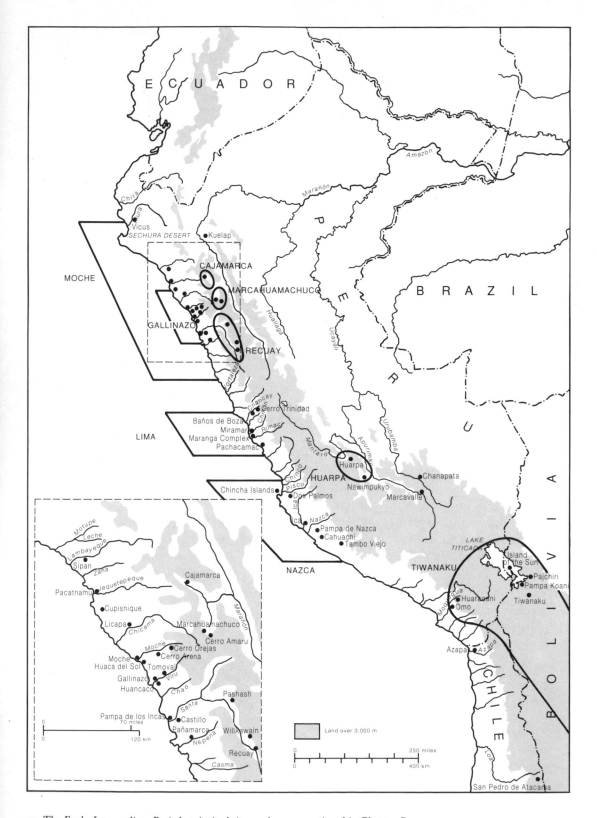

77 The Early Intermediate Period: principal sites and areas mentioned in Chapter Seven.

CHAPTER SEVEN

THE EARLY INTERMEDIATE PERIOD

In the beginning, mountain agropastoralism and desert irrigation fostered economic boom times with people spreading into under-exploited niches, prospering and increasing their numbers. Yet growth inevitably slowed, and by the time of Christ refinements of Arid Montane and Maritime-Oasis adaptations had led to the filling-in of easily exploited habitats and further agrarian expansion required substantial investment. With nature no longer permissive of unbridled growth, the tenor of life changed. The metaphysical and 'other-worldly' emphasis of early art and architecture gave way to more earthly concerns.

78 Art assumed a more worldly complexion during the Early Intermediate Period and conflict was portrayed in Moche ceramic painting.

Ceremonial centers were dramatically outnumbered by residential communities, and fortified villages and bastions were not uncommon. Rule was no doubt in the name of the gods, but now governance was in the hands of an elite class, the kuraka, who claimed special descent from founding figures. This fostered great elaboration of ancestor veneration among commoners in general and elites in particular. Employing wealth finance to distinguish privileged status, the kuraka commissioned vibrant corporate styles and the Early Intermediate Period has been called the 'Mastercraftsmen Period,' and the 'Regional Developmental Period.' Gauged by the Ica Valley ceramic sequence, the period dates between about 200 BC and AD 600. Reflecting both population growth and better archaeological preservation, it is not an easy era to characterize. Therefore, this chapter highlights economic and political transformations in the northern and southern poles of native civilization.

North coast

Plates 37, 38, 50–53

The broad outlines of north-coast developments were formulated in the 1940s by Rafael Larco Hoyle, who employed mortuary pottery to characterize a succession of early ceramic assemblages that included Cupisnique, Transitory Cupisnique, Salinar, Viru or Gallinazo, and Mochica or Moche, which was subdivided into five phases. The first two assemblages were, in part, contemporary with the flowering of the Sechín Alto Complex, while Salinar dates to the end of the Early Horizon. Gallinazo marks the emergence of a new cultural order that eventually gave rise to the Moche, a far-flung cultural and political formation based on enduring institutions of Andean statecraft.

Perhaps akin to a confederacy, Moche was the first archaic state to arise in the northern pole of Andean civilization. Uniting a politically fragmented landscape with numerous canal-based parcialidades was a complicated process. It began with consolidating the kin-based fiefdoms within a single valley, which then allowed separate parcilidades in other drainages to be picked off in piecemeal fashion. Valley size was important to the vital first act of consolidation, which was played out earliest in the small Casma drainages, as Sechín Alto testifies. Stepping up the coast to the somewhat bigger Río Viru, it was later replayed during Gallinazo times. The process then shifted to its final stage, in the moderate-sized Moche drainage. Here it was performed twice, first by Moche and later by Chimor. That state-building failed to march north into Lambayeque suggests that great valley size fostered internal fragmentation, which worked against unification. Although Lambayeque experienced several episodes of integration, its powerful señoríos never consolidated to march south and overrun their smaller neighboring valleys.

Signs of change

If Initial Period canals supported the rise of autonomous ayllu-like groups that commemorated their identity by building ceremonial centers, then a shift from defining identity to defending it is indicated by the subsequent elaboration of fortifications. It is likely that competition and hostilities increased as easily farmed land was filled in by growing populations and during episodes of drought, such as between the time of Christ and about AD 200. Although defensive works were erected at different times in different locations, strongholds on the coast and in the sierra share certain similarities. Fortified villages generally occupy the top of high ridges within an hour's walk of arable land and water. The route of easiest access to such settlements was along the ridge crest that was characteristically defended by ditches and walls. Called *pukaras*, bastions and redoubts typically occupy the summits of steep-sided hills, and consist of one or more encircling walls with defensive parapets, stocks of sling stones and narrow entrances. Ditches and dry moats often provided additional exterior protection, while interior buildings and rooms varied in number and arrangement. Admirably designed to withstand raids and armed assault, such strongholds were later discovered by the Incas to be ill equipped to withstand long-term siege because most were far from water. Thus, we can conclude that the defensive works were primarily safeguards for short-term conflicts.

Yet not every hilltop sanctuary was a fort. The grandest of them all, Sacsahuaman, was a cloistered temple as no doubt was one of the earliest, Chankillo. Perched high on the side of the Casma Valley with dates of 342 and 120 BC, Chankillo looks like an Old World citadel, with two interior towers and *Plate 50* a rectangular compound of rooms encircled by three concentric perimeter walls each replete with masonry parapets, and narrow entrances backed by bulwarks. Although long thought to be a fort, the bar-holds for lashing and securing the exterior doors are all on the outside, not the inside, of the perimeter walls!

In the mountains behind the Viru, Moche, and Chicama valleys, a survey by Canadian archaeologists indicates that fortified villages and hilltop pukaras become conspicuous during the Early Intermediate Period. Coastal concerns with defense began somewhat earlier and exhibit potential correlations with the reclamation of arable land. Valley necks and pockets of canyon land were irrigated early, because they could be reached by relatively short canals. Fortifications are often more numerous and earlier in these settings than in lower valley areas reclaimed later by larger reclamation works. From a regional perspective defenses seem earliest in the smaller southern Casma, Nepeña and southern Santa valleys where fortifications appear during the Early Horizon. With some 40 hilltop strongholds, the Santa drainage has more ancient sanctuaries than any other valley. Although the valley is a well-watered coast-sierra corridor, arable terrain totals about half that in the Viru, and occurs as discrete canyon or valley-flank pockets irrigated by independent canal systems. During Cupisnique times, the canyon and upper valley supported five separate site clusters. Each contained small habitation sites, several platform mounds and from 1 to 12 nearby sanctuaries. Most remained in use during Salinar times *Plate 52* when settlement clustered in the same areas, although one new pocket of canyon land was opened to occupation.

Lest conflict be overemphasized, we must remember that not all hilltop sanctuaries were necessarily forts, and undefended residential settlements were the norm. In the Viru Valley, Salinar sites include several fortified hilltops, numerous dispersed households on flat lands, frequent agglutinated villages of 20 to 30 residences, small rectangular compounds enclosing a dozen or so interior rooms, and low mounds of collapsed adobe buildings. Comprising spacious courts, corridors, and rooms, an excavated example of the latter served as the residence and headquarters of local elites and their retainers, including metallurgists – indicated by the presence of copper slags and metalworking instruments in some compartments. This is significant, because the privilege of residing in adobe architecture and controlling metallurgical production became exclusive prerogatives of the coastal kuraka class.

Salinar bastions are not evident in the Moche Valley, where foundations for later city life were laid at the nascent urban center of Cerro Arena. Occupied by a 2.5-sq.-km sprawl of residential building, Cerro Arena is a rocky ridge that separates the southern middle, and lower valley. A small platform occupied the ridge top. The majority of other structures were made of stone and comprised simple households of several oval or rectangular rooms containing hearths, grinding stones, culinary ceramics, storage vessels, and food remains such as shellfish, guinea pigs, llamas, maize, and fruits. Where two roadways crossed the ridge on graded passes they were flanked by distinct concentrations of large, well-made masonry buildings that included the multi-room dwellings of the local elite. Elite ceramics included certain wares with striking resemblances to pottery from the Cajamarca region. There was certainly interaction with the sierra, but perhaps not of the bellicose nature postulated for the Nepeña and Casma region.

Gallinazo political constellations

Moche or Mochica art and architecture formed a great art style associated with a discrete ideology and distinct forms of socio-political organization. Singular styles were only formulated after the corporate bodies they served had come into existence, as is clear in Inca lore. Pachacuti consolidated the Titicaca region long before he returned to Cuzco as an old man and rebuilt the city in an imperial style. Because corporate formation precedes style formation, we must look to Gallinazo developments to understand the origins of Moche, and indeed the two cultures partially overlapped in time. Although Gallinazo is present in the Lambayeque region, its better studied manifestations are in the Río Viru and adjacent southern drainages.

Utilitarian ceramics, fired in an oxidizing environment, evolved out of Salinar antecedents, whereas Gallinazo elite wares employed a decorative tech-*Plate 53* nique known as 'negative' or 'resist' painting, in which vessels were ornamented with carbon smudge applied after undecorated surfaces were shielded with wax or a similar substance that burned off during firing. Gallinazo potters borrowed this technique from elsewhere to produce a relatively coherent style of elite ceramics. It reflects a high degree of consolidation within individual valleys. The broader distribution of the wares, from the Chicama to the Santa drainages, denotes shared aesthetic tastes, if not marriage or political alliances, among governing gentry.

By the first century BC, Gallinazo populations were undergoing dramatic growth sustained by the construction of large valley-neck canals, and large canals opening the lower valleys to farming and settlement. Indeed, agriculture expanded to its limits in smaller basins, and prehistoric population levels are thought to have peaked in the Viru and Santa drainages. All valleys included abundant, widespread, and varied types of sites. Settlement size was hierarchical. Numerous small farmsteads and hamlets gave way to progressively fewer but successively larger tertiary and secondary settlements which were overshadowed by a single primary center of exceptional dimensions. This situation is thought to reflect valley-wide systems of organization based at local primary centers.

Social distinctions in architecture had crystallized. Commoners were relegated to simple quarters with cane walls on stone footings. Masonry and cane was not eschewed by the elite, particularly in canyon settings with few alternative building materials, but adobe – the subsistence of Pacha Mama – was reserved for quarters of the kuraka class and for large buildings at corporate centers. Irrigation created soils suitable for producing mud bricks, and they became a hallmark of Gallinazo and later coastal monuments. Bricks were initially made by hand and varied in shape, but as corporate architecture regained the monumentality that had abated with the fall of the great U-shaped centers, construction of ever-bigger works soon led to the mass production of mold-made adobes. Fashioned from sturdy cane, four-sided molds were employed to turn out millions of bricks during the later phases of Gallinazo building activity. Mit'a-like labor organization is reflected in what is called 'segmented' construction. When an adobe platform is viewed from the side it can be seen that the distribution of bricks is not homogeneous. Instead, the mound looks like a vast loaf of sliced sandwich bread with distinct vertical seams separating tall slabs of bricks. Slabs are four or more adobes in width, and the bricks in them are mortared together, but contiguous slabs simply rest against one another and are not bonded. With potential antecedents in the mesh-bag fill of Preceramic platforms, segmentation is a means of subdividing construction projects into the same sort of repetitive modular units of work that characterized ancient canals and other corporate works on the coast right through to Inca times.

Gallinazo builders undertook enormous projects and the most dazzling reflect new notions about relations between huacas and mountains. Whereas old U-shaped centers were often aligned with and visually focused on a particular peak, now peaks were actually built upon in grand scale. These imposing works include vast terraced platforms perched high upon steep hillsides. One occurs at Licapa, a major center in Chicama. In the Moche drainage another flight of grand terraces was erected at Cerro Orejas, where settlement stretched for several km along a valley neck canal. Down-valley a second major Gallinazo center existed near Cerro Blanco, but this was built over and largely obscured when the area was transformed into the capital of the later Moche state. To the south the most famous and spectacular of Gallinazo huacas were perched directly atop isolated valley peaks and include the majestic 'Castillos' of Santa *Plate 54* and Tomaval. Surrounded by a 70-ha residential area accommodating more than 3,000 people, the Santa Castillo was the primary political center in the Santa drainage. In Viru similar numbers may have resided around the peak-top Huaca Tomaval, but the primary focus of elite residence was in the lower valley. Here the cultural type site is a concatenation of numerous mounds formed by collapsed adobe buildings scattered over a 4–5-sq.-km area. Known as the 'Gallinazo Group,' the poorly preserved standing structures are estimated to contain some 30,000 rooms and compartments, and modern farming has no doubt destroyed a multitude of ground-level buildings between the mounds. No Gallinazo center of comparable size survives elsewhere, leading scholars to propose that this was the regional political center of a loosely confederated realm. Alliances among coastal groups were likely fostered by dry times during the first centuries AD, which saw sierra people encroach on valley canyon lands held by Gallinazo populations.

Moche

Political transformations leading to more centralized governance arose during the late Gallinazo era as drought waned when the population at Cerro Blanco gained control over the Río Moche and then attained political integration with the much larger Chicama drainage. Linkages between the two valleys were probably forged less by conquest than by coalition through marriage and kin alliances among local kuraka, who then adopted a new corporate style, Moche, as their hallmark. Continuities in settlement patterns, monumental architecture, molded adobes, extended burials, and utilitarian ceramics point to uninterrupted cultural development, and late Gallinazo and early Moche remains are basically indistinguishable, except for their corporate art and ideology. From its heartland, the Moche polity spread down the coast and formed an archaic state stretching between the Ríos Chicama and Huarmey. The corporate ideology and art also spread up the coast, where it was adopted by a number of powerful señoríos that were loosely allied with the south.

The Moche capital. At Cerro Blanco the Moche capital reflects consolidated, albeit potentially dual, power expressed by two enormous platform mound complexes some 500 m apart. Built on the flanks of the white hill, Huaca de la Luna was the smaller and more southerly. Nearer to the river loomed the largest *Plate 56* structure of solid adobes ever erected in the Andes, Huaca del Sol. The great huacas demarcated the imperial nexus and defined the apex of a regional hierarchy of administrative monuments erected by the state in its provincial coastal valleys. On the flats between Sol and Luna, Peruvian and Canadian archaeologists are exposing the magnificent buildings and residences that flanked the main north–south avenues. Extended families resided together in discrete walled compounds with internal rooms and courts where people worked and lived. Some compounds were homes of crafts personnel who produced elite ceramics and fine arts, others were the residences of noble families. Yet little of the once-splendid metropolis survives above the ground due to a combination of El Niño floods and sand-dune inundations. Although the area of former occupation reaches depths of 7 m, the site now covers little more than 1 sq. km because the Spanish destroyed the entire western portion of the city when they diverted the Río Moche to hydraulically mine Huaca del Sol for its rich tombs.

Today the Huaca del Sol platform measures 340 by 160 m and stands over 40 m high. It is one of the two or three biggest mounds ever erected in the continent, even though less than half of the original monument survives. To judge from the remaining eastern portion, the plan of Huaca del Sol once formed a giant cross with its front to the north. In profile there were four sections creating step-like changes in height. The first and lowest section was the northernmost, which probably had a ramp leading to the summit. The second section was higher and considerably wider, and gave Huaca del Sol its cross-shaped configuration. The third section was by far the highest, and no doubt the most important. The lower fourth and final section had the smallest surface area. Spanish looting focused on the third section, where gaping holes were dug

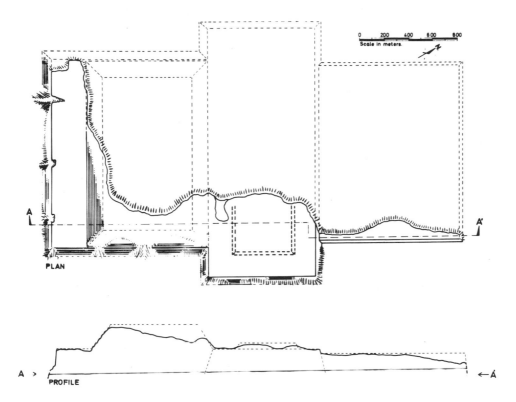

79 Shown in solid line, the intact remnant of Huaca del Sol suggests that the vast platform was originally cross-shaped.

before the river was diverted to undercut the mound and wash out its content. There is scant but important colonial documentation indicating that treasure was discovered during one or more of the large looting operations. This and other lines of evidence suggest that Huaca del Sol was the imperial palace and mausoleum for the heads of state.

Hydraulic mining cut a high profile down the length of Huaca del Sol and reveals information about how the great monument was built and used. Construction was in segments, and more than 100 million bricks were used. To avoid confusion each work-force impressed a single distinctive symbol or 'maker's mark' on the bricks it produced and laid up for its assigned section. More than 100 makers' marks are known and we can assume that an equal or greater number of communities supplied workers. Section two was built in eight stages of construction separated by episodes of use when summit rooms, courts, and corridor complexes were seats of activity. Some activities were rather mundane because refuse was allowed to accumulate on the floors of out-of-the-way rooms. A Phase I burial near the base of Sol, with the same north–south orientation as the mound, suggests that early stages of construction were underway by this time, while a Phase IV interment of a Moche couple

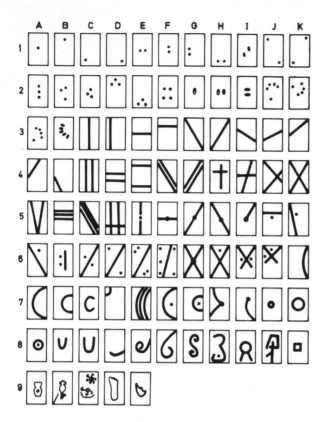

80 To account for their labor, different work forces impressed distinctive makers' marks on the millions of bricks produced to build the Moche capital.

atop the last construction stage indicates that building and use of the colossal monument spanned many generations.

Although contemporaneous with Sol, Huaca de la Luna differs in that it is a complex of three platforms that were once interconnected and enclosed by high adobe walls. Richly ornamented with polychrome murals, the northern mound was largely destroyed by looters. Recent excavations by Santiago Uceda and archaeologists from Trujillo, therefore, have focused upon the large central platform, and its small southern counterpart. The latter was built over the up-hill side of a prominent rock outcrop, leaving the high stony face exposed to viewers below. This was the ceremonial stage for rituals depicted in Moche iconography that show the mountain-top sacrifice of captive warriors whose mutilated bodies were then flung down hill. Below the outcrop platform archaeologists found more than a dozen corpses of mature males who had been dispatched by blows to the head and other violent acts, and then cast down to the ground which had been softened and muddied by a torrential El Niño downpour.

The large central platform of the Luna complex grew through multiple stages of use and construction, some of which were triggered by damage from El Niño rainfall events. Spacious summit courts were embellished with dazzling polychrome murals. The forward-facing head of a large supernatural with

Plate 60

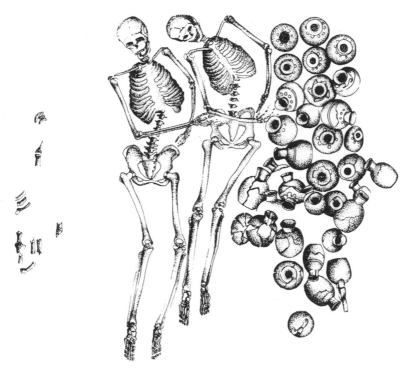

81 A man with llama bones at his side and a woman with Phase IV vessels were jointly interred atop section two of Huaca del Sol.

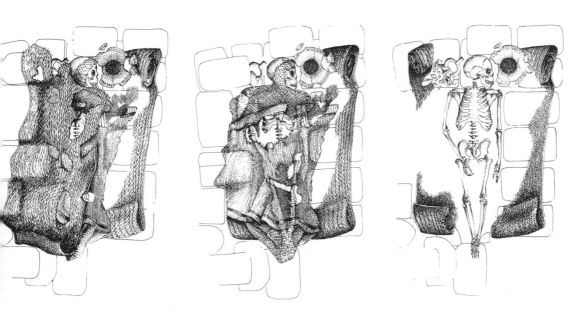

82–84 Burial within the bricks of an upper construction stage preserved mats and textiles accompanying a Phase III adolescent grave in section two of Huaca del Sol.

85 A mural motif from Huaca de la Luna.

marked canine teeth, called 'Ayapec,' was a recurrent motif, while other panels depicted spider-like creatures, anthropomorphic beings, and the parading of captive warriors. The richly ornamented courts were certainly sacrosanct settings for elaborate rituals that placated deities and maintained the social and cosmic order. Some high-status burials were interred in the Luna complex, yet it seems to have been primarily an imperial huaca adoratorio and home of the gods. Alternatively, Sol, with its dearth of murals, seems more of a huaca sepultura where the heads of state lived and were interred. Ultimately, it is difficult to prove, but tempting to see the two great monuments as reflecting dual organization at the apex of rule.

86 An anthropomorphic mural motif from Huaca de la Luna.

87 A fine line ceramic motif from the Moche Burial Theme depicts two figures using ropes to lower the coffin of an important lord while vultures dismember the corpse of a presumed healer accused of malpractice in the death of the lord.

As at other ancient capitals, Moche rulers invested substantial labor in opening new agricultural lands around their imperial metropolis. Where ancient planting surfaces survive, they reflect corporate land management, with fields laid out in a standardized manner and often divided into small rectangular plots of uniform size. Some field areas were replete with small adobe platforms that served as stations for supervisory personnel directing agricultural tasks. Working the fields was presumably an obligation or tax that the peasantry executed for the government, because there is little doubt that commoners and kurakas had become distinct classes.

Art and iconography. Fine arts were fully in the service of the political order and expressed a brilliant, often realistic, iconography that rationalized an ideology of kuraka rule and ritual. Highly symbolic and extremely standardized, Moche corporate style was expressed in many media, but it survives principally on ceramics and stirrup-spout libation vessels in particular. Most libation vessels were made in multi-piece molds. Standardization was apparently achieved by producing molds in the imperial heartland and shipping them to workshops in the political provinces. Potters lavished exceptional care upon the spouts of stirrup-spout libation vessels, and five different spout forms divide Moche art into five phases. Although the spout types were seemingly introduced sequentially, the initiation of a new shape did not preclude continued production and use of prior forms, particularly in the north. There were two different categories of spouted libation vessels. The first comprises three-dimensional forms, *Plates 61, 62* molded in highly naturalistic shapes depicting people, such as warriors, animals including felines and birds, and striking beings merging human and animal attributes that were certainly supernaturals. Among the most stunning of three-dimensional vessels are 'portrait heads' that painstakingly depicted the facial features of specific nobles. The other category comprises vessels with depictions painted in red-and-white clay slips as well as black negative or resist pigments carried over from Gallinazo technology. Beginning in Phase III, painting was done with progressively narrower brushes that culminated in magnificent *Plate 59* 'fine-line' depictions that invite comparison with Greek vase painting. Because fine-line paintings can portray many figures interacting, they provide our fullest record of iconographic characters and their behavior.

Revolutionary research on Moche arts and their mortuary associations by Christopher Donnan demonstrates that the iconography was a means of symbolic ideological communication based upon a limited number of themes. After about AD 300, the entire corpus of Moche art seems to revolve around fewer than two dozen themes or ideological stories. Similar to stories about the birth or the resurrection of Christ, the ideology being conveyed was likely analogous to that of scriptures in accounting for phenomena such as human origins, conflicts of good and evil, and proper behavior. Each Moche theme entailed a cast of characters that could include animals, humans, and supernaturals. Similar to a scene from a play, the characters interacted in repetitive manners, and some characters could appear in multiple scenes and themes and engage other players. In addition to being depicted graphically, themes were recounted orally, and acted out in regal pageants and in calendar rituals by elites made up and costumed to emulate the characters they portrayed.

The message and meaning of many themes are elusive, perhaps due to mythic content, but others are more tractable. One is clearly a burial theme recounting the demise and interment of a kingly figure in a coffin, while vultures consume a shaman apparently accused of malpractice relating to the deceased. The arts also depict human skeletal figures engaged in various activities sometimes assisted by living females who might have been mallquipavillacs. If claims of special ancestry descent justified kuraka rule, then elaborate concerns with death and the deceased seem expectable.

50 (above) Perched on a bedrock bluff above the Casma Valley, the Chanquillo fortress is surrounded by thousands of small quarry pits that supplied building stone.

51 (right) Gallinazo effigy vessel depicting a monkey.

52 (below left) A Salinar stirrup-spout vessel depicting a monkey.

53 (below right) Negative black painting decorates a Gallinazo vessel in the shape of a reed boat with a warrior at one end. The figure wears élite earspools and carries a distinctive club with a pike-like end and a pointed-disk mace head. This club form became a major Moche emblem.

Mounds and pyramids of the Early Intermediate Period

54 (left above) The hilltop Gallinazo Castillo in the Santa Valley is flanked by poorly preserved residential buildings.

55 (left below) Erected in the Nepeña Valley, the Moche administrative center of Panamarca reflected many of the architectural and iconographic features of the imperial capital. An adobe pyramid with a switch-back ramp towered over spacious courts and buildings ornamented with polychrome murals.

56 (above) Only one terraced side of Huaca del Sol ('Pyramid of the Sun') remained intact after colonial looters diverted the Río Moche to hydraulically mine the vast platform. Originally cross-shaped, Huaca del Sol was once the seat of Moche imperial government, and probably the burial place of Moche emperors.

57, 58 (*opposite and above*) *Frequent in Phase IV of the Moche sequence, portrait heads realistically depicted specific Moche individuals, probably nobles and leaders. The portraiture suggests that while rule was in the name of the gods, governance was identified with real people.*

59 (*right*) *A late Phase IV libation vessel, decorated with fine-line painting, depicts richly attired 'runners' or chaskis. Each runner carries a small bag in one hand, thought to contain beans.*

60 (*below*) *A polychrome mural of spider-like motifs ornamented a summit court at the site of Huaca de la Luna, close neighbor of Huaca del Sol in the Moche Valley.*

Moche art

Moche ceramics

61 (left) Holding a typical Moche mace-headed pike, this probably portrays a human disguised as a deer.

62 (below) A Moche vessel depicting a llama.

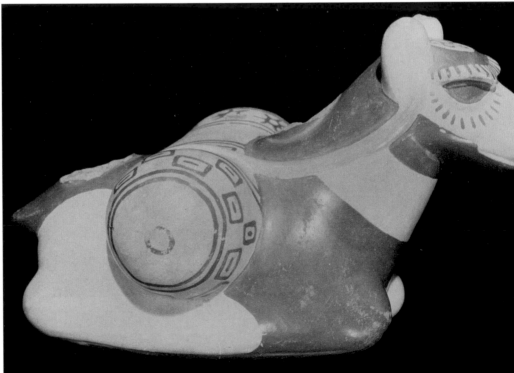

Sipan

63 (above) Flanked by dedicatory burials, the central coffin of Sipan's Tomb 1 held a 'Warrior Priest.' His many lavish garments and precious metal accompaniments constitute the richest unlooted tomb scientists have discovered in the Western Hemisphere.

64 (below) Inlaid with Ecuadorian Spondylus shell, this gold and copper feline head was one of a series in a majestic necklace looted from a royal Sipan tomb.

Moche crafts

65 (left) The emblem of Moche culture was a distinct mace-headed pike shown on the top of this vessel and carried by the painted warrior.

66 (below) Metal objects denoted status, and their manufacture was a highly sophisticated technique. Here, three metalworkers blow into tubes to sustain temperatures high enough for smelting in the dome-shaped kiln, while a fourth smith arranges the heated objects.

88 Two Moche warriors fighting: painting from a vase. Both hold maces with pointed staves. The victor, who has knocked off his opponent's helmet, holds him by the hair. He wears a shirt and helmet decorated with a design like a medieval coat of arms. The device on the left is a trophy of arms, which includes two maces, two darts and a square shield. Hummingbirds hover above.

A more common set of scenes pertains to one-on-one armed conflict among finely garbed kuraka warriors with the aim of capturing, not killing, opponents whose armor and attire were stripped and retained by the victor. The vanquished were then paraded about nude before being sacrificed. Because parading of nude captives is depicted in Huaca de la Luna murals, and in painted friezes at Huaca Cao Viejo at El Brujo in the Chicama Valley, while prisoner sacrifice is shown in murals at Pañamarca in the Nepeña Valley, it is likely that these ritual activities transpired at major Moche centers. Warrior combatants are almost always other Moche elites, and some portrait vessels depict specific individuals regally attired for combat, and then later stripped, bound, and awaiting ceremonial execution. Thus, ritual combat, and shedding one's blood and life for the good of the gods and society was, no doubt, an honorable demise.

Plates 57, 58

Important iconographic characters are individually set apart by singular head gear as well as distinctive attire and accoutrements, and it is revealing that some elite burials contain individuals with the same attire shown in the arts. The most noteworthy case is the 'warrior priest,' who is the main character in the 'sacrifice theme.' Entailing a large cast, iconographic action depicts slicing prisoners' throats, collecting their blood in a special goblet, parading of the vessel by a series of figures, including a priestess and a figure wearing an owl headdress, who then present the goblet to the impressively garbed warrior priest for his consumption. This paramount character is clearly represented among the richest unlooted tombs found in the hemisphere – those excavated by Walter Alva at Huaca Sipan in the Lambayeque drainage. In addition to dazzling funerary and much precious metal, deceased warrior priests were accompanied

Plates 63, 64

89 Defeated and stripped, vanquished warriors ascend the huaca of their noble victor in this drawing from a Moche vessel.

by a presentation goblet, as well as uniforms and headgear of the type depicted iconographically. The arts depict a spotted dog accompanying the warrior priest, and such an animal did indeed accompany the deceased. It is telling that in the Jequetepeque Valley Donnan has excavated several graves of women bedecked as the priestess of the presentation theme.

These opulent burials presumably represent a succession of individuals who held the important offices and positions defined in the iconography. We can reasonably conclude that art expressed the ideology of the kuraka nobility and defined the ranks of religious, political, and social hierarchy as well as the proper rites, rituals, and behavior of adherents. This was certainly the iconography of governing elites, because it never depicts the most fundamental of peasant activities, farming. Yet the depicted rituals of warrior bloodshedding were probably intended to placate Pacha Mama and maintain nature's productivity. It is doubtful that combat and blood sacrifice permeated everyday life. More likely, iconographic themes expressed ideological rituals that were scheduled and enacted over the course of an annual ceremonial calendar, much like the Incas' sacramental almanac.

Moche arts and interments clearly indicate that governance was in the hands of a kuraka class stratified by rank and role. Gentry holding high office, such as warrior priest or presentation priestess, were probably viewed as demigods because elite status, as in later times, was presumably justified by special creation myths that gave commoners humble origins and kurakas high origins to rule by divine right. This right was used to monopolize the fine arts and generate iconography, ideology, and ritual empowering of the nobility in an integrated manner that likely brought Gallinazo and other elites into the Moche fold.

Imperial hinterlands. On land, Moche archaeological remains are distributed from the Vicus section of the central Piura drainage in the far north, to the Río Huarmey in the south. At sea, Moche mariners established a far-flung island presence extending far down the coast to include the southern Chincha Islands. The proposition that these were the far-flung terrestrial and maritime frontiers of a single centralized state is now debated because Moche art and architecture functioned rather differently in the north from in the south. The best case for a unified state is one based at Cerro Blanco and reaching from the Río Chicama south through progressively smaller valleys down to Río Huarmey during Phase III and particularly Phase IV times. In most of these valleys the state erected a monumental administrative center of grand design. Reflecting architectural canons of the imperial capital, these seats of provincial government included Huancaco in Viru, Pampa de Los Incas in Santa, and Pañamarca in Nepeña. The last-named was ornamented with brilliant polychrome murals including a depiction of the presentation theme, and presentation rituals were probably enacted in the facilities.   *Plate 55*

Intriguingly, the Casma Valley was skipped over, but the Moche reasserted a limited presence some 70 km further south in the Huarmey drainage. It is doubtful that the Casma drainage was unconquerable, but the role of forced conquest versus voluntary conversion is much debated for Moche. All battles shown in the arts take place in uninhabited desert wilderness, never in settlements or around pukara fortifications. Indeed, pukaras are rare in the southern Moche realm, where people moved from former defensive settlements into open sites around mid- and lower-valley agricultural lands. In some valleys, such as Santa, the total amount of land occupied by dwellings decreased, perhaps reflecting a mitmaq-like resettlement policy that moved people to new locations. Nonetheless, for commoners a 'Pax Moche' prevailed as they toiled to support the kuraka nobility.

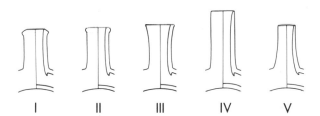

| I | II | III | IV | V |

90 Larco Hoyle employed five different spout forms of libation vessels to define five phases of Moche ceramic arts.

To the north, the nature of Moche was more varied. In the Vicus region Phase I and II ceramics make an early appearance, but the two spout forms remained in use until AD 600. Thus, the Vicus spouts must demarcate kin, class, or social affiliation that did not change for centuries but constituted conservative tradition that endured while later-phase vessels were being produced to the south. Perhaps Moche colonists reached the Piura drainage by sea and then settled Vicus, because Phase I and II vessels are rare or absent in the Lambayeque region. Here Phase III ceramics predominate at Sipan and elsewhere. One of the Sipan warrior-priest tombs has a date of AD 290, but burials including ceramics and other artifacts contain mixed attributes of several different phases. Therefore, while Sipan was certainly the center of a powerful Moche señorío, it did not march in lock step with Cerro Blanco even though elite ideology was shared. Further down the coast in the Jequetepeque Valley the picture is again mixed. Tombs at the sites of Pacatanamu and Dos Cabezas yield early Moche ceramics, but Phase IV is largely absent in spite of its predominance in the adjacent Chicama Valley. The great northern valleys also lack intrusive administrative centers such as Pañamarca.

Thus, if the magistrates at Cerro Blanco exerted political hegemony beyond the Río Chicama it entailed indirect rule at best. Indirect rule through local lords was a policy later used by both Chimor and Tahuantinsuyu in governing the northern demographic center of Andean civilization. Yet my impression of Moche is that the powerful northern señoríos were largely independent and formed only a loose confederation with the south by a vibrant ideology empowering kuraka rule. Although Moche may not constitute a single unified state it represents a remarkable evolution in statecraft, ranging from taxation and labor organization to art and ideology. For the first time the largest of coastal populations were united together by shared notions about the nature of rule and governance. Peace and prosperity were not enduring, however. Shortly before AD 600 nature turned pernicious, occasioning major upheavals that will be examined in the next chapter.

The central and south coasts

Early U-shaped monuments had their greatest frequency in the region between the Ríos Chancay to Lurin and, after the centers collapsed, corporate construction declined and became more variable as the complexion of life changed. After 400 BC, people started producing red, oxidized pottery decorated with white pigment. White-on-red ceramics from the Chancay Valley are known as 'Baños de Boza,' while 'Miramar' designates contemporary remains in the Chillon region. These are local mergers of folk and elite wares that shared a similar ceramic technology and, like Salinar in the north, they seem to reflect a time of transition and reorganization.

Lima

By about AD 200 a stronger focus of settlement and monumental construction emerged in the central Rimac Valley. Called the Lima culture, it is now beneath the modern city. The primary center was probably the Maranga complex, which included numerous adobe buildings as well as three sizable platforms. The principal huaca measured about 270 by 100 m and stood 15 m high, and was constructed of hand-made bricks. A number of extended burials have been excavated nearby. The bodies were normally extended and laid out in the same north–south orientation as the large platform. Most contained few accompaniments, but one elite individual lay on a cane litter and was accompanied by two dismembered human sacrifices. Growing out of the earlier white-on-red pottery tradition, Lima decorative ceramics employed black pigments as well as occasional negative painting, and fish and serpents with triangular heads were common decorative motifs.

The pottery was fairly widespread, and may reflect loose political linkages. It occurs in the Chancay region at Cerro Trinidad, where a long adobe wall painted in four colors was found, depicting an interlaced fish design as on the ceramics. In the Lurin Valley the local population clustered along short canals irrigating pockets of land in the canyon drainage at the beginning of the Early Intermediate Period. Gradually, longer canal systems were opened in down valley locations, and larger settlements arose nearby, as did elite residences on hilltops. Agricultural expansion into the lower valley facilitated the founding of Pachacamac, which is not far from the shore. This became a notable Lima center and also included elite residential compounds. Built over in later times, the core of the large 'Sun' huaca was probably erected at this time, as was the flanking 'Pachacamac Temple,' and another adobe platform exhibiting fish-motif murals. Numerous burials suggest that the center enjoyed sacrosanct status. Presumably the Pachacamac oracle came into existence at this time, and if so, the cult of the oracle and its priesthood endured for more than a millennium while petty kingdoms and great states rose and fell. Along with the Island of the Sun in Lake Titicaca, Pachacamac remained one of the most sacred places in the Inca realm until it was sacked by Pizarro's brother.

Nazca

A number of little streams converge at the base of the Andean foothills to form the small Nazca drainage, which never supported more than 25,000 people. Yet the by-gone inhabitants are famous for both their desert ground drawings and their vivid polychrome pottery as well as fine textiles. Although found along the coast between the Chincha and the Acari valleys, the core area of the ceramic style is the Ica and Nazca drainages. In the former valley, seated-flexed burials yield pottery accompaniments that form the master stylistic sequence of archaeological periods and horizons. Resin painting characterizes the earlier Paracas vessels style, while the onset of the Early Intermediate Period is defined by polychrome slip painting, which began around 200 BC, as the Early Horizon drought ended.

Plates 68–70

The polychrome ceramic tradition has been divided into eight epochs or phases. Nazca 1 preserved the mythical content of Paracas art, but introduced realistic subject matter in the form of birds, fish, and many kinds of fruit. Realism increased in Phases 2, 3, and 4, collectively called 'Monumental' because of bold but simple renditions of plants, animals, people, and demons against white or red backgrounds. Nazca 5 witnessed many innovations, including bodiless human heads and demon heads, as well as new vessel forms, and is known as 'Proliferous' because backgrounds are cluttered and filled in. Phases

91 A Nazca ceramic depiction of a demonic creature holding a trophy head.

92 A Nazca ceramic painting of a richly attired demonic being

6 and 7 retained earlier motifs while adding militaristic motifs and elite por-traits. At this time, some vessels exhibited design concepts similar to Moche ones, and cultural contacts may have come by way of the sea. Nazca 8 saw con-tinuing break-up of design motifs with human and demonic figures rendered in disjointed manners. Over time the trends toward elaboration and complexity conveyed a rich iconography, which was intelligible to its users but eludes us today. Unfortunately, radiocarbon assays on the Nazca sequence are character-ized as much by overlap as by sequential ordering. Although Phase 8 is estimated to end *c*. AD 600, there are seemingly associated dates of AD 755, or later. Thus, chronology remains a problem.

In addition to ceramics, Nazca is renowned for its textiles, and its core valleys have yielded more fine fabrics than any other region of Peru. Growing out of the sophisticated Paracas tradition, the technical characteristics of Nazca textiles were more precocious than those occurring in areas to the north. Textiles were the media of stylistic innovation and new motifs appeared on fabrics before ceramics. Although local use of camelid hair began early, massive quantities of alpaca wool now came into use. The north coast did not witness comparable expenditures of wool for almost a thousand years. Cultural esteem of wool, along with burials in a seated position, link Nazca with the south highland sphere of influence. The source of coastal wool must have been sierra herds, probably from the Ayacucho region which enjoyed close relationships with the coastal communities.

The corporate style was remarkably vibrant for a region characterized by small to moderate drainages and modest populations. The Río Nazca is formed by eight short drainages that cut across a wide, flat coastal pampa and then converge 35 km inland to form a single channel leading to the sea. In three cases, surface runoff disappears at a midpoint where drainages first leave the foothills. Moisture then flows under the stream beds as they begin to cross the pampa, but reappears as surface runoff down channel. Limited runoff restricted farming to the upper regions of individual drainages and resulted in a series of separate oases rather than an agriculturally unified valley. Habitation sites and small villages were frequently located on terraced hillsides adjacent to irrigated floodplains. The separate areas of surface flow were reclaimed early on and settlements clustered along the drainages above and below their dry midpoints during the first four Nazca phases. In the succeeding phase settlement distributions changed markedly in apparent response to short but severe drought that began in AD 560. People moved up some tributaries to elevations above 1,000 m, seeking more reliable water supplies. Yet along the Río Nazca itself settlements arose in normally dry sections of the drainage where there is little surface flow, but subsurface water is not deep. Because many El Niño floods have scoured the river channel, we do not know for certain how Phase 5 populations went about extracting subsurface moisture for drinking and farming in this section of the river. While sunken gardens were perhaps excavated down to the water table, some scholars propose that long tunnels were dug back into the aquifers. Similar to Near Eastern qanats, the gently sloping tunnels could have channeled flow down their course to surface impoundment tanks that sourced canals. In other valleys, however, there is scant evidence of such tunneling technology until Spanish times.

Early on, Nazca influence spread north to the Pisco Valley and the Phase 2 site of Dos Palamos, a settlement of densely compacted, contiguous rooms grouped around five separate plazas. To the south, influence reached Tambo Viejo in the Acari Valley before the end of Phase 3. This era of regional importance coincides with the florescence of Cahuachi, the short-lived Nazca 'capital' located on the south bank of the Río Nazca 50 km inland.

Cahuachi was unlike the Moche capital of Huacas Sol and Luna and more akin to the Casma Sechín complex, because the Nazca center comprised 40 mounds scattered along a riverside area of c. 150 ha. Virtually all were built during Phase 3 according to studies by Peruvian, Italian, and American investigators, which show that many people visited the site but few resided there permanently. The largest mound, the 20-m-high 'Great Temple,' encased a natural hill with a facade of elongated, wedge-shaped adobes. A spacious basal enclosure contained rooms, courts, and a spacious 47 by 75 m plaza. Labor for this monument came from many groups who also erected their own separate facilities, consisting of a kancha enclosure with a prominent mound. Of varying size, the platforms were adobe facades encasing trash piled up over natural hills. The trash in each contains abundant decorated sherds, because the garbage came from ritual feasting and drinking in the adjacent enclosure. Thus, mound size commemorated ceremonial lavishness, a practice found at the later Chimu trash-mound center of Pacatanamu. Some Cahuachi platforms held elaborate textiles stored in large vessels, while others housed well-to-do graves.

93 A Nazca geoglyph or ground drawing of a monkey.

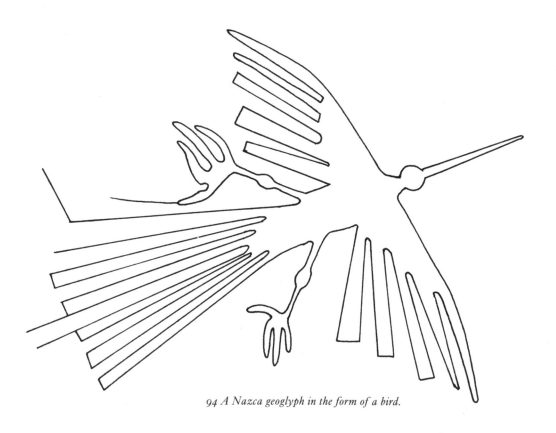

94 A Nazca geoglyph in the form of a bird.

95 A killer-whale depicted on a Nazca ceramic.

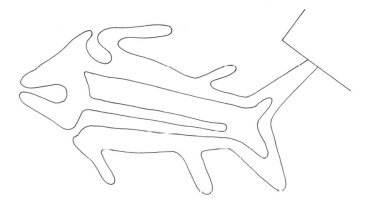

96 A Nazca geoglyph in the form of a killer whale.

If platforms reflect politics, the contrasts between the Moche and Nazca speak of centralized rule versus confederacy perhaps akin to a maximal or mountain ayllu. Cahuachi gives the impression that every parcialidad or kin group participating in the confederation asserted its identity by erecting a separate mound complex. The paucity of domestic quarters and refuse leads Helaine Silverman, who has studied the site, to suggest that the center was built and used by people who, by and large, lived elsewhere. People residing along the separate Nazca drainages presumably came together at Cahuachi on a cyclical basis to conduct rituals and carry out common business. Cahuachi seems to have maintained a highly sacred and ceremonial character that overshadowed concerns of mundane rule. Corporate construction declined dramatically at the end of Nazca 3, and in the following phase, the center was transformed into a great mortuary ground and place of votive offerings. Its status as a special burial place persisted long after Nazca times and resulted in horrendous looting of the ancient capital.

Nazca is particularly famous for its desert markings and ground drawings that occupy the pampa flats between the river's tributaries. Called 'geoglyphs,' ^{*Plate 67*} the markings were created by brushing away and removing the upper, dark, oxidized desert sediments to expose lower, lighter-colored surfaces. Experiments by Anthony Aveni and a small team of co-workers indicate that 16,000 sq. m of desert pavement can be cleared in about a week's time. Therefore, very large figures could have been created by relatively small crews. Created at many different times, geoglyphs are widely but sporadically distributed along the Andean coast, and occur from the Lambayeque region into northern Chile.

There are at least two broad categories of glyphs. One consists of figures rendered on hillsides so that they were readily visible to passers-by. Akin to billboards, these markings often depict humans, llamas, or other life forms as well as occasional geometric or abstract symbols. Occurring on flat, horizontal plains, the second category of compositions seems to have served as ritual pathways. In the Moche area I discovered a geometric line that issued directly out of the entrance of a small hut, and the figure was certainly intended to be walked on. Cleared sections of the desert are discernible at ground level, but very large compositions and long, flat lines cannot be seen in their entirety. It was only through the study of aerial photographs that Paul Kosok and Maria Reiche first discovered the exceptional concentration of glyphs on the 200-sq.-km pampa flats of Nazca. There are some early hillside figures, but the dominant compositions are flat-land forms, including 1,300 km of straight lines of varying widths, and lengths reaching 20 km or more, and 300 geometrical figures consisting mostly of trapezoids, triangles, zigzags, and spirals. Together, the linear and geometric figures cover a staggering 3.6 million sq. m, or about 2 percent of the pampa surface.

Archaeoastronomer Anthony Aveni and a team of anthropologists conducted the most systematic and extensive study yet of pampa geoglyphs and failed to find either statistically significant celestial correlations or directional correlations. However, lines were often found to radiate out from hills or high vantage points, called ray centers. Some 62 such nodes were mapped and shown to be interconnected by long, linear geoglyphs thought to be trans-pampa pathways leading from one irrigated oasis to another. Glyphs are most numerous near irrigated, settled land where younger ones regularly cross older ones, indicating that the creations were used briefly and then forgotten about. Elongated trapezoidal figures measure 40 by 400 m on average, and near river courses their skinny ends point up stream about two-thirds of the time, suggesting symbolic connections with water flow. There are about three dozen animal drawings, comprising birds, several killer-whales, a monkey, a spider, a probable fox or llama, at least one human, and a few plants. Most are small and confined to a corner of the pampa near where people lived. Unlike trapezoids these are not 'solid' compositions with cleared interior surfaces, but outlines formed by a single narrow line. The line never crosses itself and has separate starting and end points, as if the figure was intended to be walked.

Geoglyphs at Nazca and elsewhere certainly served more than one function. Calendrical significance for the lines has been suspected, but not yet demonstrated. The great concentration of figures on the Nazca pampa represents by far the largest cultural artifacts of the region's ancient inhabitants. Similar to the many mounds at Cahuachi, they are numerous and impressive, but do not represent great expenditures of energy. Although the geoglyphs are technically similar, each seems to have been created separately, used for a time, and then forgotten. New figures cross old ones in amazing profusion, and the works were obviously not part of a larger, centralized conception planned by one mind at one time. As with mounds at the capital, one is left with the impression of confederated beliefs, and while everyone agreed that geoglyphs were important, each group erected its own. Thus, individuality – with cultural coherence, but without large-scale or integrated power – were Nazca hallmarks.

The sierra

Moche and Nazca had important and often powerful neighbors in the mountains. Much of the sierra was occupied by dispersed, rural inhabitants, but sizeable populations clustered in the highland basins. Refinement of High Montane adaptations facilitated a northward thrust into the Ecuadorian sphere of tropical-influenced sierra populations, known as Kuelap. These colonized mountain settings were in a sense more tropical than Andean. Kuelap is represented by mighty masonry ruins perched high atop hills shrouded with tropical vegetation in the modern Department of Amazonas. Many of the buildings were circular, and important corporate structures were ornamented with masonry reliefs of geometric and zoomorphic figures. The nature of Kuelap political organization has not been established, but the economy was based on the exploitation of vertically stratified ecological zones, with llamas herded in high pasturelands and crops ripened in the humid valley bottoms.

To the southeast in higher mountains, Cajamarca archaeological remains occur in the lush sierra basin of the same name. They are largely represented by a long, five-phase ceramic tradition characterized by the use of kaolin paste to produce fine white vessels painted in red, black, or orange. Phase 2 is broadly contemporary with Moche. Reflecting either verticality or trade, the pottery frequently occurs at Moche sites in the lower Jequetepeque Valley. Later in time, it reached the Ayacucho and Cuzco basins, indicating that the white ware was much esteemed. Although Cajamarca ceramics reflect a distinct corporate style, it has yet to be associated with sizeable monuments indicative of political power as in the neighboring Crisnejas Basin.

Marcahuamachuco

A robust sierra polity or confederacy arose in the Crisnejas Basin, due east of the Río Moche, during the Early Intermediate Period. Perched high atop a commanding hill, its capital of Marcahuamachuco is one of the greatest of highland monuments. Research by a Canadian archaeological mission reveals that the center arose in association with economic and demographic changes during the century after the AD 1–200 drought. As conditions improved new lands were cultivated, local populations grew, and commerce increased along a sprawling network of roads, around which many settlements clustered. Marcahuamachuco was adjacent to a major north–south highway that facilitated 'horizontality' and interchange along the elevated mountain chain. An outlying hierarchy of administrative centers controlled roads descending along the western slopes of the Cordillera reflecting concerns with verticality, a folk adaptation politicized by the rise of the kuraka class and powerful coastal señoríos governing sierra access to lowland resources.

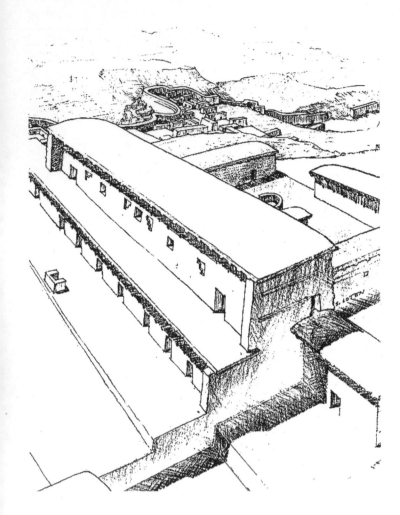

97 An architectural reconstruction of a two-story gallery at Marcahuamachuco.

Long, narrow buildings, called galleries, are the hallmark of corporate architecture in the region. Construction of such edifices began before 200 BC in the Crisnejas Basin and then underwent a long evolution. In some galleries interior floor space was left open, creating great halls. In others, internal cross walls formed rooms and compartments. Early one-story forms gave rise to very long, multi-storied galleries at the capital, where building began around AD 300.

Marcahuamachuco's many tall buildings created an imposing city visible from vast distances, because it was perched atop a high, slim, steep-sided plateau 3.5 km long. Monumental masonry construction began at the northwest end of the plateau then shifted to the central section and elaborate southern 'Castillo' region by AD 500, where building activity continued for another three centuries. Circular galleries, including the five-storied Castillo, are among the most striking buildings. They enclosed a central area, filled with other buildings and courts. Built on an elevated platform, the Castillo fronted a great plaza paved with stones and bounded by long rectangular galleries. Ornamented with niches, the massive walls of rectangular galleries framed great halls measuring

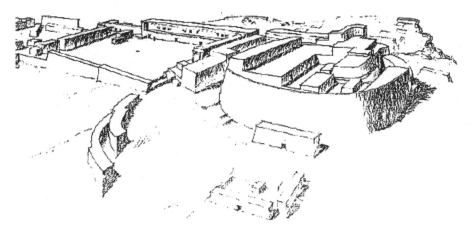

98 A reconstruction of the five-story oval Castillo that crowned the Marcahuamachuco mesa.

up to 8 by 48 m. As with Inca kallanka halls, these were seats of elite festivities and rituals which the Canadian investigators believed focused upon the deceased and ancestor veneration. Indeed, the political fabric of the city may have been woven around important progenitors interred above ground in mausoleums and chulpa-like towers scattered about the ruins. Nonetheless, people did reside in the ground floors of long curvilinear galleries often erected along the edge of the steep plateau.

Within a 10-km radius of Marcahuamachuco, there are more than half a dozen other monumental centers with similar large galleries and elite architecture. This concatenation of subsidiary sites reflects yet another imperial landscape different from Moche's, where almost all monumental construction was concentrated at the Moche capital. Significantly, Cerro Amaru, the satellite center closest to the sierra capital, seems to have served religious purposes. Votive offerings found in three elaborate reservoirs suggest that observances included ritual manipulation of water. The Marcahuamachuco sierra state was long-lived, and we will return to its political fortunes in the next chapter.

Recuay

Recuay is a vibrant corporate style found in the Callejon de Huaylas and the headwaters of the Río Santa. It is known primarily from looted collections of fine ceramic vessels generally made of white kaolin paste. Decoration employed negative painting, positive painting, and three-dimensional modeling. It is reminiscent of the Moche corporate style both in technical mastery and in portraying a standardized, repetitive iconography. There is a strong emphasis on men in arms, often bearing trophy heads. In some cases, a prominent male is accompanied by one or more female figures. Serpents, felines, and condors are common motifs and probably had supernatural connotations. Double-headed serpents, two-headed animals, and dragon-like creatures certainly had such significance.

Plate 71

Two types of stone sculptures were produced. One, a Chavín carry-over, comprised tenon heads for ornamenting important buildings. These are often realistic male heads presumed to be kuraka warriors. None have been found in their original positions, nor have any freestanding sculptures of human form, which comprise the other category of stonework. Analysis of the statues by Richard Schaedel suggests that production began early and led to two phases of *Plates 72, 73* Recuay works. Both are characterized by squat figures, about a meter tall, with oversized heads. About a third of the examples are women, while the males often carry clubs, shields, or trophy heads.

Looted long ago, important elite were interred in subterranean mausoleums, roofed with large slabs and covered with earth. At Willkawain they resemble subterranean houses with several rooms or crypts. One masonry chamber was about 1 m in height and width, and 7 m in length. Entered through the roof via a shaft, intruders had rifled the crypt leaving but a few fragmentary offerings. At the hilltop site of Pashash, Terence Grieder and Alberto Bueno excavated a much less elaborate tomb that contained 277 fine items distributed among three offering deposits. The deceased was a poorly preserved adult who must have been flexed, because the body was placed in a masonry niche built beneath the southernmost chamber of a small, three-room shrine. A large offering of magnificent vessels, figurines, jewelry, earspools, and other objects was placed on a cloth in front of the niche. A second offering of 66 ceramic and stone vessels was placed on a cloth at the doorway to the interment chamber. The chamber floors were then filled in, covering both deposits, and during the filling another offering was made. Although this included an axehead and some jewelry, it contained many vessels ritually smashed and scattered about. More fill was added and then capped with a flagstone floor. Finally, an elevated, rectangular altar was erected in the chamber above the tomb. One must wonder if the edifice was not an ancestral shrine, containing the entombed founding figure.

The shrine was but one aspect of a much larger complex of monumental architecture at Pashash, for many masonry buildings occupied the hill, including the impressive 'Caseron' which stood 15 m high and created a great platform terrace 30 m in width. The modern town of Cabana now surrounds the hill and there are indications that the settlement covers extensive ruins. There is no question that Pashash was a major Recuay center, but it is not clear yet if it constituted a capital, or one of a series of more or less equally important centers.

Recuay ceramics frequently appear at Moche settlements in the lower Santa and adjacent valleys, and it is clear that Recuay and Moche elites were exchanging corporate arts because Moche tombs have been found with Recuay vessels. This points to a higher order of interaction than folk-level verticality alone.

Huarpa

The most important archaeological manifestations in the Ayacucho Basin during the period are called Huarpa, named for the local river with which these sites are associated. The Huarpa evidence indicates a señorío associated with a rather loosely integrated corporate style beginning *c*. AD 200 and ending four centuries later. The principal decorative technique consisted of red and black painting on a white-slipped surface. Motifs began with simple forms, becoming more complex over time. They reflect marked Nazca influence, and a strong symbiotic relationship apparently linked the two populations. Huarpa people probably supplied wool, if not copper and other minerals, to their coastal counterparts, who reciprocated with salt, marine products, and other lowland produce.

The Huarpa homeland is arid and characterized by deep ravines and broken surfaces with little flatland. Where rainfall alone sustains agriculture Andean folk farm remarkably steep terrain, but it is difficult to irrigate steep terrain because water and erosion become unruly. As a consequence, sloping surfaces are terraced. Both terracing for residential purposes and canal-based farming were Preceramic in origin, and could have arisen independently in different settings. But their combination is expensive because both require substantial labor investments. Thus, steep slopes requiring terraced irrigation were the last agrarian niche that people sought to reclaim.

Huarpa people were among the first to reclaim steep slopes and they employed terraces for both irrigated and dry farming. Their hillside reclamation works were corporate undertakings. Contour terraces were laid out and erected as integrated flights of farmland, each narrow but long step being of equal length, and some flights had as many as 100 terraces from the top of a hill to the valley below. Some terraces may have been irrigated from cisterns that caught runoff from rainfall. In other cases springs fed chains of small reservoirs situated at different levels supplying different terraces. Surviving examples of Huarpa canals are several kilometers long, have widths of up to 1.6 m, and show evidence of impermeable clay linings.

Terraced agriculture supported a large, but scattered population represented by some 300 sites, most of which were small communities and dispersed farmsteads. There was a preference for residing on hilltops near arable land. Rural houses were built of irregular stonework and tended to be one or two-room affairs of circular or elliptical form. They differ from much of the architecture at Nawimpukyo, the presumed capital of the Huarpa people. This was an urban center that occupied a hilltop overlooking the modern town of Ayacucho. Buildings in the urban core are characterized by 'H-type' masonry, which comprised large, narrow rocks set vertically apart in rows with courses of smaller stone filling the intervening spaces. The center of the settlement was occupied by several platforms, on both sides of which were groups of aligned administrative buildings, spacious courts and patios, and elite residences. Fed by springs, a canal system ran through the center and supplied residents with water. Nawinpukio is not an imposing governmental center, but it laid important political and agrarian foundations for empire-building during the Middle Horizon.

Southern basins

Further south in the sierra there is little evidence of hillside terracing during the Early Intermediate Period, and large political centers have not been found. A dispersed occupation characterizes the Andahuaylas Basin. Here ridge tops wcre the preferred sites for small villages and hamlets. The settlements lack defensive walls, and warfare is not in evidence. Reflecting the exploitation of dispersed habitats, sites were strategically situated at intermediate altitudes below the tuber-growing zone, but above deep valley floors where maize is grown. Herding is indicated by both camelid burials and clay models of camelids. Thus, the occupation is thought to reflect verticality. Operating at a folk level, this apparently entailed relatively localized movement within the Andahuaylas region, because exotic goods from distant lowlands are not in evidence.

A similar Early Intermediate Period adaptation seems to characterize the Cuzco basin in the upper Urubamba drainage. Whereas earlier Marcavalle Phase sites were on the valley floor, Chanapata Phase settlements occupy somewhat higher altitudes. This suggests that they were intermediate residential bases for the exploitation of higher and lower ecological zones.

The altiplano

The sprawling altiplano around Lake Titicaca formed the southern demographic pole of Andean civilization where ideological integration first stirred in art and iconography of the Yaya-Mama tradition. The flowering of Pukara brought a degree of political integration at the north end of the lake, but the site succumbed to drought during the first centuries AD. To the south, a contemporary settlement arose, weathered dry times, and then gradually matured into the great center that would unite the cradle of high-altitude civilization. Ever since *conquistador* Cieza de León visited Tiwanaku in 1549, the imposing ruins and sensational stonework of this extraordinary city have fascinated explorers and tourists alike. The colossal monument looms out of the annals of antiquity as the highest capital of an ancient empire that the world has ever known.

Tiwanaku

Plates 74–85

Situated some 15 km east of the lake on a small river, Tiwanaku's urban core of monumental edifices and great stelae was once encircled by a shallow moat beyond which sprawled up to 10 km of adobe residential compounds, houses, and refuse. The city and its agrarian hinterland were most recently investigated by a team of archaeologists from Bolivia, Mexico, and the U.S. Radiocarbon dates reaching back to 400 BC mark the beginnings of a long five-phase occupation, which remained unpretentious until large architectural and agrarian construction projects were initiated during Phase 3 (*c.* AD 100–375), and then were further expanded in the succeeding Classic Tiwanaku era of Phase 4 (*c.* AD 375–600/700). During Phase 4 the metropolis began to attain regional hegemony, and established a hierarchy of administrative centers around the south end of the lake. Phase 5 saw the founding of far-flung colonies and caravanserai, spreading Tiwanaku influence down the Cordillera into the Chilean altiplano. The Titicaca empire then saw its fortunes decline as protracted drought set in around AD 1100 and the metropolis collapsed shortly thereafter.

67 *Seen from the air, Nazca ground drawings are linear. They are thought to have served as ritual walkways.*

Nazca: a culture of the south coast

68 (left) A Nazca vessel depicting a trophy head whose lips are pinned shut with thorns.

69, 70 (below) A grave excavated in the Nazca capital, Cahuachi, yielded these vessels. One depicts hummingbirds, and the other, decorated with painted peppers, held peanuts.

Recuay

71 (right) A polychrome Recuay vessel of a feline clutching a man. The man's earspools denote high status.

72, 73 (below left and right) Stone Recuay statues.

74 (above) A gateway lintel shows a jaguar with a collar and leash. Tiwanaku depictions of collared felines indicate that the animals were kept as pets.

75 (right) A classic Tiwanaku polychrome vessel with feline and geometric motifs.

76 (below) A monolithic model of a Tiwanaku sunken court with three flights of steps, and sockets for gateways.

Tiwanaku: south highland capital

77 (top) A tenon head ornamenting the sunken court at Tiwanaku.

78 (above) A wooden spoon handle depicting a winged figure carrying a staff. Possibly carved by artisans at Tiwanaku, it was found in the Moquegua Valley.

79 (right) This half of the Thunderbolt Stela, with a central frog motif, was found at Tiwanaku. The other half was discovered at the opposite end of Lake Titicaca.

Tiwanaku: south highland capital

80 (above) Monolithic stairs lead up to the Kalasasaya gateway, beyond which stands the Ponce Monolith.

81 (below) The Ponce Monolith depicts a richly attired figure holding a beaker and short scepter.

82 (opposite above) Carved from a single block of stone, the Gateway of the Sun is no longer in its original architectural context.

83 (opposite below) Detail of the Gateway God.

84 (above) Found in the Moquegua Valley, this Tiwanaku vessel portrays a mustached individual.

85 (below) Depicting an elderly man, this is an unusually realistic ceramic portrait for imperial-style Tiwanaku.

The urban core. Cieza de León reported that the ruined megalopolis was dominated by a man-made hill of enormous size erected upon massive stone foundations. This is our earliest account of the Akapana, the largest structure at the capital and the southernmost of great Andean platforms. Standing over 15 m high, and measuring roughly 200 m on a side, the flat-topped mound was 'T'-shaped and widest in its eastern front. In the center of the flat summit, surrounded by stone buildings, there was a prominent sunken court. Excavations on the platform sides revealed that it was terraced with mammoth stone-faced retaining walls and rose in six successively smaller steps. The two basal walls were built of cyclopean sandstone blocks several meters on a side, whereas higher retaining walls were of smaller and finely finished andesite blocks. The summit and sunken court were drained by a complex system of conduits that carried runoff to vents along the terrace tops. This allowed water to cascade freely down the platform sides in dazzling imitation of a moisture-giving apu mountain. At the base of one terrace wall a large cache of elegant kero beakers had been deliberately smashed and then covered over. Near the basal terrace dozens of dismembered male bodies were interred, the apparent victims of sacrifice.

Surrounding the great mound the eroded topography is characterized by low rises and shallow depressions of unexcavated courts and other buildings. To the east the partially explored 'Kantatayita' is a minor rise with a jumble of big slabs. It has a majestically carved stone lintel of a regal gateway and a great stone maquette of a rectangular sunken court, replete with staircases and sockets for miniature stone portals. A sunken court, measuring about 30 m square, flanks the Akapana 200 m to the west. The court walls were ornamented with numerous tenoned heads depicting males or human skulls. A large collection of stelae were once set in the court floor, including the 'Bennett' monolith, the largest known Andean stela. Rendered in Classic Tiwanaku style it depicts an elegantly garbed human figure, probably a potentate or a god, holding a kero in one hand and baton-like object in the other. Other stelae in the court and elsewhere at the site are not always Tiwanaku-style carvings. Indeed, half of one monolith, known as the Thunderbolt Stela, was found at the city and the other half at the north end of Lake Titicaca. We can reasonably conclude that imperial policies included holding subject peoples' sacred or ancestral objects hostage at the capital.

Due west of the sunken court, and aligned with it, monolithic stairs surmounted by a prominent gateway provided access to the spacious summit of the 'Kalasasaya' platform. Here a central court holding the Classic 'Ponce' monolith was framed by a northern and southern row of small, one-room buildings. Measuring more than 100 m square, and standing about two stories high, the exterior Kalasasaya walls exhibit massive H-type masonry with finely cut small blocks filling the spaces between gargantuan vertical slabs. Directly west, at ground level, the 'Putuni' rectangular building complex has been interpreted as a palace compound where the rulers of Tiwanaku resided. Sections of finely carved water conduits occur in this precinct and the others mentioned above.

Plate 76

Plate 77

Plate 79

Plates 80, 81

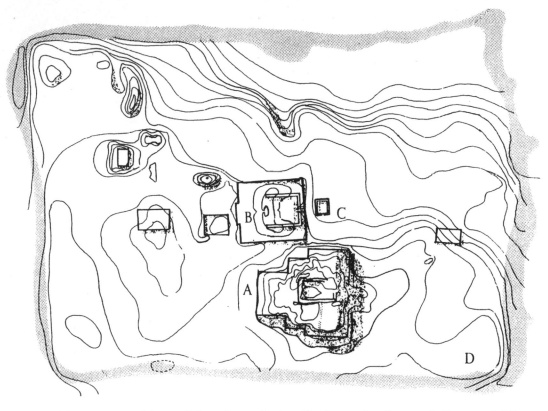

99 The civic-ceremonial core of Tiwanaku was dominated by the towering Akapana platform mound (A), which was flanked by the much lower Kalassaya platform (B) and fronted by the ornate semi-subterranean court (C) with its multitude of stelae.

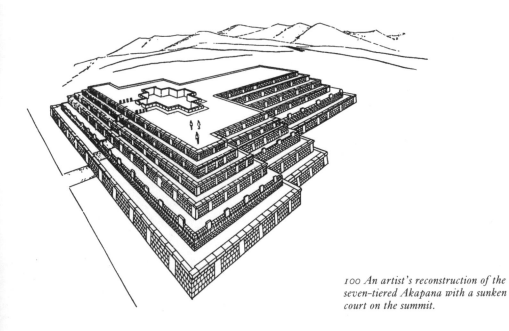

100 An artist's reconstruction of the seven-tiered Akapana with a sunken court on the summit.

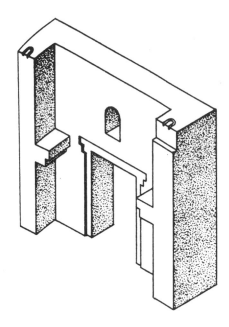

101 The Pumapunku platform was graced with monolithic gateways.

While they certainly served functional ends, the lavish amount of effort expended on them suggests that ritual manipulation of water was important.

About a kilometer away, the very finest andesite and sandstone block masonry, along with exquisitely carved gateway fragments, are found at the 'Pumapunku' platform. Standing 5 m high and measuring 150 m square, the front of the platform had a majestic megalithic facade with two or three separate stairways leading to an equal number of grand portals individually carved from single slabs of andesite weighing tons. Behind the gateways lay a sunken court that has yet to be excavated.

Among its many stunning architectural features Tiwanaku exhibits an unprecedented elaboration of ritual gateways represented by multitudes of stone lintels, both plain and decorated. The latter generally depict paired beings converging from each end of the lintel on the center in tinku-fashion. They reflect a long evolution that culminated with great portals rendered from single blocks of rock. The largest monolithic entry is the Gateway of the Sun, which

Plate 74

Plates 82, 83

102 Bas-relief motifs comprising the border of the Gateway of the Sun design panel.

103 Expressing Tinku convergence, the Gateway of the Sun depicts winged staff-bearing 'angels' converging upon the central dual-staff-bearing deity on top of a three-tiered platform.

is also the most complex statement of Tiwanaku iconography. The top of the portal is ornamented with an incised frieze of figures that converge upon a large, dominant central character called the 'Gateway God.' Standing atop a triple-tiered platform, this forward-facing anthropomorphic figure wears an elaborate headdress with 19 ray-like projections ending in circles or puma heads. Garbed in a decorative necklace, tunic, and kilt, it is singularly significant that the deity holds two vertical staffs that terminate in condor heads. Dual vara leave little doubt that the Gateway God is a resurrection and revitalization of the old Chavín Staff God, the supreme synthesizer of dual organization. On the sun portal, arranged in three horizontal rows one above the other, smaller, winged attendants converge upon the central deity from each side of the gate. Depicted in profile, the attendants have either human or avian heads and each marches toward the center of the portal in rich attire carrying a vertical staff of office. As with the black-and-white portal of Chavín, we can reasonably infer that a millennium later the Gateway of the Sun was the focal point of tinku rituals uniting the two halves of society in a cosmic whole. In overview, Tiwanaku and the altiplano were seemingly much more conservative and traditional in their ideology whereas Moche and the coast reflect a more secular and kuraka-oriented ideology.

Agrarian hinterland. In the northern Titicaca Basin the Tiwanaku occupation consisted of enclaves among local people, but Tiwanaku blanketed the south, where the empire invested heavily in improving agricultural yields and opening new farmland as a means of banking labor taxes. Hillside terracing was of little interest. Instead, reclamation focused upon the construction of ridged fields in flat, low-lying areas particularly around the lake margins. Because ridged fields require high-water-table conditions and substantial runoff, most of Tiwanaku's agrarian expansion came after AD 200 as drought gave way to normal and then abundant rainfall. Large-scale reclamation has been studied on a vast, lakeside plain called Pampa Koani, where the agrarian enterprise was managed by a hierarchy of state-controlled sites. Two major centers occupied the apex of the Koani administration, Pajchiri to the north of the pampa, and Luqurmata on the south. The latter had a long folk occupation before it became an administrative node complete with monumental masonry buildings, stone-faced platforms, sunken courts, and stelae. Scattered about the pampa were smaller centers, and multitudes of little mounds serving farmsteads dispersed among the fields.

Caravans, colonies, and outposts. Tiwanaku relied on an agropastoral economy that integrated farming and camelid herding. Although herds supplied food and fiber, llamas were the pack animals for great caravans moving commodities over long treks vertically up and down the mountain flanks and horizontally deep into Chile. Interpretation of the far-flung distribution of Tiwanaku arts and artifacts is influenced by views about the nature of its political organization. Some authorities argue for centralized, Inca-like organization, while others propose segmentary organization akin to a maximal or mountain ayllu with multitudes of internal hierarchies. Tiwanaku goods clearly moved beyond its political frontiers in the case of San Pedro de Atacama, a Chilean oasis in the salt puna some 800 km from the altiplano capital, a month-and-a-half caravan travel time. Here, among thousands of local burials less than two dozen have yielded fancy Tiwanaku textiles, small vessels, and woodcarvings with elaborate iconography, and these were apparently local people who trekked to Lake Titicaca and brought exotic goods back home without political involvement. Involvement may have been somewhat greater in the Azapa Valley of northern Chile where cemeteries have produced a minority of interments with Tiwanaku accompaniments that may reflect status as local agents of the Titicaca state.

At the north end of the lake the state seems more Inca-like. Here the Island of the Sun was wrested from a local señorío and brought under imperial management as a major shrine. To the east, some scholars argue for Tiwanaku enclaves in Bolivia's low, lush Cochabamba region. To the west, the state fostered colonization that may have been mitmaq-like in the lower, arid sierra of the Río Moquegua. In this Pacific drainage, mid-valley flatlands above 1,000 m were first irrigated by Huaracane peoples who used fiber-tempered ceramics related to Chiripa wares in the altiplano. This long occupation persisted into Tiwanaku times when a modest number of Phase IV settlers arrived from the

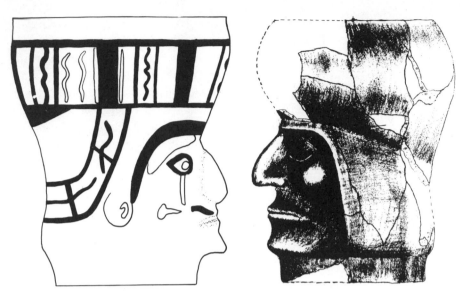

104, 105 Portrait head beakers excavated at Omo.

altiplano perhaps around AD 550–600. The majority took up residence on a spacious flat-topped bluff adjacent to land that could be irrigated. This is called the Omo Phase after the principal Tiwanaku settlement which had some 500 rectangular rooms. Built of cane, rows of several rooms formed households that were grouped into three separate plaza clusters. Imported Tiwanaku goods, and local imitations of goods with Tiwanaku iconography, dominate the artifact assemblage. Excavations revealed an interesting special-purpose structure where chicha beer was brewed and then consumed in magnificent portrait-head kero beakers originally made in the altiplano capital. The open, undefended Omo Phase sites are thought to reflect a peaceful settling of altiplano people,

Plate 78 who gradually brought the original inhabitants into the Tiwanaku cultural sphere.

In overview, Tiwanaku reflects the evolution of complex economic adaptation and political organization that cast a vast net over the south-central Cordillera and integrated the southern demographic pole of Andean civilization. The cords of unity seem loosely structured, yet they were remarkably enduring. While Moche and Nazca would fall, and a new state, Huari, would arise in Peru, the Bolivian metropolis of Tiwanaku perpetuated its political longevity far beyond that of other ancient Andean empires.

CHAPTER EIGHT

THE MIDDLE HORIZON

Triggered by deep drought, the Middle Horizon was an era of punctuated cultural change as old empires withered and new ones arose. This chapter will examine the changing fortunes of three: Moche, Huari, and Tiwanaku. Technically the horizon dates between AD 600 and 1000 in the Ica Valley. Yet it was set in motion in AD 562 when rainfall began a 25–30 percent plunge that lasted until AD 594. This was the most pronounced Andean rainfall abnormality of the last 1,500 years, second only to an exceptional precipitation increase during the initial centuries of the Little Ice Age, to judge from climate-monitoring ice cores drilled in the Quelccaya glacier situated south of Cuzco. The cores indicate dry times were accompanied by increased atmospheric dust, attributable to decreased plant cover and fields lying fallow.

Famine certainly occurred because agrarian systems in many settings stretched beyond their modern limits. We can infer that the productivity of highland rainfall farming declined proportionally by 25–30 percent and that the productivity of desert irrigation declined disproportionally by at least twice as much due to dry mountain soils absorbing scant runoff moisture. Consequently, coastal populations were more severely disadvantaged than their sierra counterparts. During drought, however, both populations were ill-equipped to deal with normal disasters, such as large-magnitude earthquakes and El Niño crises which struck in the years AD 511–12, 546, 576, 600, 610, 612, 650, 681, and later times according to ice core records. Thus, the Middle Horizon began amid stress when people were on the move, and when linguists see change in the distribution of indigenous languages and dialects.

Moche upheaval

Moche ideological integration of the north coast was described in the last chapter. By about AD 500 the southern valley populations were politically united and employed Phase IV ceramics, while their more loosely confederated northern counterparts continued to use Phase III styles. The capital at Huacas del Sol and de la Luna matured into a splendid city, having survived a number of El Niño calamities, sometimes propitiating the unwanted rains with prisoner sacrifice. Yet around the time of the AD 562–94 drought there was further disaster, and the coast was struck by one or more exceptionally erosive flood events, perhaps aggravated by a prior earthquake. Floodwaters inundated the city with such power and force that sections of the urban landscape were completely stripped away, removing several meters of deposit. Erosional scarring debilitated irrigation systems in the Moche and Jequetepeque valleys and other

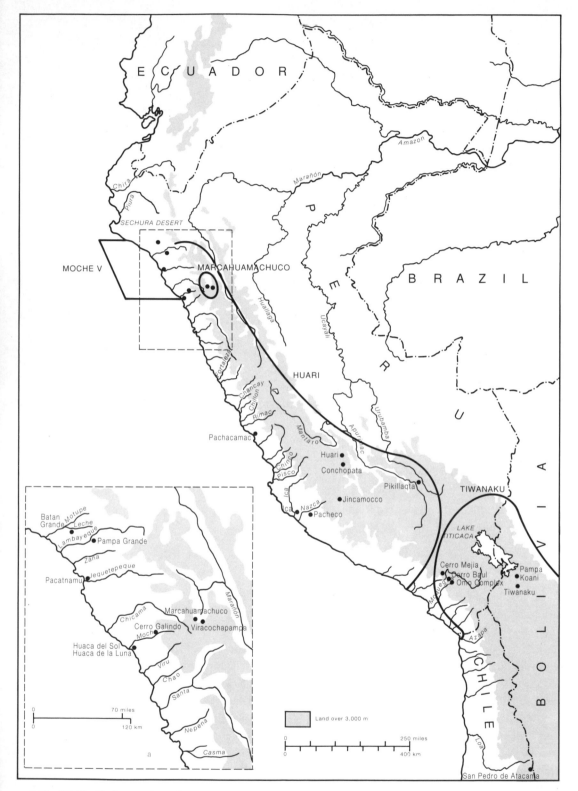

106 *The Middle Horizon: principal sites and areas mentioned in Chapter Eight.*

drainages. To judge by modern El Niños, the ancient disaster endured for 18 months or more, bringing drought to the southern mountains and rain to the desert, with intense flooding in the north where the largest irrigation systems supported the most densely settled populations. Cane and adobe houses collapsed in the rains as potable water supplies and sanitation systems broke down. Ensuing pestilence, disease, and soaring mortality rates among infants and the elderly are expectable.

The Moche landscape was so deeply scarred and altered that construction of entirely new irrigation systems was required in many areas. Yet farming confronted still another disaster in the making. Erosive flooding washed massive loads of sediment into the ocean, which the sea reworked and deposited as beach sand. Strong daily winds off the ocean moved the sand inland, forming massive dunes which crept across fields and settlements forcing farmers to retreat inland. Fishing was less perturbed and fishermen did not starve during an El Niño because there was an influx of marine life from warm equatorial waters. The sea, however, could not support everyone who depended on farming during the years it took to rebuild the irrigation systems. Significantly, a new strain of maize with large cobs and more kernels came into use after the flood, apparently introduced from the mountains to the east, suggesting that the Moche secured aid from their highland neighbors.

The capital weathered the flood, and survivors repaired Huacas Sol and Luna, heightened the platforms and gave them new facades to mask erosional damage. Significantly, one of the Luna courts was ornamented with a distinctive polychrome mural showing a large front-facing anthropomorphic being. Although the upper body and head were not preserved, the figure held a vertical staff in each hand and is highly reminiscent of the central deity on the Gateway of the Sun at Tiwanaku. The mural was executed in Moche artistic *Plate 83* canons and was later painted over by another mural with more traditional Moche subject matter. Nevertheless, the staff figure's brief appearance reflects foreign ideology and perhaps diminished confidence in the Moche pantheon's ability to mitigate natural catastrophe, and people eventually packed up their households and dispersed elsewhere, abandoning the capital and its great huacas at the close of Phase IV.

Reorganization

Opening in the aftermath of drought and disasters, Phase V dates between AD 600 and 800 and is coincident with the onset of the Middle Horizon. Revolutionary change swept the north coast as people adjusted to new environmental and economic conditions. In some littoral and sierra drainages pukaras and fortified settlements were erected as populations forged new social and political relations. I will summarize these far-reaching transformations from the traditional chronological perspective in which Phase V succeeds Phase IV in the south and Phase III in the north before assessing possibilities that the phases overlap.

The southern valleys from Huarmey through Viru, as well as upper canyon lands, were lost to the Moche realm when the former capital at Cerro Blanco

Plate 86

was abandoned and a new order arose among the northern señoríos. Transformation of the Moche Valley from imperial heartland to frontier hinterland is reflected in the Phase V occupation centered at Cerro Galindo. The site was strategically situated on the north side of the valley neck, beyond the reach of blowing sand and near the intakes of the largest operable canals. The occupation began as a fortified hillside settlement surrounded by a great wall with parapets and piles of sling stones. However, the elite soon moved out onto the lower flats, and scattered residences and other buildings eventually sprawled out over some 4–5 sq. km, according to studies carried out by Garth Bawden. Significantly, one entire section of the city, representing a fifth of the total occupied area, was set aside for small one-room structures filled with food storage vessels. This is by no means the first evidence of such facilities; they had also existed at the old Moche political center of Huancaco in Viru. But, the quantity of storage structures at Galindo points to heightened concern with centralized administration of staples.

The Phase V settlement had a large population and a great deal of masonry and cane architecture, but very few corporate structures of adobe. The largest adobe structure, reflecting a sharp break with the previous Moche tradition of erecting towering mounds, was a large, rectangular, thick-walled enclosure, measuring about 240 by 130 m. Most of the structure was occupied by a complex of spacious courts. Double doorways through the east wall led to an expansive entry plaza ornamented with murals. A small depressed rectangular court, about 1 m deep, was centered in the rear of the plaza and represents one of the last coastal vestiges of the ancient sunken-court tradition. A rectangular adobe platform two stories high lay behind the plaza and separated from it by a high wall. Although looted, the mound was once a mausoleum for elite burial. The Galindo enclosure can be interpreted as a huaca sepultura, serving as the residence and burial place of local rulers. The second largest monument, a nearby adobe platform, was probably the city's huaca adoratorio and principal shrine.

Beyond the southern frontier, Phase V ceramics have been reported up the coast and into the Vicus region of the Piura drainage, making reorganized Moche society essentially a northern north-coast phenomenon. Perhaps akin to a confederacy or maximal ayllu of nested hierarchies, the new political order seems relatively diffuse. Major centers, such as Galindo and the Jequetepeque site of San José de Moro, all produced Phase V ceramic forms. Yet iconography varied from place to place, with different themes emphasized at different settlements, and monumental architecture likewise varied.

The capital of the new order was Pampa Grande located in the Lambayeque Valley neck, 50 km from the sea. Spread over 6 sq. km, this well-preserved ceremonial city was investigated by Izumi Shimada and co-workers. The new center preserved some earlier Moche traditions, such as building gigantic pyramids, but if it were not for the corporate arts, few relationships with the old capital at Cerro Blanco would be evident. The differences are striking and invite analogy with those arising when the capital of Christendom shifted from Rome

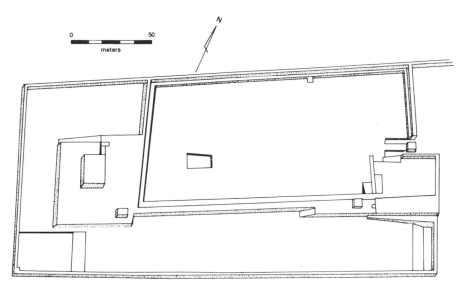

107 A reconstruction of the Galindo enclosure. The entry court housed a small rectangular sunken court behind which lay a burial platform.

to Constantinople. A few leaders may have moved, but basically power was transferred to new hands that shaped things in different ways. Agglutinated housing of commoners, workshops of artisans and coppersmiths, and rectangular walled enclosures of the elite were concentrically distributed around the urban core. One formal enclosure combined large-scale cotton processing with ceremonies in a niched court with an elevated bench where ceramic frames for drums were found along with racks of deer antlers that may have been ritual headgear. The urban core was completely dominated by a gargantuan mound, Huaca Fortaleza, at the rear of an enormous enclosure measuring 600 by 400 m. Associated adobe architecture included rows of contiguous, one-room storage facilities set in walled courts. Access was strictly controlled by check points in adjacent courts and halls. Although the original contents had been systematically removed, it is likely that the banks of storerooms stockpiled elite goods integral to wealth finance. Near the base of the pyramid, a spacious walled enclosure was used for the production of sumptuary artifacts made of Ecuadorian *Spondylus* shell. The coveted shells may have been imported by sea or by caravans of llamas that were bred and herded on the coast.

The adobe architecture at Pampa Grande is quite different from that of the Huaca del Sol and Huaca de la Luna. Bricks often bear makers' marks, but these are mixed together, indicating that brick makers and masons, if not labor taxes in general, were organized differently from how they had been at the old capital. Measuring 275 by 180 m, and standing 55 m high, the Fortaleza platform ranks as one of the largest mounds ever erected in the Andes. Yet, unlike Huaca del Sol, which was solid brick, Fortaleza achieved its great magnitude with a less labor-intensive construction technique, known as 'chamber-and-fill,' in which loose earth was dumped into walled cribs that stabilized the deposit while

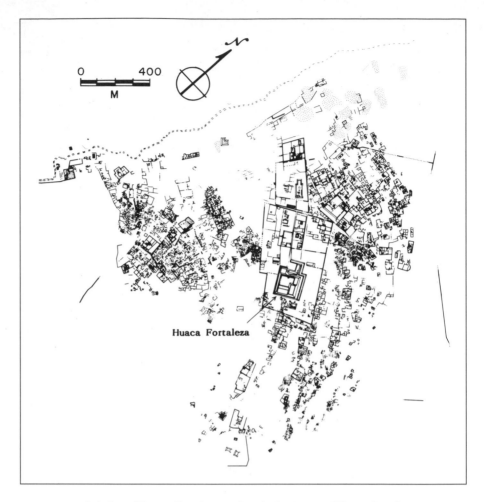

108 A plan of Pampa Grande, revealing the dominance of Huaca Fortaleza.

allowing a rapid build up of bulk. Nonetheless, at least two separate stages of major construction were needed to bring the Fortaleza structure to its final dimensions, as a four-tiered huaca. A broad basal platform, 20 m high, was surmounted by three terraces rising from the front to the towering rear of the mound. Summit buildings included courts and rooms ornamented with polychrome murals. A great perpendicular ramp almost 50 m long provided access to the first terrace. The ramp itself was probably a stage for ritual display, and it marks the beginning of a far northern architectural tradition emphasizing prominent perpendicular ramps.

The new capital was rapidly established at a time of ideological change. Scrutiny of Moche and later Chimú arts indicates that profound iconographic changes occurred at the beginning of Phase V, and the new ideology that emerged was subsequently adopted by Chimor. Much of the old Moche pantheon was dropped, but figures associated with the sea were elevated to new status and maritime themes assumed great importance. Significant figures included an elderly individual, known as wrinkle face, and an anthropomorphized iguana. These companions, depicted traveling on reed boats and shown with Strombus shells from Ecuador, were major actors in a new Phase V theme. Called the burial theme, wrinkle face and iguana are shown interring a potentate who died at the hands of a malpracticing female curer, who is fed to vultures. Concern with the sea and a maritime iconography persisted at Chan Chan. Why it replaced more terrestrially oriented iconography is a speculative matter. One proposition holds that the maritime economy was less disrupted and recovered far faster than agriculture did from the natural cataclysms that brought down the Moche state at the end of Phase IV.

Plates 101, 102

109 *Moche concerns with the sea persisted at Chan Chan with friezes depicting maritime motifs.*

Phase V was by no means calamity-free. Evidence of El Niño flooding has been found at Galindo, Pacatanamu, and at Pampa Grande. Perhaps renewed environmental stress finally broke the back of the imperial camel, or the demise of the Moche may have been for entirely cultural reasons. Whatever the case, Pampa Grande was literally abandoned in a blaze, as its inhabitants torched the city and moved elsewhere. Radiocarbon dates from recent excavations at Huaca de la Luna and adjacent buildings raise the possibility that the Phase IV occupation of the old capital persisted and overlapped with Phase V developments. If this proves true then the late political landscape was split, with Galindo allied to the north and Pampa Grande, while Sol and Luna seemingly clung to the

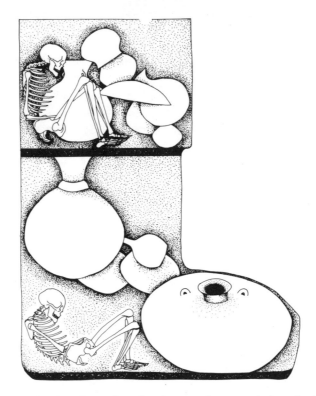

110 After the collapse of Moche culture people went to the hereafter in a seated position exhibited by these Chimú burials found near Huaca del Sol.

southern remnants of their former realm. Nonetheless, by about AD 800 the Moche had dissolved into fragmented señoríos and concepts about the hereafter changed as people went to their graves in a seated position rather than lying down.

Huari adaptive dispersal

Religion and politics were inextricably interwoven in Andean statecraft and by Middle Horizon times states had developed two expressions called *intensive* and *extensive*. Intensive manifestations, such as coastal Moche, submerged local populations under state ideology and organization. Alternatively, extensive organization saw isolated nodes of state authority scattered among local populations, as Tiwanaku did at the northern end of the Titicaca Basin. All states were intensive in their heartlands and extensive at their distant frontiers. Local ethnic heterogeneity was perpetuated under nodal arrangements, which probably arose out of folk adaptations that established scattered satellite settlements to create economic archipelagos. Because regional manifestations of religious cults, such as Chavín and Pachacamac, were also nodal and dispersed, this form of organization was not limited to economics and politics. Consequently, the extensive nature of highland Huari is debated, some authorities proposing that it was a Middle Horizon religion practiced at confederated regional centers, others arguing that it was an Inca-like, militaristic empire. Favoring a middle ground, I believe Huari wrapped appealing economic innovations in religious fundamentalism to spread state tendrils to disparate political nodes.

Huari's political and religious dominion was anchored by its capital of the same name, located at an elevation of 2,800 m in the central sierra on a hilly plateau 25 km north of the modern city of Ayacucho. From humble beginnings *Plate 87* in Huarpa times, the settlement became a ceremonial and elite residential center and by AD 600 its corporate arts reached the coastal Ica Valley, marking the beginning of the Middle Horizon. Subsequently, the metropolis matured into a 3–4-km sprawl of masonry buildings and multi-story enclosure walls, accommodating estimates of 10,000 to 35,000 inhabitants before abandonment around AD 1000.

Investigations headed by Luis Lumbreras, and later by William Isbell, indicate that the surface ruins are a late outgrowth of earlier complex changes in architectural canons, organization, and orientation. The settlement was originally surrounded by extensive irrigation, and a sophisticated system of underground conduits transported water through the city. Much of the urban core was terraced to create broad habitation surfaces, and massive walls of substantial length compartmentalized Huari into separate, irregular sections. Indeed the city was so heavily partitioned by towering sections and compound walls that it is difficult to imagine how traffic flowed through it. The architectural emphasis was on segregation rather than integration, and presumably based on kin, class, rank, and occupation. Different urban sections were occupied by numerous building compounds separated from one another by high-walled enclosures of rectilinear and irregular form measuring 40 to 100 m on a side. Within walled enclosures, buildings were two to three stories high. Early on the structures may have been arranged around oval courtyards, but the dominant pattern was one of dividing enclosures into a number of rectangular patios. Each large patio was formed by elongated, rectangular buildings reminiscent of the great halls and galleries at Marcahuamachuco. Some ground-floor rooms contain hearths, food refuse, and other domestic remains indicating that they were residences, while others were kept clean.

Some compounds were associated with specialized crafts such as ceramic, jewelry, and projectile point production. One exhibited a high frequency of serving-bowls and elaborate libation cups, suggesting ritual feasting and drinking. Another enclosure, called Cheqo Wasi, contained the remains of looted subterranean megalithic chambers, made of finely cut and carefully dressed stone slabs. The disturbed human remains in them were accompanied by abundant luxury goods, including gold and many exquisite artifacts. These may well be the tombs of Huari potentates, who once occupied the compound. Sumptuary goods from Cheqo Wasi, and elsewhere, show that Huari imported raw materials and finished products from great distances, including *Spondylus* ornaments from Ecuador, cowrie and other types of shell from different coastal locations, pottery from Cajamarca, and minerals such as chrysacola, lapis, and greenstone from distant sources. Copper, silver, and gold were also imported.

111 Staff-bearing 'angels' on Tiwanaku's Gateway of the Sun (left) were transformed by Huari weavers who conceptually subdivided the winged figures into a series of vertical panels that could be expanded, contracted, or transposed at will.

Adaptation

How is it that Huari arose and prospered at a time when Moche was brought to its knees by environmental stress? To probe for answers, we must recall that during the Early Intermediate Period most sierra farming took place at high elevations where rainfall supported potato and tuber cultivation. Complementary irrigation agriculture also took place in the bottoms of the sierra basins, but steep mountain slopes were not farmed to a significant degree. Huarpa people in the Ayacucho area were among the first to terrace and irrigate inclined terrain. However, most canals were relatively short and low, limiting the amount of land they could water. Huarpa people lived at Huari long before it assumed political stature, and William Isbell has shown that they constructed an exceptionally large and innovative agricultural system. Their system combined a high-altitude water source situated far above the city; a long primary canal routed across high-elevation contours to feed lower secondary canals; and extensive terraces that facilitated the irrigation of steep slopes. Building such a reclamation system required substantially more labor than other communities were investing in agricultural works at the time. Nonetheless, such investment gave Huari distinct economic advantages over its neighbors, and in a sense pre-adapted it to weather the great drought. Irrigation drawn from elevated streams or springs can escape many vicissitudes of irregular rainfall, and rights to it can be claimed before it reaches lower terrain.

Thus the people of Huari had developed reclamation technology that could bring into production the vast quichua zone, which had previously been under-exploited in the Ayacucho region and seemingly unexploited in other sierra settings because of the costs of building irrigated terrace systems. Bringing steep terrain into agrarian production was obviously critical during the great drought, and was one of the few ways to compensate for decreased yields in traditional farming areas. Initially, concerns with food shortages must have overriden concerns about labor costs, and once the process of reclaiming mountain

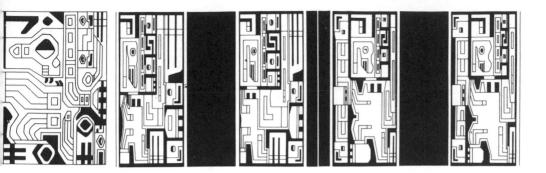

slopes began, it remained the major means for expanding highland agricultural economies long after rainfall returned to normal levels. Maize was found to grow in the quichua, and by borrowing and experimenting the Huari people added new, high-yield varieties of this crop to their farming, gaining both relief from drought and economic expansion into the last of the Andean agrarian habitats.

The residents of Huari built their own terraced irrigation system, but the political fortunes of the city were furthered by having other populations build similar systems elsewhere. In a process similar to patenting and marketing a major invention, the new technology was packaged with innovative organizational, ideological, and iconographic wrappings, and the conceptual package may have emphasized hierarchical organization and reciprocity. These changes were associated with what is called the Okros style, which saw early political expansion and consolidation. Many Huarpa settlements, including Nawinpukio, were abandoned and people relocated at Huari and Conchopata (a site on the outskirts of modern Ayacucho). The Okros style preserved local traditions, but also showed a significant increase in decorative concerns, with strong borrowings of Nazca design elements, suggesting that symbols were being sought for *Plate 89* the newly emerging political and economic order.

Major elements of Tiwanaku ritual art and architecture reached Huari and Conchopata during Okros times by uncertain means. Elements of altiplano ideology were perhaps transferred by emissaries between the Titicaca and Ayacucho capitals. Alternatively, the transfer may have been via Cerro Baul, a Huari mesa-top colony established in Tiwanaku's Moquegua Valley territory.

Among the interesting elements to appear at Huari was a magnificent rectangular sunken court, built of beautifully cut and finished stone, discovered ceremonially entombed deep beneath a later building complex. Carbon associated with initial construction has yielded a date of AD 580 ± 60. The court may have been a temple, for it was kept scrupulously clean during long use, and saw a series of renewed floors, of plain clay, white plaster, red plaster, and polygonal cut stones. One of the middle floors produced a radiocarbon date of AD 720 ± 60. Thus, the court, as well as the special activities it housed, remained important

*112 Huari spread the iconography of staff bearers far and wide. In this ceramic
painting of an 'angel' the staff base ends in a maize cob motif.*

for more than a century before the structure was carefully buried. It is probable
that this distinctive form of ceremonial architecture was borrowed from
Tiwanaku along with much of the ritual and ideology that made sunken courts
critical symbols and seats of corporate activities.

Fashioning a compelling ideology, Ayacucho savants appropriated the most
potent of Tiwanaku icons: the staff-bearing emblems of the Portal of the Sun.
Winged figures carrying single staffs were converted into secondary 'angel'
deities, while the double-staffed Gateway God was transformed into an agrarian almighty with ears of corn sprouting forth from the supernatural's rayed
headdress or from the deity's staffs or those of attendant angels. Here we must
remember that the original Chavín Staff God was born during drought and the
supernatural's Karwa depictions are replete with plant metaphors. Thus, in
renewed dry times, Huari resurrected and revitalized a very old deity to crown
a current fundamentalist ideology that propagated a new political economy
incorporating terraced maize farming.

The new fundamentalism did not emphasize tinku or spacious architecture
for converging ritual processions, but it did include ceremonies of ritual intoxication culminating in the smashing of elaborate vessels and their careful interment. The Huari staff deity figured prominently on many of these vessels,
which were principally kero beakers at Cerro Baul. Alternatively, large jars and
Plate 98 urns used to prepare and dispense chicha beer comprised the fine ceramics in
Plate 90 two caches discovered at Conchopata, one at Huari, and another at Pacheco in
Nazca. The vessels in each hoard vary in shape and decoration, suggesting that
each group was commissioned and produced for a single ceremony. Variation in
rituals is also evident at Conchopata, where young women were sacrificed and
interred adjacent to one ceramic cache.

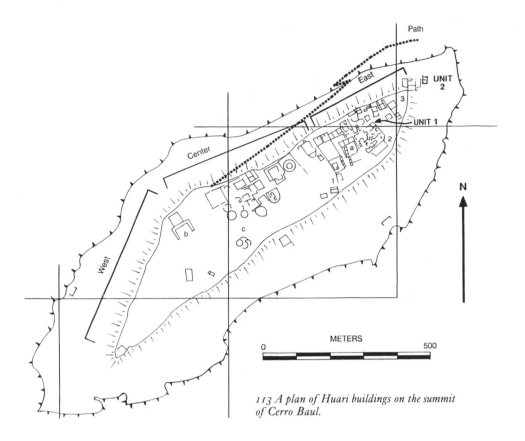

*113 A plan of Huari buildings on the summit
of Cerro Baul.*

A mesa-top colony

During and after the AD 562–94 drought, Huari's innovative agrarian adaptations allowed its political interests to spread under the guise of an appealing
ideology that promoted improved farming. Reliance on force of arms is not
evident with the possible exception of an early daring drive south by Ayacucho
people who penetrated deep into the Tiwanaku province of Moquegua and colonized Cerro Baul (2,300 m), a grand, jutting mesa 600 m high with steep sides   *Plate 88*
grading to vertical cliffs. Strategically situated above the confluence of the Río
Moquegua's major sierra tributaries, the towering mesa is a sacred apu today
and it was likely revered in the past to judge from Tiwanaku ritual architecture
at its base. Hence, Huari made a bold religious statement by seizing the hallowed pinnacle, building ceremonial facilities atop Cerro Baul, and by colonizing the promontory behind it, Cerro Mejia. Yet the statement was also bold in
its economic implications, because Tiwanaku folk living in the vicinity and at
the Omo Complex 20 km downstream were flat-land farmers largely confined
to the valley bottoms. Slopes of the rugged sierra were unfarmed and unoccu-
pied and the Huari colonists invested great labor to move into the vacant niche.
Drawing abundant water from a high-altitude tributary, they constructed a
10-km-long contour canal that negotiated broken terrain to cross the lofty

114 A Huari kero beaker from Cerro Baul depicting the head of the Staff deity.

divide between Cerros Mejia and Baul and irrigate expansive flights of terraces along the mountainsides. Thus, the newcomers transformed the Baul apu both religiously and economically.

With valley-bottom water more than an hour's walk away, the majority of colonists lived on hillside domestic terraces near the canal that distributed runoff between the two cerros. Commoner housing, with stone foundations and cane or perishable walls, consisted of discrete clusters of compartments for sleeping, cooking, and other activities arranged around a central patio. A limited number of large, well-made patio-group residences were built on the spacious summit of Cerro Mejia, which was enclosed by two large perimeter walls that lack parapets or piles of sling stones indicative of defensive design. From the pass crossed by the Huari canal, the hour-long ascent route up Cerro Baul was crossed by a number of walls that might have been defensive or simply traffic controls. Bulwarks did not reinforce the summit of the great mesa, which was occupied by compact domestic quarters in the northwest overlooking the access route. Residents included crafts personnel as well as elites in charge of one- and two-story monumental facilities in the center of the summit, built of rock quarried from the mesa top.

Following architectural canons of the Huari capital, the central facilities included storage complexes, galleries, ceremonial halls used for brewing and drinking, and D-shaped ritual centers. As at the capital, there were at least two episodes of building and remodeling, reflecting long use of the summit. Recent excavations by Ryan Williams and Peruvian colleagues indicate that the Huari colony was implanted early on when Okros pottery was in use and persisted to at least AD 900 if not later. Abandonment of the monumental buildings entailed considerable ceremony, including the smashing of libation vessels and the torching of roofs. Although the colonists seemingly coexisted in peace with their local neighbors for centuries, the Huari departure may have coincided with a time when many Tiwanaku settlements were systematically razed. Thereafter, Huari pulled its political frontiers back to the Sihuas drainage in the north.

Sierra dispersal

Although not forts, Cerros Baul and Mejia were certainly strategic, defendable installations, in stark contrast to all other hinterland administrative centers that Huari typically built in open, easily accessible flatlands. Administrative centers consisted of one, or occasionally several, large rectangular enclosures, measuring from 25 to 800 m on a side. Open courts occupied much of the interior floor space, and excavations have revealed high frequencies of serving vessels and cups suggesting corporate feasting and drinking. Some buildings are thought to have been food preparation areas for such ceremonies, and many rooms may have been produce storage areas. Others were apparently elite quarters. Some very long buildings, divided into repetitious cell-like rooms, may have been barrack-like quarters for people rendering mit'a labor. No two enclosure complexes are the same, but similarities in style and layout suggest that their construction was supervised by Huari architects. The complexes are associated with elite ceramics from Huari and copies or regional variants of such wares. However, utilitarian ceramics were locally produced and exhibit local attributes. The overall impression is that these complexes were built and used by local folk and their nobles working with a small contingent of Huari overlords.

Located near Cuzco, Pikillaqta is the largest and southernmost of the highland Huari centers. Northward for more than 1,000 km all major sierra basins, including Cajamarca, were strung together by such widely scattered, state-built administrative centers. Many were apparently instrumental in transforming local settlement and subsistence patterns, as in the Carahuarazo Basin on the route between Huari and Nazca. Jincamocco is a 27-ha Huari complex, founded on flat bottomlands adjacent to major roads that were also paved at the time. Much of the steep-sided valley was terraced and irrigated for the first time. With the opening of large tracts of new land local people abandoned high-altitude hamlets near the juncture of the herding and tuber-growing zones, and moved downslope to reside in villages and farmsteads near the terraces to grow maize and other crops.

As in Moquegua, Huari opened a vital agrarian niche in the Carahuarazo Valley, but here there is no evidence of fortified colonization or militarism. Rather, Huari policy in Carahuarazo was apparently one of promoting cooperative innovation that motivated local ethnic groups to build and benefit from irrigated terraces, as well as the state buildings, roads, and facilities that integrated the region within the national economy.

Farther north, Huari interacted with the powerful, well-established highland state at Marcahuamachuco. At the very doorstep of the thriving northern capital, less than 3 km away, lies the second largest of all Huari compounds, Viracochapampa. Measuring more than half a km on a side, the compound enclosed vast courts, and a core of systematically aligned patios, halls, and other structures arranged around a central plaza flanked by halls. As at Jincamocco, there are no indications of fortification, or of conflict with Marcahuamachuco.

Coastal influence

Huari expressions are fundamentally different on the coast. Centers such as Jincamocco or Viracochapampa are rarely found in the desert oases, nor are there great forts similar to Cerro Baul, and evidence of Huari presence is more ideological than architectural. This is probably because Ayacucho innovations in canal-fed terracing could reclaim little additional desert terrain, whereas it had far-reaching potentials for steep sierra land. Some authorities argue that the coast was invaded and conquered by Huari, and perhaps this happened in some southern oases. Alternatively long-standing verticality ties between the Ica and Nazca valleys and the Ayacucho region may have simply been politically strengthened and formalized without recourse to force of arms.

Nor is conquest evident on the north coast within the Moche realm, where, as we have seen, late murals at Huaca de la Luna depict a front-facing figure holding two staffs, that was very likely the Huari rayed deity.

Plate 92 At Pachacamac numerous Middle Horizon tomb accompaniments exhibit Huari influence, which was of an ideological nature because there is no skeletal evidence of Ayacucho people colonizing the oracle center, nor were highland-type administrative centers ever erected in desert valleys. Nonetheless, Huari stylistic and ideological elements were widely adopted along the littoral as far north as the Lambayeque region and many persisted in modified form to enrich local development.

The demise of Huari remains undated and not understood, but the original spread of its appealing ideology, featuring a resurrected Staff God, was far-reaching due to accompanying agrarian innovations. By introducing mountain-slope, terrace farming to many highland regions Huari preadapted sierra populations to drought, the longest of which was yet to come.

Tiwanaku

Tiwanaku's integration of the southern, highland pole of Andean civilization shifted from ideological to more of a political nature in the aftermath of the AD 562–94 drought when Phase 5 opens with strong sectarian concerns related

Plate 93 to agricultural management in both the imperial heartland and in dispersed regional nodes of state control. Tightened managerial reigns led to prosperity when rainfall returned to normal or higher levels allowing the capital and its hinterlands to flourish. Yet this episode of altiplano integration was undone and Tiwanaku collapsed when four centuries of drought began to grip the Andes in about AD 1100.

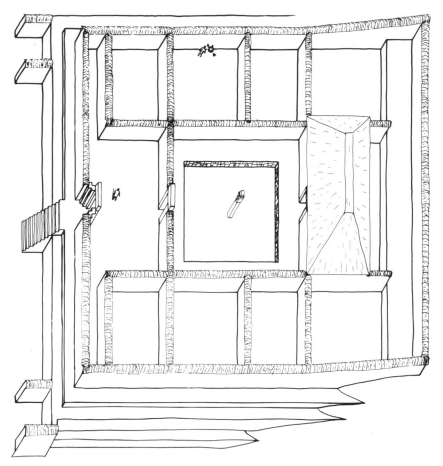

115 An idealized reconstruction of the Omo platform summit depicting the summit court.

The Moquegua hinterland

Tiwanaku Phase 4 occupation of the Moquegua drainage began modestly when several communities of altiplano farmers settled in the lower sierra adjacent to the valley bottom. There was no apparent resistance from the local Huaracani population, and the new arrivals founded their largest community at the Omo Complex, an area with five sites spanning three sequential Tiwanaku occupations. Excavations by Paul Goldstein suggest that after a century or so the Omo community was deserted, and altiplano colonists abandoned the sierra for some time. Colonial settlement was resumed on an imperial scale early in Phase 5 – the Chen Chen Phase, named after a looted cemetery near modern Moquegua. Transformation of the region from a former folk colony into an imperial province was marked by a large influx of settlers and by agricultural expansion. The focus of reclamation was on flatlands, irrigated by long canals built with corporate labor. Chen Chen agrarian works expanded mid-valley farming far beyond the confines of contemporary cultivation, growing maize, tubers, beans,

Plate 91

peanuts, squash, pumpkin, fruit, and other crops for local consumption and presumably for export to Tiwanaku 300 km away.

Tiwanaku's colonies were organized hierarchically by size differences and by elaboration of corporate construction. A new settlement at the Omo Complex sat at the apex, covering 7.7 ha with dense housing remains and deposits of cultural debris. The exceptional status of Omo was demarcated by monumental architecture and the only Tiwanaku platform mound to be erected outside the Titicaca Basin. Built of adobe, with cut stone blocks, the platform was banked against a hill and measured 120 m in length. It rose in three tiers, each forming a spacious plaza, the highest of which had rectangular compartments arranged symmetrically around a sunken court. Free of domestic refuse, excavations produced two finds: an offering of a llama fetus accompanied by a starfish, and an elaborate tapestry fragment depicting a staff-bearing figure. The monument may have housed statuary, for the head of a stela, carved in Classic Tiwanaku style, was discovered on the surface of a nearby area. It depicted an anthropomorphic face with round eyes and a wide headband of the type represented on monoliths at the capital. It was apparently made of stone from the Moquegua region and represents the first truly Tiwanaku monolith fragment found outside the altiplano. Another stone sculpture, of the same material and found at the site years ago, is different, depicting an oval human face, with a protruding nose, round eyes, and a grinning mouth. This work is vaguely reminiscent of the tenon heads ornamenting the rectangular sunken court at Tiwanaku. Yet another surface find of the same type of stone is a maquette of the Omo platform.

Surrounding the terraced platform, but separated from it, a large residential area comprised densely packed cane dwellings arranged round a series of spacious plazas. The settlement was in turn ringed by a series of separate cemeteries where different kin groups were buried. Tiwanaku people considered cranial deformation a mark of beauty and bound the heads of babies to shape their skull growth. Individuals in a cemetery shared the same deformation pattern, and patterns varied from one Omo graveyard to another. The cranial osteology of these people confirms that they were colonists originally derived from the altiplano.

After long prosperity the Chen Chen occupation came to a very violent end when canals were destroyed and virtually all houses and buildings were systematically razed. Cemeteries were violated and tomb lids were prized open, exposing the deceased to the elements. Destruction and desecration were truly extensive and intensive, but who was involved and why is not understood due to vague dating of the upheaval. Perhaps it was related to the retreat of the Huari colony at Cerro Baul, or it may have transpired later as an internal revolt associated with the collapse of Tiwanaku.

The ensuing Tumilaca Phase shows occupation of a different tenor – one that was folk rather than state oriented. It started very late in Tiwanaku Phase 5 times and seems to have lasted a century or more after the collapse of the altiplano imperium. Ceramics lack their former standardization, as altiplano imports disappeared and local communities each produced their own wares. Mid-valley canal systems contracted back to their present confines, and there

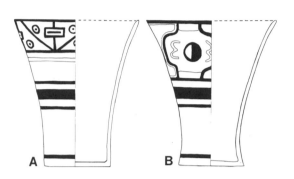

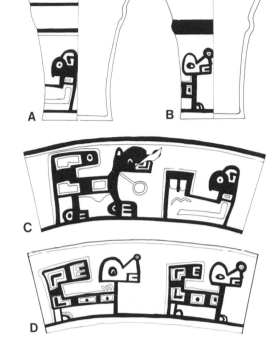

116 Two Tiwanaku Phase 5 kero vessels from Moquegua.

117 Two Chen Chen Phase kero beakers (A, B) and their painted motifs (C and D respectively).

were relatively few settlements. A new Tumilaca settlement was erected at Omo, occupying a defensible hill spur fortified with an enclosing wall and a dry moat. Although houses were of cane construction as they had been earlier, there was no public architecture here or elsewhere. Most other settlements were also enclosed by ramparts and walls. The political fabric of the region seems to have dissolved into one of independent, competitive communities.

The Tumilaca Phase saw a gradual change to irrigated terrace farming. Settlements shifted up-valley, first to the base of Cerro Baul where relatively short canals could irrigate steep terrain. The Tumilaca works were low, small, and often attempted to cultivate the tops of flat ridges. Their modest size indicates that reclamation was in the hands of individual communities. By the close of the phase a few farmsteads had appeared in the high sierra. Here the

118 Tumilaca Phase ceramic motifs.

emphasis was still on irrigating flat ridges rather than investing labor in ter-races, but this marks the opening of the high sierra, where vast terrace systems were later erected by Aymara-speaking colonists from the altiplano. Huari's brief intrusion seems to have left an agrarian legacy that would restructure Moquegua sierra farming centuries later.

The coastal region of the Río Moquegua was not colonized by Tiwanaku during Phase 5 or earlier times, although a few graves have yielded highland ceramics that probably reflect trueque exchange. Yet, following Chen Chen's violent destruction some sierra groups did move, including Tumilaca people who had settled at Loreto Viejo, Algodonal, and several other lower-river local-ities by at least *c.* AD 1000. Living in unfortified communities the new arrivals constructed the very largest of the lower-valley canals, thereby opening new lands to cultivation. Polychrome painting was introduced and elaborated upon by descendant populations to create the brilliant Chiribaya style, which perpet-uated aspects of Tiwanaku's legacy long after the altiplano imperia collapsed.

The Titicaca heartland

Linked to distant provinces and administrative nodes by large llama caravans, Tiwanaku became the ideological and political quintessence of high montane adaptations and a true agropastoral state. To a large degree, the opulent capital and its nobility were sustained by surpluses from ridge-field farming of enor-mous tracts of flat lowlands around Lake Titicaca where the water table was high. Constructed in parallel sets, the ridges were long, narrow, artificially ele-vated planting surfaces, with maximum dimensions reaching 15 by 200 m. Many were made simply by excavating parallel trenches and piling earth in the center to create a flat-topped ridge bound by trenches. However, during Phases 3 and 4, the state-built ridges on Pampa Koani had permeable footings of boul-ders and cobbles capped by a meter or more of good soil hauled in from distant hills. The labor invested in reclamation was prodigious because an estimated 100,000 ha of ridge fields were in production during Tiwanaku times, including 75 sq. km of wetlands on Pampa Koani.

Archaeologists working with indigenous people have experimentally rebuilt and reactivated plots of ridge fields at the northern and southern end of the lake, and in both cases agricultural yields were double or more than those from plowed fields in the same region. Essential to high productivity is constant water in the trenches on either side of a ridge, because the liquid warms during the day and then releases night-time heat to mitigate frost damage. Furthermore, the ditch water is rich in nutrients and nitrogen-fixing plants, and when the muck is cleaned out and dumped on the planting surfaces it is a potent source of natural fertilizer. Due to these qualities, the ancient farming technol-ogy produces two harvests a year, whereas rainfall farming yields produce but one of lesser quality. Yet the technology was delicate because lake levels fluctu-ate, up to 4 m a decade in historic times, and Tiwanaku engineers canalized rivers and springs and built massive aqueducts to move runoff where it was needed as well as remove excessive water from planting areas.

Tiwanaku's agrarian fortunes were undone by the AD 1100 onset of pro-tracted drought that ultimately dropped lake levels by some 12 m and depressed the water-table levels proportionally, thereby creating dry standing ridged fields. We know from recent altiplano droughts associated with the 1982–3 and 1997–8 El Niño events that Titicaca people lose half their potato harvests, and impoverished pastureland leads to widespread disease and starvation of llama and alpaca herds. The collapse of Tiwanaku was therefore seemingly preor-dained by four centuries of dry climate. Populations subsequently dispersed from around the lake margins to pursue high-mountain rainfall farming, which remains the general norm. Although rainfall now approximates long-term norms, government attempts to reactivate large-scale ridge-field farming have failed miserably because water-table conditions are not what they once were. Thus, when Tiwanaku's vast reclamation works collapsed population levels in the Titicaca region entered a persistent, long-term decline.

The capital

The religious and political nexus of the altiplano was abandoned as desiccation undercut its agrarian support base. Perhaps the metropolis simply atrophied as most people dispersed elsewhere, leaving stelae and monuments to collapse on their own. Yet, similar to the torching of Pampa Grande, closure of the center may well have involved intentional destruction of major edifices, including the upper terrace walls of the Akapana, and the prizing up of megalithic blocks in the base of the Pumapunku. I suspect, but cannot prove, that as nature turned pernicious the common populace rose up against their lords who ruled by the divine right of keeping heaven and earth on an even keel. Nonetheless, by delib-erate action or by prolonged negligence a point was reached when all the great stone gateways were toppled and all the fine masonry buildings were in ruins.

Then, a marvelous process of righting the wrong began long after the col-lapse. The Akapana walls were repaired, but in a markedly haphazard manner, mixing stone blocks from different contexts. Megalithic gates at the Pumapunku were also righted, yet their faces were marred by large holes for reinforcing rods, needed to anchor the works in a vertical position. The Gateway of the Sun was moved from the Pumapunku to its now-incongruous *Plates 80, 82* position in the northwest corner of the Kalasasaya platform that leads nowhere, and the same can be said of the nearby Gateway of the Moon that now stands prominently atop an otherwise formless mound. Obviously, somebody believed in the sanctity of the city, but lacked either the where-with-all, or the knowledge to restore it to its original condition. The presence of numerous Inca artifacts at the site leads me to suspect that the masters of Tahuantinsuyu had a major hand in resurrecting the ruins. Imposing stelae provided fossil evidence for the con-tention that giants once ruled the world, and royal mythology held that Viracocha later came to Tiwanaku to fashion the primordial human race from sacred lake clay. What better place for an Inca park validating imperial lore?

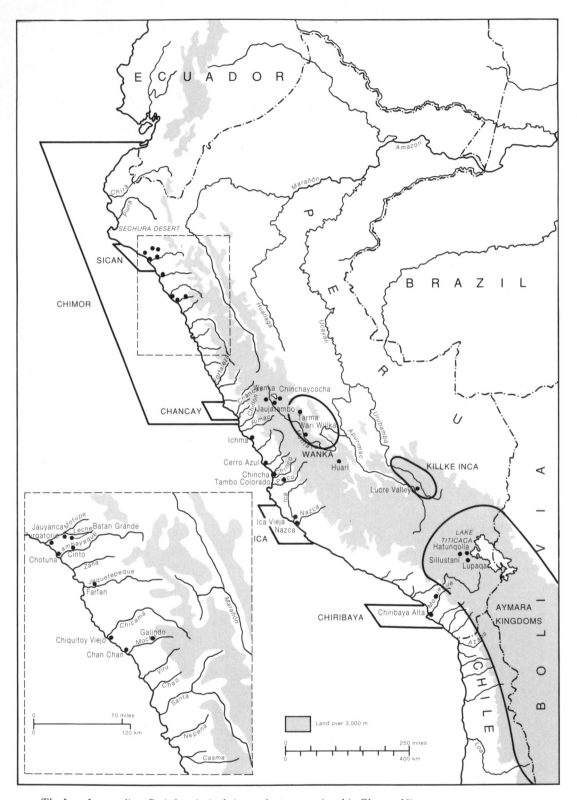

111 *The Late Intermediate Period: principal sites and areas mentioned in Chapter Nine.*

THE LATE INTERMEDIATE PERIOD

The Late Intermediate Period is exceptionally fascinating historically and environmentally. Historically, colonial documents greatly enrich the archaeological record with limited but important accounts of native remembrances about events and conditions that preceded the Inca conquest. Spanish records suggest the lords of Cuzco incorporated the coastal Ica Valley in 1476, thus ending the Late Intermediate Period, which technically began in AD 1000. Many developments that shaped the period began several centuries earlier, when rainfall was average or above average. Then, beginning around AD 1100, four centuries of climate change saw precipitation decline and reach a 10–15 percent below-normal nadir shortly after AD 1300. Drought endured until AD 1500, and we can see a range of human responses to the waxing and waning of protracted stress. Sierra populations dispersed to higher altitudes where rainfall could still support farming, albeit with large investments in terracing mountain slopes. There was also migration into the wet eastern face of the Cordillera, where terracing was again essential. Desert farmers fared very poorly because runoff to littoral valleys dropped on the order of 20–30 percent or more. The only agricultural option was to exploit subsurface runoff by digging enormous sunken gardens down to ground water, and this was only tenable in limited areas with high water-table conditions near the coast. We will start this chapter in the southern altiplano and work north to conclude with coastal Chimor, the great rival state of Tahuantinsuyu.

The Titicaca region

Many 16th-century accounts of the Titicaca Basin describe so-called 'Aymara Kingdoms,' particularly of the powerful Colla and Lupaka nations on the northwest and southwest lake borders, as well as other señoríos including the Cana, Canchi, Charca, Umasuyo, and Pacaje. Linguists debate whether Aymara had always been the indigenous language of the lake region, or whether its speakers arose in more northerly settings and swept into the altiplano after the fall of Tiwanaku. The issue is unresolved because the archaeological record points to both continuity and change, and the understudied biology of mortuary populations remains mute. Nonetheless, the pre-Inca altiplano was a landscape of combative señoríos that the lords of Cuzco played off against one another and conquered in piecemeal fashion.

With drought, both Lake Titicaca and adjacent water tables declined by many meters and digging kocha sunken gardens was often impossible. Consequently, most people moved uphill to pursue rainfall farming, but inclement weather at 4,000 m and above required terracing to control erosion, and shorter growing seasons limited crop diversity. Drought, the world over, is marked by competition for scarce resources, and seeking to safeguard what they had, people generally lived in pukara-type walled settlements throughout the altiplano and southward through San Pedro de Atacama. The grandest of all was the Pukara de Juli, near the modern city of the same name on the lake's west side. The builders erected many kilometers of defensive walls to entirely encircle the large Juli hill, thereby protecting residences, corrals, and terraced farmland. Lake region surveys by UCLA's Charles Stanish and national colleagues indicate that most walled settlements were associated with corrals for llamas and alpacas and that herding facilities were far more prevalent than in earlier times. Indeed, wealthy Lupaka lords reportedly owned flocks of 50,000 animals. Thus, intensification of pastoralism was an important response to drought.

A few settlements covered 150 ha or more; others were on the order of 30 ha. The most frequent were smaller villages and hamlets. Sometimes dwellings were arranged in two discrete clusters reflecting dual organization. Houses were circular in some regions, and rectangular in others. Old altiplano traditions involving sunken courts, platform mounds, and stelae had been rejected, as had vibrant polychrome arts. Seated burials in below-ground circular cysts endured, but kuraka elites adopted a new practice of interment in burial towers, or *chulpas*, one to three stories tall, erected adjacent to settlements and in separated groups. Located west of Puno, Sillustani is a famous tower cluster with *Plate 94* round and square chulpas of magnificent masonry. Serving as huacas sepulturas and family mausoleums, most chulpas contained numerous bodies of adults and children and were likely overseen by mallquipavillac ministers. Use of the towers continued during the Inca occupation, and many contain Inca-style artifacts indicating that local lords were incorporated into provincial administration and rewarded for their service to Cuzco.

The Incas conquered the lake region as drought waned and gave way to exceptionally wet conditions that permitted farming to be renewed at lower, less hostile elevations. Consequently, Tahuantinsuyu often moved people out of fortified hilltops and resettled them in low-lying localities that gave better yields, afforded easier political control and were closer to the imperial highway system. For the Colla, resettlement included building a new capital at Hatunqolla, near modern Puno. John Murra's original exposition of Andean verticality drew heavily on Spanish accounts of distant Lupaka colonies in low-altitude habitats, one of which was the Río Moquegua sierra. This holding was not a traditional one, but a grant from the Incas to loyal Lupaka lords who used it more for personal enrichment than community betterment.

The late prehistory of the Moquegua sierra was closely interlinked with its lower coastal valley, where descendants of earlier Tumilaca colonists formed the Chiribaya señorío. Never conquered by Tiwanaku or Huari, the small southern valleys from the Río Vitor well into northern Chile pursued their own Maritime-Oasis lifeways, developing in parallel with no evidence of overarching coastal states. Unlike dour upland arts of the time, several Pacific populations developed ornate corporate styles expressed in ceramics and textiles, including the San Miguel and Gentilar styles of the Arica drainage. Chiribaya was by far the most vibrant, with ceramics painted in lively polychromes, and textiles using threads of many colors to depict mythical creatures and ornate emblems. The capital, Chiribaya Alta, was located somewhat inland on a high bluff overlooking the valley. Covering about 1 km square, the settlement was made up of elite rectangular dwellings with masonry footings that supported walls of cane. Here nobles were buried in rectangular stone-lined crypts with splendid finery, objects of precious metal and sometimes with female companions. Elsewhere, elites were interred in low, 'proto-chulpas,' while commoners were contained in below-ground rectangular tombs and fishermen were often accompanied by miniature log rafts with reed sails.

Plate 96

When highland rainfall and coastal runoff had been abundant Chiribaya farmers expanded irrigation systems beyond their modern limits and populations in the arid sierra were brought into the Chiribaya fold which focused upon flatland farming. Prosperity changed to austerity with drought, cases of anemia rose in mortuary populations, and a thick rampart of loose earth was mounded up to encircle Chiribaya Alta. Then, exceptionally severe El Niño flooding decimated the Chiribaya populace, its settlements, and agrarian infrastructure around AD 1365. Ongoing drought inhibited economic recuperation and the former señorío dissolved into impoverished folk communities.

Freed of coastal constraints, sierra survivors and their descendants moved into the higher wet mountains and dropped all trappings of Chiribaya iconography and ideology, in favor of an austere plain style called Estuquina. Relying principally on irrigated terracing, Estuquina reclamation of the high watershed was vast, far surpassing Huari's earlier introduction of the technology. In comparison, the coastal populations declined by at least 50 percent, but this loss was more than made up for by demographic expansion into the wet sierra. Expansion was folk- and community-based, without overarching political integration. There is little mortuary evidence of physical conflict, but people lived in walled settlements atop hills and ridges. Just beyond the perimeter walls local elites were interred in stubby chulpas surrounded by below-ground circular cyst-tombs of commoners. One chronicler says Moquegua highlanders retreated to Cerro Baul to fend off Inca forces, but protracted siege starved them out. After submission many communities were resettled on lower open terrain and Lupaka holdings were established in the region.

The southern sierra

Whereas historic lore portrays Tahuantinsuyu and its splendid capital as very short-lived, archaeologists trace Inca development back to the beginning of the Late Intermediate Period in association with two art styles, Killke in the northwestern Cuzco Basin, and Lucre to the southeast. The latter has certain antecedents at Pikillaqta, Huari's largest provincial center. Covering more than 1 sq. km, Pikillaqta was formally planned with symmetrical, contiguous buildings grouped in sectors enclosed by walls up to 10 m high. Some facilities were residential, others were for storage, while large halls with interior wall niches were ritual settings focusing upon ancestor veneration, according to excavator Gordon McEwan. When Huari collapsed and the center was abandoned, a nearby settlement, Chokepukio (meaning 'Golden Spring,') rose to prominence. Perhaps this thermal spring was a local *pacarina* or mythical origin place, because its long occupation began before 300 BC. Later it became the production center for the Lucre-style ceramics, which preserved the earlier Huari penchant for polychrome painting. Joint investigations by Cuzco archaeologist Arminda Gibaja and McEwan reveal that fancy Inca buildings at Chokepukio were preceded by two distinct phases of sizeable corporate construction, the first emphasizing discrete buildings and the second, large kancha-like enclosures with internal structures. While many facilities served elite residential and storage functions, others were temples and ritual structures where rites included ancestor veneration. It is not clear to what degree the hot springs were a ceremonial center versus the center of a small señorío, but arts and architecture of Chokepukio provided local foundations for later Inca elaboration.

Found in the immediate vicinity of Cuzco and to the northwest, Killke pottery shares similarities with Lucre ceramics but is less colorful and employs black-and-red geometric motifs on cream or buff surfaces. The style has traditionally been associated with the ethnic beginnings of the Incas, but Chokepukio may prove to have inspired the later imperial arts if not architecture, because Killke is not known for monumental construction. Killke settlements and those in the Lucre region are not fortified, and tend to occupy low, open settings near good water supplies and arable land. The lack of pukara fortifications negates lore that Emperor Pachacuti had to subdue bellicose, warring neighbors. Indeed, in several immediately adjacent provinces, inhabited by 'Incas of Privilege,' but not by blood, people resided in open undefended settlements and produced their own pottery styles, but later imported and emulated the Killke ceramics without changing where they lived. Site surveys in the region lead Brian Bauer to conclude that the spread of Killke reflects early, gradual expansion of Inca hegemony that was nondisruptive. Thus, Killke Cuzco was apparently a young señorío, likely confederated with Chokepukio by about AD 1200.

Lower down the Urubamba drainage, some 80 km from Cuzco, research by an Anglo-Peruvian project reveals that local people producing their own style of ceramics initially resided in defensive hilltop settlements near rainfall farmland. Then there was a downward shift from hilltops to locations near the valley floor during the latter part of the Late Intermediate Period, when Killke ceramics spread through the area. Occupation of many lower communities then continued uninterrupted into imperial Inca times. Here again Cuzco's incremental expansion transpired long before the birth of Pachacuti or the rise of imperial-style construction that was artfully employed in terracing the Urubamba and transforming it into the magnificent 'Sacred Valley.'

86 *A large rectangular enclosure and élite buildings (bottom right) occupy the flatlands of Cerro Galindo in the Moche Valley. Above a dry moat and high wall, residential terraces cover the hillside.*

87 (above) *Huari seen from a hillside cave overlooking the ruins.*

88 (below) *Deep within Tiwanaku territory, Huari established a fortified colony atop the natural bastion of Cerro Baul.*

Huari

89 (above) A classic Huari-style polychrome vessel.

90 (above right) A Huari-style urn from a ceremonial cache at the site of Pacheco.

91 (right) A Tiwanaku-style four-cornered hat from Chen Chen in the Moquegua Valley.

92 (below left) A vessel from the coastal Huacho Valley exhibiting Huari stylistic influence.

93 (below right) A Tiwanaku portrait head vessel found in the Moquegua Valley.

94 (left) *Ruins of a chullpa burial tower at Sillustani near Puno.*

95 (right) *Depicting a human figure holding a libation beaker, this is a typical Chancay black-on-white funerary vessel.*

96 (below) *A Chiribaya-style polychrome vessel.*

97 (right) With wings on his shoulders, the Sican Lord is depicted on the handle of a gold tumi or ceremonial knife.

98 (far right) A Chimú wooden figure discovered at Huaca Tacanaymo.

99 (below) Air view of the city of Chan Chan, capital of Chimor, with its vast rectangular compounds reserved for members of the élite.

Chan Chan

100 (above) Typical of late U-shaped offices of the ruling nobility, this Tschudi audiencia *had two large niches in each interior wall.*

101 (right)   An adobe frieze in the Uhle Compound at Chan Chan depicts fish, sea fowl, mythical creatures and wave motifs, reflecting an interest in the sea.

102 (below right) Detail of a Chan Chan adobe frieze showing fish.

103 (overleaf) Guardian figures lined the entry to Ciudadela Rivero at Chan Chan; each wooden sentry once held a staff or spear.

Impressive imperial stonework characterizes all the valley's major centers from Machu Picchu through Ollantaytambo and Pisac. Consequently, they are all relatively late in the process of Inca state formation because distinct corporate styles, such as imperial Inca, only arose after the corporations they identify were firmly established and viable. Nor did a style crystallize across all media at the same time. For Andeans, unique attire and textiles come first, and then distinctive jewelry, ceramics, utensils, and architecture follow in various orders.

Although Cuzco's hegemony was expanding by AD 1200, the imperial corporate style did not crystallize in different media until *c.* 1375 to 1425. This very late formulation reinforced historical lore that a very late ruler, Pachacuti, invented statecraft and the arts of civilization. Yet lore is belied by the archaeological record. Clearly, the dual-organized Incas had many more kuraka heads and potentates than ten, and early processes and events set in motion by Pachacuti's distant ancestors were at best claimed by him for his own aggrandizement. Thus, while truthful aspects reside in what Incas told *conquistadores* about the growth of Tahuantinsuyu, the rendering of Inca history that reaches us is a mytho-poetic epoch of heroic proportions, because centuries of development were compressed into the narrow span of three lifetimes: that of a purported extraordinary ruler, his reputedly exceptional son, and a more earthly grandson who, as emperor, died of smallpox.

The central and northern sierra

Throughout the central and northern sierra drought prompted many people to move to higher, moister elevations and to the wet eastern face of the Cordillera. Agricultural terracing was frequently imperative, residing in pukara-type settlements often expedient, and climatic stress fostered class separation with kurakas being interred in chulpas or other special mortuary monuments. Pushing north as dry times waned, Cuzco's forces often encountered little organized opposition. Yet Inca expansion into the central sierra met stiff resistance from a powerful ethnic group known as the Wanka or Huanca. They occupied the region where Lake Junín feeds the upper Río Mantaro and highlands to the east in the Río Tarma headwaters of the Río Chanchamayo, where other groups known as the Tarma and Chinchaycocha also lived. Here herding had long been emphasized over farming. The adoption of large-kerneled varieties of maize and intensification of farming did not begin until *c.* AD 1000, much later than in other regions. The intensification process was associated with dramatic settlement changes in the verdant Yanamarca Valley, if not in other Mantaro tributaries. Reflecting a shift from low to high population densities, small, low-lying sites were replaced by larger, more numerous walled communities defensively situated atop hills. With Huari less than 200 km away, the complex of corporate buildings at Wari Willka, the Wanka capital, was influenced by Ayacucho style. But elsewhere in the Mantaro area there was surprisingly little Huari influence. The later residence patterns fit Inca descriptions of the Wanka as a people fraught with internal hostilities. Nonetheless, there was a pronounced size hierarchy, grading from many hamlets of 5-10 ha, through a few between 15 and 40 ha, to one of more than 100 ha. Most sites had fewer than 50 buildings per ha, but numbers more than twice as high characterized several of the larger Wanka sites in the rich Yanamarca area.

Dwellings were predominantly round, and clusters of up to half a dozen structures around open patios formed household groups. As with contemporary sierra settlements there was little formal planning, but dual organization is suggested by villages split into two spatially distinct subdivisions, or by pairs of adjacent settlements. Following the Inca conquest, an imperial administrative center was erected at Jaujatambo in the Yanamarca area and inhabitants of the region were encouraged to resettle in lower zones. Agriculture was reorganized to emphasize production for the state and vast numbers of qollqa warehouse facilities were erected.

In the headwaters of the Tarma region and the lower Chanchamayo Valley, the Campa or Amuesha peoples pursued Amazonian adaptations in the montaña zone of the lower valley up to about 1,800 m, above which manioc staples did not grow. Concentrated on alluvial terraces near the river, their houses were primarily of wood and thatch, and stone architecture was generally absent or poorly executed. Their pottery was entirely different from that of the sierra, and very limited interchange is indicated by negligible amounts of sierra wares in Campa sites and vice versa.

Spanning a vertical range of almost 3,000 m, the highlanders traversed an extraordinary gradient of environmental zones from the lower montaña at *c.* 2,000 m up through the sierra valleys to the high, wet puna. Apparently the Wanka, and more particularly their Tarma and Chinchaycocha neighbors, each maintained a contiguous vertical swathe of territory crossing these altitudinal extremes, rather than discrete satellite holdings typical of Aymara kingdoms in the drier south. Territorial holdings transecting multiple altitudinal zones also seem to characterize the lower, moister northern sierra. Here drought prompted significant demographic influx into the Kuelap area and the rugged mountain forests of Chachapoyas region noted for its Gran Pajaten ruins.

In overview, from northern Chile through northern Peru drought prompted mountain people to move higher, as well as eastward where rainfall could still sustain farming and herding. Opening these vast reaches of the Cordillera to intensive production required extensive investments in terracing and agricultural infrastructure, but they sustained significant population growth in spite of dry times. This changed the demographic balance of power in favor of the sierra, as coastal populations wilted in the wake of protracted drought.

The central and south coasts

Because runoff for desert irrigation declined more dramatically than did rainfall for mountain farming, AD 1100 saw coastal civilizations enter centuries of deprivation and stress, contributing to an often feudal landscape of competitive señoríos. There were important exceptions, including the Ichma whose territory embraced the large Rimac Valley and the smaller Lurin drainage, which was home to the great oracle center at Pachacamac. An architectural florescence transpired at the sacred city during the Late Intermediate Period, and many of its splendid sanctuaries and elite architectural compounds were erected at this time. The temple of Pachacamac, where the oracle resided, was the supreme huaca adoratorio, but the numerous other temples and shrines at the center reflect a rich and cosmopolitan pantheon. It is likely that some sanctuaries were commissioned and built to serve deities foreign to the Ichma. This was certainly the case in Inca times when Topa Inca had a shrine erected dedicated to the cult of the Sun. In part this reflects a particularly close relationship between the Incas and the Ichma, who formed a military alliance for purposes of attacking and defeating their great northern adversary of Chimor.

Shortly before the Inca–Ichma alliance was struck, ethnohistorical sources indicate that Chimor expanded its frontiers south through the Chancay Valley and perhaps into the Chillon drainage. A vibrant corporate style, known as Chancay, occurs in these two valleys and suggests that they achieved a degree of political integration prior to Chimor's late intrusion. Chancay ceramics are characterized by black and occasionally red painting on a whitish slip. Vessels *Plate 95* exhibit a matte finish. Motifs are usually geometric, but plants, animals, and people were occasionally depicted, and many vessels have modeled and painted human faces. Some were molded in the form of birds and llamas, and large human figures, generally females, were common. Mold-made ceramics are common and reflect mass production of corporate wares.

Chancay tombs contained seated figures, and are notable for their textiles, which include elaborate gauzes, brocades, openwork fabrics, and a great deal of

120 Painted decoration on a Chancay textile.

painted cloth. Corporate architecture is noteworthy for its use of *tapia* construction, in which sections of walls, foundations, or floors were framed in wooden molds. Moist adobe was then poured and pounded into the forms and allowed to dry. Relative to more arduous brickwork, tapia is a means of mass production, and it was used to create many impressive monuments on the central coast. In a sense Chancay reflects an industrialization of corporate art and architecture that permeated many Andean polities to varying degrees during the Late Intermediate Period. More people had access to mass-produced ceramics and textiles, but the nobility still guarded its symbols of privilege by monopolizing the production and use of precious metals.

To the south of the Chancay and Ichma states, the señorío of Huarco controlled the lower Cañete Valley. Here, on a high rocky promontory jutting into the sea, Cieza de León described '. . . the most adorned and handsome fort that there was in the kingdom of Peru, built upon great square slabs, with very well-made facades, reception rooms, and large patios.' This monument, Cerro Azul, still retains marvelous Cuzco-style masonry, and its beautiful stonework is unique among Inca coastal works, which elsewhere were generally of adobe.

Cerro Azul rose to prominence during the Late Intermediate Period as a prosperous maritime center. There were at least ten monumental complexes of large multi-room tapia constructions, surrounded by numerous smaller buildings and dwellings. Excavations did not reveal evidence of subsistence farming, but of an economy based on net fishing. Emphasizing surplus production, anchovies and sardines were dried and then packed by the thousand into storage rooms and filled over with dry sand to ensure the conservation of the catch. From the warehouses the fish were presumably exported to farmers in the rest of the señorío, if not beyond. Cerro Azul was probably founded by the Huarco nobility when this small state initially organized economic production, and fishing would have been formally organized through the social hierarchy.

Parallel developments seem to have transpired in the neighboring valley to the south. Here the Chincha señorío reportedly had 30,000 male tribute-payers, including 12,000 farmers, 10,000 fishermen, and 6,000 merchants. Chincha merchants are of particular interest, but what is known about them comes primarily from ethnohistorical sources. Their exchange network handled many commodities, but they were particularly noted for travels to Ecuador to procure Spondylus shell. The sacred shell was shipped back to Chincha to supply the Incas and the nobility of their conquered realms. It is not unlikely that Chimor had previously monopolized the *Spondylus* trade, and following Inca conquest it was turned over to the Chincha.

Still farther south people residing in the Ica and Nazca drainages continued their long tradition of producing fine textiles and distinctive polychrome ceramics, known as Ica. This artistic tradition witnessed a particularly strong influx of Huari iconographic and ideological influence that gradually faded and underwent local reinterpretation over time. Burying the deceased in a flexed and seated position persisted, accompanied by cloth, pottery, and other offerings. Unifying ceramic characteristics are polychrome wares with white and black painting on red surfaces. Motifs are predominantly geometric, but fish and sea birds are also depicted. The Ica style is corporate in nature, but its broader distribution reflects prestige more than political power.

Old cultural links with the Ayacucho region persisted as indicated by the occasional occurrence of Ica ceramics in highland sites in the Río Pampas area. On the coast the pottery has also been found with tombs in the Chincha señorío. Yet within its heartland there is little to suggest that the style was associated with a powerful state. Large urban settlements are not evident in the Nazca drainage at this time, and the only noteworthy center is Ica Vieja, 10 km south of the modern city of Ica. This complex of structures, built on mounds, was probably the node of local government because it was taken over by the Incas to serve as a bureaucratic center.

Although the Incas may have preferred working through established centers, they also erected new ones, of which Tambo Colorado in the Pisco Valley is the most noteworthy and best preserved in the desert lowlands. Here adobe buildings, ornamented with trapezoidal niches, fronted a great plaza with an *usnu* platform.

Chimor and the north

Embracing 1,000 km of Pacific coastland, Chimor is the second-largest native state in South America that can be documented both by archaeological remains and by ethnohistorical accounts. At its height, the empire encompassed two-thirds of all irrigated land along the desert and, by inference, two-thirds of the coastal population. In evolutionary perspective, Chimor synthesized the Maritime-Oasis trajectory of lowland development and integrated the northern demographic pole of the Andes within a single nation. Residing at the metropolis of Chan Chan, the governing royalty bitterly contested Inca territorial ambitions until the coastal nation was defeated by Cuzco's forces *c.* AD 1470. Brutal dismemberment followed as the Incas exiled hostile groups to distant colonies, and carved the nation up into independent señoríos loyal to Cuzco. Then smallpox and the first New World pandemics further ravaged survivors of the old state.

Plate 99

Thus the *conquistadores* encountered only a few, fragmentary accounts of the royal dynasties that had forged Chimor into the continent's penultimate empire. Four Spanish writers briefly mention native oral accounts about the founders and governing lords of the two coastal empires. The first was the Taycanamu dynasty, based at Chan Chan and comprising the rulers of Chimor. The second was the Naymlap dynasty of the Lambayeque region, which Chimor came to incorporate.

The term dynasty is somewhat misleading because these were probably dual rulerships rather than monarchies. Furthermore, Naymlap lore describes a political confederacy, whereas Taycanamu lore describes centralized rule. Unfortunately, neither royal succession is described in detail. The lore clearly contains myth and allegory, but also mentions places and events identifiable in the archaeological record. To judge from radiocarbon dates on associated sites the deeds and events are related in correct chronological order; transpired over the course of many centuries; but were compressed by native accounts into a short span of ten or twelve generations.

Naymlap lore describes developments in the Lambayeque Valley after the abandonment of the Moche capital at Pampa Grande. Correlated with the archaeological record, the dynastic story probably begins in the early Sican Phase between AD 700 and 900. Landing at the valley mouth with a flotilla of balsa boats, a lord called Naymlap arrives with his wife, a greenstone idol, and a large entourage, including a retinue of 40 officials. Saying he was sent from afar to govern, Naymlap builds a palatial court at a place called Chot, thought to be Chotuna, a complex of platforms and ruins 4 km from the sea. In prosperous old age, as death approaches, the patriarch has himself entombed, but commands his offspring and followers to spread the tale that Naymlap sprouted wings and flew away to the hereafter. A senior son, Zolzdoni, has 12 sons who with other followers go off to found a dozen new Lambayeque settlements.

Beginning with the dynastic founder, there are 12 named rulers in the dynasty. It ends with Fempellec, who is tempted by a sorceress to move Naymlap's stone idol, a sin which occasions '30 days' of disastrous rains and devastating floods, followed by famine and pestilence, and causes the potentate's vassals to rise up and cast him into the sea. Following an interregnum of unknown duration, Chimor conquers the region and holds it through a brief succession of three governors before the Incas subdue the area.

The number 12 is a recurrent motif in the story and its limitation to the number of months in a year leads some ethnohistorians to argue that the story had calendrical significance. Arrival by sea may be a fanciful embellishment meant to confer special status on ancestral founders and Naymlap's large entourage bespeaks a new elite. (The Taycanamu story begins similarly but the leader arrives alone.) Many nobles in this retinue bear official titles that reflect specialized tasks, such as Lord of the Feathered Cloth Makers, suggesting the guild-like economic specialization prevalent when the Spanish arrived.

As yet, there is no archaeological evidence of an incursion of seafaring foreigners at Chotuna or in the valley, although commerce with Ecuador is later evident. The region did, however, experience profound upheaval following the collapse of the Moche polity at Pampa Grande. When centralized rule disappeared and coastal communities were on their own, highlanders from Cajamarca seem to have pushed into lower elevations along the mountain slopes, introducing new artistic elements. Noteworthy aspects of Huari iconography were also adopted. Combined with older Moche traditions, there was also a synthesizing surge in local innovations and this brought forth a new regional style, called Sican. This saw the introduction of ceramic ornamentation by stamping moist clay surfaces with decorated paddles that leave design imprints. Decoration by modeling and painting persisted, but black ware vessels and double-spouted libation vessels became increasingly common.

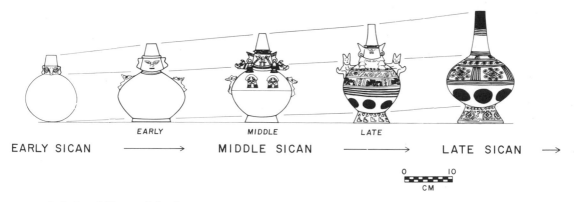

EARLY

MIDDLE

LATE

EARLY SICAN   ⟶   MIDDLE SICAN   ⟶   LATE SICAN   ⟶

0   10
CM

121 Seriation of Sican-style bottles.

There is but scattered evidence of monumental construction at this time, but construction activity increased dramatically during the Middle Phase (AD 900–1100), when Sican crystallized as a sharply defined corporate style. The central design element is a male figure called the Sican Lord. The richly attired image is often depicted with small wings on each shoulder, a beak-like nose, and occasionally with talons instead of feet. On libation vessels he is often shown in a flight-like attitude atop a serpent with a head at each end of its body. On double-spouted vessels the serpent forms a handle bridging the two spouts. On single-spouted vessels, the head of the Sican Lord was often modeled on the spout and flanked by two serpent heads, as well as by smaller human attendants shown in ritual flight. The double-headed serpent is an old Moche motif often associated with the sky, and the Sican Lord is a very strong iconographic candidate for Naymlap.

Plate 97

Reflecting the vast size of the greater Lambayeque irrigation complex, this region contains more large cities and settlements than other Andean regions. Many centers, including Chotuna, arose during Sican times, but precisely when is not clear in most cases. Including the imposing ruins at Cinto, Tucume, and Juayanca, at least five of these cities may be sites reputedly established by Naymlap's grandsons. Large Sican centers are sufficiently numerous to accommodate the claim that all 12 heirs founded important settlements. Yet, here the dynastic lore is best understood in an allegorical sense and seen as rationalizing the emergence of a confederation of local city-states. (On the basis of archaeological site clusters and ethnohistorical information, it has been suggested that there were ten.) Several others no doubt occupied the nearby Zaña drainage to the south.

These ethnic centers probably arose independently at different times and only later put forward claims of descent from Naymlap as a means of forging alliances. Alliances were critical for building and maintaining the great interval-ley canal systems that carried abundant water from the Río Lambayeque to drier northern and southern drainages. Here, for example, the Lambayeque city of Cinto sat at the beginning of the Taymi Canal supplying water to the area around the city of Tucume in the Leche Valley. Therefore, lore purporting that both urban centers were founded by Naymlap's heirs provided a kinship charter for mutual cooperation. Inter-valley canals involved not only great labor and engineering skills, but sensitive claims to water and land. An inter-valley system extending south from the Zaña and north from Jequetepeque was fully completed except for its narrow, mid-point linkup. Here each great canal simply turned down slope and did not bond with its counterpart. Thus, what was technologically feasible was not always politically attainable.

Chotuna was occupied from early Sican times into the Late Horizon to judge from excavations by Christopher Donnan. The civic core of important buildings grew over time, but early construction was largely removed by catastrophic flooding *c.* 1100, and the remnants covered by later reconstruction. Building apparently began with a modest, but ornate set of rooms and courts attached to a small platform, Huaca Gloria, two stories high. Later, this architectural nucleus was isolated and enclosed by tall brick walls built and remodeled several times. Two high platforms overlooking Huaca Gloria were erected against opposite, exterior sides of the spacious court, and adjacent to the long ramp leading to the top of the larger mound, there was an enclosure housing buildings used for metalworking, particularly small copper items. Huaca Gloria was ornamented with distinctive friezes depicting double-headed serpents and other figures, but the Sican Lord is absent, and looters did not leave behind sufficient evidence to tell who or what was buried in the small platform. Nevertheless, it is tempting to see Huaca Gloria as Naymlap's shrine.

Chotuna was neither the biggest settlement nor the largest monumental center in the region. Its special status was as an ancestral center bonding a confederation rather than as a political capital dominating the region. Batan Grande, in the Leche Valley, was the region's pre-eminent center up to the end of the middle Sican Phase. Covering an enormous area, this complex of domestic and monumental buildings probably contains more mounds of exceptional size than any other Andean center of comparable antiquity. Called the Sican Precinct, the civic core covers 4 sq. km and includes more than a dozen truncated pyramids. Huaca Corte is among the largest and measures 250 m square. Many architectural elements were carried over from Pampa Grande, including an emphasis on large platforms with prominent perpendicular ramps, summit colonnades, chamber and fill construction, and the use of marked adobes.

The pyramids of Batan Grande tower over a landscape that resembles the pitted surface of the moon, because grave robbing has been practiced here for centuries, and even include gaping holes carved by bulldozers. People were buried in a flexed and seated position, reflecting new beliefs after the collapse of Moche, and were often richly accompanied. Izumi Shimada's detailed studies indicate that the graves number in the tens of thousands, reminiscent of Pachacamac's vast cemeteries, and one must wonder if more people were not buried at Batan Grande than resided in the center. The center may have been a religious capital similar to today's Vatican. Much of the plundered Peruvian goldwork now in private collections and museums reputedly came from elite

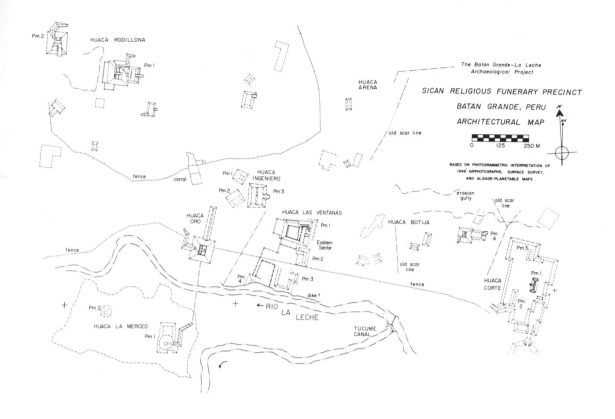

122 A plan of the Sican Precinct of Batan Grande.

burials at Batan Grande. A single tomb in the central precinct yielded some 200 gold and silver necklaces, mummy masks, repoussé vases, *tumi* knives, other artifacts, and quantities of shell, turquoise, lapis lazuli, emerald inlays, and other adornments. Another tomb held 17 human sacrifices, quantities of Ecuadorian *Spondylus* shells, lapis lazuli and precious metal items, as well as some 500 kg of copper artifacts including orderly stacks of *naipes* arranged 500 to a stack.

Naipes were common grave accompaniments at Batan Grande, but rare elsewhere. They are small, flat I-shaped objects of hammered and cut sheet copper, ranging from 5 to 7 cm long and from 3 to 5 cm wide. When found stacked together the specimens are often of similar size. Similar objects found in western Mexico and coastal Ecuador are called 'copper axe money' and are thought to have served as money. Copper deposits are rare in coastal Ecuador, and the metal for axe money, if not the objects themselves, must have been imported. The 6,000 seafaring Chincha merchants traveling to Ecuador are reported to have used copper as a medium of exchange, and it seems likely that Batan Grande was a mint for the production and distribution of naipes. Copper arsenical cores were locally mined and there is abundant evidence of smelting and crafting of metal artifacts from about AD 850. Combined with seafaring trade, metallurgical production was clearly a key contributor to the Middle

Sican florescence of Batan Grande. During this florescence much of the Chira and Tumbes regions of northern Peru first entered the Andean cultural fold, a transformation undoubtedly fostered by lively coastal commerce.

After several centuries of good runoff and prosperity, irrigated valleys along the Pacific were suddenly decimated by an exceptionally severe El Niño in AD 1100, which was then followed by generations of drought. Unlike Chotuna, Batan Grande was not rebuilt after massive floods swept through the metropolis. Instead, wood and brush were piled up against the towering pyramids, and the city was burned and abandoned in a dramatic conflagration reminiscent of the final rites that accompanied the earlier demise of Pampa Grande and Cerro Baul. If the lords of Batan Grande ruled as divine intermediaries between the cosmos and humanity, then in the wake of unmitigated natural disaster the populace seemingly concluded they had been duped by false gods and prophets and torched shrines and temples alike. Ideological upheavals were far reaching, and the Sican Lord, Naymlap's apparent emblem, was conspicuously excised from late-phase iconography. The center of power shifted down the Leche Valley to Tucume or Tucume Viejo, which became the region's pre-eminent metropolis. Studies headed by Thor Heyerdahl, Daniel Sandweiss, and Peruvian archaeologists reveal that the northern tradition of erecting colossal mounds culminated at Tucume in the construction of Huaca Larga, a gargantuan platform ranking among the five largest in the continent. The metropolis remained a major center after it was conquered by Chimor c. 1370, but may have joined with the Incas a century later to overthrow this yoke, because the city enjoyed great privilege under the rule of Tahuantinsuyu.

Dynastic lore of the Naymlap dynasty mentions starvation following flood-induced political collapse, and famine was certainly accentuated by the onset of prolonged drought. Coastal irrigation systems were rebuilt after the AD 1100 El Niño, but depleted runoff curtailed long-term recovery. Reminiscent of Cahuachi with its many ceremonial mounds, the Jequetepeque platform mound complex of Pacatanamu, which was stricken by the AD 1100 El Niño event, produced numerous interments displaying anemia, and lack of food leading to demographic decline, which was widespread along the coast. Drought engenders conflict, and in the Andes two ethnic groups turned this into conquest, but one – the highland Incas – commanded better economic and demographic resources than did their adversaries – desert Chimor.

The dynastic lore of Chimor is meagre and vague, listing only nine to eleven pre-Inca rulers. Arriving alone by boat, a man called Taycanamu says he was sent from afar to govern, and settles in the Moche Valley, presumably at Chan Chan. A son subjugates the lower drainage, and his son, Nancenpinco, consolidates the upstream portion of the valley, then carries out the first stage of external expansion, extending the imperial frontiers from the Río Santa to the Río Jequetepeque. Five to seven unnamed rulers supposedly follow, leading up to the reign of Minchançaman. Initiating a second stage of expansion, he reputedly conquers the coast from the Río Chillon through the Río Tumbes, but is defeated by the Incas and taken off to Cuzco. An heir is installed as a puppet, and his heirs lasted into the Spanish colonial period.

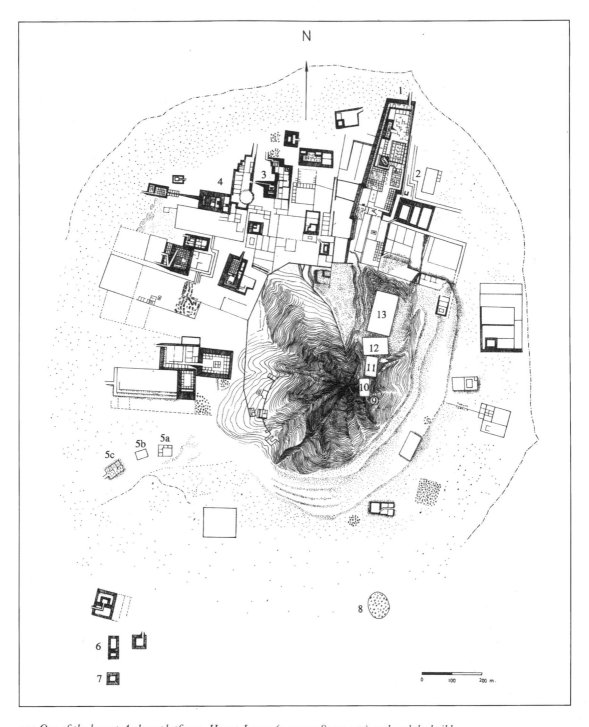

123 One of the largest Andean platforms, Huaca Larga (1,700×280×20 m) anchored the build-ings (2, 5) and many mounds (3, 4, 6, 7) of Tucume Viejo sprawling around La Raya Mountain. Above a sacrosanct cave (9) the towering peak was artificially stepped and built over (10, 11, 12, 13) to create a grand Apu temple in Inca times.

A different Spanish account says that the Jequetepeque Valley was subdued by a general from Chimor called Pacatnamu, who became the first provincial governor and who built an administrative center that came to bear his name. Pacatnamu's exploits pertain to the first episode of expansion, and the center he built is Farfan. Dates from Farfan and fortified sites closer to the Moche Valley indicate that the first stage of expansion was actually a composite episode of incremental conquests that spanned many generations. The same can be said for the second stage because Lambayeque was incorporated several generations before Minchançaman's reign. Other Spanish sources indicate that the imperial artisans at Chan Chan were moved to Cuzco and that there was at least one violent coastal revolt against the Incas.

According to ethnohistorical accounts, prosperous coastal lords resided in walled compounds with spacious courts and appropriate facilities for receiving their subjects and entertaining kuraka elites. The grandest were vast rectangular enclosures with towering adobe walls and an interior mortuary mound that comprised the dominant monuments of Chimor's imperial heartland. Although associated with political administration, the mighty structures bespeak rule by divine right and ancestor veneration uniting noble kin-lines for purposes of governance. Built more or less sequentially over the course of a millennium, 12 such palatial monuments still stand to commemorate graphically the political fortunes of the desert valley. The earliest was built in the valley-neck at the Moche V city of Galindo. Later the majority, including the largest and most elaborate, were erected at Chan Chan near the sea. Finally, with the demise and dismemberment of Chimor, the last great enclosure, Chiquitoy Viejo, was built under Inca aegis on the south side of the Chicama Valley to control the main road leading to the former capital.

With the abandonment of Galindo the valley reverted to the petty city-states encountered by Taycanamu. This was a time when Huari influences melded with local customs to bring forth the new artistic and iconographic tradition *Plates 101, 102* called Chimu, and best represented at Chan Chan. Sea creatures and maritime themes dominate adobe friezes gracing the interior courts and walls of buildings within imperial enclosures. Marine motifs first rose to prominence in the wake of drought during Moche V times, and their later elaboration during dry centuries may reflect beliefs that the ocean was a far more constant provider than the land. Indeed, the sea, called *Ni*, was a primary deity, and the tide-pulling moon was considered more potent than the sun. Maritime motifs often *Plate 100* embellish small, but exceptionally important U-shaped buildings called audiencias. Foreshadowing later U-shaped Inca masmas, those at Chan Chan are usually set in a small court and elevated slightly above the court floor. About 4 m square, they have interior wall niches and gabled roofs. Standing in the center of the building, iconographic depictions show a richly garbed figure holding audience with people assembled outside the front of the structure. The architectural form recalls the great U-shaped ceremonial centers of the Initial Period, but at Chan Chan, instead of housing gods, these special buildings were offices of the god-kings of Chimor and its ruling nobility.

VELARDE

SQUIER

GRAN CHIMU

BANDELIER

LABERINTO

UHLE

RIVERO TSCHUDI

CHAYHUAC

PACIFIC OCEAN

MAIN CIUDADELA WALLS
OTHER WALLS
CANAL
DISUSED CANAL
WALK-IN-WELLS
PONDS

GENERAL PLAN OF
CENTRAL CHAN CHAN

0 100 200 300 400 500 600 700 800 900 1000
SCALE IN METERS

*124 At the height of Chimor's political prosperity the imperial capital of
Chan Chan was dominated by palatial compounds.*

125 Adobe friezes were reserved for royal palaces and exceptionally important buildings. This Gran Chimú example depicts interlocking birds with a border of monkeys wearing hats.

The Taycanamu narrative lists nine to eleven pre-Inca rulers, and, depending on how certain of the earliest edifices are categorized there are nine to eleven monumental enclosures at Chan Chan. There is also evidence of at least two large enclosures that were razed and buried. This situation suggests that the heads of state not only manipulated imperial lore by compressing events and eliminating rulers from the dynastic rosters, but that they also selectively retained and eliminated the monuments of previous rulers.

Nonetheless, in final form Chan Chan was a vast metropolis. Its northern city wall bracketed some 20 sq. km of the valley mouth, much of which was open, seemingly set aside for further urban expansion. The densely packed civic center of great enclosures and other buildings covered 6 sq. km. Different types of architecture and construction material distinguish class and occupation. The lower class metropolitan majority lived and worked in quarters comprising small patios and irregular rooms of cane construction. Evidence excavated in these structures indicates that they were occupied by technicians and craftsmen. There was wood and lapidary work, but the dominant concern was large-scale metallurgical production, complemented by weaving. These people enjoyed the social privilege of wearing ear tubes, married among themselves – metalsmiths taking weavers as wives – and were buried in their own cemeteries. It is estimated that some 26,000 craftsmen and women resided in densely packed neighborhoods along the southern and western margins of the civic center when the city was at its height. Another 3,000 lived immediately adjacent to different royal enclosures, which they served directly. By this time neither farmers nor fishermen were allowed to live in the city, which was exclusively concerned with rule and governance.

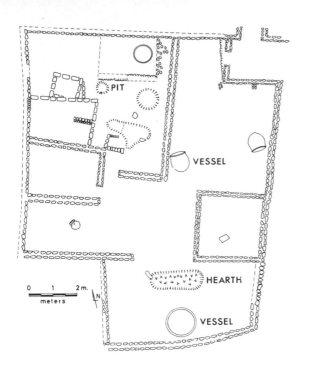

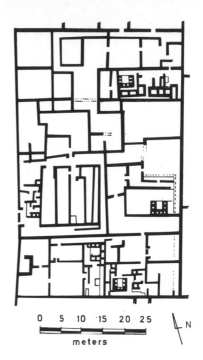

126 (above left) Living and working in cramped quarters made of cane, thousands of artisans and technical personnel resided at the Chimú imperial capital of Chan Chan.

127 (above right) The lesser nobility at Chan Chan resided in irregularly organized adobe compounds that had U-shaped offices but lacked friezes and burial mounds.

128 (right) To serve a ruler and his family in life, as well as death, Ciudadela Rivero at Chan Chan was equipped with U-shaped audiencias for offices, store rooms for wealth finance, and a burial platform for a mausoleum.

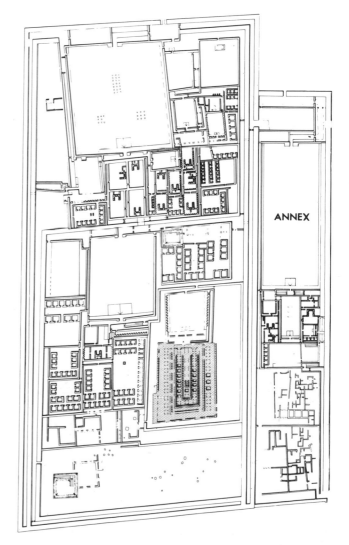

ANNEX

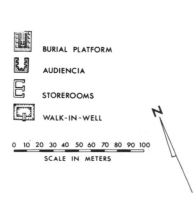

BURIAL PLATFORM
AUDIENCIA
STOREROOMS
WALK-IN-WELL

0 10 20 30 40 50 60 70 80 90 100
SCALE IN METERS

At its height the urban minority of rulers, lords, and kuraka may have numbered 6,000 or less. They lived and worked in two classes of detached brick enclosures. The lesser nobility lived in 30 small compounds with low walls, while paramount rulers held court in the palatial enclosures described above. With political consolidation of the valley around AD 850, monumental construction began with two compounds housing large mounds, and two early enclosures, Tello and Uhle, that were composite complexes of three and four separate compounds, which were eventually joined together. Standardization started with two middle-phase compounds (c. 1125–1350), followed by four late-phase (c. 1350–1470) palaces of highly repetitive form called *ciudadelas* ('citadels'). The palatial complexes are named after early explorers and archaeologists. Within a particular architectural phase two enclosures often exhibit close chronological pairing, and interpretations differ as to which was built first, not surprising if propositions that the ordering of the great enclosures and their spatial distribution were governed by principles of dual rural and moiety organization which split the metropolis into eastern and western sections.

Plate 100 The final pair of enclosures, Rivero and Tschudi, are classic ciudadelas, built shortly before the conquest of Chimor. Tschudi yielded otherwise rare specimens of Chimu-Inca ceramics and is a potential candidate for Minchançaman's court. Both complexes were enclosed by thick walls towering three stories high. Erected in segments by mit'a labor, the lofty walls seclude the royalty and graphically distinguish their grandiose quarters from the lesser nobility and the rest of humanity. Other than a royal family and servants few people lived in the Plate 103 stately compounds, even though the smallest, Rivero, is six times the size of a football field. Entry was through a narrow northern gateway and limited to single-file traffic. High curtain walls partitioned the interiors into northern, central, and southern sectors, and sometimes a fourth, eastern sector. Residing in humble cane quarters, retainers lived in the southern sector, which lacked brick buildings. The northern and central sectors each held a large centrally positioned entry court, often ornamented with carved friezes. A ramp at the southern end of the reception court led up to an elevated complex of maze-like corridors connecting smaller courts housing U-shaped audiencias and warehouses comprising rows of cell-like rooms for the storage of elite goods. Often Plates 101, 102 embellished with maritime friezes, audiencias were hierarchically arranged and controlled access to one another and to certain storage facilities.

In late ciudadelas the northern sectors contained many more audiencia offices than the central sectors, which sometimes had only one – possibly a throne room. Alternatively, more warehouses occupied central than northern sectors, and these facilities were probably imperial coffers serving wealth finance. It is likely that the paramount royalty held court and resided in the central sector, while attendant nobles worked in the northern offices, but lived outside the palaces either in annexes or in small enclosures of their own.

The largest construction associated with almost all the imperial compounds was a huaca sepultura. This was secluded within a high-walled court and generally set within the central sector. Platforms were one, two, or more stories

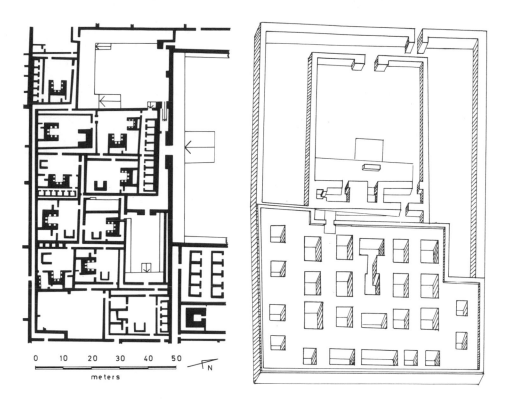

129 *A plan of the hierarchical organization of U-shaped audiencia offices in Ciudadela Tschudi at Chan Chan.*

130 *Chimú heads of state were interred in huacas sepultura. The smallest and best-preserved, Huaca Avispas, had a central T-shaped chamber and ancillary cells that once contained great wealth and the bodies of young women.*

high, and all had multiple interior chambers and cells. The Tschudi huaca and other late mounds were built with rectangular cells symmetrically arranged around a central chamber. This compartment was distinguished by great size and a T-shaped ground plan. The T-shaped chamber presumably held the corpse for which the platform was built, and the richest of the accompaniments placed in the cells at the time of interment. It is significant that in many cases a smaller platform, itself containing a number of smaller T-shaped cells, was later annexed to the principal huaca. These cells were apparently put into service over a span of time to accommodate a number of important, yet less richly accompanied, elite. Excavations of looters' dregs in cells, chambers, and votive deposits around the platforms reveal a 'shrine complex' of rich and distinctive remains, including abundant *Spondylus* and Conus shells, llama bones, bones of numerous human juveniles (largely young women) and phenomenal concentrations of fine textiles, pottery, and other elite goods. Spanish documents record that the Chan Chan huacas sepulturas also contained inordinate quantities of precious metal.

Among later ciudadelas each burial platform is thought to be the mausoleum of the ruler who built the associated compound to serve as his imperial court. This lord was the founding ancestor of a kingly lineage and important heirs were subsequently buried in T-shaped chambers of platform annexes. If this interpretation is generally correct, then rule was in the hands of multiple royal kin-groups associated with different palaces in the eastern or western moieties. The ruling lineages seemingly proliferated over time and new enclosures and ciudadelas were built. However, each palatial compound witnessed an initial era of use when substantial architectural remodeling went on, followed by a critical turning point when all interior construction ceased and the monument was simply maintained, 'frozen' in immutable form. Rituals within the grand enclosures apparently focused more upon the dead than the living. Wooden models of ciudadela entry courts complete with miniature figures and objects mounted on cloth have been found accompanying late Chimú tombs at Huaca de la Luna. The models depict processions of dignitaries, priests, and probable mallquipa-villac entering the plazas with gifts, llamas, and bound prisoners to be offered up to noble mummy bundles, the paramount figures at the rear of the court! Thus, as with the ayllu, the apex of Chimor was glued together by corpses and ancestor veneration.

The growth of Chan Chan was tied to its political fortunes and to its potable water, which came from large open wells with walk-down ramps. In an era of relatively abundant rainfall and runoff, the earliest monuments were erected near the sea where relatively shallow wells could tap the aquifer. Canal reclamation focused upon higher flatlands to the north and west, lying up-slope from Chan Chan where irrigation charged the urban aquifer. Consequently, agrarian expansion elevated the water table and allowed the well-dependent metropolis to grow inland onto higher ground. Over several centuries, the vast canal system above the city was expanded under the direction of rural administrative buildings with audiencias similar in form to those in the Uhle enclosure. The severe El Niño flood of AD 1100 damaged this enclosure and much of the city while completely devastating the entire irrigation system in the Moche Valley and those in other coastal drainages. Arduous reconstruction followed, and canals in the imperial heartland were reshaped with trapezoidal cross-sections and stone lined to increase hydrological efficiency. Yet those recharging Chan Chan's urban aquifer carried meager water and then none because river flow declined with the onset of drought and relatively little land could be watered.

The capital continued to grow inland during its middle phase, but this required excavation of extremely deep wells. Attempting to recharge the urban aquifer, the Lords of Chimor initiated construction of an enormous inter-valley canal, more than 70 km long, designed to irrigate the land above the city with water from the Río Chicama. The entire course was trenched, but only the first portion of the channel was lined and completed. Where this section ends, the canal now runs uphill suggesting that the builders unsuccessfully tried to cross an active fault. Failure of the inter-valley canal curtailed inland expansion and forced the metropolis to grow back toward the sea where wells could reach the depressed water table. Enormous sunken gardens were excavated along the ocean side of the city, and multitudes of smaller gardens were laboriously dug from the river delta up to 5 km inland. Yet, in the imperial heartland and elsewhere, vast investments in sunken garden farming fell far short of mitigating the loss of irrigated land due to drought. Settlement surveys in the Viru and other littoral valleys reveal a dramatic decline in the size of late prehistoric populations.

Incremental conquest and territorial expansion beyond the Moche Valley were underway during the city's early phase, when great labor was also being invested in land reclamation around the city. When the El Niño floods of 1100 rendered such investments inoperative and curtailed further reclamation, the lords of Chimor turned their attentions to obtaining agricultural land by force. By about 1200, General Pacatanamu had won the Jequetepeque region and erected Farfan as an imperial administrative center there. This center and a similar state-built facility in the Viru Valley have audiencias similar in style and date to the final section of the Uhle enclosure at Chan Chan. Both sites also have a burial platform, suggesting Pacatanamu and his southern counterpart governed as vice royalty.

But this pattern of rural rule changed by the time the Lambayeque region was incorporated, when administrative centers were erected with audiencias, but not burial platforms. Governors ruled indirectly through local kuraka, while the kings of Chimor monopolized the privilege of platform burial. Subjugation of Naymlap's former dominion fostered dramatic changes at Chan Chan as its last architectural phase opened. The victory was attributed to the western moiety, previously the junior family of royal kin groups. Formerly, western palaces were not built with burial platforms, but they were now erected with great mausoleums, and mortuary mounds were even added to earlier ciudadelas which originally lacked them. The urban population also changed, and it is estimated that almost 10,000 skilled metallurgists and craftsmen and women from the north were brought into the city to serve their new masters.

From the perspective of multilinear evolution, the long trajectory of lowland Maritime-Oasis development culminated in Chimor and Chan Chan; while the evolution of highland Arid Montane adaptations climaxed with the Incas and Cuzco. From a geopolitical perspective, the rise of these competitive nations pitted the two great demographic centers of the Andes against one another in a protracted struggle for sovereignty over the Cordillera. Protracted drought tipped the economic and demographic balance of power, and the greater forces of the southern mountains prevailed over those of the northern desert. This brought about the final political synthesis of the Andes that was known as Tahuantinsuyu, and the Late Horizon of unity was the last.

EPILOGUE

Tracing the evolution of Andean civilization has allowed us to share thoughts about world-class monuments and marvelous antiquities. Terrorism made many great ruins unsafe to visit and the destruction of others proceeded at an alarming rate when I wrote the first edition epilogue for this book. Fortunately, tourists now enjoy secure access to all the grand monuments. Unfortunately, each is fast becoming a small 'antiquity preserve,' because the devastation of sites and wasting of archaeological landscapes is ever increasing. If the present learned from the past, then things might be different, but this is not the case in the Cordillera or elsewhere. People colonized the Andes during the Pleistocene and civilization blossomed during the Holocene, but we currently live in what scientists are calling the 'Anthropocene,' an era in which human alteration of the atmosphere and ocean has detrimentally changed earth's climatic habitats. Indeed, the Cordillera has warmed to the point that mountain glaciers supplying long-term climatic records are now melting for the first time in thousands of years.

The Anthropocene has its foundations in Columbus' New World landfall, which opened an unprecedented evolutionary episode of escalating environmental alteration. Forces of the new era, which destroy habitats and drive species extinction, impacted first upon Native Americans. With these people largely gone, their archaeological remains are now being obliterated by the same forces. The era opened when Tahuantinsuyu was arguably the largest nation on earth and then saw its dismemberment among half a dozen modern countries. Some of these countries have witnessed more coups and changes of government than years of statehood, while others have seen a majority of their national territory in insurrection and beyond control. Social and governmental instability will increase with Anthropocene climatic change as we have repeatedly seen in the past. Maintaining rule and order has never been easy in the Cordillera, but some forms of government are certainly more appropriate than others. Tahuantinsuyu was grounded in institutions of statecraft that evolved out of folk adaptations to global extremes in environmental conditions. Consequently, government embraced symbiotic relationships that complemented the well-being of its host populations. This symbiosis dissolved in the wake of European pestilence, people, and political economy. The alien order has never reproduced itself well in anoxic mountain habitats where large indigenous populations survive. Accordingly, seats of government and industry are in lower, warmer settings where Old World people, plants, and animals could successfully replace New World species.

Spatially segregated, native mountain people became a denigrated ethnic underclass governed indirectly from distant capitals of Spanish establishment, and ruled remotely by the Caitlin Crown and now by international financial institutions. Failing to recognize basic adaptations of high-altitude life, no government has ever recognized the existence of verticality procurement. Indeed, because the essential role of direct commodity procurement to highland communities is based upon scattered, discontinuous land-holding patterns, the adaptation has remained an anathema to Old World notions about territorial and economic organization. Beginning with Spanish land-ownership practices and continuing through recent agrarian reform policies, vertical procurement adaptations have been systematically undercut for 500 years. Thus there is very good reason for popular unrest among highlanders and the instability of European-style statecraft which will become ever more tenuous as the climate changes yet again.

The past and future of Andean civilization is tied to agriculture, and we have seen that abandoned farming systems are by far the largest of human works in the Cordillera. Well-preserved remains of ancient agrarian systems cover millions of hectares, and in many regions people farmed 25 to 95 percent more land before Columbus arrived than is in production today. Visiting Machu Picchu today it must be remembered that this pinnacle sanctuary was formerly flanked by vast agrarian terraces that are now in thick forest where no one farms. Because they are the largest and most widespread of archaeological remains in the continent, abandoned farmlands have long fascinated me. Finding ancient canals that now run uphill prompted interest in plate tectonics and chronicling earth movement. Fields washed away by enormous floods promoted an ongoing chase for documenting ancient El Niño events, some of which are far larger than historical records attest to. Finally, those formerly extensive farming systems where no water flows today provide important testimony to climatic swings and changes. I believe that the loss of farmland is a continuing process driven by ongoing environmental processes which contemporary political and agrarian planners are neither aware of nor immune to. Consequently, I believe that notions of 'sustainable' agricultural development in the Andes are nothing more than an ill-founded myth propagated by the current political economy. The myth allows international financing and western technology to sponsor the investment in Andean countries of the construction of very sizeable reclamation projects. Many of the very biggest projects are erected within the ruins of more expansive ancient agricultural works, and all modern undertakings proceed with absolutely no study or knowledge of why the earlier, larger systems collapsed in the first place. Systematic destruction of past sites and agrarian landscapes that might reveal both what the Anthropocene will bring and how to adapt is the product of an unstated premise that western technology is divorced from the past. Proceeding on deliberate ignorance, the scale of archaeological destruction by Andean reclamation and development projects far exceeds that of Egypt's Aswan Dam. Yet there is absolutely no international hue and cry to save great Andean monuments, and little measurable assistance to salvage ruins and antiquities slated for eradication. More is the pity in the Anthropocene age because what is being destroyed records both climatic change and successful and unsuccessful responses to it. However, the myth of sustainable development rests upon the untenable premise of environmental stability which allows governments to raise their national debt to build yet another dam in the Cordillera. From an evolutionary perspective this is expectable, because those in political power trace their ancestry to Spain and the Old World. Salvaging prehistory from the bulldozer's plow is not a priority, because it is associated with the denigrated ethnic underclass of the mountains. With few to claim it as their own, Andean civilization is the orphan of the ancient world. Consequently, the adage that the present learns from the past does not apply to the past of other people whom we do not understand.

SOURCES OF ILLUSTRATIONS

Numerals in *italics* refer to line illustrations; numerals in **bold** refer to plates

M. Allison et al. 'Chinchorro, momias de preparacion complicada. . .', *Chungara* 13 (1984): *42* • American Museum of Natural History **86** • Jose Canziani Amico, *Asentamientos humanos y formaciones sociales en la costa norte del antiguo Perú* (del Paleolitico a Moche V), 1989: *50, 60* • Ferdinand Anton, *The Art of Ancient Peru*, Thames and Hudson, London 1972: *41, 43, 78, 92, 102, 103* • Ferdinand Anton, *Ancient Peruvian Textiles*, Thames and Hudson, London 1987: *3, 21, 24, 45, 49, 64, 67, 75, 91, 112, 120*; **89** • George Bankes, *Peru before Pizarro*, Phaidon, Oxford 1977: *66* (drawing Michael Jones) • R. Braunmüller, Museum für Volkerkunde, Munich **69, 70, 90** • British Museum **61** • Geoffrey H. S. Bushnell, *Peru*, Thames and Hudson, London 1965: *7, 32* (drawn by Mrs G. E. Daniel), *88* (redrawn from Larco) • Cambridge University Museum of Anthropology and Ethnography **10, 19, 22, 23, 68, 92** • Chan Chan-Moche Valley Project *79–86, 107, 109, 110, 124–130*; **35, 36, 60, 100, 102** • C. Chauchat *39* • K. and S. Chavez *63* • Cleveland Museum of Art **21** (The Norweb Collection, CMA 40.530) • William Conklin *62*; **87** • Christopher B. Donnan *15, 17, 18, 87, 89, 90*; *66* • Simon S. S. Driver *37* • José Emperaire, Annette Laming-Emperaire, and Henry Riichlen, 'La Grotte Fell et autres sites de la région volcanique de la Patagonie Chilienne', *Journal de la Societé des Américanistes*, 1963: *38* • Patricia A. Essenpreis **12, 42** • Robert Feldman *52, 53, 113*; **25, 26, 41, 78, 91, 93, 96** • Robert Feldman and Ryan Williams *114* • Field Museum of Natural History, Chicago **26, 88** • Carlos Fernando Fuentes *99* • Paul Goldstein *33, 104, 105, 115–118* • Terence Grieder, *Galgada Peru: A Preceramic Culture in Transit*, 1988: *51* • Abraham Guillen M. **97** • Ann Kendall, *Everyday Life of the Incas*, Batsford, London 1973: *13* • Alan Kolata *100*; **74, 83–85** • George Kubler, *The Art and Architecture of Ancient America*, Penguin Books, Harmondsworth and Baltimore 1962: *48, 57, 58,*

76, 101 (drawings by K. F. Rowland) • Rafael Larco Hoyle **37, 38, 44, 46, 51, 52, 53** • Vincent R. Lee *34* • S. Loton *97, 98* • Thomas F. Lynch *40*; **27, 28** • Hans Mann **1, 3, 4, 8, 9, 11, 18, 31, 67, 101** • Craig Morris and Donald E. Thompson *Huánuco Pampa: an Inca City and its hinterland*, Thames and Hudson, London and New York 1985: *26, 27, 31* • Michael E. Moseley *11* (drawing by Tracy Wellman), *12* (modified from Paul Kosok, drawing by Tracy Wellman), *19* (drawing by Tracy Wellman), *29, 46, 47, 54, 65, 68* (after Lumbreras), *93, 94, 96*; **30, 32, 33, 34, 43, 47, 48, 49, 55, 72, 73, 76, 77, 79, 80, 98, 99** • Musée de l'Homme **71, 75** • Museo Arqueologico, Cuzco **24** • NASA **7** • National Museum of Archaeology, Lima **95** • The Newark Museum **20** • Kristine Olsen **64** • Peabody Museum, Harvard University **57, 58, 62, 65, 103** • Annick Peterson *1, 2* (redrawn by Tracy Wellman), *10, 36, 44, 55, 69, 77, 106, 119* • Philadelphia University Museum **45** • Guaman Poma *4, 16, 20, 22, 23, 28, 30, 31* (above left) • R. Ravines *61* • John H. Rowe *35, 72, 73, 74* • Dan Sandweiss *123* • Alan R. Sawyer, *Tiahuanaco Tapestry Design*, 1963: *111* (drawing Milton Franklin Sonday, Jr; courtesy the Museum of Primitive Art, New York) • Servicio Aerofotografico Nacional, Peru **5** (photo Hans Mann), **6, 29, 50** • Izumi Shimada *108, 121, 122* • Shippee-Johnson Expedition, American Museum of Natural History **2, 39, 54, 55, 56, 86** • Bunny Stafford **13, 81, 82** • Nicholas J. Saunders, *People of the Jaguar: the living spirit of ancient America*, Souvenir Press, London 1989: *25* (after Roe 1974, Fig. 29a), *70* (after Rowe 1967, Fig. 11), *71* (after Roe 1978, Fig. 1) (all drawings by Pauline Stringfellow); **17** • Frank Spooner Pictures (photo Carlos Angel) **63** • H. Ubbelohde-Doering, On the Royal Highways of the Inca, Thames and Hudson, London, 1967: *16* • Tracy Wellman *5* • Carlos Williams, 'A Scheme for the Early Monumental Architecture of the Central Coast of Peru', in Christopher B. Donnan (ed.), *Early Ceremonial Architecture in the Andes*: *56, 59* • Nicholas Young **14**

Adorno, R. 1986 *Guaman Poma: Writing and Resistance in Colonial Peru*. Austin: University of Texas Press.

Allen, C. 1988 *The Hold Life Has: Coca and Cultural Identity in an Andean Community*. Washington, D.C.: Smithsonian Institution Press.

Antúnez de Mayolo, S. E. 1981 *La Nutrición en el Antiguo Perú*. Lima: Banco Central de la Reserva del Perú.

Baker, P., and M. Little (eds.) 1976 *Man in the Andes*. Stroudsburg, PA: Dowden, Hutchinson, and Ross.

Bastien, J. 1978 *Mountain of the Condor: Metaphor and Ritual in an Andean Ayllu*. St. Paul: West Pub. Co.

Betanzos, J. D. 1996 *Narrative of the Incas [1557]*. Austin: University of Texas Press.

Castro, A. 1992 *Hanan Huanca. História de Huanca Alta y de los Pueblos del Valle del Mantaro desde sus Orígenes hasta la República*. Lima: Asociación Editorial Stella.

Classen, C. 1993 *Inca Cosmology and the Human Body*. Salt Lake City: Univ. of Utah Press.

Cobo, B. 1979 (1653) *History of the Inca Empire: An account of the Indians' customs and their origin together with a treatise on Inca legends, history, and social institutions [1653]*. Austin: University of Texas Press.

Collier, G., et al. (ed.) 1982 *The Inca and Aztec States, 1400–1800*. New York: Academic Press.

Conrad, G. W., and Arthur A. Demarest 1984 *Religion and Empire: The Dynamics of Aztec and Inca Expansionism*. Cambridge: Cambridge University Press.

Cook, D. 1981 *Demographic Collapse: Indian Peru, 1520–1620*. Cambridge: Cambridge University Press.

Davies, N. 1995 *The Incas*. Niwot: University Press of Colorado.

Duviols, P. 1986 *Cultura Andina y Represión: Procesos y Visitas de Idolatrías y Hechicerías, Cajatambo, Siglo XVII*. Cuzco: Centro de Estudios Rurales Andinos 'Bartolomé de Las Casas'.

Elkin, D., et al. (ed.) 1994 *Zooarqueologia de Camelidos: Perspectivas Teóricas y Metodológicos*. Grupo de Zooarqueologia de Camelidos, Año 1. Buenos Aires.

Espinosa, W. 1987 *Artesanos, Transacciones, Monedas, y Formas de Pago en el Mundo Andino. Siglos XV y XVI*. Lima: Banco Central de Reserva del Peru.

Flannery, K., J. Marcus, and R. Reynolds 1989 *The Flocks of the Wamani: A Study of Llama Herders on the Punas of Ayacucho, Peru*. New York: Academic Press.

Flores Ochoa, J. (ed.) 1988 *Llamichos y Paqocheros – Pastores de Llamas y Alpacas*. Cuzco: Consejo Nacional de Ciencia y Tecnología.

Gelles, P. 2000 *Water and Power in Highland Peru: The Cultural Politics of Irrigation and Development*. New Brunswick: Rutgers University Press.

Harrison, R. 1989 *Signs, Songs, and Memory in the Andes: Translating Quechua Language and Culture*. Austin: University of Texas Press.

Holmes, R. 1986 *Irrigation in Southern Peru: The Chili Basin*. Chicago: University of Chicago.

Huanca, L. T. 1989 *El Yatiri: En la Communidad Aymara*. La Paz: CADA.

Isbell, B. J. 1978 *To Defend Ourselves: Ecology and Ritual in an Andean Village*. Austin: University of Texas Press.

Julien, C. 1991 *Condesuyo: The Political Division of Territory under Inca and Spanish Rule*. Bonn: Bonner Amerikanistische Studien.

Julien, C. 2000 *Reading Inca History*. Iowa City: University of Iowa Press.

Kuznar, L. 1994 *Awatimarka: The Ethnoarchaeology of an Andean Herding Community*. Fort Worth: Harcourt Brace.

Lehman, D. (ed.) 1982 *Ecology and Exchange in the Andes*. Cambridge: Cambridge University Press.

MacCormack, S. 1993 *Religion in the Andes – Vision and Imagination in Early Colonial Peru*. Princeton University Press.

Masson, L. 1984 *Las Terrazas Agrícolas: Una Tecnología Olvidada en el Perú*. Lima: Banco Continental.

Masuda, S., I. Shimada, and C. Morris (ed.) 1985 *Andean Ecology and Civilization: An Interdisciplinary Perspective on Andean Ecological Complementarity*. Japan: University of Tokyo Press.

Masuda, S. (ed.) 1988 *Recursos Naturales Andinos*. Tokyo: University of Tokyo Press.

Mayer, E., and R. Bolton (ed.) 1980 *Parentesco y Matrimonio en los Andes*. Lima: Universidad Católica del Perú.

Millones, L., and H. Tomoeda (ed.) 1982 *El Hombre y su Ambiente en los Andes Centrales*. Senri Ethnological Studies No. 10. Osaka, Japan: National Ethnological Museum.

Millones, L. C. 1990 *El Retorno de las Huacas: Estudios y Documentos del Siglo XVI*. Lima: Instituto de Estudios Peruanos.

Mitchell, W. P., and D. Guillet (ed.) 1994 *Irrigation at High Altitudes: The Social Organization of Water Control Systems in the Andes*. Am. Anthropological Assoc., Society for Latin American Anthropology, Pub. Series Vol. 12.

Murra, J. 1972 'El "Control Vertical" en un Maximo de Pisos Ecológicos en la Economía de las Sociedades Andinas' in *Visita de la Provincia de Leon de Huanuco en 1562*. J. Murra. Huanuco, Peru. 2: 427–476.

Murra, J. 1980 *The Economic Organization of the Inka State*. Greenwich, Conn.: JAI Press.

Murra, J., et al. (ed.) 1986 *Anthropological History of Andean Politics*. Cambridge: Cambridge University Press.

Oliver-Smith, A. 1986 *The Martyred City: Death and Rebirth in the Andes*. Illinois: Waveland Press.

Orlove, B., and D. Guillet 1985 'Theoretical and Methodological Considerations in the Study of Mountain Peoples: Reflections on the Idea of Subsistence Type and the Role of History in Human Ecology', *Mountain Research and Development* 5 1: 3–18.

Parssinen, M. 1992 *Tawantinsuyu: The Inca State and its Political Organization*. Helsinki: Societas Historica Finlandiae.

Patterson, T. 1991 *The Inca Empire: The Formation and Disintegration of Pre-Capitalist State*. New York: Berg.

Pease, G. 1992 *Curacas, Reciprocidad y Riqueza*. Lima: Pontifica Universidad Católica del Perú.

Piperno, D. and D. Pearsall 1998 *The Origins of Agriculture in the Lowland Neotropics*. San Diego: Academic Press.

Platt, T. 1976 *Espejos y Maiz: Temas de Estructura Simbólica Andina*. La Paz: CIRCA.

Poma de Ayala, F. G. 1936 (1st ed. *c.* 1600) *Nueva Crónica y*

Buen Gobierno. Valladolid, VA: Spain, Libreria Maxtor.

Ramirez-Horton, S. 1997 *The World Upside Down: Cross Cultural Contact and Conflict in Sixteenth Century Peru*. Stanford: Stanford University Press.

Rasnake, R. 1989 *Autoridad y Poder en los Andes: Los Kuraqkuna de Yura*. La Paz: HISBOL.

Rostworowski de Diez Canseco, M. 1981 *Recursos naturales renovables y pesca, siglos XVI Y XVII*. Lima: Instituto de Estudios Peruanos.

Rostworowski de Diez Canseco, M. 1988 *História del Tahuantinsuyu*. Lima: Instituto de Estudios Peruanos.

Rostworowski de Diez Canseco, M. 1992 *Pachacamac y El Señor de Los Milagros*. Lima: Instituto de Estudios Peruanos.

Sallnow, M. 1987 *Pilgrims of the Andes – Regional Cults in Cusco*. Washington, D.C.: Smithsonian Institution Press.

Salomon, F., and George Urioste 1991 *The Huarochirí Manuscript, a Testament of Ancient and Colonial Andean Religion*. Austin: University of Texas Press.

Salomon, F. 1986 *Native Lords of Quito in the Age of the Incas: The Political Economy of North Andean Chiefdoms*. Cambridge: Cambridge University Press.

Silverblatt, I. 1987 *Moon, Sun, and Witches: Gender Ideologies and Class in Inca and Colonial Peru*. Princeton University Press.

Silverman, G. 1994 *El Tejido Andino: Un Libro de Sabiduria*. Peru: Banco Central de Reserva del Peru.

Spaulding, K. 1984 *Huarochiri: An Andean Society under Inca and Spanish Rule*. Stanford University Press.

Spier, F. 1992 *Religious Regimes in Peru: Religion and State Development in a Long-Term Perspective and the Effects in the Andean Village of Zurite*. Amsterdam.

Thompson, L. G., E. Mosley-Thompson, J. F. Bolzan, and B. R. Koci 1985 'A 1,500-year record of tropical precipitation in ice core from the Quelccaya ice cap, Peru', *Science* 229: 971–973.

Treacy, J. M. 1989 *The Fields of Coporaque: Agricultural Terracing and Water Management in the Colca Valley, Arequipa, Peru*. Ann Arbor: University Microfilms.

Tschopik, H. 1951 *The Aymara of Chucuito, Peru. Pt. 1: Magic*. New York: American Museum of Natural History.

Urton, G. 1981 *At the Crossroads of the Earth and Sky: An Andean Cosmology*. Austin: University of Texas Press.

Urton, G. D. 1990 *The History of a Myth: Pacaritambo and the Origin of the Inkas*. Austin: University of Texas Press.

Villanueva, H., and J. Sherbondy 1983 *Cuzco: Aguas y Poder*. Cuzco: Centro de Estudios Rurales Andinos Bartolome de Las Casas.

Von Hagen, A., and C. Morris 1998 *The Cities of the Ancient Andes*. London and New York: Thames and Hudson.

Zuidema, R. T. 1964 *The Ceque System of Cuzco: The Social Organization of the Capital of the Inca*. Leiden: E. J. Brill.

Zuidema, R. T. 1990 *Inca Civilization in Cuzco*. Austin: University of Texas Press.

ARCHAEOLOGICAL BIBLIOGRAPHY

Albarracin-Jordan, J., and J. Mathews 1991 *Los Asentamientos Prehispánicos en el Valle de Tiwanaku*. Volume 1. La Paz, Bolivia: Producciones CIMA.

Albarracin-Jordan, J. 1996 *Tiwanaku: Arqueología Regional y Dinamica Segmentaria*. La Paz: Editores Plural.

Alconini, S. 1995 *Rito, Simbolo e História en la Piramide de Akapana, Tiwanaku: Un análisis de Cerámica Ceremonial Prehispánica*. La Paz: Editorial Acción.

Aldenderfer, M. 1998 *Montane Foragers: Asana and the South-Central Andean Archaic*. Iowa City: University of Iowa Press.

Aldunate, C., and V. Castro 1981 *Las Chullpas de Toconce y su Relación con el Poblamiento Altiplanica en el Loa Superior, Período Tardío*. Santiago: Ediciones Kultrun.

Allison, Marvin J., et al. 1984 Chinchorro, momias de preparación complicada: métodos de momificación. *Chungará* 13:155–174.

Alva, W. 1993 *Las Salinas de Chao: Un Asentamiento Temprano, Observaciones y Problematica*. Munchen, Germany: Kommission fur Allgemeine und Vergleichende Archaoligie des Deutschen Archaologischen, Institus Bonn, Band 34.

Alva, W., and C. Donnan 1993 *Royal Tombs of Sipan*. Los Angeles: Fowler Museum of Culture History, University of California at Los Angeles.

Anton, F. 1987 *Ancient Peruvian Textiles*. London: Thames and Hudson.

Arriaza, B. and A. Aufterheide, et al. 1993 'Análisis antropológico fisico de la inhumación de Acha-2' in *Acha-2*

y los Orígenes de Poblamiento Humano en Arica. I. Muñoz, B. Arriaza, and A. Aufterheide. Arica, Chile, Ediciones Universdiad da Tarapacá: 47–62.

Arriaza, B. 1995 *Beyond Death: The Chinchorro Mummies of Ancient Chile*. Washington, D.C.: Smithsonian Institution Press.

Aveni, A. (ed.) 1991 *The Lines of Nazca*. Philadelphia: The American Philosophical Society.

Bakewell, Peter 1984 *Miners of the Red Mountain: Indian Labor in Potosi, 1545–1650*. Albuquerque: University of New Mexico Press.

Bauer, B. 1992 *The Development of the Inca State*. Austin: University of Texas Press.

Bauer, B. 1998 *The Sacred Landscape of the Inca: The Cuzco Ceque System*. Austin: University of Texas Press.

Bauer, B. and C. Stanish 1990 'Killke and Killke-Related Pottery from Cuzco, Peru, in the Field Museum of Natural History', in *Fieldiana Anthropology*. Chicago: Field Museum of Natural History.

Bawden, G. 1996 *The Moche*. Cambridge: Blackwell Publishers Inc.

Benavides, M. 1984 *Carácter del Estilo Wari*. Ayacucho, Peru: Universidad Nacional de San Cristobal de Humanga.

Benfer, R. 1990 'The Preceramic Period Site of Paloma, Peru: Bioindications of Improving Adaptation to Sedentism', *Latin American Antiquity* 1(4):284–318.

Berman, M. 1994 *Lukurmata: Household Archaeology in Prehispanic Bolivia*. Princeton University Press.

Binford, M. W., A. L. Kolata, M. Brenner, J. W. Janusek,

M. T. Seddon, M. Abbott, and J. H. Curtis 1997 'Climate Variation and the Rise and Fall of an Andean Civilization', *Quaternary Research* 47:235–248.

Bird, J. 1985 *The Preceramic Excavations at the Huaca Prieta, Chicama Valley, Peru*. New York: American Museum of Natural History.

Bonavia, D. 1982 *Los Gavilanes, mar, desierto y oasis en la historia del hombre*. Lima: Editorial Ausonia.

Bonavia, D. 1985 *Mural Paintings in Ancient Peru*. Bloomington: Indiana University Press.

Bonavia, D. 1991 *Peru: Hombre e História de los Orígenes al Siglo XV*. Lima: Fundación del Banco Continental para el Fomento de la Educación y Cultura.

Browman, D. (ed.) 1987 *Arid Land Use Strategies and Risk Management in the Andes*. Boulder, Colorado: Westview Press.

Bruhns, K.O. 1994 *Ancient South America*. Cambridge: Cambridge University Press.

Buikstra, J. 1990 'Sumario de investigación de restos humanos de Omo, Moquegua y San Gerónimo, Ilo', in *Trabajos Arqueológicos en Moquegua, Perú*. M.M. L. Watanabe, and F. Cabieses, (ed.) 59–68, Vol. 2. Lima: Editorial Escuela Nueva.

Burger, R. 1984 *The Prehistoric Occupation of Chavin de Huantar, Peru*. Berkeley: University of California Press.

Burger, R. 1992 *Chavin and the Origins of Andean Civilization*. London: Thames and Hudson.

Canziani, J. 1992 'Arquitectura y urbanismo del período Paracas en el Valle de Chincha', *Gaceta Arqueológica Andina* 22:87–188.

Cardenas M., Mercedes, et al. 1993 *Materiales Arqueologicos del Macizo de Illescus: Sechura-Piura*. Lima: Pontificia Universidad Catolica del Peru.

Cardich, A. 1964 *Lauricocha: Fundamentos para una Prehistória de los Andes Centrales*. Buenos Aires: Studia Praehistorica III, Centro Argentino de Estudios Prehistóricos.

Carneiro, R. 1970 'A theory of the origin of the state', *Science* 169:733–738.

Castillo, L.J., and C. Donnan 1994 'La ocupacion Moche de San Jose de Moro, Jequetepeque', in *Moche: Propuestas y Perspectivas*. S.Uceda and E. Mujica (eds.) 79, 93–146. Lima: Travaux de l'Institut Francais d'Etudes Andines.

Chauchat, C., E. Wing, J. Lacombe, P. Demars, S. Uceda, and C. Deza 1992 *Préhistoire de la Côte Nord du Pérou: Le Paijanien de Cupisnique*. Bourdeaux: CNRS-Editions, Centre Regional de Publication de Bordeaux.

Chavez, K. M. 1989 'The Significance of Chiripa in Lake Titicaca Developments', *Expedition* 30(3):17–26.

Cieza de Leon, Pedro de 1976 *The Incas of Pedro Cieza de Leon* [Part 1, 1553 and Part 2, 1554]. Harriet de Onis, transl. Norman: University of Oklahoma Press.

Cobo, Bernabe 1990 *Inca Religion and Customs [1653]*. Roland Hamilton, transl. Austin: University of Texas Press.

Conziani Amico, Jose 1989 *Asentamientos Humanos y Formaciones Sociales en la Costa Norte del Antiguo Perú*. Lima: Instituto Andino de Estudios Arqueológicos.

Cook, A. 1994 *Wari y Tiwanaku: Entre el Estilo y la Imagen*. Lima: Pontifica Universidad Católica.

D'Altroy, Terence N. 1992 *Provincial Power in the Inka Empire*. Washington D.C.: Smithsonian Institution Press.

Defrance, S. 1996 'Iberian Foodways in the Moquegua and Torata Valleys of Southern Peru', *Historical Archaeology* 30(3):20–48.

Denevan, W. M., K. Mathewson, and G. Knapp (eds.) 1987 *Pre-Hispanic Ridged Fields in the Andean Region*. Volume 359 (ii). Oxford: BAR International Series.

Dillehay, T., and P. Netherly (ed.) 1988 *La Frontera del Estado Inca*. Volume 442. Oxford: BAR.

Dillehay, T. 1989 *Monte Verde: A Late Pleistocene Settlement in Chile*. Vol. 1: Paleoenvironment and Site Context. Washington, D.C.: Smithsonian Institution Press.

Dillehay, T. (ed.) 1995 *Tombs for the Living: Andean Mortuary Practices*. Washington, D.C.: Dumbarton Oaks.

Dillehay, T. 2000 *The Settlement of the Americas*. New York: Basic Books.

Donnan, C., and C. Mackey 1978 *Ancient Burial Patterns of the Moche Valley, Peru*. Austin: University of Texas Press.

Donnan, C. (ed.) 1985 *Early Ceremonial Architecture in the Andes*. Washington, D.C.: Dumbarton Oaks.

Donnan, C., and G. Cock (eds.) 1986 *The Pacatnamu Papers, Vol. 1*. Los Angeles: UCLA Museum of Cultural History.

Donnan, C. 1993 *Ceramics of Ancient Peru*. Los Angeles: Fowler Museum of Cultural History, University of California at Los Angeles.

Earle, T., et al. 1987 *Archaeological Field Research in the Upper Mantaro, Peru, 1982–83: Investigations of Inka Expansion and Exchange*. Los Angeles: Institute of Archaeology, UCLA.

Engel, F. 1991 *Un Desierto en tiempos Prehispánicos*. Lima: Centro de Investigaciones de Zonas Aridas.

Erickson, C. 1995 'Archaeological Methods for the Study of Ancient Landscapes of the Llanos de Mojos in the Bolivian Amazon', in *Archaeology in the American Tropics: Current Analytical Methods and Applications*. P. Stahl (ed.) Cambridge: Cambridge University Press.

Farrington, I. S. (ed.) 1985 *Prehistoric Intensive Agriculture in the Tropics*. Volume 232. Oxford: BAR.

Frost, P. 1989 *Exploring Cuzco*. Lima: Nuevas Imagenes, S.A.

Fung, R. 1969 *Las Aldas: Su Ubicación dentro del Proceso Histórico del Perú Antiguo*. Volume 5, Nos. 9–10. Sao Paula, Brazil: Museu de Arte e Arqueología, Univ. de Sao Paulo.

Gasparini, Graziano, and Luise Margolies 1980 *Inca Architecture*. P.J. Lyon, transl. Bloomington: Indiana University Press.

Goldstein, P. 1993 'Tiwanaku Temples and State Expansion: A Tiwanaku Sunken-Court Temple in Moquegua, Peru', *Latin American Antiquity* 4(1):22–47.

Golte, J. 1994 *Los Dioses de Sipán, II: La Rebelión contra el Dios Sol*. Lima: Instituto de Estudios Peruanos.

Gonzalez, A. 1992 *Las Placas Metálicas de los Andes del Sur Contribución al Estudio de las Religiones Precolombinas*. Mainz am Rhein, Germany: Verlagphilipp von Zabern.

Grieder, T., A. Bueno, C. Smith, and R. Molina 1988 *La Galgada, Peru: A Preceramic Culture in Transition*. Austin: University of Texas Press.

Guaman Poma de Ayala, Felipe 1980 *El primer nueva coronica y buen gobierno [1615]*. 3 vols. Jorge I. Urioste, transl. Mexico City: Siglo Veintiuno.

Haas, Jonathen, Shelia Pozorski and Thomas Pozorski (eds.) 1987 *The Origin and Development of the Andean State*. Cambridge: Cambridge University Press.

Hastorf, C. A. 1993 *Agriculture and the Onset of Political Inequity Before the Inca*. Cambridge: Cambridge University Press.

Hecker, W., and G. Hecker 1991 *Die Huaca 16 in Pacatnamú. Eine Ausgrabung an der Nordperuanischen Küste*. Berlin: Dietrich Reimer Verlag.

Hemming, J., and E. Ranney 1992 *Monuments of the Inca*. Albuquerque: University of New Mexico Press.

Heyerdahl, T., D. Sandweiss, and A. Navaez 1995 *Pyramids of Tucume: The Quest for Peru's Forgotten City*. London: Thames and Hudson.

Hidalgo, L., Jorge, Virgilio Chiappacasse F., Hans Niemeyer F., Carlos Aldunte Del S., & Ivan Solimano R. 1989 *Culturas De Chile Prehistoria: Desde Sus Origenes Hasta Los Albores De La Conquista*. Santiago, Chile: Editorial Andres Bellos.

Hocquenghem, A. 1987 *Iconografía Mochica*. Volume 2. Lima: Pontifica Universidad Catolica del Perú.

Hyslop, J. 1984 *The Inca Road System*. New York: Academic Press.

Hyslop, J. 1990 *Inka Settlement Planning*. Austin: University of Texas Press.

Isbell, W. 1977 *The Rural Foundations for Urbanism*. Illinois: University of Illinois Press.

Isbell, W. and G. McEwan (ed.) 1991 *Huari Administrative Structure: Prehistoric Monumental Architecture and State Government*. Washington, DC: Dumbarton Oaks.

Isbell, W. 1997 *Mummies and Mortuary Practices: A Postprocessual Prehistory of Central Andean Social Organization*. Austin: University of Texas Press.

Izumi, S., and Terada, K. 1972 *Andes 4: Excavations at Kotosh, Peru, 1963 and 1966*. Tokyo: University of Tokyo Press.

Izumi, S., et al. 1972 *Excavations at Shillacoto, Huanuco, Peru*. Tokyo: University of Tokyo.

Julien, C. 1983 *Hatunqolla: A View of Inca Rule from the Lake Titicaca Region*. Berkeley: University of California Press.

Kendall, A. (ed.) 1992 *Current Archaeological Projects in the Central Andes: Some Approaches and Results*. Oxford: BAR.

Kolata, A. (ed.) 1989 *Arqueología de Lukurmata 2: La Tecnología de la Producción Agrícola en el Estado Tiwanaku*. La Paz, Bolivia.

Kolata, A. L. 1993 *The Tiwanaku: Portrait of an Andean Civilization*. Cambridge: Blackwell.

Kolata, A. (ed.) 1996 *Tiwanaku and its Hinterland: Archaeology and Paleoecology of an Andean Civilization*. Volume 1: Agroecology: Smithsonian Institution Press.

Kosok, P. 1965 *Land, Life and Water in Ancient Peru*. New York: Long Island University Press.

Larco Hoyle, R. 1948 *Cronologia Arqueologica del Norte del Peru*. Buenos Aires, Argentina: Sociedad Geografica Americana.

Lavallee, D., et al. 1987 *Telarmachay, Tome 1*. Lima: Institut Francais d'Etudes Andines.

Lechtman, H., and A. Soldi (ed.) 1981 *La Tecnología en el Mundo Andino*. Mexico City: Univ. Nac. Aut. de Mexico.

LeVine, Terry (ed.) 1992 *Inka Storage Systems*. Norman: University of Oklahoma Press.

Llagostera, A. 1992 Fishermen on the Pacific Coast of South America. *Andean Past* (3):87–109.

Lumbreras, Luis G. 1981 *Arqueologia De La America Andina*. Lima: Editorial Milla Batres.

Lumbreras, L. 1989 *Chavin de Huantar en el Nacimiento de la Civilización Andina*. Lima: Inst. Andino de Estudios Arqueológicos.

Lumbreras, L. 1989 *Visión Arqueológica del Perú Milenario*. Lima: Editorial Milla Batres.

Lynch, T. 1967 *The Nature of the Central Andean Preceramic*. Volume No. 21. Pocatello.

Lynch, T. (ed.) 1980 *Guitarrero Cave: Early Man in the High Andes*. New York: Academic Press.

MacCormack, Sabine 1991 *Religion in the Andes: Vision and Imagination in Early Colonial Peru*. Princeton: Princeton University Press.

MacNeish, R. S., R. K. Vierra, A. Nelkin-terner, R. Lurie, and A.Garcia Cook 1983 *Prehistory of the Ayacucho Basin, Peru, Volume IV, The Preceramic Way of Life*. Ann Arbor: University of Michigan Press.

Maldonado, E. 1992 *Arqueología de Cerro Sechín, Vol. 1: Arquitectura*. Lima: Pontifica Universidad Católica del Perú, Lima.

Malpass, M. (ed.) 1993 *Provincial Inca: Archaeological and Ethnohistorical Assessment of the Impact of the Inca State*. Iowa City: University of Iowa Press.

Manzanilla, L. 1992 *Akapana: Una Pirámide en el Centro del Mundo*. Mexico City: Instituto de Investigaciones Antropológicas.

Marcus, Joyce 1987 *Late Intermediate Occupation at Cerro Azul, Peru*. Ann Arbor: Museum of Anthropology, University of Michigan.

Matos, R. (ed.) 1988 *Sociedad Andina Pasado y Presente – Contribuciones en Homenaje a la Memoria de Cesar Fonseca Martel*. Lima: Fomecienias.

McEwan, Gordon F. 1987 *The Middle Horizon in the Valley of Cuzco, Peru: The Impact of the Wari Occupation of the Lucre Basin*. Oxford: British Archaeological Reports.

Menzel, D. 1977 *The Archaeology of Ancient Peru and the Work of Max Uhle*. Berkeley: R.H. Lowie Museum.

Millones, L., and Y. Onuki (ed.) 1993 *El Mundo Cerremonial Andino*. Osaka: National Museum of Ethnology.

Moore, J. 1996 *Architecture and Power in the Ancient Andes: The Archaeology of Public Buildings*. Cambridge: University of Cambridge Press.

Morris, C., and D. Thompson 1985 *Huanuco Pampa: An Inca City and its Hinterland*. London: Thames and Hudson.

Morris, C., and A. Von Hagen 1992 *The Inka Empire and its Andean Origins*. New York: American Museum of Natural History.

Moseley, M., and K. Day (eds.) 1982 *Chan Chan: Andean Desert City*. Albuquerque: University of New Mexico Press.

Moseley, Michael E., and Alana Cordy-Collins (eds.) 1990 *The Northern Dynasties: Kingship and Statecraft in Chimor*. Washington D.C.: Dumbarton Oaks Research Library and Collection.

Muñoz, I., B. Arriaza, and A. Aufderheide (eds.) 1993 *Acha-2 y Los Origenes del Poblamiento Humano en Arica [N. Chile]*. Chile: Universidad de Tarapacá.

Niles, Susan A. 1987 *Callachaca: Style and Status in an Inca Community*. Iowa City: University of Iowa Press.

Nuñez, L., and B. Meggers (eds.) 1987 *Investigaciones Paleoindias al Sur de la Línea Ecuatorial*. San Pedro de Atacama, Chile.

Nuñez, L. 1991 *Cultura y Conflicto en los Oasis de San Pedro de Atacama*. Santiago: Editorial Universitaria.

Ortloff, C. R. and A. L. Kolata 1993 'Climate and collapse: Agro-ecological perspectives on the decline of the Tiwanaku state', *Journal of Archaeological Sciences* 20:195–221.

Oyuela-Caycedo, A. (ed.) 1994 *History of Latin American Archaeology*. UK: Avebury, Aldershot, Hampshire.

Patterson, T. 1991 *The Inka Empire: The Formation and Disintegration of a Pre-Capitalist State*. New York: Berg Publishers.

Paul, A. 1990 *Paracas Ritual Attire: Symbols of Authority in Ancient Peru*. Norman: University of Oklahoma Press.

Paul, A. (ed.) 1991 *Paracas: Art and Architecture, Object and Context in South Coastal Peru*. Iowa City: University of Iowa Press.

Pillsbury, J. 1996 'The Thorny Oyster and the Origins of Empire: Implications of Recently Uncovered *Spondylus* Imagery from Chan Chan, Peru', *Latin American Antiquity* (7):313–340.

Pillsbury, J. (ed.) 2001 *Historiographic Guide to Andean Sources in Art History and Archaeology*. Oklahoma: University of Oklahoma Press.

Ponce, C. 1989 *Arqueología de Lukurmata 1: Ensayo de Historia del Avance Científico (1985–1988)*. La Paz: Sui Generis.

Ponce, C., et al. 1992 *Arqueología Subacuática en el Lago Titicaca*. La Paz: Editorial La Palabra Publicaciones.

Pozorski, Shelia, and Thomas Pozorski 1987 *Early Settlement and Subsistence in the Casma Valley, Peru*. Iowa City: University of Iowa Press.

Protzen, J.P. 1993 *Inca Architecture and Construction at Ollantaytambo*. New York: Oxford University Press.

Quilter, J. 1989 *Life and Death at Paloma: Society and Mortuary Practices in Preceramic Peruvian Village*. Iowa City: University of Iowa Press.

Quilter, J., et al. 1991 'Subsistence Economy of El Paraíso, and Early Peruvian Site', *Science* 251:277–283.

Raffino, R. (ed.) 1993 *Inka – Arqueología, História, y Urbanismo del Altiplano Andino*. Buenos Aires: Ediciones Corregidor.

Ravines, R. 1982 *Panorama de la Arqueología Andina*. Lima: Instituto de Estudios Peruanos.

Ravines, R. (ed.) 1986 *Arte Rupestre del Perú*. Lima: Instituto Nacional de Cultura.

Regal, A. 1970 *Los Trabajos Hidraulicos del Inka*. Lima: Imp. 'Graf Industrial'.

Reiche, M. 1949 *Mystery on the Desert: A Study of the Ancient Figures Near Nasca, Peru*. Lima.

Reinhard, J. 1988 *The Nasca Lines: A New Perspective on their Origin and Meaning*. Lima: Los Pinos.

Reinhard, J. 1991 *Machu Picchu: The Sacred Center*. Lima: Nuevas Imagenes, S.A.

Rice, Don, Charles Stanish, and Phillip R. Scarr (ed.) 1989 *Ecology, Settlement and History in the Osmore Drainage, Peru*. Volume 545. Oxford: BAR International Series.

Richardson, J. 1996 *People of the Andes*. Washington, D.C.: Smithsonian Institution Press.

Rick, J. 1980 *Prehistoric Hunters of the High Andes*. New York: Academic Press.

Rick, J. 1983 *El Precerámico Peruano: Cronología, Clima, y Subsistencia*. Lima.

Rosas, H., and R. Shady 1970 *Pacopampa – Un Centro Formativo en la Sierra Nor-Peruano*. Lima: Univ. Nacional Mayor de San Marcos.

Rowe, J. 1962 *Chavin Art: An Inquiry into its Form and Meaning*. New York: The Museum of Primitive Art.

Rowe, J. 1979 'An Account of the Shrines of Ancient Cuzco', *Ñawpa Pacha* 17:2–80.

Rowe, A. (ed.) 1986 *The Junius B. Bird Conference on Andean Textiles*. Washington, D.C.: The Textile Museum.

Sakai, M. 1998 *Reyes, Estrellas y Cerros en Chimor: El Proceso de Cambio de la Especial y Temporal en Chan Chan*. Lima: Editorial Horizonte.

Sandweiss, D. 1992 *The Archaeology of Chincha Fishermen: Specialization and Status in Inka Peru*. Pittsburgh.

Santoro, Calogero, and Lautaro Nuñez 1987 'Hunters of the dry puna and salt puna in the northern Chile', *Andean Past* 1:57–109.

Schiappacasse, Virgilio, and Hans Niemeyer (eds.) 1984 *Description y analysis interpretativo de un sitio Arcaico Temprano en la Quebrada de Camarones*. Museo Nacional de Historia Natural, Universidad de Tarapacá Publicacion Ocasional No. 41.

Schreiber, K. 1992 *Wari Imperialism in Middle Horizon, Peru*. Ann Arbor: University of Michigan Museum of Anthropology.

Shady, R. S. 1997 *La Ciudad Sagrada de Caral-Supe en Los Albores de la Civilizacion en El Peru*. San Marcos: Universidad Nacional Mayor de San Marcos.

Shady, R., and H. Rosas 1976 *Enterramientos en Chullpas de Chota, Cajamarca*. Lima: Museo Nacional de Antropología y Arqueología.

Shimada, I., C. B. Schaff, L. G. Thompson and E. Mosley-Thompson, 1991 'Cultural impacts of severe droughts in the prehistoric Andes: Application of a 1,500-year ice core precipitation record', *World Archaeology* 22:247–270.

Shimada, I. 1994 *Pampa Grande and the Mochica Culture*. Austin: University of Texas Press.

Shimada, I. (ed.) 1994 *Tecnología y Organización de la Producción de Cerámica en los Andes*. Lima: Pontifica Universidad Católica del Perú, Fondo Editorial.

Silverman, Helaine 1993 *Cahuachi in the Ancient Nasca World*. Iowa City: University of Iowa Press.

Silverman, Helaine 1996 *Ancient Peruvian Art· An Annotated Bibliography*. New York: G.K. Hall and Co.

Stanish, C. 1991 *A Late Pre-Hispanic Ceramic Chronology for the Upper Moquegua Valley, Peru*. Chicago: Field Museum of Natural History.

Stanish, Charles 1992 *Ancient Andean Political Economy*. Austin: University of Texas Press.

Stanish, C., and L. Steadman 1994 *Archaeological Research at the Site of Tumatumani, Juli, Peru*. Chicago: Field Museum of Natural History.

Stanish, C. (ed.) 1997 *Archaeological Survey in the Juli-Desaguadero Region of Lake Titicaca Basin, Southern Peru*. Chicago: Field Museum of Natural History.

Stone-Miller, R. 1995 *Art of the Andes: From Chavin to Inca*. London: Thames and Hudson.

Stothert, K. 1990 *La Prehistória Temprana de la Península de Santa Elena: Cultura de Las Vegas*. Guayaquil, Ecuador: Museos del Banco Central del Ecuador.

Tello, J. 1956 *Arqueología del Valle de Casma*. Lima: Universidad Nacional San Marcos.

Tello, J. 1960 *Chavin: Cultura Matriz de las Civilizaciones Andinas*. Lima: Universidad Nacional San Marcos.

Tello, J., and T. M. Xesspe 1979 *Paracas, II Parte: Cavernas y Necropolis*. Lima: Universidad Nacional Mayor de San Marcos.

Terada, K., and Y. Onuki 1985 *The Formative Period in the Cajamarca Basin, Peru: Excavations at Huacaloma and Layzon, 1982*. Tokyo: University of Tokyo Press.

Topic, J. 1992 'Las huacas de Huamachuco: precisiones en torno a una imagen indígena de un paisaje andino', in *La Persecución del Demonio: Crónica de los Primeros Augustinos en el Norte del Perú*. T.V.R.E. Deeds, L. Millones, J. Topic, and J. González (eds.) Málaga, Spain: Algazara.

Treacy, J. 1994 *Las Chacras de Coporaque: Andenería y Riego en el Valle del Colca*. Lima: Instituto de Estudios Peruanos.

Uceda, S., and E. Mujica (eds.) 1993 *Moche: Propuestas y Perspectivas*. Lima: Universidad Nacional de Trujillo.

Uceda, S., E. Mujica, and R. Morales (eds.) 1997 *Proyecto Arqueologico Huacas de Sol y de la Luna: Investigaciones en la Huaca de la Luna 1995*. Trujillo: Universidad Nacional de la Libertad.

Uhle, M. 1903 *Pachacamac: Report of the Wm. Pepper Expedition of 1896*. Philadelphia: University of Pennsylvania.

Valencia, A., and A. Gibaja 1992 *Machu Pichu: La Investigación y Conservación de los Monumentos Arqueológicos después de Hiram Bingham*. Cuzco, Peru.

VanBuren, Mary 1996 'Rethinking the Vertical Archipelago: Ethnicity, Exchange, and History in the South Central Andes', *American Anthropologist* 92(2):338–351.

Watanabe, L., M. Moseley, and F. Cabieses (eds.) 1991

Trabajos Arqueológicos en Moquegua, Peru. Lima: Museo Peruano de la Salud.

Wheeler, J. C. 1984 'On the origin and early development of camelid pastoralism in the Andes', in *Animals and Archaeology. III. Early herders and their Flocks*. BAR International Series 20, J. Clutton-Brock, and Grigson, C. (eds.) 395–410.

Willey, G. 1953 *Prehistoric Settlement Patterns in the Viru Valley, Peru*. Washington, D.C.: Smithsonian Institution.

Williams Leon, C. 1980 'Complejos piramides con planta en U, patron arquitectonico de la costa central', *Revista del Museo Nacional* (1978–80) 44:95–110.

Wilson, D. J. 1988 *Prehispanic Settlement Patterns in the Lower Santa Valley, Peru: A Regional Perspective on the Origins and Development of Complex North Coast Society*. Washington, DC: Smithsonian Institution Press.

Wing, E., and J. Wheeler (eds.) 1988 *Economic Prehistory of the Central Andes*. Volume International Series No. 427. Oxford: BAR.

Ziólkowski, M., and R. Sadowski (eds.) 1989 *Time and Calendars in the Inca Empire*. Oxford, U.K.: British Archaeological Reports.

Zuidema, R. Tom 1986 *La Civilisation Inca au Cuzco*. Paris: Presses Univeritaires de France, Collège de France.

INDEX

Numerals in *italics* refer to line drawings; numerals in **bold** refer to plates

Acari valley 197
achira 113, 128
adobe 143, 159, 162, 177, 178, 197, 199, 225, 226, 227, 240, 260, 261, 264, 267, *52*, *125*, *127*, **101**
agriculture 31, 41, 50, 51, 52, 53, 55, 73, 77, 78, 107, 112, 133–36, 144, 157, 199, 207, 232, 239, 242, 245, 257, 258, 277, *13*, *16*
agropastoralism 41, 44, 45, 47, 55, 70, 102–03, 107, 110, 131, 144, 157, 173, 221, 242
Aiapec 68
Akakana 217, 243
Aldenderfer, Mark 98
Algodonal 242
alpaca 41, 42, 44, 72, 104, 143, 155, 162, 198, 243, 246, **4**
altars 126, 137, 206
altiplano 26, 32, 41, 46, 68, 99, 119, 208, 220, 221, 222, 233, 238, 239, 240, 242, 243, 245, 246
altitude 7, 8, 27, 28, 31, 41, 44, 47, 72, 73, 131, 143, 154, 177, 232, 235, 258
Alto Salavery 119
Alva, Walter 193
Amazon 7, 26, 30, 42, 50, 103, 109
Amotape phase 93
Amuesha 258
Anahuaylas Basin 207
ancestry 53, 55, 56, 65, 69, 75;

ancestor veneration 100, 173, 205, 248, 274
Ancon Bay 113
Ancon-Chillon 95
Andahuaylas Valley 154, 208
Andamarca 154
Andes 9, 11, 13, 17, 19, 20, 26, 27, 28, 30, 41, 43, 44, 49, 53, 56, 68, 79, 80, 87, 88, 89, 91, 96, 99, 102, 105, 107, 108, 111, 131, 133, 135, 154, 155, 167, 169, 170, 178, 238, 261, 266, 272, 275, 276, 277, *13*
animals 10, 27, 29, 30, 44, 47, 52, 87, 88, 92, 95, 100, 102, 104, 117, 143, 246, 276; totemic 79; *see also* named animals, iconography, motifs
anoxia 8, 27, 44, 50, 88, 89, 103, 276
Anthropocene 276, 277
Antisuyu 41, 42, 82; mountains 3
apu 51, 52, 65, 66, 69, 119, 129, 217, 236
archaeology 17–21, 41, 47, 48, 84, 102, 107, 261, 262, 263
architecture 18, 43, 68, 79, 80–81, 84, 95, 109, 113, 118, 121, 129, 156, 168, 173, 226, 227–28, 234, 248, 257, 270, **15**, **16**, **17**; ceremonial 136–37, 144, 234; corporate 260; monumental 178
Argentina 7, 91, 95, 103
Arica 247
Arid Montane lifeway 25; adaptations 27, 31, 43, 44–48, 53, 59, 131, 154, 173, 275, **2**, **3**, **4**

Asana 98, 99, 156
Asia site 115, *47*
Aspero 114, 123, 124, 126, 128, 142
Atacama Desert 7, 26, 32, 41, 99, 100
Atacama Maritime Tradition 92, 99–100
Atahualpa 11, 12, 69
Atalla 171
Atlantic 26, 42
atlatl (spear thrower) 88, *37*
audiencias 137, 272, 274, *129*
Aveni, Anthony 201, 202
avocado 103
axe money *see* naipes
Ayacucho 48, 97, 105, 154, 170, 171, 198, 203, 206, 207, 231, 232, 234, 235, 238, 257, 261
ayllu 53–55, 67, 69, 70, 71, 72, 74, 75, 79, 82, 84, 103, 160, 174, 221, 226, 272, *19*
Aymara 20, 32, 46, 55, 74, 137, 242, 245, 258
Azapa 48, 99, 129, 156, 160, 221

Bandurria 123, 126
barter 30, 44, 46, 49, 113; *see also* trueque
bas-reliefs 167, *70*, *102*
basketry 115, 122, 125, 126, **19**
Batan Grande 264–66; Sican Precinct 264; *122*
Bauer, Brian 248
Bawden, Garth 226
beakers *104*, *105*
beans 103, 105, 108, 109, 112,

113, 133, 239
Betanzos 83–84
Bird, Junius 91
birds 74, 94, 97, 99, 109, 117, 121, 153, 166, 167, 197, *70*; condor 117, 120, *46*; marine 41; partridge 52; sea birds 48
blood types 87–88
bofedales 98
Bolivia 17, 26, 55, 68, 77, 221
bone 11, 88, 89, 90, 92, 93, 94, 95, 96, 100, 109, 110, 115, 121, 273, *81*, **65**
bottles, double-spout-and-bridge 160; Sican-style *121*; stirrup-spout 170
bowls 159, 231
Brazil 91
bricks 177, 227, 272, *80*
bronze 157
Bueno, Alberto 206
Burger, Lucy 141
Burger, Richard 140, 141, 163, 169, 171
burial theme 229
burials 11, 19, 68, 92, 93, 94, 95, 101, 124, 153, 161, 162, 178, 179, 182, 194, 196, 197, 226, 247, 270, 275, *82–84*, **64**, *76–78*; 'Cavernas'-type pits 66; Chimú *110*; 'Necropolis'-type crypts 66; seated 198, 246, 260, 264, *110*; 'temple interment' 118; *see also* chulpas

Caballo Muerto Complex 135, 138, 143, **35**, **36**

Cabana 206
Cahuachi 199, 201, 202
Cajamarca 7, 11, 48, 136, 137, 144, 153, 176, 203, 237, 262
Callejon de Huaylas 48, 96, 97, 104, 109, 120, 205
Camana, Río 99
camelids 90, 96, 97, 103, 109, 121, 144, 155, 170, 171, 221
Camino 113
Campa 258
Cana 245
canals 32, 43, 49, 52, 54, 77, 108, 109, 133–35, 160, 174, 175, 197, 207, 232, 235, 239, 240, 242, 264, 274, 39
Canchi 245
cane 94, 111, 125, 176, 222, 225, 226, 236, 272, 126
Cañete Valley 260
cañihuas 41, 103
Carahuarazo 237
Caral 112, 114, 119, 120, 123; 'amphitheater' complex 127
Cardal 140–41
cargo systems 67, 69, 135
carving 8, 20, 144, 159, 171, 217, 221
Casma 19, 123, 131, 136, 142, 168, 174, 175, 176, 195, 199; Río 43, 95, 96, 113, 121, 143; Valley 195
Catequil 68
Cayman 168, 73
cemeteries 17, 18, 65, 157, 239, 240, 264, 270
Central Andean Tradition 95–99
ceques 82
ceramics 18, 76, 77, 78, 84, 107, 122, 128, 131, 133, 144, 153, 155, 157, 158, 160, 163, 169, 170, 171, 174, 176, 183, 196–97, 198, 203, 205, 206, 223, 226, 227, 231, 234, 237, 240, 247, 257, 259, 260, 262, 22–24, 37, 38; Baños de Boza 196; Chimú-Inca 272; Ica 260, 261; Killke style 84, 248; Lucre style 84, 248; Miramar 196; Moche 196, 17, 29, 32, 78, 88–90, 61, 62; Nazca 91, 92, 95; painting 78; portraits 85; Tumilaca Phase 118; see also pottery
cereals 77, 103
ceremony 77, 114; centers 115, 128, 136, 143, 144, 158, 178, 248, 99; facilities 119, 123, 132, 135, 163
Cerro Amaru 205
Cerro Arena 175
Cerro Azul 260
Cerro Baul 234, 235, 236, 238, 240, 241, 247, 266, 113, 114, 88
Cerro Blanco 177, 178, 195, 196, 225, 226
Cerro El Calvario 113
Cerro Galindo see Galindo
Cerro Julia 113
Cerro Mejia 235, 236
Cerro Orejas 177
Cerro Sechín 142, 143, 25, 57, 58, 31, 32, 33, 34
Cerro Trinidad 197
Chachapoyas 258
Chamaya Basin 144
chamber-and-fill technique 227
Chan Chan 17, 18, 49, 52, 76, 79, 135, 229, 261, 266, 267, 270,

273, 274, 275, 109, 124, 126, 128, 129, 99–103
Chanapata Phase 208
Chanca 14, 15
Chancay 140, 197, 259, 260; Río 114, 143, 196
Chanchamayo, Río 257
Chankillo 175
Chanquillo fortress 50
Chao, Río 123, 143; Valley 7
Charca 245
charqui 77
chaskis 74, 59
Chavez, Karen and Sergio 158
Chavín 153, 160, 163–68, 169, 170, 206, 220, 230, 234, 64; Chavín de Huantar 20, 119, 132, 141, 158, 163, 170, 47, 48, 49; Castillo 163–66, 168, 169, 68, 69, 43; Lanzón stela 164–65, 68, 49; New Temple 165, 70, 72; Old Temple 163–64; Raimondi Stela 167; 74
Chavín style 44, 45, 46
Chen Chen 240, 242, 117
Chen Chen Phase 239
Cheqo Wasi 231
Chicama 177, 178; Río 43, 123, 176, 178, 195, 196, 274, 12; Valley 94, 193, 196, 267
chicha beer 67, 77, 82, 222, 234
Chinchaysuyu 82
Chilca 105, 110, 112
Chile 7, 15, 19, 26, 48, 79, 87, 89, 91, 95, 99, 100, 107, 110, 129, 157, 201, 221, 246, 258
chili peppers 51–52, 105, 109, 121, 168
Chillon 140, 196, 259; Río 43, 123, 128, 140; Valley 127, 61
Chimor 17, 43, 48, 49, 52, 68, 69, 75, 77, 79, 111, 137, 144, 174, 196, 228, 245, 259, 261–62, 266, 267, 274, 275
Chimú 228, 267, 126, 98
Chincha 49, 160, 162, 195, 197, 260, 261, 265
Chinchamayo 258
Chinchaycocha 257, 258
Chinchaysayu 42, 43, 74
Chinchorro 100–01, 110, 111, 122, 129, 157; see also mummies
Chipacigarro 123
Chiquitoy Viejo 267
Chira, Río 93, 144, 266
Chiribaya 246, 247; style 242, 96
Chiribaya Alta 247
chirimoya 103
Chiripa 155–56, 157, 158, 221, 62
Chokepukio 248
Chongos 48
Chotuna 262–64, 266
chrysacola 231
chulpas (burial towers) 246, 247, 94
chuño 44, 77
Chupas 171
Cieza de León, Pedro 8, 12, 15, 18, 85, 208, 217, 260
Cinto 263
ciudadelas 272, 274
Ciudadelo Rivero 272, 128, 101, 103; Tschudi 272, 273, 129
class, social 70, 114–15, 171, 195, 231
clay 13, 98, 100, 115, 124, 207, 233, 243, 42, 53

clothing 162, 257; hats 91; kilts 220; tunics 220, 10
clubs 32, 53
coca 41, 45, 46, 66, 68, 103, 15
Cocha Mama 68
Cochabamba 221
cochas 32, 160
Colla 14, 245, 246
Collasayu 32, 74, 82
Colombia 26, 28, 42, 107, 170
Columbus, Christopher 7, 15, 18, 276, 277
Compañón, Martínez de 18
Con 68
Conchopata 232, 233, 234
Conklin, William 138, 156, 170
conquistadores 7, 8, 13, 17, 72, 82, 84, 85, 208, 257, 261
copper 49, 157, 170, 207, 227, 231, 264, 265, 63
cord 88, 28
Cordillera 8, 10, 11, 13, 15, 17, 18–20, 25–26, 27, 29–31, 41–45, 46, 47, 48–52, 73, 77, 79, 89, 91, 92, 97, 99, 101, 102, 103, 107, 111, 115, 131, 136, 144, 153, 157, 170, 171, 203, 245, 257, 258, 275, 276, 277; Blanca 26; colonization of 87–105; Negra 26, 41, 49
Coricancha 8, 14, 15, 68, 82, 84, 85
corporate activities 234
corporate arts 84, 226; construction 201, 240; organizations 134; style 79, 80, 160, 198, 205, 206, 247, 257; works 118, 158
Cotapachi 77
cotton 41, 48, 74, 103, 104, 108, 109, 112, 113, 124, 128, 133, 162, 170, 18
crafts 49, 78–79
Cral 127
cranial deformation 240
Crisnejas Basin 204
crocodiles 168, 73
crops 31, 41, 43, 44, 46, 47, 49, 52, 73, 103, 109, 112, 113, 128, 133, 144, 153, 157, 160, 168, 233, 240; see also named crops
Culebras, Río 113, 115, 123
Cuntisuyu 42, 82
Cupisnique 94, 174, 37, 38
Cuychu 84
Cuzco 7, 8, 10, 11, 12, 13, 14, 15, 17, 18, 19, 32, 42, 43, 48, 49, 55, 65, 68, 70, 71, 72, 73, 74, 75, 76, 77, 79, 80, 81, 82, 83, 84, 85, 154, 160, 176, 223, 237, 245, 246, 248, 257, 260, 266, 267, 275, 10, 35; Basin 41, 154, 203, 208, 247

dead, cult of the 66, 100, 122
deer 49, 92, 95, 109, 121, 227
dialects 48, 223
diet 100, 110–11, 113, 128, 171
Dillehay, Tom 90, 93, 157
disease 11–12, 225, 243; see also smallpox
domestication 47, 102–05; plant 41, 102
Donnan, Christopher 184, 194, 264
Dos Cabezas 196
Dos Palomos 199
drink 66, 67, 70, 71, 75, 77, 78,

117, 231, 236, 237; ritual intoxication 67; see also libations
drought 27, 28, 29, 31, 32, 44, 49, 70, 72, 73, 74, 77, 82, 84, 129, 158, 171, 197, 221, 223, 225, 232, 233, 234, 243, 245, 246, 247, 257, 258, 266, 274, 275

Early Horizon Period 119, 131, 158–71, 174, 175, 197, 55
Early Intermediate Period 21, 173–222, 232, 77
earthquakes 28, 31, 51, 68
Earthshaker see Pachacuti
economy 79, 109, 110
Ecuador 7, 10, 15, 17, 26, 28, 42, 49, 68, 79, 91, 92, 107, 112, 117, 144, 170, 229, 231, 260, 265
El Brujo 193
El Inga 91
El Jobo Points 90
El Niño 20, 28, 42, 51, 70, 178, 180, 199, 223, 225, 229, 243, 247, 266, 275, 277
El Paraiso 123, 126, 127–29, 138, 140, 54, 29, 30
elephants 89, 90
emblems 79, 25
embroidery 162, 67, 20
emeralds 8, 265
Encantada 144
environment 25, 54, 87, 107
Estero phase 93
Estuquina 247

Faldas el Moro 156, 157
Farfan 268, 275
farming 28, 29, 30–32, 41, 43, 44, 46, 47, 48, 49, 53, 71, 72, 73, 74, 79, 103, 109, 110, 112, 113, 117, 129, 131, 133, 134, 135, 144, 153, 157–58, 177, 199, 207, 221, 225, 232, 234, 235, 239, 241, 243, 245, 246, 247, 248, 257, 258, 275, 277
feathers 74, 100, 109, 121, 70, 10
Feldman, R. 114
felines 142, 159, 74
Fempellec 70, 262
figurines 126, 206, 53
fish 41, 47, 48, 92, 94, 95, 100, 111, 117, 121, 128, 142, 153, 155, 160, 163, 197, 46; anchovies 41, 110, 111, 113, 260; sardines 111, 260; seafood 74, 99, 113; shellfish 93, 113, 176
fisherfolk 95, 108, 112, 114
fishing 43, 44, 48, 49, 95, 99–100, 110, 134
food 26, 27, 28, 44, 45, 52, 56, 66, 67, 68, 70, 71, 72, 73, 75, 77, 78, 88, 94, 96, 99, 100, 104, 107, 110, 155, 176, 221, 226, 231, 232, 266; ritual feasting 90, 117, 231, 237; see also diet
Formative Period 131, 154
Fortaleza de Paramonga 5
Fortaleza, Río 43, 143; Valley 112, 137
fortifications 175, 225, 238, 248
fruits 41, 45, 90, 103, 104–05, 108, 109, 112, 128, 133, 176, 197, 240; see also named fruits
funerary objects 109
fur 126

Galindo 226, 229, 267, 107, 86

Gallinazo 174, 176–77, 178, 184, 194; Castillo 54; vessels **51**, **53**
game 87, 88, 89, 90, 94, 97
Garagay 140, 141, *61*
gardens 8, 93, 275; *see also* sunken gardens
Gateway God 220, 234
Gentilar style 247
geoglyphs 201–02, *93, 94, 96*
Gibaja, Arminda 248
goiter 45, 113
gold 7, 8, 17, 74, 76, 77, 84, 154, 157, 162, 170, 171, 231, 264, 265, **25**, **63**, **97**
Goldstein, Paul 239
gourds 45, 48, 77, 92, 108, 109, 112, 113, 115, 117, 124, 168, *15, 43*; gourds *48*
grains 41, 45; *see also* canihua, quinoa
Gran Pajaten ruins 258
grave goods 18, 19, 122, 153, 264
graves 18, 167, 194, 199, 264, *82–84*
Grieder, Terence 206
guanaco 42, 91, 121
Guayaquil Gulf 92
guinea pigs 109, 176
Guitarrero Cave 95, 97, 104, 105, *40*, **27**, **28**
guyaba 113

Hatun Xauxa 77, 80
Hatunqolla 246
headdresses 167, 220, 227
herding 30, 41, 43, 44, 46, 47, 52, 53, 102, 109, 131, 133, 157–58, 221, 246, 257, 258
hide 88, 90, 94, **28**
Higueras, Río 109
Himalayas 7, 8, 25, 44
Holocene 276
Honda phase 93
horizontality 30, 203
House of the Sun *see* Coricancha
Huaca Avispas *130*
Huaca Cao Viejo 193
Huaca Corte 264
Huaca de la Luna 178, 180, 182, 193, 199, 223, 225, 227, 229, 238, 274, *85, 86*, **60**
Huaca de los Idolos 124, 125, 126, *52, 53*
Huaca de los Sacrificios 124
Huaca del Sol 17, 18, 135, 178–80, 182, 199, 223, 225, 227, 229, *79, 81, 82–84, 110*, **56**, **75**, **76–78**
Huaca Fortaleza 227–28, *108*
Huaca Gloria 264
Huaca Larga 266
Huaca Los Reyes 138–39, *60*, **35**, **36**, **37**, **38**, **39**
Huaca Moxeke 142
Huaca Prieta 115, 117, 123, *45, 46, 48*
Huaca Sipan 193
Huaca Soto 162
Huaca Tomaval 177
Huacaloma 137, 144
Huacaloma Phase, Early 144; Late 144
huacas 14, 51, 65, 67, 68, 69, 71, 80, 82, 84, 85, 96, 124, 127, 136, 142, 169, 177, 228, 273, *89*; *adoratorios* 52, 139, 226, 259; *sepulturas* 52, 70, 122, 246, 272, 273, *130*
Huacaypata 81, 85
Huacpata 82
Huallaga, Río 109, 153
Huanaco 109
Huancaco 195, 226
Huancavelica 170, 171
Huánuco Pampa 77, 80, *27, 31*
huaqueros 17–18
Huara Valley 123
Huara, Río 137
Huaracane peoples 221
Huaracani 239
Huarago 91
Huarco 260
Huari 43, 48, 222, 223, 230–31, 233, 234, 236, 237, 238, 240, 242, 247–48, 257, 260, 262, 267, *24, 113*, **87–90**, **92**
Huaricani 156, 157
Huaricoto 113, 120, 121, 153, 170
Huarmey 195, 225; Río 113, 143, 178, 195
Huarpa 206–07, 231, 232
Huascar 11
Huatanay Valley 13, 14
Huatanay, Río 14, 84
Huaura valley 138
Huaura, Río 143
Huaynuna 113, 123, 126–27
Humboldt Current 30
Humboldt, Alexander von 18, 102–03
hunter-gatherers 97–99, 105
hunting 44, 49, 91, 93, 96, 97, 108, 109, 110
Hunu Kuraka 70
Huri 232
hurin 81, 82, 83
Huyanaputina, Mount 28
hypoxia 27

Ica 161, 197, 260; Desert 95; Valley 19, 21, 42, 48, 158, 173, 223, 231, 238, 245
Ica Vieja 261
Ice Age 87, 88, 89, 107
Ichma 259, 260
iconography 78, 198, 208, 226, 267, *33, 34*; felines 20; marine *45*; maritime 229, *109*; Moche 180; raptorial birds 20; serpents 20; *see also* motifs
iguana 229
Illapa 84
Inca Urcon 14
incest taboos 88
infanticide 111
Initial Period 21, 113, 119, 121, 122, 131–58, 170, 174, 267, *55*
inlay 265
Inti 8, 11, 13, 15, 68, 75, 82, 84, 142
irrigation 17, 28, 29, 32, 43, 46, 47, 48, 49, 80, 82, 108, 109, 110, 128, 131, 133–36, 144, 156, 157, 175, 177, 199, 207, 232, 233, 236, 237, 241, 242, 247, 258, 261, 263, 266, 274, *13*
Isbell, William 231, 232
Island of the Sun 68, 124, 197, 221

jaguars 164, 167, *74*
Janabarriu Phase 163, 170, 171
Jaujatambo 258
Jaywamachay 91

Jequetepeque 137, 223, 226, 264, 275; Río 43, 137, 138, 143, 266; Valley 48, 194, 196, 203, 267
jewelry 76, 122, 153, 206, 231, 257; beads 8, 109, 124, 126, 171; crowns 171; disks 109; earspools 76, 141, 164, 171, 206, **53**, **71**; necklaces 126, 141, **63**; nose ornaments 162; pectorals 171
Jincamocco 237, 238
Jivaro 115
Juayanca 263
Juli hill 246
Junin, Lake 96, 257

kallanka halls 80, 204
kancha-wasi 81, 85, 248, *34*
Kantatayita 217
Karwa 169, 170, *75*
keros beakers 77, 159, 234, *33, 114, 116, 117*
Killke style 84, 247
kinship 47, 53, 54, 55–56, 65, 66, 69, 79, 81, 82, 84, 88, 101, 114, 135, 136, 141, 174, 178, 195, 231, 240, 264, 267, 274, 275, *19*
Koani 221
Kosok, Paul 202
Kotosh 109, 110, 119, 120, 121, 123, 126, 127, 136, 141, 153, 171; Chavín Phase 171; Mito Phase 109; Religious Tradition 109, 120–23, 144, 153
Kroeber, A.L. 19
Kuelap 203, 258
Kuntur Wasi 171
kurakas 68, 69–70, 74, 75, 77, 78, 85, 107, 135, 153, 160, 162, 171, 173, 173, 177, 178, 183, 184, 193, 194, 195, 196, 203, 206, 220, 257, 272, 275

La Cumbre 94
La Florida 140, 141
La Galgada 109, 110, 113, 115, 119, 121–22, 128, 136, 137, 138, 153, 154, *51*
La Leche, Río 43, 137; Valley 136, 264, 266
La Paloma 101, 111
Lambayeque 43, 49, 70, 79, 93, 174, 176, 193, 196, 201, 261, 262, 263, 267, 275; Río 43, 153, 263; Valley 226, 262
landslides 28
language 10, 14, 48, 88, 95, 267
Lanzón cult 169, 167, 170
lapidary 18, 76, 78, 270
lapis lazuli 231, 265
Larco Hoyle, Rafael 174
Las Vegas culture 92
Late Archaic Period 107
Late Horizon Period 19, 264, 275
Late Intermediate Period 21, 245–75, *119*
Lauricocha Cave 96, 97, 109
Layzon 144
Laz phase 95
legumes 77, 133
libations 77, 82; vessels 67, 77, 78, 159, 160, 183–84, 195, 231, 237, 262, 263, *32, 90*, **59**, **95**
Licapa 17, 19, 43, 95, 112, 113, 140, 177, 196–97
Lithic Period 21, 87, 98, 99, 107, 108, 110, 118, *36*
Little Ice Age 29, 223
lizards 94, 95, 159
llamas 8, 30, 41, 42, 44, 46, 47, 72, 91, 95, 133, 143, 144, 155, 159, 176, 202, 221, 227, 240, 242, 243, 246, 273, 274, *17, 23, 81*, **4**, **11**, **62**, **75**
Llamas platform 143
llapa 68
Loa, Río 99, 157
Loma Negra 17
lomas 42
looting 17, 180, 201, 205, 226, 239, 264; looting 273; *see also* grave robbing, *huaqueros*
Loreto Viejo 242
Los Gavilanes 113
Los Morteros 123
Los Toldos 91
Lucre style 84, 247, 248
lucuma 104
Lumbreras, Luis 160, 161, 163, 231
Lupaka 14, 45, 46, 246, 247
Luqurmata 221
Lurin, Río 17, 140, 196, 259; Valley 68, 138, 140–41, 197
Lynch, Thomas 96

Machu Picchu 42, 73, 85, 257, 277, 3, **16**, **17**
maize 8, 29, 41, 45, 46, 71, 113, 133, 153, 157, 176, 225, 233, 239, 257, *16*
Mala, Río 138, 171
mallquipavillac 65–66, 100, 122, 247, 274
Mama Kilya 68
Mama Oqlyo 14
Manchay Bajo 141
Manco Capac 14, 65, 84, 127
manioc 29, 41, 103, 144, 153, 168
Mantaro, Río 257
Maranga complex 196
Marañón, Río 109, 110, 163
Marcahuamachuco 203–05, 231, 237, 238, *97*; Castillo 204; *98*
Marcavalle 154, 208
Maritime-Oasis lifeway 25, 246, 261, 275; adaptations 27, 43, 48–50, 131, 173, **5**, **6**, **7**
marriage 53, 54, 55, 69, 75, 88, 111, 178, 270
masmas 80
masonry 71, 80, 82, 84, 114, 121, 124, 127, 144, 158, 163, 166, 176, 203, 207, 217, 226, 243, 247, 260, **14**, **15**, **16**, **30**
mastodons 89, 91
Mayu *see* Milky Way
McEwan, Gordon 248
metals 76, 78, 154, 264, **66**; precious 17, 49, 79, 193, 247, 260, 273; *see also* named metals
metallurgy 49, 76, 79, 157, 265, 270, **25**, **26**
Mexico 7, 265
Middendorf, E.W. 20
Middle Horizon Period 207, 223–43, *106*
Middle Phase 263
Milky Way 32, 52, 81
millaquis 69
Mina Perdida 141
Minchançaman 266, 272
mindala 49
mit'a 55, 56, 70, 72, 73, 74, 75, 77, 78, 177, 237

mitamaqs 10, 73
Mito Phase 121
Moche 48, 143, 144, 174, 177,
   178–96, 198, 199, 201, 202, 203,
   206, 220, 222, 223, 225, 226,
   229, 230, 232, 238, 262, 263;
   architecture 176; art 176,
   183–84, 228, 57–60; Burial
   Theme 87; crafts 65, 66; iconography 183–84; people 18; Río 17,
   18, 43, 178; Valley 17, 18, 19,
   94, 119, 135, 141, 175, 266, 267,
   274, 7, 35, 36
moieties 54–55, 66, 67, 88, 135
Molina, Cristobal de 80
mollusks 41, 48, 92, 111
monoliths 240, 25, 31, 32; Ponce
   Monolith 80, 81
montaña 41, 42, 153, 258
Monte Verde 87, 89–91
Moquegua 47, 235, 237, 239, 240,
   242, 247, 33, 116; Río 28, 29, 99,
   156, 221, 235, 242, 246; Valley
   42, 156, 160, 233
mortuary practices and rituals
   117, 136
mosaics 142, 153, 58
Mosna 163
motifs 160, 207, 67, 102, 116, 117,
   118 ; animal 259; Ayapec 182;
   bird 159, 124; ceramic 87;
   condor 205; demonic figures
   198; 91, 92; design 78; eyes 171;
   feline 155, 159, 171, 205, 171,
   64, 21; fish 197, 261, 101; frog
   79; geometric 248, 259, 261;
   human head 159; llamas 159;
   maize cob 112 ; maritime 229,
   267, 109; militaristic 197;
   monkey 124; mural 85, 86;
   mythical creatures 101; plant
   259; Preceramic 117; sea birds
   261, 101; serpent 197, 205, 263,
   49, 70; spider 60; Staff God 167,
   169, 74, 75; tapestry 76; textile
   24, 45, 46, 47; wave 101
Motupe, Río 43
mounds 43, 123, 124, 126, 127,
   139, 153, 171, 178, 180, 199,
   201, 217, 264, 273, 59, 39, 54,
   55, 56
Moxeke 143
mummies 54, 56, 121, 161, 162,
   265, 272, 22, 65; Chinchorro
   100–01, 122, 42
mummification 19, 56, 100–01,
   111
murals 182, 197, 225, 59
Murra, John 45, 46, 246
musical instruments 155
Muyu Moqo 154

naipes 49, 265
Nancenpinco 266
Nanchoc 93, 118
Nawinpukio 233
Naxca, geoglyphs 201–02, 93, 94,
   96
Naymlap 261, 262, 263, 264, 266,
   275
Nazca 19, 25, 48, 160, 161,
   197–203, 207, 222, 233, 234,
   237, 260, 261,
   67, 68–70; Río 198, 199; Valley
   19, 48, 238
Nepeña Valley 175, 176, 193, 195, 7
Netherly, Patricia 93

Northwestern Lithic Tradition
   92, 95
Nudo de Vilcanota 26, 28, 32
Nuñez, Lautaro 99, 157
nutrition see food
nuts 90

obsidian 89, 99, 100, 111, 170
oca 41, 103, 104, 113
Ocucaje 171
offerings 51, 121, 123, 138, 141,
   163, 260
Okros 233; pottery 236
Ollantaytambo 42, 85, 257, 34
ollas 155
Omo 115
Omo 235, 239, 240, 241, 115; Río
   95
Orinoco Basin 103
Owl Cave 153

pacae 113
Pacaje 245
pacarina 248
Pacatanamu 196, 199, 229, 266,
   275
Paceco 234
Pacha Mama 51, 52, 119, 131,
   177, 194
Pachacamac 17, 19, 68, 124, 142,
   169, 197, 230, 238, 259, 264, 6;
   'Pachacamac Temple' 197
Pachacuti 13, 14, 15, 79, 83, 84,
   176, 248, 257
Pachamachay Cave 96, 97, 143
Pacific 26, 42, 46, 48, 97, 133,
   221, 246, 261, 264
Pacopampa 144, 171
Paijan people 99; Tradition 92,
   93–95
Paita 144
Pajchiri 221
Paleo-Indians 87, 92
Paloma 112
Pampa de Los Incas 195
Pampa de los Llamas-Moxeke
   Complex 132, 142, 143
Pampa Grande 226, 227, 229, 243,
   262, 264, 266, 108
Pampa Koani 221, 242
Pampas, Río 261
panaka 81, 82, 84, 85
Panama 11, 87, 88
Pañamarca 193, 195, 196, 55
Paracas 19, 160–62, 169, 171, 197,
   198, 64, 65, 67
Paraiso Tradition 137–41
Paramonga, Río 5
parcialidades 10, 49, 174
Paricaca 68
Pashash 206
pastoralism 246
Pativilca, Río 43; Valley 112, 137
Pax Incaica 10
Pax Moche 195
peanuts 103, 240
Pechiche 144
Peru 7, 19, 20, 21, 26, 28, 42, 48,
   87, 89, 91, 92, 95, 99, 101, 103,
   104, 107, 108, 110, 111, 114,
   117, 119, 126, 131, 143, 144,
   153, 170, 198, 222, 260, 266, 5,
   6, 7, 8
Piedra Parada 119, 123, 127, 137

Pikillaqta 237, 247
pikimachay 91
Pisac 42, 257
Pisco, Río 136; Valley 199, 261
Piura 195, 226; Río 93, 144
Pizarro, Francisco 7, 10, 11, 12,
   17, 42, 43, 68, 69, 85, 197
plants 10, 27, 28, 29, 30, 32, 41,
   42, 44, 47, 48, 52, 87, 88, 89, 90,
   93, 94, 97, 102, 104–05, 108,
   109, 111, 112, 121, 124, 126,
   128, 143, 155, 156, 276, 14;
   cactus 71; medicinal 90, 104
platform mounds 68, 80, 118–19,
   121, 123, 127, 128, 135, 139,
   144, 153, 154, 162, 163, 175,
   177, 199, 201, 225, 240, 261,
   264, 274, 275, 99, 101, 128
plazas 81, 82, 85, 159, 165, 199,
   240, 246, 261; hundidas 119, 120
Plaza Hundida Tradition 123
Pleistocene 89, 91, 92, 93, 102,
   276
Poma de Ayala, Felipe Guamán
   12, 3, 4, 16, 22, 23, 28
Ponce Monolith 217, 80, 81
Ponce, Carlos 157
Poopó, Lake 26, 99, 156, 157
Portal of the Sun 234
portrait heads 57, 58
potatoes 30, 41, 44, 71, 89, 90,
   103, 105, 113, 155, 232, 243
pottery 8, 17, 19, 21, 80, 107, 109,
   133, 141, 144, 153, 154, 155,
   156, 160, 170, 171, 174, 176,
   184, 196, 197, 260, 273, 18;
   Chiripa 156; Faldas del Moro
   157; Qaluyu 156; Waira-jirca 153
Pozorski, Thomas and Shelia 143
Preceramic Period 21, 107–29,
   133, 134, 135, 138, 153, 156, 177,
   207, 44
projectile points 95, 100, 231, 40;
   El Jobo; fluted 91–92, 95, 38;
   Paijan 93, 95, 39
Pucallpa 153
Pukara 41, 43, 72, 73, 154,
   158–60, 161, 171, 208, 246, 248,
   257, 40, 41, 42
Pukara de Juli settlement 246
pukaras 174, 175, 195, 225, 28
pumas 84, 85, 220, 35
Pumachupan 84, 85
Pumapunku 243
pumpkin 240
puna 7, 26, 41, 44, 45, 46, 72, 87,
   96, 97, 98, 99, 109, 156
Puno 246, 94
pyramids 264, 266, 55, 56; pyramidal mounds 43
Pyramid of the Moon see Huaca
   de la Luna
Pyramid of the Sun see Huaca del
   Sol

Qaluyu 154
qollqa 71–72, 77, 258, 26, 27, 31
qomba 74
Quebrada Cuculicote 94
Quebrada Jaguay 99
Quebrada Las Conchas 99, 100
Quebrada Tacahuay 99
Quebrada Tiviliche 99–100
Quechua 10, 14, 20, 52, 53, 55,
   65, 66
Quelccaya glacier 223
Quero 91

quichua 232, 233
quinoa 41, 103, 133, 155
quipu 12, 74, 3, 4, 31
quipukamayogs 76
Quirihuac Shelter 94
Quito 42, 91

radiocarbon dating 19, 84, 87, 89,
   90, 91, 93, 98, 99, 123, 128, 157,
   160, 229, 233, 262
rainfall 26, 27, 28–29, 31, 32, 41,
   42, 44, 49, 52, 72, 73, 77, 107,
   108, 112, 132, 133, 134, 153,
   154, 158, 160, 180, 220, 221,
   223, 233, 242, 245, 247, 248,
   258, 262, 274, 12
Ravines, Rogger 137
reclamation of land 31, 32, 72,
   232, 238, 243, 247, 277
Recuay 205–06, 71–73
reeds 8, 48, 92, 94, 111, 112, 114,
   118, 155, 229, 247, 8
Reiche, Maria 202
religion 18, 67–68, 71, 79, 88, 131,
   136, 141–43, 169, 231; cult of
   the Sun 259; Lanzón cult 167,
   169, 170
rhizomes 90, 104
Rick, John 96
Rimac, Río 32, 43, 140, 240;
   Valley 68, 196, 259
Ring Site 99
ritual combat 193
road networks 74
roads 1, 2
Rock of the Sun 68
Rostworowski de Diez Canseco,
   Maria 48
Rowe, John 19, 154
Runa Simi 10, 52

sacrifice 85, 124, 194, 217, 265
Sacsahuaman 72, 85, 175, 35, 12,
   13, 14
Salinar 174, 175, 196, 52
Salinas de Chao 119, 123
salt 26, 41, 45, 90, 111, 157
San Bartalo Bay 111
San Jacinto 141
San José de Moro 226
San Miguel style 247
San Pedro de Atacama 99, 107,
   157, 221, 246
sanctuaries 52, 126, 136, 138, 142,
   153, 164
Santa Castillo 177
Santa Elena Peninsula 92
Santa Rosa 144
Santa, Río 26, 43, 95, 97, 109,
   113, 121, 133, 137, 138, 175, 176,
   205, 266
Santiago Uceda 180; Valley 175,
   195, 206, 7
Schaedel, Richard 206
sculpture 160, 166, 206, 240
sea mammals 41, 111
Sechín Alto 19, 132, 138, 140,
   142, 163, 174, 56
Sechín Bajo 142
Sechin, Río 142, 143
Sechura Desert 144, 171
Seco, Río 114, 119, 123, 126, 128
seeds 90, 96, 109, 111, 155
señorios 10, 49, 67, 68, 69, 72, 79,
   135, 178, 196, 203, 206, 221, 226,
   245, 246, 247, 248, 259, 260, 261
Shady, Ruth 113, 114–15

shamans 88
sharks 129
sheep 42
shell 93, 97, 100, 109, 115, 121, 153, 171, 122, 124, 231, 229, 265, 273; *Spondylus* 49, 111, 126, 227, 231, 260, 265, 273, **63**
shellfish 176
shicra 118
Shillacoto 153
Shimada, Izumi 226, 264
shrines 7, 68, 80, 126, 138, 206, 221, 226, 266, 273
Si 68
Sican Lord 263, 264, 266, **97**
Sican Phase 262 63, 264, *121*
Siches phase 93
sierra 26, 32, 41, 42, 47, 48, 65, 73, 87, 89, 96, 97, 98, 99, 108–10, 113, 114, 117, 118, 121, 128, 131, 132, 144, 153, 157, 161, 175, 176, 177, 198, 203, 207, 221, 223, 225, 232, 232, 237–38, 239, 242, 245, 246, 247, 257–58
Sihuas 237
Sillustani 246, **94**
silver 7, 8, 17, 74, 76, 77, 84, 170, 171, 231, 276, **26**
Silverman, Helaine 201
Sipan 196, **63, 64**
smallpox 11, 15, 257, 261
Smiling (Snarling) God 165
snails 94, 95, 100, 155
Spanish 12, 17, 27, 31, 47, 48, 56, 65, 67, 65, 67, 69, 80, 83, 85, 178, 266; Conquest 9, 11, 12, 20; *see also conquistadores*
spinning 74
squash 108, 109, 112, 113, 128, 133, 240
staffs 67, 220, 234, *24, 25, 111, 112*, **78**
Staff God 167, 169, 170, 220, 234, 238, *74, 75, 114*
Stanish, Charles 246
statecraft 9, 12, 14, 51–85, 104, 174, 231, 257
stelae 15, 20, 159, 217, 240, 243, 246, *63*; 'Bennett' monolith 217; Lanzón 164–65, *68, 49*; Raimondi 167; Thunderbolt 217, **79**
stone 8, 9, 20, 80, 88, 90, 91, 92, 95, 109, 115, 125, 143, 144, 153, 157, 159, 169, 171, 206, 219, 231, 233, 236, 240, 247, 257, 260, **72, 73**
stress, chronic 26–27; episodic 27–29
sunken courts 120, 121, 127, 136–37, 163, 165, 217, 219, 233, 240, 246, *100*, **42, 76, 77**

sunken gardens 32, 48, 245, 275
Sunturwasi 82
Supe, Río 43, 112, 115, 123, 124; Tradition 123; Valley 112, 127, 137, 168, *76*
suyu 52, 54, 55

Tablachaca, Río 109
Taguatagua 91
Tahuantinsuyu 7, 8, 9, 10, 11, 12, 13, 15, 17, 19, 25, 32, 41, 42, 43, 49, 51, 69, 70, 72, 73, 75, 79, 80, 81, 84, 91, 196, 243, 245, 246, 247, 257, 266, 275, 276
Tambo Colorado 261
Tambo Viejo 199
Tampu Machay **15**
tapestry 170, 240, *76*
tapia construction 260
Tarma 257, 258; Río 257
Taukachi-Konan 142
taxation 17, 70, 71–72, 75, 77, 78; agricultural 71–72, 75; textile 71, 74, textile 75; tithes 70, 169
Taycamanu 261, 262, 266, 267, 270
Taymi Canal 263
Telarmachay Cave 143
Tello enclosure 272; Obelisk 168
Tello, Julio C. 19, 20, 161
temples 7, 52, 68, 82, 84, 85, 122, 163, 167, 175, 248, 266
terracing 2, 72, 80, 121, 127, 133, 144, 158, 207, 221, 232, 233, 234, 236, 237, 241, 242, 245, 246, 247, 248, 257, 258, 277, **2**
textiles 18, 56, 68, 70, 74, 76, 78, 104, 115, 116–17, 122, 124, 125, 153, 157, 160, 162, 169, 170, 198, 221, 247, 259, 260, 273, *20, 24, 46, 47, 75, 120*, **18, 19, 20, 21**; Nazca 198; Paracas *49*; *qomba* 74
Thunderbolt Stela 217, **79**
Tierra del Fuego 26, 91
time, conception of 12, 19
tinamou 97
tinku 66–67, 81, 84, 167, 219, 234, *103*
tithes *see* taxation
Titicaca 24, 29, 43, 46, 107, 141, 157, 158, 162, 176, 221, 233, 243, 245–47, *9*
Titicaca Basin 14, 28, 32, 48, 77, 98, 113, 110, 131, 143, 154, 156, 157, 160, 170, 221, 230, 240, 245; Lake 13, 14, 15, 18, 26, 28, 32–33, 68, 124, 132, 136, 137, 154, 155, 157, 158, 208, 217, 242, 245
Tiwanaku 13, 15, 18, 19, 41, 43, 48, 68, 77, 84, 119, 156, 157, 160, 208, 220, 221, 222, 223,

230, 233, 234, 235, 237, 238, 240, 242–43, 245, 246, *33, 99*, **74, 77–79, 80, 81, 82, 83, 84**; Akapana platform mound *99, 100*; arts 221; Classic Tiwanaku style 217; Gateway God **83**; Gateway of the Moon 243; Gateway of the Sun 82, 219–20, 225, 243, *102, 103, 111*; Kalasasaya gateway **80**; Kalasasaya platform 217, 243, *99*; Pumapunku platform 219, *101*; 'Putuni' complex 217; ritual art 233
Tomaval Castillo 177
tombs 17, 18, 65, 136, 171, 196, 206, 238, 240, 247, 259, 261, 265; Chancay 259; Chimu 274; Sipan Tomb I **64**; *see also* burials, grave robbing, graves
tools 94, 98
Topa Inca 13, 15, 83–84, 259
Toquepala caves 98
Transitory Cupisnique 174
Tre Ventanas Cave 105
trepanation 161
Tropical Forest lifeway 25; adaptations 27, 44, **8, 9, 10, 11**
trueque 44, 46, 48, 49
Trujillo 180
trumpets 155, 159
tubers 41, 44, 71, 77, 90, 103, 104–05, 133, 155, 232, 239; *see also* jicama, oca, potatoes, ulluco
Tucume 263, 264, 266, *123*
Tullumayu, Río 84, 266; Valley 144
Tumibamba 10, 11, 80
Tumilaca 241, 242, 246
Tumilaca Phase 240–41
Tutishcainyo 153
twining 88, 115, 170

U-shaped centers 80, 123, 129, 132, 136, 137, 138, 139, 140, 141, 142, 143, 153, 154, 163, 177, 196, 267, 272, *56, 61, 65, 69, 127, 128*, **39, 100**
Ucayali, Río 153
Uhle enclosure 272, 274, **101**
Uhle, Max 18–19, 20, 21, 124
ulluco 41, 103, 105, 113
Umasuyo 245
Urabarriu Phase 163
Urubamba 208, 248; Valley 42, 73, **2**
Uruguay 91
Ushumachay 91
usnu 81, 82, 85

Valcarcel, Luis E. 20
Valdivia 117, 144
Vega, Garcilaso de la 85

Venezuela 90
Ventanilla Bay 113
ventilation systems 72
verticality 30, 44, 45, 47, 109, 133, 206, 246, 277
vessels 154, 155, 160, 176, 193, 197, 199, 203, 205, 206, 221, 226, 259, 262, **24, 41, 44, 51, 62, 65, 68–71, 75, 89, 92, 96**; aryballoid **22, 23**; Chancay **95**; Gallinazo **51, 53**; Paracas **45**; portrait head **93**; stirrup-spout *46, 52*; Tiwanaku **75, 84**; *see also* libations
vicuña 96
Vicus 195, 196, 226
Viracocha 13, 15, 68, 84, 243
Viracochapampa 238
Viru 174, 177, 195, 225, 226; Río 43, 143, 176; Valley 175, 275, 7
Vitor, Río 246
vizcacha 94, 97
volcanoes 20, 28, 51

Wacheksa 163
Waira-jirca 153
Wanka 257, 258
Wankarani complex 156, 157
Wari Willka 257
wasi 80, 81, 84, *34*
water 29, 30, 32, 52, 54, 70, 73, 82, 89, 103, 114, 128, 129, 133, 134, 153, 163, 174–75, 235, 236, 242–43, 263, 264, 274, 277
Wayna Capac 10, 15, 80
Waywaka 154
weather 26, 31, 41, 44, 77, 246
weaving 70, 74, 76, 115, 122, 133, 157, 170, 270, *20, 29, 111*, **19, 20**; weaving *29*; *see also* twining
Wichqana 154
Williams, Carlos 129, 137, 138, 140
Williams, Ryan 236
Willkawain 206
Wiñay Wayna 42
wood 18, 68, 78, 88, 90, 92, 104, 221, 260, 266, 270, **78, 98**
wool 44, 72, 74, 133, 162, 207, *67, 20*; alpaca 162, 198; camelid 170; vicuña 74

Yanamarca Valley 257, 258
Yaya-Mama Religious Tradition 158, 208; *63*
yuca 113
Yupanqui 14

Zana, Río 43, 93, 95, 108, 133, 153, 263, 264
Zolzdoni 262